Women and Gender in Ira

CW01468203

Since the US-led invasion and occupation of Iraq in 2003, the challenges of sectarianism and militarism have weighed heavily on Iraqi women. In this book, Zahra Ali foregrounds a wide range of interviews with a variety of women involved in women's rights activism, showing how both everyday life, and political and intellectual lives have developed since the US-led invasion. In addition to this, Ali offers detailed historical research on social, economic, and political contexts since the formation of the Iraqi state in the 1920s.

Through a transnational and postcolonial feminist approach, this book considers the ways in which gender norms and practices and Iraqi feminist discourses and activism are shaped and developed through state politics; competing nationalisms; religious, tribal, and sectarian dynamics; wars; and economic sanctions. The result is a vivid account of the everyday life in today's Iraq and an exceptional analysis of the future of Iraqi feminisms.

Zahra Ali is Assistant Professor of Sociology at Rutgers University-Newark. Her research explores the dynamics of women and gender, social and political movements in relation to Islam(s), the Middle East, and contexts of war and conflict with a focus on contemporary Iraq. Ali is also a Muslim feminist activist involved in antiracist and anti-imperialist struggles.

Cambridge Middle East Studies

Editorial Board

Charles Tripp (general editor)

Julia Clancy-Smith

F. Gregory Gause

Yezid Sayigh

Avi Shlaim

Judith E. Tucker

Cambridge Middle East Studies has been established to publish books on the nineteenth- to twenty-first-century Middle East and North Africa. The series offers new and original interpretations of aspects of Middle Eastern societies and their histories. To achieve disciplinary diversity, books are solicited from authors writing in a wide range of fields including history, sociology, anthropology, political science, and political economy. The emphasis is on producing books affording an original approach along theoretical and empirical lines. The series is intended for students and academics, but the more accessible and wide-ranging studies will also appeal to the interested general reader.

A list of books in the series can be found after the index.

Women and Gender in Iraq

Between Nation-Building and Fragmentation

Zahra Ali

Rutgers University–Newark

CAMBRIDGE
UNIVERSITY PRESS

CAMBRIDGE
UNIVERSITY PRESS

University Printing House, Cambridge CB2 8BS, United Kingdom

One Liberty Plaza, 20th Floor, New York, NY 10006, USA

477 Williamstown Road, Port Melbourne, VIC 3207, Australia

314–321, 3rd Floor, Plot 3, Splendor Forum, Jasola District Centre,
New Delhi – 110025, India

79 Anson Road, #06–04/06, Singapore 079906

Cambridge University Press is part of the University of Cambridge.

It furthers the University's mission by disseminating knowledge in the pursuit of
education, learning, and research at the highest international levels of excellence.

www.cambridge.org
Information on this title: www.cambridge.org/9781107191099
DOI: 10.1017/9781108120517

First published 2018

Printed in the United Kingdom by TJ International Ltd. Padstow Cornwall

A catalogue record for this publication is available from the British Library.

Library of Congress Cataloging-in-Publication Data
Names: Ali, Zahra, author.
Title: Women and gender in Iraq : between nation-building and fragmentation /
Zahra Ali, Rutgers University-Newark.
Description: New York : Cambridge University Press, [2018] | Series:
Cambridge Middle East studies
Identifiers: LCCN 2018005018 | ISBN 9781107191099
Subjects: LCSH: Women – Iraq – Social conditions. | Sexism – Iraq – History. |
Women's rights – Iraq. | Muslim women – Attitudes. | Feminism – Religious
aspects – Islam.
Classification: LCC HQ1735 .A625 2018 | DDC 305.409567–dc23
LC record available at https://lccn.loc.gov/2018005018

ISBN 978-1-107-19109-9 Hardback
ISBN 978-1-316-64162-0 Paperback

For my mother, Raja Musa Shaaban, for all her suffering and sacrifices, forever in exile

إلى والدتي رجاء موسى شعبان التي تحملت وعاشت كل معاناة وتضحيات الغربة والمنفى

In memory of my father, Ali Kadhim al-Adhadh, killed in Baghdad on November 18, 2006, by a terrorist sectarian armed group

إلى روح والدي الشهيد علي كاظم العضاض الذي قتل في بغداد يوم ١٨ تشرين الثاني ٢٠٠٦ على يد مجموعة مسلحة إرهابية

Contents

Figures

Maps

Acknowledgments

This research was made possible by all the Iraqi women activists and scholars who generously gave their time and shared their thoughts and personal and political trajectories with me. I can never thank them enough for these insightful, fascinating, deep, intense, passionate, and long interviews and discussions. I hope each of them gets the chance to read and comment on this research, and I hope that it contributes to our common struggle for justice and equality.

Despite being a very lonely and individual process, this book is also the product of collective material, moral, affective, and intellectual support from family, friends, and colleagues. I am very grateful to Institut Français du Proche-Orient (IFPO) for funding my research and fieldwork and for being a real home for me in both Syria and Iraq. I want to especially thank François Burgat, head of IFPO at the time, for his trust and support, as well as Hosham Dawod and Jessica Giraud for welcoming me in Erbil. Joining the Centre for Gender Studies at the School of Oriental and African Studies (SOAS) in London as a visiting research student would not have been possible without a grant from the Académie Française; I want to thank them for their valuable support. At the Iraqi National Library, Saad Eskander's help in accessing all the resources I needed was priceless; I am grateful to him and Sayyid Isma'il for kindly and generously facilitating my bibliographic research there. I am also grateful to the Centre for Gender Studies at SOAS for welcoming me; my time there was essential in shaping my intellectual journey. I also want to thank the British Institute for the Study of Iraq (BISI) for funding my recent fieldwork trip to Baghdad, Najaf-Kufa, Karbala, and Nasiriyah.

My sweet and brilliant Khala Muluk, you welcomed me in our home in al-Kazimiyya and looked after me throughout all these years, while you were also taking care of our sweet Bibi. I can never thank you enough for the time we spent together; it changed my life and deeply touched my soul. Thanks to all my aunties, uncles, and cousins who filled my time in Baghdad with love, tenderness, humor, and joy. 'Amu Abu Manal, thank you for everything, for your support, your trust, your help, and your wonderful friendship. You made this journey possible.

This book is based on my doctoral research, and I want to thank my supervisors, at Ecole des Hautes Etudes en Sciences Sociales (EHESS) in Paris Nilüfer Göle and at SOAS in London Nadje Al-Ali. Nilüfer has followed me since my master's degree and has furthered my personal and intellectual growth. Thank you so much for your support and your valuable and insightful comments and revisions throughout this research. Your office represented a real intellectual shelter for me, and EHESS would not have been the same without your presence. Nadje, I cannot thank you enough for welcoming me at the Centre for Gender Studies at SOAS and allowing me to access the most amazing spaces of work and life in London. Your generosity, kindness, warmth, and great support made it possible for me to materially, morally, and emotionally produce this research. Your own research deeply inspired this work at its every stage; your comments, remarks, and corrections helped to deepen and enrich this research. I also want to thank very much Lila Abu-Lughod for her enriching and challenging comments on my initial manuscript that pushed my reflection and understanding further throughout the completion of this book.

Pierre-Jean Luizard, Charles Tripp, and Sarah Bracke's valuable comments as examiners of my thesis manuscript have been very valuable in the process of writing this book. I thank them very much for that. I also thank Oliver Scharbodt and Yafa Shanneik at the Chester Center for Islamic Studies for being great and generous mentors during the time I was transforming my initial manuscript into this book. Thank you for offering me the environment that enabled me to prepare this work and broader my research horizons. At Cambridge University Press, I am very grateful for Maria Marsh for her constant support and great role as facilitator. I also thank very much the anonymous reviewers whose comments have been central in finalizing this book.

Maria Alabdeh, thank you for your friendship and your unending support and love throughout all these years. I know, *Insha'Allah*, that we will continue our struggle for a better future in our countries, Syria and Iraq. Souad Lamrani, thank you for your unconditional and warm support, for being a guardian angel all the time, and for accompanying this transformative period of my life. Thanks so much to my friends in London: Faridha Karim, for your kindness and love and for the infinite hours of chilling and chatting, and Farrah Sheikh, for your stunning generosity and kindness. Naima Bouteldja, your unlimited support and kindness throughout this process have been central in making the existence of this book possible. Thank you also Robin Virgin for motivating me and believing in this project.

Hassouni and Hamoudi, my dearest big brothers, thank you for your love and tenderness, especially in these difficult times you both face. I want to tell you that the love and care we have for one another can overcome everything. Mameh, this research is for you, for your sacrifices, your suffering, your unending love, sweetness, and grace. Noor, my big sister and second mother, thank you infinitely for being the *nur* of my life, supporting me and loving me. Fatoumeh, my other big sister, my second half and best friend, there is not a single word in this book that you have not brilliantly commented on; you always cheer me up, make me laugh, reassure me, love me, trust me, and support me all the way.

Organizations, Networks, and Groups

Women's Organizations, Groups, and Networks

Al-Rafidain Women's Coalition (RWC)
Association for Women's Revival
Association of Women for Women
Assyrian Women's Association
Asuda
Baghdad Women's Association (BWA)
Center for Widows' Progress and Training
Chaldean Women's Association
Civilian Women (*al-Nisa' al-Medeniyyat*)
Iraqi Independent Women's Group
Iraqi Mothers' League
Iraqi Muslim Women's League
Iraqi Women Journalist's Forum (IWJF)
Iraqi Women Network (IWN)
Iraqi Women's League (*al-Rabita*)
Iraqi Women's League of Kurdistan (*al-Rabita al-Kurdistaniyya*)
Iraqi Women's Will (IWW)
Islamic League for Iraqi Women (ILFI)
Jewel of al-Rafidain
Kurdistan Islamic Sisters Union
Organization for Muslim Women in Iraq (*Hawa'una*)
Organization for Women and Future
Organization of Women's Freedom in Iraq (OWFI)
Mihaniat Organization
Model Iraqi Women Organization
National Union of Women of Kurdistan
New Life Organization for Anfal Women
Rasan OrganizationRewan Center
Sisters of Kurdistan Organization

Society of Modern Women
Tory Hawbesh
Women Empowerment Organization (WEO)
Women for Progress Center (WPC)
Women Leadership Institute (WLI)
Women's Alliance for a Democratic Iraq (WAFDI)
Women's Association for Reform and Development
Women's Union of Kurdistan (*Zhinan*)

Civil Society Organizations, Groups, and Networks

Al-Ansar Charity Association
Civil Initiative to Preserve the Constitution (CIPC)
Iraqi al-Amel Association (al-Amel)
Iraqi Civil Society Solidarity Initiative (ICSSI)
Iraqi Council for Peace and Solidarity (ICPS)
Iraqi Democratic Future Network
Iraqi Human Rights Society
Office of the Iraqi Child
Organization for Development in Kurdistan
Organization for Family Well-Being
Organization for Social Solidarity
Start Social Development Organization
Tammuz Organization for Social Development (TOSD)

Political Parties, Coalitions, and Unions

Al-Da'wa Party or Da'wa
Al-Fazila Party
Federation of Worker Councils and Unions in Iraq
Iraqi Communist Party (ICP)
Iraqi National Alliance
Iraqi National Movement
Islamic Group of Kurdistan
Islamic Supreme Council of Iraq (ISCI)
Kurdistan Democratic Party (KDP)
Kurdistan Islamic Union
Left-Worker Communist Party of Iraq
Mustamarun Movement
National Democratic Party
National Reformist Trend or Tayar al-Islah

Patriotic Union of Kurdistan (PUK)
Sadrist Movement or *Tayar al-Sadri*
Worker-Communist Party of Iraq

Cultural, Ethnic, and Religious Groups and Centers

Al-Batul Cultural Center
Ashur Banipal Cultural Association
Islamic Institution for Women and Children
Khanzad Social and Cultural Center
Yazidi Cultural Forum

Research Institutions and Centers

Al-Thakalain Study Center
Gender and Violence Studies Center (Sulaymaniyah University)
Iraqiyat Study Center

Governmental Institutions

Bayt al-Hikma al-'Iraqi
High Council in Charge of Women's Affairs (Erbil)
Ministry of State in Charge of Women's Affairs (Baghdad)
Office in Charge of the Struggle against Gender Based Violence (Erbil)
Parliamentary Committee for Women and Children (Iraqi Parliament)

Note on Translation and Transliteration

This book is meant as much for a general reader as it is for specialists. I have preserved Arabic terms when it was possible for words commonly used by non-Arabic speakers and names of places such as cities, neighborhoods, and institutions. I have generally followed the transliteration guidelines of the *International Journal of Middle East Studies* but have not used diacritical long vowel marks.

Introduction

Many sociological questions about this research on women, gender, and feminisms in Iraq were answered by my experience of the everyday life in postinvasion Iraq. For a day of fieldwork in the capital city center, we have to pass at least a dozen checkpoints as our car, driven by 'Amu[1] Abu Manal[2], leaves my family house in al-Kazimiyya on our way to central Baghdad. Such checkpoints are situated between the different areas of the capital we are crossing, and some are more imposing than others. Framed by concrete walls, a checkpoint can consist of pulling into a hall where the car is parked and the motor turned off; a soldier then passes a mirror under the car's wheels, and another walks with an explosive detector around the car. Sometimes we would have to get out of the car, and its trunk would be searched. In such cases, 'Amu Abu Manal would be searched from head to toe by soldiers while standing in front of the car, and I would be taken behind a window where my bag would be searched and my body patted down by women security guards. Such checkpoints are rare and mostly found in areas such as al-Kazimiyya, which is often visited for the al-Kazimayn shrines, or between some Sunni and Shi'a neighborhoods. For most other checkpoints, 'Amu Abu Manal would not have to turn off the motor or park the car; he would simply lower his window and salute the soldiers, who would always salute back, while one of the soldiers would run an explosive detector alongside the car as it passed the concrete walls. Passing checkpoints is more or less difficult and time-consuming depending on the security climate in the country. If there was a car bomb, an assassination of a political leader, or any kind of security-related events during the week, the circulation in Baghdad would be slowed down due to

---

[1] 'Amu is a familiar and affectionate word that means "uncle," and it can be used to designate a paternal uncle or an elder man, as in this case.

[2] *Abu Manal* means literally the "father of Manal." In Iraq, most adults are commonly addressed as "father of" or "mother of" their eldest son, and less frequently eldest daughter, as in the case of Abu Manal, who has three daughters and whose eldest is named Manal.

1

increased checkpoint inspections. In such environments, we would have
to leave home earlier; if an explosion happened while we were on the road
in a nearby area of Baghdad, we would have to wait hours for the soldiers
to allow us through the checkpoints, especially if we were trying to cross
neighborhoods of different sects.

Every day in Baghdad carries its uncertainties, surprises, and often
frustrations and tensions. Baghdad is segmented by checkpoints and
concrete walls that divide its neighborhoods according to ethnic, religious
and sectarian belonging; such barriers also exist around governmental
buildings and surrounding the Green Zone where some of the country's
most important institutions (Parliament, Council of Ministries, etc.), the
US Embassy, the United Nations, and other international agencies are
situated. Although these walls are often covered in paintings of the Iraqi
flag, scenes highlighting national unity, and various symbols of ancient
and modern Iraq,[3] these art works hardly affect the atmosphere of conflict, chaos, and degradation and impoverishment. On our way to central
Baghdad, between buildings marked by bullets or traces of explosions,
hanging electricity wires, and dirt, I witness heart-wrenching scenes of
women beggars. Often holding a swaddled baby in their arms, they would
sit in the dust wearing a ripped black *'abaya*[4] or stand selling small packets
of tissues to car drivers. Next to them, children whose faces have been
burned by the sun sell all kinds of biscuits, sweets, and small bottles of
water. In the evenings, the women beggars approach families sitting on
restaurant terraces, at ice cream parlors, or in cocktail shops to sell small
packets of chewing gum. Always presenting themselves as widows, these
women would ask for help to feed their children. They are the only
women hanging around the streets, because most women are merely
passing by, entering or leaving a shop, or sitting in family-dedicated
spaces. The rest of the capital's public outdoor spaces are occupied by
men, and armed male soldiers and police officers stand at every corner
(see Figures I.1 and I.2).

While we approach central Baghdad, 'Amu Abu Manal said to me: "'Amu
Zahra, al-Rashid is not a good place to walk around, especially for a young
woman like you. It is full of *muhasheshin* ['junkies'] and loose men. Let me

[3] In 2008, the occupying Multi-National Forces (MNFs) decided to erect checkpoints and
mural divisions in the form of the T-walls all over the capital in their attempt to "secure"
the different areas of Baghdad, which were divided according to sectarian belonging after
the 2006–7 explosion of violence. In 2008, the US army, the Iraqi government, and several
foreign associations commissioned a $100,000 budget for what was called a "beautifica-
tion campaign" for the T-walls, which was led by local municipalities. This resulted in the
creation of a series of paintings, mostly inspired by ancient Mesopotamia symbolism, all
over Baghdad (Damluji 2010; Pieri 2014).
[4] A traditional piece of women's clothing in Iraq consisting in a long section of black tissue.

Figure I.1 Central Baghdad (April 2012)

drive you directly to al-Mutannabi Street." I replied: "I would like to walk around there, in Bab al-Mu'azem, al-Midan, the 'old Baghdad' and also al-Rashid and al-Nahar Street before going to al-Mutannabi." 'Amu Abu Manal was right, it is not pleasant to walk around this area nowadays, but I still enjoyed going there because of its association with my family: my mother used to work on al-Rashid Street as an accountant at the Orosdi Company, which is where she met my father, and, in the 1970s, al-Nahar Street is where my mother would go shopping for fashionable clothes and spend time with her friends. Today, these streets have been converted into depositories and wholesale shops for all kinds of products. This area of Baghdad used to be the cultural and social heart of the city; when my parents first met in their mid-twenties, this area was full of theaters, cinemas, shops, cafés, restaurants, and places for young Baghdadis to relax, socialize, and walk around. Now the beautifully white and flowery balconies and colonnades are covered in dirt, and the theaters, cinemas, and cafés have disappeared. The area has become a stomping ground for poor, lurking men and has the reputation for hosting all kinds of underground business. Despite harassing looks and remarks from the men with tattered clothing who hung

Figure I.2 Al-Shuhada' Bridge (May 2017)

around aimlessly, I often walk around there – either alone or accompanied – before heading to al-Mutannabi (see Figures I.3 and I.4).

In Baghdad, I visit al-Mutannabi area on an almost weekly basis. Friday is the day this street, which is dedicated to books and stationary, unveils its treasures and wonders: booksellers display their books along the street as scholars and students of all fields, poets, musicians, writers, painters, political activists, and idealists of all ages walk along. Usually a cultural event is organized in Dar al-Mada bookshop or in the cultural center recently restored at the end of the street, after which people sit at the al-Shabendar Teahouse and discuss things over black or lemon tea. Al-Mutannabi is the only street in central Baghdad that has been refurbished; it was nearly destroyed in 2007 after a dramatic car bomb killed thirty people and wounded a hundred. Every Friday afternoon I feel that I am on an island far away from the realities of Baghdad. In the little garden at the end of the street, around al-Qishla clock tower[5] on the edge of the Tigris River, a group of young musicians often sits at a wooden kiosk singing old Iraqi songs and playing Maqam with their ouds while others improvise verses of poetry.

---

[5] Built during the Ottoman period in 1855.

Figure I.3 Al-Rashid Street (March 2010)

There one can meet famous Iraqi scholars and artists, as well as meet with activists and liberal and leftist politicians (see Figures I.5 and I.6).

There are not so many women, young or old, walking around in this area nowadays; middle-aged or older academic and other highly educated men are in the majority. Most of the women I meet, apart from activists and scholars with whom I have a specific appointment, are mothers who come to buy schoolbooks for their children (see Figures I.7 and I.8).

Sadly, apart from small little islands like al-Mutannabi and university campuses, most outside public spaces in Baghdad are male dominated, particularly by young and middle-aged army soldiers or police officers. Poor widows begging in tattered black 'abaya are the primary female figures in the streets. Even the gorgeous Abu Nuwas promenade, which is bordered by gardens and flowering trees at the edge of the Tigris River, is no longer the place for lovers. Its restaurants, where my maternal grandparents brought their children to eat their famous *samach mesguf* ("smoked fish") on the banks of the Tigris, are today empty and in disrepair. The French Cultural Center where I sometimes study is situated on Abu Nuwas, and I am often the only woman walking alone

Figure I.4 Al-Rashid Street (May 2017)

there, several times being harassed by soldiers at checkpoints or lurking men. I later heard from relatives that this area had become a landmark for prostitution, understanding then why I was constantly told to avoid this area without anyone verbalizing the reason. When I asked my female cousins of a similar age about their experiences walking in central Baghdad, they said emphatically that it is no place to walk at all, especially for women. A few weeks after I settled in Baghdad, I realized that "going out" with my cousins and relatives meant going to "family-dedicated places" – restaurants, shopping areas, or homes. Often my male cousins would leave the family gathering after a while and continue the evening together in a coffee or a *shisha* place. Many cafés in the capital are exclusively open to men after 7 P.M., and most restaurants are divided into two spaces: the *shabab* ("young men") area for men and the *'awa'il* ("family") area for women.

The militarization of Baghdad's public space makes it a real challenge to photograph the streets of the capital, and I received many warnings from soldiers when I attempt to do so. I told that taking photographs was forbidden, especially in areas related to the Green Zone (some

Figure I.5 Al-Mutannabi (May 2017)

of the Green Zone is visible from Abu Nuwas and central Baghdad), official buildings, political party offices, and checkpoints. In order to evade such warnings, I bought a little pink camera that looked like a girlish telephone in the hopes that it would confuse the army soldiers and police officers standing at every corner. I initially thought the soldiers would not forbid a young woman to take random pictures in the streets, and most of the time my performance of innocence and naiveté convinced them that I was taking pictures without intention or agenda. Being a young woman and mastering the urban middle class gender codes in dress and behavior really help me to access many places without being systematically stopped and searched. A man standing, observing, or taking pictures alone in the city would be regarded with suspicion because most of the kidnappings, assassinations, and explosions are perpetrated by males. Dressed casually, I am perceived as harmless while observing and taking pictures, eliciting smiles from male officers rather than suspicion. Nevertheless, most of the time I am so exhausted by trying to move around Baghdad that I have no energy to play the role of simple-minded, girlish photographer. As a result, I take most pictures from inside

Figure I.6 Al-Mutannabi (May 2017)

offices or while sitting with other people at a café or restaurant so as not to garner the attention of security services.

From this brief ethnographic account, the first question that arises is, How did one of the most advanced countries in the Middle East and North Africa, in terms of women and men's education, work, and personal status, turn into this militarized, armed-men-dominated, and fragmented place that is so difficult to live in for its inhabitants, especially for women?

This book explores women, gender, and feminisms in Iraq. My sociological approach merges in-depth ethnography and social, political, and oral histories to provide an understanding of Iraqi women's social, economic, and political experiences that allows me to analyze the content, realities, and political significance of the different forms of their social and political activism and feminisms. My initial argument here is that women and gender issues as well as feminist struggles in Iraq must be analyzed through a complex, relational, historical, and multilayered lens of analysis that moves away from the use of "culture" or an undifferentiated "Islam" to explain women's social, economic, and political realities. Looking at Iraq's social histories from – at least – the very formation

Figure I.7 Crowd at the end of al-Mutannabi, in front of the Shahbender Teahouse (May 2017)

of the postcolonial state appeared essential to me, as much as avoiding an approach marked by the "post-2003 rupture" (Harling 2012)[6] or through the reductive lens of an undifferentiated and millinery violence (Al-Rachid and Méténier 2008). Clearly, this book is as much about women, gender, and feminisms in Iraq as it is a feminist book about Iraq. As such, it seeks to contribute to critical feminist debates as well as to propose a feminist analysis of Iraq's contemporary social and political history.

With and Beyond the Postcolonial: Looking at the Materiality and Heterogeneity of "Culture"

Since the publication of Edward Said's *Orientalism* (1977), significant steps have been made in academic approaches to the Middle East and Muslim majority contexts. Mostly influenced by Fanon's groundbreaking

[6] As rightly pointed out by Peter Harling (2012), the lack of historiographical continuity of many research on Iraq starting the study of its current realities in 2003 poses a serious problem to the understanding of its social, economic and political histories.

Figure I.8 Al-Qishla Park, poetry in a kiosk (May 2017)

works (1952, 1961), Said provides a strong critique of Western scholarship's tendency to essentialize the so-called Orient, depicting it as in opposition to a supposed West. In this dichotomous equation, the "Orient" is depicted as fundamentally archaic, barbaric, and inclined to despotism; the "West," by contrast, is defined as modern, progressive, and liberal. Said also shows that by depicting the "East" in essentialist and negative terms, Western writers and researchers constructed a positive representation of the West, justifying its colonial enterprise and so-called mission of civilization. Throughout his work, Said always insists on the importance of deconstructing essentialism, seeing neither the East nor the West as homogeneous realities but instead as representational constructs built on and according to the interests of European colonialism. While denouncing Western imperialism by revealing the functioning of its discursive mechanisms, in line with Fanon (1961), Said remained cautious about the risk of falling into reverse essentialism. In *Culture and Imperialism* (1994), he provides a critique of several forms of identity politics–based cultural resistance and a homogenized representation of the West. According to Said, "Occidentalism" means accepting the racial, religious, and political divisions imposed by imperialism itself. Moreover, Zubaida (1989) also shows the importance of deconstructing Western/Eastern dichotomies in refusing to situate the roots of concepts – such as modernization and feminism – in the West. He insists on dismantling linear and simplistic evolutionist readings of Western history and showing the conflicting dynamics of modernization in the geographic spaces considered as the West and the East.

The gender dimension of cultural imperialism was pointed out in Gayatri Chakravorty Spivak's famous quote: "White men saving brown women from brown men" (1988). Moreover, postcolonial feminism has showed that Eurocentric modernist categories of "women's rights" and agenda are based often on the objectification of the "Third World woman" considered as the bearer of difference. In her groundbreaking article "Under Western Eyes" and its revisited version, Chandra Talpade Mohanty (1986, 2003b) argues that assumptions of privilege and ethnocentric universality, on the one hand, and inadequate self-consciousness about the effect of dominant Western scholarship on the "Third World" in the context of a world system dominated by Western economic, military, and political powers, on the other, characterize white feminist scholarship on women in the "Third World". It is in the production of this "Third World difference" that white feminisms appropriate and colonize the constitutive complexities that characterize the lives of women in the colonized countries. It is in the homogenization and systematization of the oppression of women in the "Third World" through "culture" and "religion" that white feminist scholarship exists and finds the definitions of its own self. Regarding Muslim contexts, Leila Ahmed's work (1992) reveals the colonial roots of modern debates on women and gender in relation to Islam, looking specifically at the Egyptian context. She shows how the "woman question" was constructed during the colonial period and depicted "Muslim woman oppression" as caused by an undifferentiated, essentially patriarchal, and archaic "Muslim culture" that stood in opposition to a Western culture supposedly favorable to women's rights and dignity. According to Ahmed, the construction of the "Muslim woman question" guides debates on women and gender in Muslim contexts and frames the way political resistance to Western domination was formulated. This is at the core of the dilemma faced by women's rights activists in Muslim majority contexts as according to Ahmed they have to choose between "betrayal or betrayal" in contexts where their defense of gender equality is often associated with "Westernized demands" (Ahmed 1982). Ahmed also looks at the process of "re-veiling" in Muslim majority contexts, as well as within Muslim communities in the United States, depicting it as representing a form of "cultural resistance" to Western models of modernity (Ahmed 2011).

As much as I sympathize with Ahmed's approach, especially in revealing the colonial roots of the "Muslim woman question," I also emphasize the necessity of looking at the plurality of Islam(s) and the complexity and diversity of what constitutes Muslim women's realities. Moreover, in line with Zubaida's *Beyond Islam* (2011), I suggest that colonialism also represented a discursive process that had an impact on cultural representations of "modern" and "traditional." As Zubaida argues, colonial modernity was also the introduction of modern capitalism in the Middle East and, as a consequence, of transformations of social relations, powers, and authorities brought about by sweeping socioeconomic forces. These forces, according to Zubaida, produced different patterns of cultural and political transformations depending on local historical and cultural conjunctures. These differences are not the West versus the "Rest" but include both the West and the "Rest." In shedding light on the material realities of colonialism, Zubaida managed to deconstruct the overemphasis on its discursive and representational realities. Moreover, he insists on deconstructing the undifferentiated and decontextualized use of the "Islamic" adjective, which is often added to the word "culture," in showing the complexity and diversity of realities and dynamics deemed as "Islamic."

I concur with Zubaida's argument; in this research, I suggest going beyond analyses based on "discourses and representations" and grounding "culture" in its material contexts. By doing so, I suggest that discursive dimensions are insufficient to understand the complex and multidimensional aspects of women's lives in contexts broadly qualified as "Muslim." Without undermining the importance of the discursive, I argue that by focusing on the discursive and representational dimensions of "culture," its concrete realities can be omitted and that both representations and their concrete material realities of deployment should be considered in the analysis. In other words, I argue that the use of "Islamic culture" or "in Islam" has no meaning unless situated economically, politically, and socially and analyzed according to a context or a situation. These expressions are not only misleading, they can also easily fall into a form of essentialization.

This is why Lila Abu-Lughod's "Writing against Culture" (1991) echoes so much in my research process. Abu-Lughod refused to use the word "culture" because she reacted to its generalizing and homogenizing tendency within the field of anthropology. The use of the terms "culture" and "Muslim culture" not only homogenizes complex and multidimensional realities but also push away analysis of the material realities in which "culture" is shaped, reshaped, lived, and experienced. Abu-Lughod also proposes to avoid generalization and favor the focus on "particular individuals and their changing relationships" in order to "subvert the most problematic connotations of culture: homogeneity, coherence, and timelessness" (Abu-Lughod 1991: 473–76).

   In line with Abu-Lughod's perspective, another essential dimension is to be considered that has been pointed out by Deniz Kandiyoti regarding the limit of adopting a postcolonial approach in the field of Middle East gender studies. She argues that it can also be negatively affected by the arguments of Orientalism through the fact that social analysis and ethnography have been devaluated in favor of an analysis of representations that relies mainly on secondary sources. Kandiyoti also argues that binary thinking about East and West has trained researchers to focus too much on the West and not enough on the internal heterogeneity of Middle Eastern societies. The anti-Eurocentrism criticism standpoint can also reinforce indirectly these very binary categories by deflecting attention away from local institutions such as "family, school, the military, the market and cultural processes that are implicated in the production of gender hierarchies and in forms of subordination based on gender" (Kandiyoti 1996: 16–18). I entirely concur with Kandiyoti's concerns, which are also echoed in Ella Shohat's (2006) comment about the fact that knowledge about the Middle East in some feminist scholarship focused on Orientalist discourse about "them" while "they" remain safely locked in area studies.

New Feminists Praxis

My proposition in this book is to analyze both discursive and material realities of Iraqi women's social, political, and economic realities and activisms through an approach that not only moves away from analysis involving "culture" or an undifferentiated Islam but also enriches critical feminist analysis. The feminist approach that I propose here considers contextuality, complexity, relationality, and historicity as essential to the study of women and gender issues in any place in the world. As such, it merges analysis common to intersectional, Black, Third World, transnational, postcolonial, relational, and decolonial feminisms that are often labeled differently to express this essential approach. Intersectional analysis was born out of Black feminist scholarship that considers complexity, relationality, power, social context, social inequality, and social justice as essential dimensions in considering human's realities (Bilge & Collins 2016). Black, intersectional, transnational, and postcolonial/decolonial feminist scholarship questioned a so-called sisterhood supposed to gather all women together, pointing out the differences existing between women (Brah & Phoenix 2004; Collins 1989; Crenshaw 1991, 1989; Davis 1981; Hooks 1986; Lazreg 1994; Lorde 1984; Lugones 2010; Mohanty 1988, 2003). These feminist scholars argue that class, gender, race, ethnicity, sexuality, ability, and religion are interconnected in women's everyday lives and thus also agree on the importance of grounding feminist analysis within these "borders." Yuval-Davis, for example, points out that there is no definition of women that is not ethnicized, racialized, classed, aged, sexualized, etc. (Yuval-Davis 2007).

Transnational feminist analysis choice for the "trans" instead of the "inter" national reflects both the need to destabilize rather than maintain boundaries of nations, race, gender, sexuality, etc. (Grewal and Kaplan 2006) and a criticism of a so-called "global feminism" supposed to gather all women together. This "global sisterhood" relies on Eurocentric middle-class neoliberal notion of solidarity to define what "women of the world" need and what are their priorities of struggle (Enloe 2004). This scholarship discusses globalization in the transnational context showing that diverse forms of nationalisms promote new forms of patriarchy in which women are deemed "bearer of the nation." The "nation" in question is defined in essentialist and exclusivist terms and relies on militaristic male-dominated notions of citizenship in which the definitions of normative gender roles and identities are central. Inderpal Grewal and Caren Kaplan (2006) argue for the need to articulate the relationship of gender to scattered hegemonies such as global economic structures, patriarchal nationalisms, traditions, local structures of domination, and legal-juridical oppression on multiple levels. Central to a transnational feminist approach is to recognize the link between women, not through a fake universality of being and condition – that is, in reality, Eurocentric, middle class, and neoliberal – but between women's involvement in social and political dynamics that affect other women. In relation to Iraq, Ali-Ali and Pratt (2009) have pointed out the instrumentalization of a "feminist" discourse to justify the US-led occupation and invasion in the name of "saving Iraqi women."

For Mohanty, the globalization is an economic, political, and ideological phenomenon that actively brings the world and its various communities under connected and interdependent discursive and material regimes. The lives of women are connected and interdependent, albeit not the same, no matter which geographic area we happen to live in (Mohanty 2003a: 192–221). Thus, for Alexander and Mohanty (1997), feminist praxis in global contexts would involve shifting the unit of analysis from local, regional, and national "culture" to relations and processes across borders of these "cultures" defined by nations, ethnicity, race, class, sexuality, and so on. It is indeed very important to look at local feminist praxis and at the same time to understand the local in relation to larger, cross-national processes. Thus this framework challenges the originary status of Western-centric feminisms. It does not simply position Third World feminism as a reaction to gaps in Western feminism. Instead, it provides a position from which to argue for a comparative, relational feminist praxis that is transnational in its response to and engagement with global processes of colonization and imperialism (Mohanty and Alexander 1997: xx). Instead of the white Eurocentric and neoliberal frame of "simultaneity of women's oppressions," Mohanty, Russo, and Torres (1991) propose that feminist praxis should be grounded in the histories of racism and imperialism, capitalism, and neoliberal nation-states projects.

In the same line, Ella Shohat argues convincingly for a relational analysis that addresses the operative terms and axes of stratification typical of specific contexts, along with the ways these terms and stratifications are translated and reinvoiced as they "travel" from one context to another. She argues that the question of difference among so-called Western and Third World women is not to fix the difference in terms of culture but to look at different positioning vis-à-vis histories of power, especially since the advent of colonialism. It is to show the complicated histories and communities for "dialogical encounters of differences" (Shohat 2006: 1–16).

Many feminists have criticized the growing "trinity of race, class, and gender" in much of intersectional scholarship, as well as its use in simply applying additive or multiplicative analysis of the different dimensions of women's social, economic, and political realities. What I argue here is that approaching Iraqi women's lives and activism through a complex intersectional/relational lens does not mean that one has to look at gender, class, kinship, and ethnic, religious, and sectarian belonging in the same way as realities and entities added to one another. It means grounding Iraqi women's experiences in sociological analysis. This implies in-depth ethnography on which I apply a historical lens – through the use of social, political, and oral histories – exploring carefully what the relationships between gender, class, kinship, ethnic, religious, and sectarian belongings and the nature of the state and nationhood mean differently in a particular space and time. It also means grounding Iraqi women's experiences in their specific contexts and local positions while, at the same time, seeing the transnational dynamics that shape their lives. It is analyzing the complex and multilayered ways in which the different forms of power and position function and interact with one another. In other words, pointing out the transnational/intersectional/relational dimensions of feminism is a way to say that what is commonly called "local" is in fact not limited to a specific time and space and is also defined by transnational/regional dynamics. In the same line, what is deemed "global," instead of merging different local interests or being applied across national borders, can in reality represent very specific – neoliberal – interests and concerns. Careful not to fall into the trap of simplistic identity politics, I also pay attention to the nonfixity of these categories and to the need to permanently renew the analysis according to their changing dynamics.

I believe that concerns for complexity, contextuality, historicity, and relationality have an impact on how one "does" the research. My ethnographic account of Iraqi women's political activism since 2003 was guided by an intersectional look that pushed me to carefully consider the diverse dimensions of their everyday realities that I encountered during my fieldwork in Baghdad, Erbil and Sulaymaniyah (Iraqi Kurdistan), Najaf-Kufa, Karbala, and Nasiriyah. In addition to asking Iraqi women activists about their family, education, professional, and social and political trajectories, I also paid significant attention to their concrete conditions of life and activism. Adopting this approach to the ethnographic study of Iraqi women's political activism also means studying their everyday lives, as well as their offices and the places where they gather, mobilize, and demonstrate. Thus I acknowledge the diverse dimensions of Iraqi women's lives and activism in my exploration of the different private and public spaces they occupy and within which they circulate. This means observing their houses and their neighborhoods, the streets of the cities and neighborhoods in which they live, the university campuses where many work or study, the cultural and social spaces where they socialize, and the different cultural centers in which they organize gatherings and activities. In multiplying the spaces of observation linked to Iraqi women activists' personal lives and activism, I obtain a broader perspective of and in-depth look into the concrete and material realities in which they work and mobilize for women's rights. In so doing, I gather a complex understanding of Iraqi women activists' "discourses and representations" of women's rights, gender norms, and representations and thus am able to go beyond the overemphasis on the "discursive" and look at the concrete realities of their lives and activism. Then my collection of Iraqi women political activists' oral histories over two years of in-depth fieldwork, followed by several shorter fieldwork trips and the use of exhaustive historical materials on the social, political, and economic transformations and evolutions of Iraq, allows me to provide a complex analysis of women and gender issues and feminisms in contemporary Iraq.

Approaching Women, Gender, and Feminisms in Iraq

Women, Gender, Nation, State, Religion, and Beyond

Nadje Al-Ali's *Iraqi Women: Untold Stories from 1948 to the Present* (2007) started me on the path of researching women and gender in Iraq. Al-Ali's study is based on ethnographic research conducted among diasporic Iraqi women in London, Amman, Detroit, and San Diego. Al-Ali's research breaks with approaches that look at women and gender in the Middle East through the lens of undifferentiated "Islam." Her research provides a nuanced and in-depth reading of Iraqi women's social, economic, and political history; it looks at the state's different gender politics, as well as the impact of wars, sanctions, displacement, and exile. After reading Al-Ali's book, I was eager to further explore Iraqi women's social and political history and to expand on this analysis by conducting research inside Iraq.

Postcolonial feminist scholarship applied in Middle Eastern contexts proposes that the study of women and gender in the Middle East should adopt a postcolonial perspective that takes into consideration the varied processes of nation-building, politics, colonialism, imperialism, and economic changes that include class politics, the ideological and political use of Islam, and debates around its status in the state, law, and public spheres. In *Women, Islam and the State* (1991), Deniz Kandiyoti argues that analyses of women's position in Muslim majority societies must be grounded in detailed examinations of nation-states' political projects and historical transformations. Thus, looking at the establishment of nation-states in colonial and postcolonial contexts, along with the different ways the notion of citizenship was elaborated and experienced, is necessary to understand women and gender issues in the Middle East. The postindependence trajectories of modern states, the varied uses of Islam in different nationalisms, state ideologies (nationalism, secularism, etc.) and oppositional social movements, and the varied processes of economic change are central to understanding women's conditions. For Lila Abu-Lughod (1998) colonial constructions of "Eastern women" shaped anticolonial nationalisms and feminist projects in the Middle East but in a way that is not simplistic rejection/acceptance of Western dominant ideas. There has been a selectiveness and reappropriation in the translation of Western ideas and models into local contexts. Her argument means that condemning feminism as a Western import is as inaccurate as considering it as a purely local and indigenous project. Suad Joseph (2000) looks at the gendered dimensions of citizenship in the Middle East. She argues that the enterprise of state-building emerged less as an expression of specific class formations and more in conjunction with the demise of empires, resulting in top-down citizenship. Parallel to these processes has been the ongoing enmeshment of state and civil society, state and kinship, and kinship and civil society. The fluidity of the boundaries between the governmental, the nongovernmental, and kinship has often resulted in continuities in patriarchal practices in a multitude of domains. Women have experienced citizenship differently from men not only because they are women but also because they are women and members of particulars classes, races, ethnicities, and religions – all of which gender them in complex and contradictory ways.

Hisham Sharabi (1966, 1988) contributes to the analysis of women and gender issues in the postcolonial states and societies of the Middle East. Sharabi defines "neopatriarchy" as "modernized patriarchy," as the outcome of modern Europe's colonization of the patriarchal Arab world; thus neopatriarchy is the marriage of imperialism and patriarchy. Neopatriarchy's concrete historical formation was thus shaped by both internal and external forces. Arab societies' forced introduction to "dependent capitalism" within a "Western-dominated world market" via nineteenth- and twentieth-century colonization was an essential dimension of these forces. In line with Sharabi's conceptualization of neopatriarchy, but looking more specifically at the formation of modern nation-states, Floya Anthias and Nira Yuval-Davis (1989) show the centrality of women and gender in the process of modernization. They argued that control over women and sexuality is at the core of national and ethnic processes. Women are deemed "mothers of the nation," the bearers and reproducers of ethnic/national groups and the signifiers of national difference. Thus Yuval-Davis (1997) argues that a "new modern nation" can produce structures that are just as limiting and normative as traditional tribal or kin groups because gender relations and women's reproductive roles and identities are at the core of nationalist projects and ideas of citizenship.

In my analysis of the way Iraqi women deal with neopatriarchal structures, I have been much inspired by Deniz Kandiyoti's "Bargaining with Patriarchy" (1988). Kandiyoti argues that analysis of women's strategies and coping mechanisms leads to a "more culturally and temporally grounded understanding of patriarchal systems" than the abstract notion of "patriarchy." She breaks with simplistic feminist theories that define "patriarchy" as "monolithic male dominance," using it as a blanket term to explain very complex realities. Instead, Kandiyoti shows how women strategize within a concrete set of constraints, which she termed "patriarchal bargains." Kandiyoti highlights the various forms of patriarchy, as well as the contexts in which they are deployed, which present women with distinct "rules of the game" and strategies to "maximize security and optimize life options" with varying potentials for active or passive resistance. In line with Kandiyoti, I explore the social, political, and economic terms in which women "bargained with patriarchy" in contemporary Iraq, according to class, education, and ethnic, religious, and sectarian belonging.

Kumari Jayawardena's *Feminism and Nationalism in the Third World* (1986) was a foundational work in the study of the women's movement in non-Western contexts. Jayawardena shows how feminist movements in the "Third World" emerged from within nationalist struggles that drew on anticapitalism and anti-imperialism. She argues that this emergence corresponded with a move toward secularism, which was dominated by leftist ideologies and prominent among the emerging modern, indigenous middle classes. Since this pioneering work, a wide range of scholarship has further studied the complex link between nationalism and feminism, ethnicity and gender in Middle Eastern contexts (Abu-Lughod 1986, 1998; Afshar 1996; Badran 1995; Baron 2005; Charrad 2001, 2011; Dayan-Herzbrun 2005; Esposito & Haddad 1998; Göle 1993; Hatem 1993, 1994, 1998, 2005; Joseph 2000; Kaplan, Alarcon, & Minoo 1999; Kandiyoti 1991, 1996, 1999, 2007; Kian-Thiébaut 2010, Meriwether & Tucker 1999; Mikdashi, 2013; Tucker 1993).

Most of these studies have shown that although feminist movements emerged from within anti-imperialist struggles and gender was an important component of nationalist discourses, the relationship between nationalist ideologies and leaders and women's rights activists was complex and multilayered. Afshar shows that women have used different strategies to enhance their "traditional" rights and life conditions, such as using their position as "mothers" in "national" struggles in order to gain space within the political sphere (Afshar 1996). Badran (1995) and Dayan-Herzbrun (2005) show how, in the case of postcolonial Egypt, women's rights activists were asked to be both "modern" and represent the "authentic culture" of the independent nation simultaneously. As Charrad (2001, 2011) points out, the issue of the "Personal Status Code" (PSC) – a set of laws often also called "Family Laws" outlining issues such as marriage, divorce, child custody, inheritance, alimony, and so on – represented the *field of struggle* between women activists, nationalists, and tribal and religious leaders in most postindependence contexts. The PSC is the field where indigenous modernist representations of the nation, nationalists' claim for "cultural authenticity" against "Westernization," and tribal and religious authorities competed for powers. The postindependence nation demanded a "new woman"; however, the struggle around how to define this "new modern woman," her legal and political rights, education, and dress code divided women's rights activists, conservative and progressive nationalists, and leftists and communists, as well as religious and tribal authorities. I explore this field of struggle in the Iraqi context and analyze how issues of gender, nationhood, the nature of the state, kinship, and religion were articulated. I show how the changing discourse and reforms regarding the PSC – since its implementation in 1959 – reveal important political, ethnic, religious, sectarian, social, and economic dynamics in contemporary Iraq.

Feminisms, Islam, and Islamisms

Sharabi (1988) describes Islamism as the product of neopatriarchy, as a movement of political emancipation and cultural revival that opposed Westernization and criticized nationalism's, communism's, and socialism's inability to oppose imperialism. On this point, Sharabi's depiction is close to the analysis of Zubaida (1989) and Burgat (1996) on the emergence of Islamism in postcolonial Muslim majority countries. In contrast with essentialist approaches that build historical continuity between a supposed "Islam" and its political expressions, Zubaida and Burgat situates Islamism within the framework of nation-state formation and the process of modernization imposed by colonization. Looking more specifically at the Iranian context, Moghadam (1994) and Mir-Hosseini (1999) show how Islamism and the process of Islamization – present in many Middle Eastern societies since the 1970s – are also gendered processes. Mervat Hatem (1993, 1994, 1998, 2005) and Lila Abu-Lughod (1998) reveal the gender commonalities between contemporary nationalists and Islamists in Egypt: they both promote a modern, middle-class, patriarchal nuclear family model that emphasizes domesticity as central to the definition of femininity. I examine the realities of Islamism in Iraq and analyze the gender dimensions of its different movements. However, I argue that, in the case of Iraq, analysis of Islamism and gender must be complemented by a careful look at the state, as well as the competing nationalisms of the state and the tribal, ethnic, religious, and sectarian dynamics of society.

Later, in the 1970s context of the rise of Islamist movements, the realities and debates around women's legal and political rights carried an "Islamic" tint. Since the 1990s, the Middle East's social and political realities were characterized by growing Islamization, and scholarship dealing with women and gender paid particular attention to the emergence of women's activism within groups and movements affiliated with political Islam or Muslim pietist movements (Ahmed 1992; Deeb 2006; Göle 1993; Karam 1998; Mir-Hosseini 1999; Mahmood 2005). Such literature presents Islamist or Muslim-affiliated women's activism as the manifestation of alternative experiences and definitions of modernity within Islam, and analyzes Islamist women's activism and pietist women's movements as separate from or in opposition to "secular" forms of activism. Reacting to the increased attention to "Islamist" women's activism, Nadje Al-Ali's (2000) research on the Egyptian women's movement focuses on "secular-oriented" forms of activism. Al-Ali seeks to break with Western/Eastern dichotomies, proposes a contextual reading of Egyptian women activists, and problematizes notions of secularism and feminism through a postcolonial reading. She shows that women's rights activism reflects the Egyptian social and political culture. All such studies, whether they focus on "Islamist" or "secular" forms of women's agency and activism, analyze "secular" and "religious" forms of agency and activism as separate, distinct, and, at times, oppositional. Thus, I argue that while trying to show complexity and homogeneity, most of the research on women's activism in Muslim majority contexts still use a secular/Islamist paradigm in their analysis.

More recently, Zakia Salime's research (2011) takes a more nuanced approach to the dichotomist study of secular/Islamist women's rights activists, analyzing the debates around the *mudawwana* ("family law") in Morocco. She offers a relational, rather than a comparative, ethnographic study of the "feminist" and "Islamist women's movement." Salime (2011) argues that exploring feminist politics requires, on the one hand, an examination of how the feminist movement has been both enabled and circumscribed by Islamist women's activism over the past two decades, and on the other hand, such an exploration also entails identification of the various ways in which feminist movements have shaped the politics of protest among Islamist women. Salime thus describes these changes as the "feminization" of Islamist women and the "Islamization" of feminist movements. Afsaneh Najmabadi (2000), in the context of postrevolutionary Iran, argues that the configurations of Islam, feminism, nationalism, and secularism have been hybridized by two decades of power of the Islamic Republic and thus cannot be analyzed through previously dominant and accepted political paradigms. She insists on the fact that Islam, secularism, nationalism, and feminism are historically defined and in changing relationship and should be analyzed as such. My approach is very close to those of Salime and Najmabadi because I explore Iraqi women's activism from diverse religious, ethnic, sectarian, and political backgrounds in relation to one another, not as separate entities, and contextualize feminism, secularism, and Islamism. In this book, I provide an ethnographic account of diverse women's groups and networks. In my analysis, I do not apply a different *grille de lecture* ("reading grill") for Islamist and secular women activists; on the contrary, I explore such activisms in relation to one another, as part of a shared context. I analyze this context and activism in imbricating experiences of class, education, and ethnic, religious, and sectarian belongings.

Here, I show the heterogeneity of both Islamist and secular women's activism. Such activism must be analyzed according to a complex framework – a framework that includes a historical analysis of the overlapping of gender, nation, state, and Islam, as well as an examination of the diverse aspects of women's lives, such as class, education, place of residence, and ethnic, religious and sectarian belongings. In line with Niamh Reilly, who proposes to "rethink secularism as a feminist principle" (2011), I argue that the "secular" itself has to be contextualized and read within a complex framework in order to be understood. Moreover, the "religious" – notions of "Islamism" and "Islamization" – also have to be contextualized and approached through a complex analytical framework. Deeb and Harb (2013) adopt a multilayered approach to morality and piety, showing that these notions cannot be read as "purely religious" because they also contain political and social dimensions. I concur with Reilly (2011) and Deeb and Harb (2013) as I argue that the "purely religious" or "purely secular" do not exist; Iraqi women's activism has social, political, economic, and religious dimensions. The significance of each of these dimensions varies according to the context, i.e., according to state policies, state-society relations, diverse notions of nationhood, and different expressions, practices, and understandings of Islam within society as a whole.

Because this research problematizes the significance of the terms "secular" and "Islamist" women's activism, I give these words practical preliminary definitions. Throughout this book, I use the word "secular" as a qualifier for "nonreligious" – in the Iraqi context, this mainly means non-Islamist – or "pluralistic" modes of activism depending on the circumstances. For example, I use secular as pluralistic in situations where Christian organizations or Islamist groups are involved in coalitions and networks that do not have religious aims. Thus I use "secular" and "Islamist" to designate forms and modes of activism, not individuals. In this book, an "Islamist activist" is a person involved in an organization that specifically identifies Islam as an essential dimension of struggle and identity; such a person could also be involved in a secular group or secular institution. Similarly, a "secular activist" is a person involved in an organization that does not refer to religion as an essential dimension of struggle and identity. However, by often avoiding labeling individuals as "secular" or "Islamist" and instead choosing to qualify forms of activism, I problematize these notions. In so doing, I also show that an activist involved in a secular organization can, at a personal level, consider Islam to be an essential dimension of struggle and identity; likewise, a person involved in an Islamist organization can consider pluralistic notions of struggle and identity.

"NGOization" of Women's Activism

Since the 2000s, a growing number of studies on women's movements in the Middle East have noted the impact of global dynamics on local women's associations and networks. In contexts marked by the rise of Islamism, nationalism, neoliberalism, and privatization and the decline of the welfare state as a direct result of structural adjustment policies, all of which affected women's lives, rights, and activism, Moghadam (2009) analyzes women's movements as part of transnational movements for "global justice." Islah Jad (2003) analyzes the "NGOization" of women's activism in the Middle East, which she characterized as the "depoliticization" of women's initiatives and alignment with US-led, International Monetary Fund (IMF)'s agendas and World Bank agendas that highlight "civil society" groups as part of their neocolonial policies of "democratization" in the Middle East. Many studies have further analyzed the complex link between the global – US, UN, IMF, and World Bank oriented – and local agendas in the field of women's activism in contexts such as Jordan (Latte-Abdallah 2009; Pietrobelli 2013), Palestine (Richter-Devroe 2008, 2009), and Egypt (Abdelrahman 2007).

Kandiyoti (2007) notes that the investment of international policymakers occurs under the banner of the "internationalization of state-building" after imperialist military interventions in countries such as Afghanistan and Iraq. She argues that the focus of the United Nations and nongovernmental organizations (NGOs) on women's rights, despite being the product of transnational feminist activism, occurs in a context where military interventions and neoliberal politics have had a negative impact on women's basic human's rights and plunged entire countries into "underdevelopment" and humanitarian crises. In the case of post-invasion Iraq, Al-Ali and Pratt (2009) reveal the contradictory terms in which, on the one hand, the US administration emphasized Iraqi women's rights as justification for its imperialist invasion and occupation and, on the other hand, provoked a situation of political and humanitarian crisis that questions the very notion of citizenship and basic human rights. Mojab's analysis (2009, 2007) of women's activism in Iraqi

Kurdistan is also very critical of international and US donors' investment in women's groups and organization since 1991.

Both Jad (2007) and Mojab (2003, 2004, 2007, 2009) – in "post-Oslo Palestine" and "post-1991 Iraqi Kurdistan," respectively – point out the gap between "grassroots women's groups" and "women's NGOs" funded by the United States, the United Nations, and international donors. In Abu-Lughod's latest work (2013), she questions the relation between women activists involved in rights-based agendas, who use an "Islamic framework of rights," and "those in whose name and on whose behalf they work." She points out two essential critiques to women activists using an "Islamic framework of rights": first, she asks whether their initiatives can be understood outside the frames of global governance that are tied to class privilege and education and which vocabulary is saturated by democratic liberalism, even though the participants work with a shared sense of religious community and religious knowledge. Abu-Lughod also asks whether any legalistic framework of rights – human rights, Islamic frame of rights, etc. – or gender equality can do justice to the complexity of women's lives and suffering. According to Abu-Lughod, there is a profound disconnect between the lives of "grassroots" women and the terms in which they are "imagined" in the field of rights, including Islamic feminist versions (Abu-Lughod 2013: 173–200).

My research follows and aims to enrich these studies. Categories such as class, kinship, and nationhood; the nature of the state, ethnicity, and religion; and the social formations related to them (such as communism, socialism, tribalism, nationalism, authoritarianism, militarism, Islamism, and sectarianism) need to be analyzed in relation to each other, keeping in mind their changing and transnational dimensions. Thus, instead of applying them to my fieldwork as predefined and static realities, I use them as guiding social and political phenomena and tried to read them in their historical evolutions and transformations.

Conducting Fieldwork in Postinvasion Iraq

I first settled in Damascus in 2009 with the intention of researching Iraqi women political activists living in Sayyida Zaynab and Jaramana. From 2006–7, Damascus became the first place of exile for Iraqis fleeing sectarian violence (Chatelard & Doraï 2009). Iraqis mainly lived in the Damascus suburbs, such as Jaramana and Sayyida Zaynab, with its *shari' al-Iraqyyn* ("Iraqis' street"). After the 'Askeri shrine in Samarra was attacked in February 2006, the level of violence in Iraq skyrocketed, reaching 1,000 deaths per week. The dramatic circumstances of Iraqis' everyday lives was marked not only by the number of killings but also by the nature of the violence itself: gun shootings, kidnaps for ransom, torture, civilian corpses were everywhere in Baghdad. It was a mixture of gang violence, armed sectarian militias, politicosectarian mercenaries, targeted kidnappings, and assassinations. Most of Baghdad's neighborhoods experienced sectarian separation by the politicosectarian groups that ruled the streets. More than 60 percent of Baghdad's population was displaced either inside the capital, in other Iraqi provinces, or abroad. In an attempt to "secure" the different areas of Baghdad, the occupying Multinational Forces (MNF) decided to erect checkpoints and mural divisions in the form of T-walls all over the capital in 2008 (Damaluji 2010; Pieri 2014). This completely altered Baghdad. In addition to its general sanctions-induced poverty, Baghdad has become entirely fragmented by checkpoints and concrete walls. Today the inhabitants of al-Kazimiyya, a predominantly Shi'a area, feel completely distant from those in the Sunni-dominated al-A'zamiyya neighborhood, although only a short bridge divides them (see Maps 1 through 3 showing the evolution of the ethnic and religious population distribution in Baghdad in 2003, 2006, and late 2007).

After visiting Baghdad in March 2010 to get a sense of the security climate, I decided to settle there in October 2010 and stayed in my grandmother's house in al-Kazimiyya until June 2012, sharing my everyday life with Bibi,[7] my bedridden grandmother, who passed away a few months before the completion of this manuscript, and Khala[8] Muluk. 'Amu Abu Manal – the forty-four-year-old husband of Khala Um Manal, father of three girls, and longtime neighbor and friend of my family – has been a taxi driver since the mid-1990s and has lived in Baghdad all his life. He used to run a small biscuit factory but had to close it due to the assassinations of several of his employees during the sectarian war. He knows every corner of Baghdad; his knowledge of the best way to navigate, areas to avoid, and the right time to circulate made my fieldwork possible. Moreover, his unfailing friendship, kindness, generosity, and willingness to support the research process helped me get to know Baghdad's realities and inhabitants. His assistance was central to my acquiring the skills to move around the capital on my own. After about six months, thanks to his advice, I was able to use public transport more often and move around in familiar neighborhoods. In one day, despite checkpoints, weekly explosions, and violent events, he might accompany me to an interview in al-Kerrada, then al-Mansur, and finish in al-Zu'faraniyya. He was my strength during this tough fieldwork, my confidant and teacher of everything about Iraqis' daily lives. Despite all 'Amu

---

[7] Bibi is the familiar word for grandmother.   [8] Khala means maternal aunt.

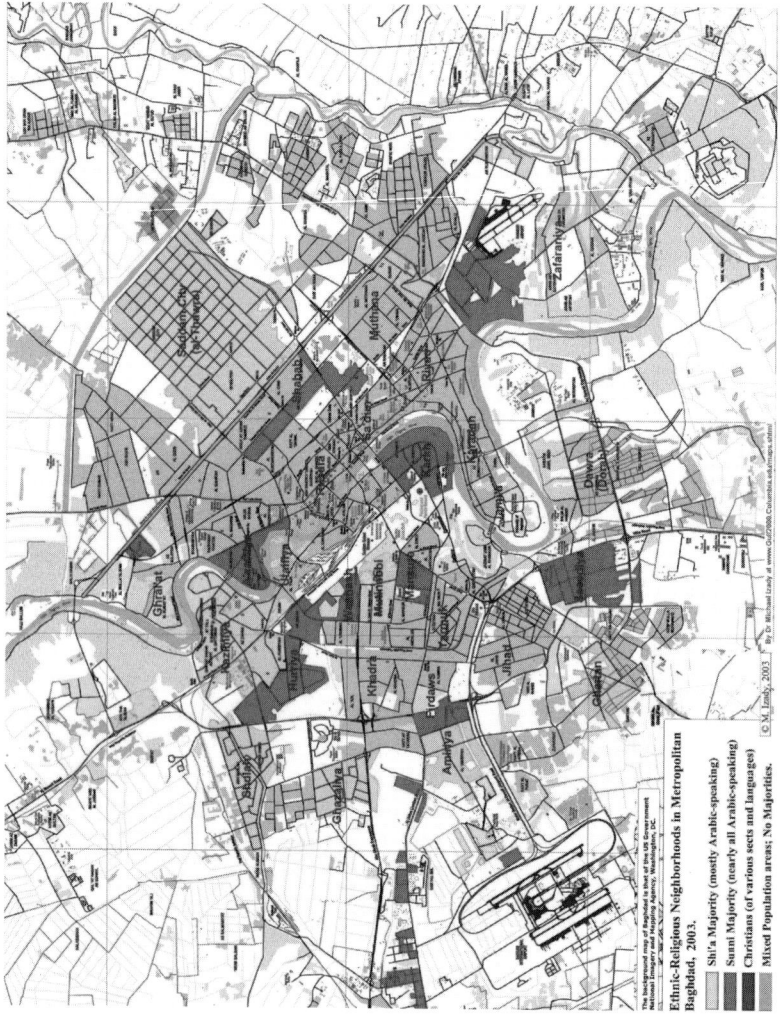

The background map of Baghdad is that of the US Government
National Imagery and Mapping Agency, Washington, DC.

**Ethnic–Religious Neighborhoods in Metropolitan
Baghdad, 2003.**

Shi'a Majority (mostly Arabic-speaking)
Sunni Majority (nearly all Arabic-speaking)
Christians (of various sects and languages)
Mixed Population areas; No Majorities.

© M. Izady, 2003   By Dr Michael Izady at www.Gulf2000.Columbia.edu/maps.shtml

Map 1 Ethnoreligious population distribution in Baghdad in 2003

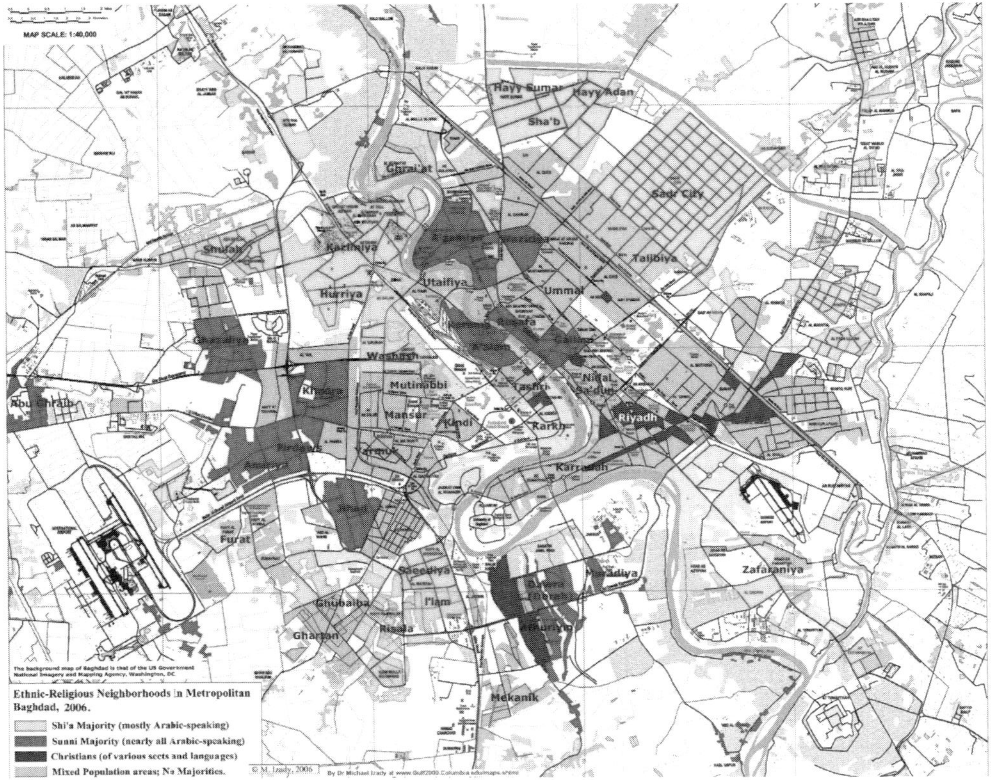

This development map of Baghdad is used by the UK Government National Mapping and Imaging Agency, Washington, DC

Ethnic-Religious Neighborhoods in Metropolitan Baghdad, 2006.

Shi'a Majority (mostly Arabic-speaking)

Sunni Majority (nearly all Arabic-speaking)

Christians (of various sects and languages)

Mixed Population areas; No Majorities.

Map 2 Ethnoreligious population distribution in Baghdad in 2006

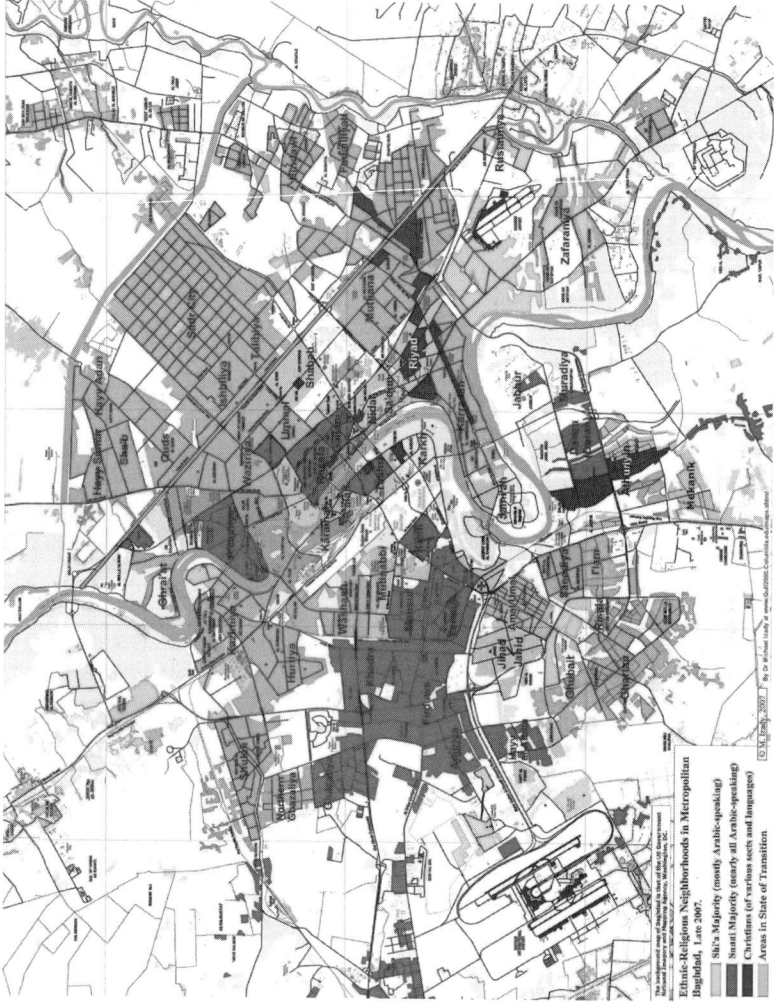

Map 3 Ethnoreligious population distribution in Baghdad in late 2007

Abu Manal had experienced in Baghdad, his love for Iraq and determination to remain in Baghdad are unbreakable. He gave me the determination to do my fieldwork, and his encouragement was essential for me at every stage of the process.

Circulation within Baghdad is very uncertain; it is difficult to plan an appointment in advance because a neighborhood can become inaccessible after a violent event, such as a car bomb or sectarian assassination. Despite returning to their "normal" lives after the violence of 2006–7, many members of my family felt traumatized and afraid, especially regarding areas of Baghdad in which they experienced or witnessed a violent event. Nevertheless, and despite the difficulties mixed couples face in finding a safe place to settle, I attended many family weddings in Baghdad involving mixed Shi'a and Sunni couples. However, despite the fact that many areas of Baghdad are now open to individuals from every sect, ethnicity, and religion, most Iraqis I met explained that they still follow a specific route when traversing neighborhoods in order to avoid certain homogeneously sectarian areas. Many Baghdadis feel that they no longer know their city; even if it is physically possible to circulate safely within different areas, the psychological barriers seem insurmountable. Thus most people remain within their own neighborhoods for their everyday needs – e.g., shopping and socializing. The fear of being trapped in traffic due to a closed checkpoint or car bomb is always present, whether traveling to school, university, or work.

However, my life in Baghdad during those two years was very lively, animated, and culturally and intellectually rich. The strong social bond that unites family members, neighbors, and friends from all religious, ethnic, and sectarian backgrounds still fulfills our lives in the most loving and warm way. On an almost daily basis, my maternal aunts 'Aziza, Naziha, Lamya, Hanaa, as well as 'Amma[9] Rabab, Khalu[10] Abdallah, and my numerous cousins, would visit us in al-Kazimiyya. Even if Baghdadis' everyday lives are marked by unspeakable violence, their lives are certainly not reduced to this violence. Over the weekends and downtimes in my fieldwork, I spent time with cousins and relatives at house gatherings and weddings. My aunts, uncles, and cousins live in different areas of Baghdad: some come from upper-class neighborhoods, such as al-Mansur; others from middle-class neighborhoods, such as al-Kerrada; and others from lower middle-class areas, such as Hay Ur. Al-Kazimiyya is a place of pilgrimage for Shi'as. There, funerals and religious ceremonies are the most common gatherings, which include moments of hearty socializing. The evening gatherings

---

[9] 'Amma means paternal aunt.   [10] Khalu means maternal uncle.

during special occasions – such as 'Ashura or the birth of Imam al-Kazem – are filled with intense socializing and joy. My family and I also went shopping, ate at restaurants, went to ice cream and fruit cocktail shops, attended poetry events in Nadi al-Sayd,[11] and – on occasions such as al-Eid – took my cousins' children to the al-Zawra' amusement park.

When the security climate deteriorated, my family and I limited our activities to our neighborhood and avoided visiting relatives in distant areas of Baghdad. I will always remember the day of the Sayyidat al-Najjat Church attacks on October 31, 2010, which was at the very beginning of my time in Baghdad. It was evening, and I was interviewing three women activists in the office of the Iraqi Women's League (Rabitat al-Mar'a al-Iraqiyya), which is only a couple blocks from the Sayyidat al-Najjat Church. The four of us were shaken by explosions; we had no idea what was going on, and our hearts raced at the sound of gunshots. We swiftly collected our things and tried to return to our homes. However, because the area was barricaded by the Iraqi army and the soldiers at the checkpoint would not let anyone enter or leave, we all had great difficulty making our way. We finally managed to exit the area; I was able to get home with the help of 'Amu Abu Manal, who guided me on the phone and waited for me on the other side of one of al-Kerrada's checkpoints. My family and I were all deeply shocked when we heard what had happened to the people in Sayyidat al-Najjat Church, who had gathered for evening mass: fifty-eight worshippers, priests, policemen, and bystanders were killed and seventy-eight wounded. However, there was no time to regain our grounding because there were several bad explosions in al-Kazimiyya the next morning. I stayed home for a couple of days after these incidents. Usually, everyday life in Baghdad stops for only a couple hours near the site of an explosion and then everything carries on as "normal".

I also conducted three months of fieldwork in Erbil and Sulaymaniyah, from November to December 2011 and March to April 2012. In Erbil, the Institut Français du Proche-Orient (IFPO) branch provided me with a place to stay and valuable contacts in Iraqi Kurdistan. In Sulaymaniyah, I spent some time in a hotel and then rented a flat in the Bekhtyary neighborhood, near the city center. As I describe in Chapter 5, my fieldwork in Iraqi Kurdistan was very different from my experience in Baghdad. I flew from Baghdad to Iraqi Kurdistan for my first trip; my second journey was done in collective taxis, which took about six or seven hours, but was very safe at the time. Although I had expected Iraqi Kurdistan to be just

[11] A cultural center in al-Mansur.

another Iraqi province, despite its autonomy since 1991, I experienced it as a foreign region; I was asked to show my passport and ID to cross the border. The Kurdish police, the *asaysh*, also considered me a "foreigner." For example, I had to undertake a very long administrative process in order to rent a flat in Sulaymaniyah.

Fieldwork in Iraqi Kurdistan was also radically different from that in Baghdad due to the overall atmosphere of security and stability. When I traveled on my own in a collective taxi, the Kurdish men with whom I traveled gave me additional regard and care. I did not experience any kind of harassment and felt looked after by my travel companions, who rarely questioned me about why and where I was traveling. I noticed that I was the only woman traveling alone; most other women in collective taxis were accompanied by male family members. Perhaps some thought I was a musician because I carried an oud with me that I was learning to play. Circulating, meeting new people, and interviewing women activists in Iraqi Kurdistan were much less tense and tiring than the same activities in Baghdad, although I felt less connected to and immersed in Kurdish people's realities, since I neither speak the language fluently nor am I related to any Kurdish families. It felt as if I was conducting fieldwork in another country of the region. Moreover, I conducted all my interviews with Kurdish women activists in Arabic, which represented a significant barrier because the younger generation does not speak fluent Arabic.

After these two years of intense fieldwork focused in Baghdad and secondarily in Erbil and Sulaymaniyah (2010–12), on which this book relies mainly, I conducted shorter fieldwork trips in Baghdad, Najaf-Kufa, Karbala, and Nasiriyah. During these shorter fieldwork trips (spring 2013, 2016, and 2017), I extended my research questions and explored youth and civil society activism especially related to massive popular protests that started in 2015. This more recent ethnographic research allows me to enrich and update the analysis of the social and political developments in Iraq, especially since the invasion of the Islamic State Organization (IS) in June 2014 and its aftermath.

Collection of Life Stories, Semistructured Interviews, and Participant Observations

I began most of my interviews with Iraqi women political and civil society activists with the following question: *Shenu eli khalatsh atkunin nashita*

niswiyya? ("What made you become a woman or feminist activist?").
Beginning my interviews with this question allowed me to listen to Iraqi
women activists' life stories, starting from their position and engagement
as activists within various women's civil society organizations, political
groups, and networks that emerged or reemerged after the fall of the Ba'th
regime in 2003. I listened to their experiences of the different social,
economic, and political events that marked Iraq's recent history.
The women political activists I interviewed ranged from twenty-one to
seventy-four years of age; hence I have gathered a transgenerational oral
history of the evolution of women's lives, political activism, and gender
issues in Iraq since the 1950s. I spoke with Iraqi women activists from
across the ethnic, religious, sectarian, and political spectrum: Arabs,
Kurds, Muslims, Christians, Sunnis, Shi'as, communists, nationalists,
Islamists. Almost all interviews consisted of two parts. In the first part,
I listened to their life narratives about their life trajectories, upbringing,
education, family, professional life, experience of activism, and exile for
some. I also asked detailed questions about Iraqi women activists' experiences and readings of the various wars (Iran-Iraq War, 1991 Gulf War,
2003 invasion and occupation, and the subsequent sectarian war), the
sanctions period, Ba'th authoritarianism, the fall of the Ba'th regime, and
the coming to power of a new regime. After listening to the activists' life
stories, which constituted the main part of the interview, the second part
involved more of a discussion between us. I asked each activist to describe
her group's current activities and comment on various issues, such as the
PSC, the constitution, and the most recent civil society and women's
groups' mobilizations. I also asked how each activist would describe her
activism, women's rights advocacy, and the way she defines gender equality and women's rights. I did not remain neutral during these exchanges;
I engaged in deep discussions about women's issues and rights in Iraq
with each activist.

Nashita niswiyya is the term most commonly used to describe women
political activists in Iraq; it usually describes "a women's rights activist" or
"a feminist activist." Since 2003, *al-nashitat al-niswiyyat* ("women activists") are the women who became involved in women-focused civil
society and political groups that (re)emerged after the fall of the Ba'th
regime. These groups can be women's organizations and networks dedicated to the defense of women's social, economic, and political rights;
women's branches of political organizations or parties; or charitable,
human rights, and social development organizations – religious or secular – that primarily address women's material life conditions. Some
organizations, despite being forbidden under the Ba'th regime, existed
before 2003 and re-emerged after the regime's fall. Many activists used

the term *al-haraka al-niswiyya* ("the women's movement") to define the women's groups and networks that emerged after 2003. For many activists, *al-haraka al-niswiyya al-iraqiyya* ("the Iraqi women's movement") also refers to what they consider the "historical women's movement," i.e., the women's groups that emerged in Iraq during the formation of the Iraqi state in the 1920s. In the context of nationalist, leftist, and anti-imperialist struggles, these groups flourished and were politicized in the 1940s and 1950s.

"Feminism" is a very charged and politicized word; for most women activists in Iraq, it oftens refers to radical egalitarian demands or Western conceptions of women's issues and rights. Thus very few activists involved in women's rights issues in Iraq use "feminism" to define themselves or their activism. However, the nuance between the word *nisa'i* ("that which relates to women") and *niswi* ("feminist") was not clearly articulated by most women activists I met. In fact, most activists used both terms interchangeably and often prioritized the use of *niswi* without necessarily meaning "feminist." Most activists used the English word "feminist" to describe, in their view, a radical political stand for equality; some criticize such a stand, but some embrace it. During my interviews, I used the terms *nashita niswiyya* and *haraka niswiyya* broadly, letting the interviewee use their own definitions and meanings, and the English word "feminist" to refer to radical egalitarian demands.

The preliminary list of individuals and groups I wanted to interview that I gathered before starting my fieldwork did not contain any kind of ethnic or sectarian indications. The list was composed of four categories: leftist, human rights, Islamist, and independent (nongovernmental) women's groups. I started researching women's activism consciously, ignoring the sectarian divide that has characterized Iraqi political and social life since 2003. My denial of sectarianism was based on the fact that none of my family members, either inside or outside Iraq, have ever thought or spoken in a sectarian way. Nevertheless, as I will show it in this book, the new Iraqi political system – which was set by the US-led Coalition Provisional Authority (CPA) – is based on ethnic, religious, and sectarian quotas rather than ideological or political affiliations, such as communist, socialist, Islamist, or liberal. It was only when I settled in Baghdad that my preliminary list of individuals and organizations took a communal shape. I added the Islamist, Sunni, and Shi'a categories, as well as Christian (Chaldean, Assyrian), Turkmen, and Kurdish (Sunni, Faili). My list of women activists and groups was thus composed of leftists, communists, Islamists (Sunni, Shi'a, and Kurdish),

Christians, Kurds, Turkmens, and independents. In this new incarnation, "independent" meant nonsectarian, nonethnic, and nonreligious organizations rather than nongovernmental ones.

I conducted eighty semistructured interviews: twenty-five in-depth life stories and fifty-five formal interviews. Most of my formal interviews consisted of a ninety-minute discussion with a single individual; there were a few instances of interviewing several individuals together. The twenty-five in-depth life stories were each about three to four hours of discussion with an activist over several meetings and, when possible, in different settings (at her organization's office and at her home). All interviews were recorded with the interviewee's consent. After six months of fieldwork in Baghdad – visiting offices and attending gatherings, meetings, and demonstrations, sometimes remaining silent and other times actively participating – I was familiar with many of the activists and thus did not always need to formally interview them. Nevertheless, I decided not to quote conversations and discussions outside the recorded interviews unless it was something said in a public conference or talk. I told all the women activists I met that the interviews would be anonymized; throughout this book, I use pseudonyms rather than the activists' actual names.

I was really moved and surprised by most activists' regard and consideration for my research; they always gave me their time, attention, and trust. They were eager to talk about their lives and personal, educational, professional, and political experiences, as well as share their thoughts.

Although I always stated clearly that I was present as a researcher at meetings and gatherings, I also participated in discussions as any other member of the assistance. I considered my position to be both a researcher and a feminist activist, listening mostly and speaking sometimes. I listened to activists' life stories and thoughts on the promise to provide a meaningful research for "us," feminists activists and scholars. I also spent a considerable amount of time observing cultural centers and university campuses and shared my analyses and thoughts with several academics and researcher at Baghdad University. I tried to diversify the places and positions of observation in order to enrich my research, and I considered the context in which interviews occurred as important as the content of the interviews themselves.

The Personal Is Academic

Pierre Bourdieu's (1980) contribution on the "condition of the possibility of knowledge" tackle the cultural, social, political, and economic situatedness of knowledge producers, complementing Foucault's (1966) unveiling of the link between knowledge and power. This perspective is strongly applied in feminist theories questioning notions of totalizing objectivity and introducing feminist standpoint knowledges, which contest both relativism and totalizing objectivism (Haraway 1988; Harding 1992). The remarkable works of Enrique Dussel (2000) and Boaventura de Sousa Santos (2007) on alternative knowledge epistemologies brings a decolonial perspective to the critique of the supposed neutrality and universality of dominant Western scholarship. Gayatri Chakravorty Spivak's (1999) critique of the "native informant" insists on the positionality of knowledge producers. Thus it is clear that my own trajectory and positionality, as well as *why* I chose my research subject and *how* I decided to undertake it, are essential aspects of the research process. Objectivity is, after all, a positioned rationality that has to be explicitly expressed and explained, because everyone is socially and politically positioned in one way or another in relation to a subject and the spaces and people associated with it.

As a young woman in her midtwenties who grew up in exile in France, living and doing fieldwork in postinvasion Iraq gave me a very concrete sense of the everyday life in Iraq, especially in Baghdad, which my family had to leave in the early 1980s. This experience allowed me to deconstruct my own diasporic preconceptions of Iraq built through my upbringing in a household dominated by a very politicized sense of what my Iraqi "cultures" ought to be. I grew up in an environment structured by the idea of return to the "motherland," an idea strengthened by the experience of racism and Islamophobia in France. My childhood and early adolescence were shaped by this dream of "returning" to Iraq, which was recalled to me as a kind of paradise. My mother originally from Najaf, was not a political activist and never wished to be one. Originally from Nasiriyah my father's personal and political paths were marked by the trajectory of the Iraqi political and religious figure Muhammed Baqer al-Sadr. In his wish to follow Shahid al-Sadr, my father became an Islamist. He openly opposed Saddam's regime, joining the political opposition, and funded an organization that supported victims of human rights abuses in Iraq.

Our home in Ferney-Voltaire, a small French town on the Swiss border, was full of Iraqi refugees – families and women and men alone – who had fled war and violence in Iraq, many of whom had experienced torture and repression under the Ba'th regime. My early youth was structured by Iraqi refugees' narratives of suffering and abuse and by the deep sadness, so intense in my mother's eyes, of being cut off from our family and homeland. Many times I wondered how our lives might have been if the 1991 uprisings had succeeded,[12] if the regime had fallen at that time. I am convinced that our

---

[12] As I show later in this book, many Iraqis, myself included, believe that the 1991 uprisings were a success, but the US-led coalition forces decided otherwise, leaving hundreds of thousands of Iraqis at the mercy of the brutal Ba'th regime.

lives, and the lives of most Iraqis, would have been totally different if popular uprisings against the Ba'th regime, both before and after 1991, had led to the fall of Saddam's regime, instead of such being accomplished by an imperialist invasion and occupation. A couple of weeks after the fall of the regime in 2003 – I was in high school at the time – my parents returned to Iraq. After more than twenty-three years of harsh, almost unbearable exile, they finally saw and embraced their family and friends. On November 18, 2006, my father was assassinated by an armed group responsible for much sectarian violence in Baghdad. His lifetime dream of *shahada* ("martyrdom") was accomplished, and our dream of returning to Iraq was violently broken.

Prior to study of the Iraqi context, I completed a master's research on Muslim antiracist feminist activism in France,[13] which represented my first attempt to theorize my own positioning as an activist articulating Muslim, antiracist, and anticapitalist understandings of feminism.[14] When I started fieldwork in Iraq, I was also preparing the edited book *Féminismes Islamiques* (2012), in which I suggested that Islamic/Muslim feminist contemporary intellectual movements challenge both Muslim and feminist orthodoxies. In this book, while I situated Muslim feminisms alongside Third World, postcolonial, and Black feminisms, I also argued that in its renewal of reformist Islam around the concept of *al-Tawhid* ("God's unicity") and engagement with Muslim juridical and spiritual traditions, contemporary Muslim feminist thought was bringing "faith" and "dynamics of piety" into feminism. I suggested that Islamic feminist activism and scholarship allows one to go beyond the secular/religious divide and propose alternative readings and practices of modernities and feminisms. Moreover, by presenting the contribution of Muslim feminist scholar-activists from Europe, North America and Muslim majority countries, I interrogated the simplistic Western/Islam dichotomy by showing the transnational dimension of Muslim feminists' claims.

However, I am also aware that a misleading overemphasis on Islamic/Muslim feminist claims could lead to reverse Orientalism. The desire to

---

[13] My master's dissertation, under the supervision of Nilüfer Göle at EHESS, was on the emergence of a Muslim feminist consciousness in France. It was based on an ethnography of the antiracist Muslim feminist movement in which I was involved and analyzed via an examination of the analysis of the imbrication of racialization, gender, and religion.

[14] I participated to the formation of the antiracist feminist organization Collectif Féministes pour l'Egalité created in 2004 in the context of the headscarf controversy in France with Christine Delphy, Monique Crinon, Ismahane Chouder, Ndella Paye, Hamida Ben Sadia, and Marina Da Silva. I was an active member of al Huda – the Muslim Women's Organization of Rennes – and very involved in the antiwar movement as well as the anticapitalist movement. I participated in the anti-G8 summit in Evian (2003) and the European Social Forum in Paris/Saint-Denis (2003) and London (2004).

provide a "Muslim version" of feminism could create an "Islamic" stand that outlines a normative definition of both Islam and feminism instead of revealing their changing and transforming dynamics and the necessity to ground their expressions and practices in their specific social, political, and economic contexts. Moreover, I also argue that an analysis of the politics of location of Muslim feminists' discourses is essential in order to avoid falling into the game of identity politics. My personal engagement with Islam as a religion present in my everyday life and my spiritual and intellectual understanding of it are in constant evolution. Having grown up in diasporic conservative Iraqi family environment, been myself a veiled Muslim feminist, I had always spontaneously questioned several simplistic dichotomies: secular/Islamist, modern/patriarchal, and feminist/religious. Such dichotomies never worked for me, as much as the equations modern = feminist, secular = pro women's rights, and religious = patriarchal also held no water. My encounter with the post-2003 Iraqi context and Iraqi women political activists simultaneously informed, questioned, confirmed, and challenged my perceptions of and assumptions about all these issues.

When living in postinvasion Iraq, I also experienced a new positionality. Because I had been part of marginalized communities in France for most of my life, living in an impoverished *banlieue* and experiencing discrimination as an immigrant, I am very sensitive to and distrustful of hegemonic powers and normative definitions of nationhood and uneven citizenship. It felt very strange when I settled in Baghdad to live in a privileged neighborhood and carry the ID of the new political elite being viewed as the daughter of a *shahid* ("martyr"). Despite my new symbolic position in the post-2003 era, I relied on my experience of antiracist struggles in France to remain sensitive to and aware of power and political leadership throughout my research and fieldwork. Living in al-Kazimiyya situated me at the forefront of what is commonly called the "Shi'a revival" in Iraq. I witnessed how a politicosectarian culture moved from decades of marginalization to the center of power after the fall of the Ba'th regime. Muharram, 'Ashura and religious ceremonies related to the birth or death of the twelve Shi'a Imams were celebrated with much zeal and emotion. The story of al-Husain martyrdom in Karbala resonates with those whose lives have been marked by injustice, scarcity, and the loss of loved ones.

Toward a "Poetics of Relation"

The epistemological background of this book questions essentialism, refusing any idea of roots or original essence, the existence of anything authentic. Edouard Glissant (1990, 1997) conceptualizes his refusal of universalism and cultural essentialism in *Poétique de la Relation* (1990), where he elaborates on his rejection of the *identité-racine* and where he insists on the interconnectedness of the world. Glissant refutes the idea of rooted origins and posited, instead, that the different and changing positionalities of contemporary humans are characterized by colonial modernity, a modernity in which colonial imperialism and slavery have shaped contemporary capitalism. According to Glissant, the world is one *un tout*; the global affects the everyday lives of most individuals as either beneficiaries, victims, or both at the same time. He proposes to poetically, rather than analytically, consider the products of the violence inherent in the expansion of colonial modernity. Thus one cannot predict what comes as the product of violence. Moreover, every being in the world is linked, in one way or another, to every other human being in a *Tout Monde*.

Glissant's philosophical ideas can be related to Stuart Hall's approach to the identity of the contemporary subject as fragmented, not fixed, but in constant redefinition and reshaping. His concept of identity (Glissant 1996a) is not an essentialist but a strategic and positional one; it considers that identities are never unified, never singular, but multiply constructed across different, often intersecting and antagonistic discourses, practices, and positions. The rise of global capitalism and, as a consequence, the weakening of nation-state borders and their local forms of identities all contributed to create "new ethnicities" (Glissant 1996b). Hall proposes a way of understanding how "ideological" elements manage in certain conditions the creation of a coherent set of identity and a way to question how and according to which articulations this set is constructed socially and politically (Hall 1996b). Distancing himself from the narrow and often colonial notions of ethnicity, he proposes a new definition based on the realities of the contemporary conjuncture characterized by the contradicting features of globalization that both incorporate and simultaneously produce difference (Hall 1996b). The politics of difference suggested by Hall is marked by a conception of identity being the articulation of a field of difference within the individuals and simultaneously another larger field of sociocultural differentiation. Moreover, Hall defines articulation as the connection that unifies two different elements under certain conditions. However, this linkage is not necessary, absolute, or fixed (Hall 1986). Thus, for Hall, the global and local are two aspects of the same phenomenon, the binary expression of late capital formation. He does not simply condemn globalization as cultural homogenization but notes the oppositional nature of the modern condition: the return to the local as response to homogenization and globalization of culture. According to Hall, the mystification of the local is not better than the global. He finds the boundary-crossing aspects of the contemporary conjuncture as expressed in debates on transnational culture and identity imbued with contradictory but powerful possibilities (Hall 1990, 1997).

The approaches of Glissant and Hall deeply affected my thinking, especially in my attempt to define my multiple positionalities. Refusing generalizations or one-word definitions, approaching the contemporary world through complexity, power, historicity, and relationality, and thus refusing dichotomous paradigms – such as modern/traditional, West/ Islam, culture/economy, discursive/material – are the epistemological and ethical propositions I take throughout this book.

Structure of the Book

Chapter 1 deals with the colonial and early postcolonial period (1917–63) and shows how women and gender issues were shaped by different power struggles involving competing ideas of nationhood and definition of the state and struggles between social and political forces such as the emerging urban middle class, the *ulemas*, tribal Shaikhs, and the emerging women's movement. First, I propose to reflect on pioneering research in order to refine my approach of Iraqi society. Then I explore the Mandate (1917–32) and the Hashemite (1932–58) periods and analyze how the nature of the relationship between the colonial state and different groups such as the *ulemas*, tribal Shaikhs, and the political forces of the emerging urban middle class shaped gender politics and women's political activism. I then analyze the importance of the revolutionary period (1958–63) in the codification of women's legal rights, and I explore the nature of the divergences between the two competing women's movements, the communist and the nationalist. Finally, I show how the achievements in terms of equalitarian notions of citizenship resulting in the dominance of anti-imperialist political culture will be undermined by the first Ba'th coup (1963–68).

Chapter 2 deals with the Ba'th period (1968–2003) and analyzes the relationship between gender issues, patrimonial authoritarianism, state rentierism, tribalism, and Islamism. I analyze the impact of different state ideologies and politics, wars, and sanctions on the Iraqi social and cultural fabric, as well as on women's conditions of life. First, I show the impact of the Ba'th authoritarian-patrimonial regime on the very definition of citizenship. I explore its gender politics during the 1970s, characterized by economic, social, and cultural growth incited by oil wealth that helped to enhance women's life conditions and legal rights. Then I explore its shifting politics in the 1980s corresponding to the war with Iran and the militarization of Iraqi society that had a great effect on women's lives and gender relations. I also explore the regime's communal anti-Kurd and anti-Shi'a politics and their gender dimensions. Then I analyze the profound changes provoked by the 1991 invasion of Kuwait, the US-led coalition bombings, and the terrible sanctions that represented the final blow to the Iraqi state and society. I explore how post-1991 Iraq corresponded to a period of social, political, and economic brutalization of Iraqi society that deeply affected on its functioning and cultural fabric. I show how this period of generalized impoverishment and social and political conservatisms redefined women's lives and gender norms and practices.

Starting with the account of a meeting with an activist in Medina al-Sadr, Chapter 3 is dedicated to the postinvasion period (2003–17) and explores the main features of Iraq's social, economic, and political realities and their impact on women's conditions of life and activism. First, I explore how women political activists experienced the invasion and occupation. Then I analyze how the context of generalized violence and social, political, and economic crisis provoked by the invasion and occupation shape women's lives and their social and political engagement. Finally, I look particularly at women's representatives in the new regime and explore how the communalization of the Iraqi political system has affected their existence and activism.

Chapter 4 opens with an account of the observation of postinvasion Baghdad's university. It presents the (re-)emergence of women's political and civil society groups since 2003. I start by reflecting on the relationship between local and global dynamics in shaping women's groups' agendas in the Middle East and third-world countries. Then I explore the ways in which women's social and political groups emerged after the fall of the regime and started to organize. Then I explore their relationship to the new regime and to the networks of United States, United Nations, and international funding targeting women's issues. I present the different groups and organizations, the nature of their activism, and their actions, mobilizations, and agenda of struggles.

In Chapter 5, after providing a sense of my fieldwork in Iraqi Kurdistan, I explore Kurdish women's activism and analyze their agendas and discourses in relation to the "Kurdish state" and Kurdish nationalisms. Then I turn to an analysis of Islamist women's activism and explore its evolution as well as the nature of religious forms of women's activism in Iraqi Kurdistan. Finally, through the example of a woman activist who refuses to join any formal organization, I explore the very impact of the NGOization of women's rights activism in Iraqi Kurdistan.

Chapter 6 deals with the mobilizations around the PSC in postinvasion Iraq beginning with the observation of the International Women's Day celebrations in Baghdad. First, I analyze the fragmentation of the field of women's legal rights linked to the institutionalization of communal-based identities and the rise of conservative political groups in power since 2003. I explore particularly the divergences between Sunni and Shi'a Islamist women's activist regarding the PSC despite their common representations on gender issues. I then propose an analysis of the relationship between gender issues and competing notions of nationhood. Finally, I look at the ways in which women involved in secular or religious forms of activism define women's rights and gender norms and propose to go beyond secular/religious feminisms.

Finally, Chapter 7 starts with a reflection of the commonalities between the different activists' discourses on what an "Iraqi woman" should be. I explore Iraqi women activists' different feminisms and their definition of gender norms and relations in an analytical framework linking the personal to the political. First, I propose to reflect on the relationship between gender and conservatisms, issues of piety, morality, and respectability, as well as on Muslimness, Islam, and feminisms. Then I present the different trends of feminisms existing in Iraq in relation to women's rights activists' discourses on gender equality, norms, and relations. Finally, I look at the ways in which Iraqi women activists define respectability and womanhood in relation to their lives and struggles.

1   Genesis of the "Woman Question"
The Colonial State against Its Society and the Rise and
Fall of the New Iraqi Republic (1917–1968)

Introduction

Going back to the period of the formation of the Iraqi state is central to
understanding the present. The social, political, and economic dynamics
characterizing colonial times shaped the genesis of what has been commonly called the "woman question": the way in which women and gender
issues were raised and debated by various social and political actors since
the colonial period. In line with Edward Said's work on Orientalism, Leila
Ahmed's seminal *Women and Gender in Islam* (1992) offers an in-depth
look at the ways in which the "woman question" was shaped in the
colonial period in Egypt. She shows how Islam was defined by the
colonizers as representing the essential difference separating the "civilized" West from the "barbaric" Muslim East. Western colonizers' depiction of Muslim women as oppressed by a "Muslim patriarchal culture,"
particularly through veiling, had an impact on the way women and gender
issues were posed by nationalists and Muslim reformists. Women symbolized the natural, biological bearer of the nation, which was always
depicted through feminine symbolism – for example, as shown in research
about Egypt (Booth 1998, 2001; Baron 2005).

Family, women, and their condition of life and status represented the
bearer of cultural authenticity and were at the core of colonizer/colonized
discourses. In the postcolonial period, at the time of independence,
women and gender issues were central to the discourses and politics of
modernity and nationalism. Yuval-Davis and Anthias (1989) show how
much gender relations and women's reproductive roles and identities are
at the core of nationalist projects. Gender relations are central in the
development of nationhood and ideas of citizenship.

Even in countries that were not colonized, such as Turkey, women's
rights, dress code, and identity were considered essential to the process of
modernization and thus an "issue of civilization," as described by Göle
(1993). The establishment of modern nation-states in the European
model was thus marked by tensions and contradictions: on the one

hand, the process involved the modernization of societies along Western lines (i.e., science, technology, social organization); on the other hand, the process involved the assertion of national identities based on past histories and in contrast to Western influences. In the context of the formation of new, independent Arab states, cultural nationalism and Islam appeared as practically interchangeable. The establishment of the personal status codes (or family laws) in the framework of *shari'a* was central to debates surrounding the definition and shape of the "new nation." Mounira Charrad (2001) proposes to approach state policies and gender in the Maghrib region in considering the central importance of tribal kin groupings. Through the ways in which the personal status codes or family laws were established, it is possible to read the nature of the relationship state–tribe alliances. She argues that the more state politics favor kin-based social groups, the more family laws are conservative, such as in postcolonial Morocco. Conversely, the more the state evolves in relative autonomy from tribal kin groupings, the more it promulgates a liberal family law, such as in Tunisia in 1956. Charrad's analysis of the very establishment of a legal frame shaping women's rights is very relevant to our study in this chapter on gender issues and feminism in colonial and postcolonial Iraq.

Several pioneering studies elaborated on and added further complexity to Ahmed's reflection on the colonial building of the "woman question." In her groundbreaking edited volume *Women, Islam and the State* (1991), Deniz Kandiyoti proposes to break with Orientalist and simplistic approaches to women and gender issues in the Middle East; such approaches consistently take the position of an undifferentiated Islam representing the essential and radical cultural difference between the West and the "Muslim world." Kandiyoti argues that an adequate analysis of the position of women in Muslim majority societies must be grounded in a detailed examination of the nation-states' political projects and historical transformations. Thus, looking at the establishment of nation-states in the colonial and postcolonial contexts, along with the different ways in which the notion of citizenship was elaborated and experienced, is necessary to understanding women and gender issues in the Middle East. The postindependence trajectories of modern states, the variation in the use of Islam in different nationalisms, state ideologies (nationalism, secularism, etc.) and oppositional social movements, and the varied processes of economic change are of central relevance to understanding the conditions of women.

Lila Abu-Lughod's edited volume, *Remaking Women: Feminism and Modernity in the Middle East* (1998), brings significant horizons regarding the ways in which women deemed "bearer of the nation" participated in the debates around their social, economic, and political conditions. Abu-Lughod also explores the different and complex ways in which "the West and things associated with it, embraced, repudiated and translated, are implicated in contemporary gender politics" (1998: 3–31). Approaching the way in which colonial modernity affected discourses and politics on gender means for the author of *Remaking Women* looking at the ways the ideas and practices deemed "modern" brought by Europe's colonies and taken up by the emerging local elites introduced both forms of emancipation and new forms of social control. It also means looking at the class dimensions of the "woman question" and at what kinds of identities – class, national, communal – are shaped through women and gender discourses and politics. Abu-Lughod deepens Deniz Kandiyoti's analysis when she argues that colonial constructions of "Eastern women" that shaped anticolonial nationalisms and feminist projects in the Middle East cannot be read through the simplistic rejection/acceptance of Western-dominant ideas. For feminists in the region, there has been a selectiveness and reappropriation in the translation of Western ideas and models into local contexts (1998: 3–31). This precise issue can be explored for the British Mandate and Hashemite periods explored in this chapter with the support of the work of Orit Bashkin, Sara Pursley, and Noga Efrati.

Regarding women's activism during the colonial period in the Middle East, in her article, "The Other 'Awakening': The Emergence of Women's Movements in the Middle East, 1900–1940," Ellen Fleischmann (1999) identifies three stages in the evolution of women's movements that appeared simultaneously or in succession from the beginning of the twentieth century to 1940. The first stage was characterized by the importance given to the "woman question" in public debates and the emergence of women's groups advocating for girls' education, as well as women's welfare and charity groups. The second stage related to the direct connection between nationalism and women's emancipation: the formation of more politicized women's groups that linked the idea of citizenship to that of gender equality. The third stage was characterized by the politics of "state feminism" undertaken by new, independent nationalist regimes. In fact, Kumari Jayawardena's *Feminism and Nationalism in the Third World* (1986) shows how much feminist movements in the Third World emerged within nationalist struggles that drew on anticapitalism and anti-imperialism. She also argues that such an emergence corresponded with a move toward secularism, which was characterized by the dominance of leftist ideologies and carried by the emerging modern indigenous middle classes.

Much has been written about the emergence of the "woman question" and the development of women's activism in Muslim majority countries during the first decades of independence. However, while much attention has been paid to places such as Egypt and Iran, very few studies were dedicated to Iraq. This chapter seeks to examine the relationships among gender, issues of nationhood, citizenship, and women's activism in the context of colonial (British Mandate and Hashemite periods) and early postcolonial Iraq (1958–68) and explores the following questions: How was the "woman question" posed in colonial and early postcolonial Iraq? How and in which contexts did women's activism develop during that period?

I start with a reflection on pioneer research in order to introduce my approach to Iraqi society. Then I explore the British Mandate (1917–32) and the Hashemite (1932–58) periods and analyze how the nature of the relationship between the colonial state and different groups such as the *'ulemas*, tribal Shaikhs, and the political forces of the emerging urban middle class shaped gender politics and women's political activism. I then analyze the importance of the Revolutionary period (1958–63) in the codification of women's legal rights, and I explore the nature of the divergences between the two competing women's movements, the communist and the nationalist. Finally, I show how the achievements in terms of equalitarian notions of citizenship resulting in the dominance of anti-imperialist political culture will be undermined by the first Ba'th coup (1963–68).

Reflecting on Pioneer Research

Ali al-Wardi (1913–95), the founder of sociology in Iraq, is one of the first to have done exhaustive analysis of Iraqi society, which appears in his two pioneer and thrilling works, *A Study into the Nature of Iraqi Society* (1965) and *Lamahat*[1] (*Insights*) (1978). Al-Wardi's research attempts to define the principles structuring Iraqi society, providing a modern understanding of Ibn Khaldun's concept of *'asabiyya* ("social bond and solidarity"). Three principles structured al-Wardi's depiction of what he called the "Iraqi personality": first, the struggle between sedentary lifestyle and nomadism, Bedouin lifestyle and urbanism; second, the spirit of social discord lying behind the fragmentation and divisions of Iraqi society; and third, the sociocultural schizophrenia of the modern Arab individual, who is torn between attachment to tradition and religious and ideological

---

[1] *Lamahat Ijtima'iyya min Tarikh al-'Iraq al-Hadith*, translated into English under the title *Social Insights of Iraq Modern History*.

ideals, on the one hand, and the social and material realities that are circumstantial and contingent on modern existence, on the other. Even if al-Wardi's analysis can be defined as binary and more inclined to psychoanalysis than to strict sociology, he still provides an in-depth and very well documented study of Iraqis' social and political life from Ottoman times to the first decade of the new Iraqi state. Although the gender dimensions of the Bedouin/urban and modern/traditional are absent from his analysis, it still constitutes an interesting starting point for thinking about the structure of the social and cultural fabric of Iraqi society, as marked by oppositional and diverging forces. Al-Wardi's depiction of the urban/rural opposition has influenced most studies on modern Iraq, including Hanna Batatu's study of Iraqi society.

Batatu's pioneering work, *The Old Social Classes and the Revolutionary Movements of Iraq* (1978), is not the most instructive research as it pertains to women and gender issues. This study is the result of two decades of in-depth research on Iraq's old landed and commercial classes, communists, Ba'thists, and Free Officers; it is a men's social and political Marxist-oriented social history of Iraq. In addition, Pierre-Jean Luizard provides a critique of Batatu's work as a study focused on what the author considered to be the movements inclined toward "modernity" – i.e., the Communist Party, the Ba'thists, and the Free Officers – and thus entirely overlooks religious movements (Luizard 2002: 10). Luizard asserts that Batatu did not take the Constitutionalist movement launched by the Shi'a *'ulemas* opposed to British imperialism, or the "defeated" in Luizard's description, into serious consideration.[2] Batatu's work also completely neglected the emergence of the women's movement within nationalist and communist ranks in the 1920s; he invokes women's political and legal rights only through the writings and activism of male nationalists and communists.

In Batatu's study, women's life conditions are only referred to once in a pitiful description of the "women of the peasants" in the 1920s and 1930s. Here women are described as submissive to their authoritarian fathers and husbands, as well as bought and sold between tribesmen (Batatu 1978: 144). Apart from this passage, women and gender issues are addressed only when the author mentions the intellectual dynamic around the journal *al-Sahifa*, which was first published in 1924. Batatu mentions that in this journal Husain al-Rahal wrote about women's liberation and the need to reform archaic and oppressive religious and

---

[2] When Batatu speaks of the Shi'a resistance of Najaf and the south in the 1920s, he presents it as mainly a revolt of large landowners who wanted to preserve their privileges and refused the taxes imposed by the British rather than a proper nationalist uprising.

cultural practice regarding women and suggested that Marxism was introduced in Iraq under a feminist garment (Batatu 1978: 396).[3]

Despite its approach and omissions, Hanna Batatu's study is an essential reference for understanding the social, political, and economic structure of Iraqi state and society. Under the monarchy, Iraq was characterized by the diversity, or "incohesiveness" in Batatu's words, of its inhabitants (Batatu 1978: 34) and the formation of its state by the colonial British Empire "against its society" (Luizard 1991), which relied on the Ottoman Sunni Arab elite's marginalization of the Shi'as and rejection of Kurdish autonomy. According to Batatu, "religion" in Iraq was an "element of division" rather than cohesion. However, it is clear from his work that the overlapping relationships and divisions between ethnic (Arab, Kurd, Turkmen, Aramean, Armenian), sectarian (Muslim Sunni/ Muslim Shi'a), and religious (Muslim, Christian, Jew, etc.) belongings within Iraqi society took different meanings, forms, and articulations throughout time, space (rural, urban), and social and political contexts. By reading Batatu, one understands that being an educated, urban Sunni Arab under the monarchy implied belonging to the urban social and political elite; in the late 1960s, in contrast, this identity could mean belonging to the political elite only if affiliated with the regime by family, tribe, regional kinship, or allegiance to the Ba'th Party. Being an Iraqi Jew living in Baghdad until the first half of 1940s[4] meant belonging to the wealthy commercial elite privileged by the British and entirely integrated into Iraqi society and "culture." After the establishment of Israel, being an Iraqi Jew meant belonging to a persecuted minority[5] suspected of threatening Arab nationalism. Finally, a Shi'a Arab under the monarchy would not be part of the urban, educated political elite.[6] A Shi'a

[3] Batatu mentioned that Husain al-Rahal succeeded Jamil Sidqi al-Zahawi: the first to call openly for Iraqi women's liberation. Batatu also mentioned the leftist and secular journal *Jam'iyyat al-Ahrar*, founded by Yusuf Salman, Da'ud Salman, and Ghali al-Zuwayyed, which dedicated their 1929 declaration of intent to "the liberation of the Arab woman." Women linked to the Communist Party are also mentioned in Batatu's work – such as Amina al-Rahal (sister of Husain al-Rahal), who was a member of the Communist Party's Central Committee from 1941 to 1943 and presented as one of the first women to take off the veil in Baghdad. The appointment of Naziha al-Dulaimi – a gynecologist and leader of the League of Defense of Women's Rights (رابطة الدفاع عن حقوق المرأة, *Rabitat al-Difa' 'an huquq al-mar'a*) – as Minister of Municipalities (first Arab woman to be appointed as minister) in 1959 is presented by the author as the result of 'Abd al-Karim Qasim's strategy to please the communists, who were the main political force at the time (Batatu 1978: 221).
[4] Until 1947, Jews constituted 15 percent of Baghdad's population (Batatu 1978: 285)
[5] From representing 2.6 percent (117,000) of the Iraqi population in 1947, Iraqi Jews represented only few thousand just several years later.
[6] Mainly urban Sunni Arabs, Christians, and Jews accessed education under the monarchy, forming the political, administrative, and military elite.

Arab could be part of the small, rich, commercial urban class but would more likely belong to the poor, exploited rural peasants and tribesmen.

In other words, while reading Batatu, an essential theoretical point can be argued: ethnic, sectarian, and religious belongings have to be read in relation to social class, location (rural/urban), kinship relations (tribes and families), and political and symbolic powers (administrative, military, religious, tribal) while also keeping in mind these belongings' changing dynamics. In line with postcolonial feminist analysis, I argue that being a woman is also being positioned within these groups and that ethnicity, sect, religion, class, location, kinship relations, and political and symbolic powers are all gendered in multiple and complex ways.

Under British Rule (1917–1932) and the Monarchy (1932–1958): State-Society Relations, Women's Rights, and Activism under British Domination

The Colonial State and Multiple Senses of Belonging

The Iraqi population was heterogeneous in its ethnic (Arab, Kurd, Turkmen, Armenian, etc.), sectarian (Sunni, Shi'a), and religious (Muslim, Christian, Jews, etc.) composition. The Iraqi state established under the British Mandate (1920–32), which began as a military occupation in 1917, was a contested and weak state. It was born in the face of popular movements repressing the Constitutionalist movement launched by the Shi'a *'ulemas* in the first decade of the twentieth century, the movement against British occupation, and the Kurdish refusal to be incorporated into an Arab state. This Iraqi state relied on the ancient elite of the Ottoman Empire; Sunni Arabs exclusively comprised its leadership, administration, and army. In Baghdad, Sunni Arab religious, political, and economic figures – whether *'ulemas*, heads of *Tariqas* (such as 'Abd al-Rahman al-Gilani), Sayyid related to the tribal leadership (such as 'Abdul Muhsin al-Sa'dun), Ashraf, land owners, or wealthy merchants – generally collaborated with and got involved based on the wishes of the British occupying authorities. Although some Iraqi Shi'a families belonged to the wealthy commercial elite, the urban educated elite was dominated by Sunni Arabs because they benefited from secondary and higher education under both Ottoman and British rule, unlike the Shi'as. Christians and Jews were also part of the educated urban elite because they were favored by the British Empire. The power of the new state was effective only in urban areas; the countryside was managed by tribesmen who, at the time, were more heavily armed than the state army.[7]

The Ottoman policy in the nineteenth century was to reduce the power of the tribes by settling the tribes in permanent villages and playing one tribe against the other. Many tribesmen resisted by refusing to register their land. While presumably intending to promote the formation of an integrated nation-state, the governments both under the Mandate and under the monarchy (1932–58) perpetuated tribal relations through tribal and land-tenure policies. These policies halted the decline and disintegration of tribal leaders' power, which had been occurring toward the end of the Ottoman period, by providing administrative and fiscal powers, as well as land grants, to selected Shaykhs. Such policies enabled the Shaykhs to tax and control those who subsequently became "their" tribesmen; thus British policy contributed to the transformation of a free cultivating peasantry into a population of serfs tied to the land of sharecroppers. (Davis 2005; Dodge 2003; Marr 2004; Farouk-Sluglett & Sluglett 1991, 1987; Jabar 2003). Under the monarchy, nation-building relied on traditional status groups – ethnic and religious – and overlooked the growth of the new, modern middle and working classes in the cities. The division in Iraqi society between the urban use of Civil Law and the rural, predominantly Shi'a[8] use of Tribunal Criminal and Civil Disputes Regulation (TCCDR), more commonly called the "tribal law," is the most revealing aspect of this reliance.

For Zubaida (2002), the four main social groups at the head of the society – the *effendiyya* or "urban officials," the ex-Ottoman officers that came to Iraq with Faysal, the clerics (Shi'a and Sunni), and the tribal leadership of the mid-Euphrates as well as Tigris districts – all constituted the "fragments" that imagined differently the new nation-state. Thus, as shown by Fattah (2012: 95–103), Davis (2005), Tripp (2000), and Bashkin (2009), the social process of becoming Iraqi was very complex and fluid, a constant negotiation between unequal partners by virtue of the undemocratic and unsystematic nature of the new Iraqi state. Moreover, it can be argued that at any given moment in the history of the Iraqi nation, there has not been a single national narrative or a single memory of the nation but rather competing visions advanced by the state and opposition forces.

Since 1921, the constitution had been drafted and redrafted; it was finally adopted in March 1925. Iraq was to function as a Western-style constitutional monarchy, with a king, cabinet, two legislative chambers,

---

[7] In 1933, tribes possessed more than 115,000 guns, whereas the army had only 15,000.
[8] In 1900, according to Luizard (1991), 75 percent of tribes were Shi'a Arab and 25 percent Sunni Arab.

and democratic rights for the population. In practice, the constitutional system allowed Britain, the royal family, and former Ottoman officers (Sunnis) to effectively control formal politics for decades. The nascent state divided Iraqis into "original" and "nonoriginal." Nationality Law No. 42 of 1924, which was enacted in the 1925 Constitution (*al-Qanun al-Asasi*), deemed "original" Iraqis to be those registered as Ottoman subjects, the Sunnis, and the Kurds. Shi'as were registered as "Iranian dependency" (*taba'iyya*) and hence second-class citizens because they were not Ottoman subjects prior to the establishment of the Iraqi nation-state due to geographic and political reasons.[9] The Law for the Election of the Constituent Assembly went even further in defining Iraqis as "every Ottoman subject now residing in Iraq and not claiming foreign citizenship" (Luizard 1991, 2006; Nakash 1994; Shaaban 2010), imparting that any Sunni, even non-Iraqi, had more rights than Iraqi Shi'as. Most Shi'as had to apply for Iraqi citizenship, even when they belonged to well-known and established Arab families.[10]

The Constitution also provided a base for the election system in Iraq that alienated an important segment of the population; the Electoral Law of 1924 provided a two-tiered electoral system in which primary electors were to nominate secondary electors, who were, in turn, to vote for deputies. Only male taxpayers older than twenty could be primary or secondary electors, and only male taxpayers older than thirty could become deputies. Thus the Electoral Law excluded the lower class, men younger than thirty, and women from serving in Parliament, and the system was mandated in such a way that it was difficult for men of the opposition to be elected, whereas, in contrast, tribal leaders were well represented.

With the formation of the Iraqi state, the Shi'a movement against the British became a subaltern memory, whereas elite social groups found their place in the emerging nation-state. At a time when pan-Arab nationalism was a growing ideology in the region and fitted very well many Sunni Arabs, Iraq's ideologies regarding issues of nationalism and

---

[9] Some Shi'as lived in areas far from the central administration, and most wanted to avoid military conscription and excessive taxation. More generally, many Shi'as did not feel related to a Sunni empire that marginalized them.

[10] Muhammed al-Jawahiri, the greatest Arab Iraqi poet, had a very famous story about this matter. Because al-Jawahiri belonged to a very famous Arab family from Najaf, he had to gather an incredible amount of documentation to prove his "Iraqiness." He was removed from his teaching position by Sati' al Husri, a theoretician of Arab nationalism and head of higher-education institutions in 1928, who was well known for speaking Arabic with a Turkish accent. He accused al-Jawahiri of having written a poem that glorified Iran, which was already considered an act of treason at the time. For more details, see Luizard (1991) and Zubaida (1989, 2002), as well as al-Musawi (2006) on the role played by al-Jawahiri in Iraqi political and intellectual culture.

belonging were diverse and competing during the Hashemite period. As Luizard (1991), Nakash (1994), and Jabar (2003) explore it in their research on the Shiʿa movement and Haddad (2010) thouches on in his study of sectarian relations in Arab Iraq, Sunnis and Shiʿas did not share a unified national narrative, symbolism, or ideology. As pointed out by Zubaida (1991, 2002) and Davis (2005), neither Sunnis, Shiʿas, nor Kurds represented homogeneous groups because class, kin-based positions, regional belongings, and political affiliations (nationalists, communists, etc.) were also important to their identities and consciousness.

It has often been argued that when nationalism began to spread as a new political ideology in Iraq, Sunnis, Shiʿas, and Kurds supported competing versions of nationalism: Iraqi-oriented nationalism – "Iraqism" – was favored by the Shiʿas and Kurds; pan-Arab nationalism, linked to the rest of the predominantly Sunni Arab region, was favored by the Sunnis. However, according to Farouk-Sluglett and Sluglett (1987, 1991), pan-Arab nationalism was never dominant neither among the intelligentsia, nor as the ideology promoted by the state, apart from a brief period when it dominated Iraqi politics in the later 1930s and early 1940s as also argued by Wien (2006, 2012). If most members of Arab nationalist parties were Sunnis, and the Iraqism-leaning Communist Party was predominantly composed of Shiʿas, and the Kurds had their own national memory and symbolism related to the ideal Kurdish nation-state, Kurdistan, as Zubaida (2002) and Davis (2005) argue, the Iraqi population was fragmented into different "nation imaginaries" that were often competitive, conflicting, and grounded in sectarian, class, and geographic divisions.

Bashkin's (2009) research on intelligentsia under the monarchy shows convincingly that these competing imaginaries – pan-Arab nationalism and Iraqism – were more blurred than it is often thought. She argues that the question that occupied many intellectuals of this period was not whether there should be a nation-state but rather what nature this state should assume to accommodate a variety of hyphenated identities (Iraqi-Shiʿi, Arab-Jew, Iraqi-Kurdish, etc.). More importantly regarding women and gender issues, the production of organic intellectuals, on the one hand, and the inability to control their radicalization, on the other, is one of the features of the Hashemite period (Bashkin 2009: 127–56).

Women and the Colonial State: Between the Shaikhs and the ʿUlemas

The Constitution adopted in 1925 divided Iraqi citizens in three different classes regarding the law and established three different courts: civil and religious courts in the urban areas and TCCDR for tribesmen in rural areas.

The Constitution divided the religious courts into *shari'a* courts for the Muslims and Spiritual Councils for other religious communities. It affirmed that *shari'a* courts only were to handle matters of personal status – issues of marriage, divorce, and inheritance (thus related to family and women's rights) – and in accordance to each sect. Thus, under the Mandate, women's legal rights were divided according to religion (Muslim, Christian, Jew, etc.), sect (Sunni, Shi'a), and location (rural, urban).

According to Efrati (2012) and J. Ismael and S. Ismael (2007), the legal system of colonial Iraq led to the "tribalization of women." Women were tribalized in the rural areas not only in their construction as tribal, subject to separate "tribal law," but also in the British involvement in determining tribal law. Even in urban areas, people could involve "tribal motives" when it came to crimes committed in the "name of honor." Two main social groups advocated against the very establishment of the TCCDR: urban intellectuals – Sunnis and Shi'as – depicted it as backward, unfair to women, and halting the modernization of the emerging nation, whereas tribal Shaikhs considered it as a direct threat to their power over tribesmen. Although J. Ismael and S. Ismael (2007) describe tribal law as "inherently misogynous" and its very existence as detrimental to women, Efrati (2012: 30–50) introduces a more nuanced analysis on the matter. The Tribal Code advocated by many Shaikhs during the Mandate and monarchy periods and aimed at reducing the power of the state over the tribes was characterized by a certain leniency and pluralism concerning women's issues. This leniency could be a reflection of the reality in the Iraqi countryside where customs regarding women were dynamic and diverse and not necessarily as harsh toward women as it was represented by the British and the urban elite. According to Efrati (2012: 35), extramarital relations did not automatically mandate a death sentence; in some places, murder for adultery was very exceptional, and there was a diversity of views regarding the way to settle blood disputes in which the handing over of women was not the rule. The British refused the Tribal Code proposed by the Shaikhs and wanted to set their own tribal law. Thus tribal law tribalized rural women not only in their construction as tribal, subject to separate "tribal law," but also by the British involvement in determining tribal law, affecting rural women as harsh and uncompromising.

In the urban areas, in addition to being exposed to the possibility of the advocacy of "tribal motives," women were ruled by *shari'a* courts, divided into Sunni and Shi'a courts. Efrati (2012: 80) explores the reasons why both the British Mandate and the Iraqi monarchy maintained *shari'a* courts in the cities, despite increasing criticism from urban intellectuals, especially leftists, demanding a civil code similar to the secular Turkish judicial system. Examining the argument developed by Charrad based on North African countries, which found that the breadth of state-tribe relations correlated directly with the liberalness and egalitarianism of family law, Efrati highlighted that the state-mosque relationship was central under the monarchy. It is tempting to argue that because the Iraqi ruling elite emerged from the Mandate period in close alliance with tribal kin groupings, the state was about to adopt a conservative personal-status legislation that protected extended male-centered patrilineage. Nevertheless, because the personal-status legislation governed only the urban population (Anderson 1953), the rest of the population was ruled by the TCCDR; in reality, it was the state-*ulemas* relation that was central to debates around personal-status legislation. Preserving *shari'a* courts allowed the influential and respected *'ulemas* class, from which the *qadis* were drawn, a share in the country's administration and thus ensured their loyalty and support to the ruling elite.

The dominant trend of British politics under the Mandate and in the following years of the monarchy, as I will show it in the next section, was to emphasize the "different needs" of Iraqi society and to establish a differentiated legal system in which citizens were granted different "rights" according to their religious and sectarian belonging as well as to their location and gender. Differences existed among women: Muslim and Christian women were not granted the same rights regarding personal matters, neither Sunni nor Shi'a, and the gap was even stronger between rural and urban women. This differentiated system was highly criticized among the intelligentsia, and the emergence of women's organizations challenged the fragmented and uneven colonial system.

The "Woman Question" under the Monarchy: Education and Political Activism

As shown by al-Shaikh Da'ud (1958), al-Derbendi (1968), and al-Zublef and Said's (1980) study dedicated to women's education and literacy from 1920 to 1979, as well as by Pursley (2012, 2013), the British did not push for progress in women's education. The first girls' school was opened in 1899 with the support of the famous poet Jamil Sidqi al-Zahawi (1863–1936).[11] The evolution of primary education at the

---

[11] Jamil Sidqi al-Zahawi's very famous article, "Women and Her Defense," criticizes the wearing of the traditional black *'abaya*, men's mistreatment of women, and men's privileges in marriage, divorce, and inheritance. This article provoked his dismissal from Baghdad Law School.

beginning of the twentieth century, girls' secondary education[12] in the 1930s, and mixed education beginning in 1928 were limited to the urban elite composed mainly of Sunni Arabs; Christians and Jews funded their own schools. In 1932, Baghdad Medical School welcomed its first female student; the faculty of law also accepted Sabiha al-Shaikh Da'ud in 1936. Omnia Shakry describes the debates around motherhood and women's education in colonial Egypt among the intelligentsia as characterized by "cultural translation and hybridizations" instead of a bad copy of the European model (Shakry 1998: 126–70). The same can be said regarding the debates around girls' education in Hashemite Iraq, although it was clearly marked by the will of Western-aligned Iraqi bureaucrats and Western, mainly American advisors to "produce gender differences," according to Pursley (2012: 119–41). While in the 1920s the education system was dominated by Arab nationalists such as Sati' al-Husri, who view education as a way to produce future nationalists, men and women, since the 1930s the implementation of American policymakers' recommendation by Iraqi officials introduced differences in boys' and girls' curricula, with courses related to domesticity for girls. This resulted in a situation where the more girls mixed with boys and women with men in the public sphere, the greater was the impetus to produce differences in their learned modes of being and thinking. According to Pursley (2012: 119–41), one aspect of the shift was a conceptual reorientation of women's household labor from the sphere of production to that of consumption at a time when foreign goods were invading the growing consumer market. As shown by Shakry (1998: 126–70) in the case of colonial Egypt, "ideal mothers" should carry the model of the bourgeois domestic way of life, and in Iraq as well, ideas of creating new desires and promoting bourgeois domesticity were at the core of these reforms of the education system built on gender differences.

However, despite these measures of mandatory female education in domesticity, in the 1950s, the political radicalization of society, especially students, created a sense among Iraqi officials that the education system, instead of producing modern mothers raising strong and healthy citizens, was producing a generation of educated Iraqi women who were resistant to marriage, domesticity, and motherhood and who were more attracted to political activism than managing a household (Pursley 2012: 119–41) More generally, the political elite aligned with Western powers was extremely worried about the politicization of the youth attracted by the ideas of the radical anti-imperialist left (Pursley 2013).

---

[12] The first secondary school for girls was opened in 1931.

Bashkin (2008) shows how much writing about women in Hashemite Iraq became an important mode of political and social identification. It was used to denote whether one belonged to the left or the right, to the religious or the secular camp, and how one conceptualized Iraqi law, independence, and electoral structures. She argues that the changes in the representations of women mirrored the radicalization of the Iraqi intelligentsia. While during the 1920s and 1930s the conversation about gender roles was mostly conducted among men who debated education, seclusion, veiling, and domesticity, in contrast, in the 1940s and 1950s, social democrats, communists, and radical pan-Arabists used the mistreatment of women as a way to criticize the Hashemite state. These groups argued that the Hashemite state preserved the tribal and premodern, where women's conditions represented the markers of the state's indifference toward Iraqi society. As in colonial Egypt (Shakry 1998: 126–70), the discourse on "women's backwardness" in Iraq symbolized the "nation's backwardness"; the ways in which women were viewed in Iraq were related to other sets of representations, such as those of peasants and tribesmen, and, more broadly, to the ways in which the Iraqi intelligentsia imagined the nation. For Bashkin (2008), in the 1940s, this discourse was far more specifically Iraqi than in the past, although the transregional dimensions remained powerful as the intelligentsia spoke about the problems of *Arab* women and hybridized colonial perceptions of *Muslim* women.

According to Batatu (1978), Bashkin (2008), and Efrati (2012), leftists, Marxists, and communists advocated for women's rights as part and parcel of the struggle for social justice and equality – the most egalitarian conception of women's rights – whereas nationalist and liberal political groups considered women's social and political rights (education and the vote) as a means to "educate" and "raise nationalist consciousness" in families. For nationalists and liberals, women primarily represented "mothers" and "educators" of the young generation, and they could be granted political rights only through a "gradual modernization" because they were not deemed ready for full political rights. In Iraq and other Middle Eastern countries, *al-Nahda al-Niswiyya* ("the Women's Awakening") advocated for women's emancipation within a modernist, reformist understanding of religion and marked a rupture with traditional kin-based powers, criticizing "archaic traditions" and "tribal mentality." The British played a key role in the antisuffrage movement, especially through some of its leading representatives – such as Gertrude Bell and Edgar Bonham-Carter. Bell, for example, considered that raising children was women's essential task and described the school opened by the British authorities in Baghdad in January 1920 as a way to "create proper mothers" (Al-Derbendi 1968; Efrati 2012).

According to Efrati (2004, 2012), it appears that in Iraq – unlike other Arab countries – faith-based charitable societies did not precede secular, more overtly social and political organizations: the first women's organization was secular, and a number of organizations developed later in parallel. In addition, the emergence of new women's organizations on the "nationalist stage" had less to do with "periods when nationalist feelings were at their peak" and more to do with governmental control. The anti-British movement in Baghdad was composed of the few Sunni Arabs opposed to British rule (e.g., Shaikhs Ahmed Da'ud and Yusef al-Suwaydi), Shi'a clerics (e.g., Muhammed al-Sadr), and wealthy Shi'a merchants (e.g., Ja'far Abu al-Taman). Women's participation in all movements against the British – the Shi'a-led 1920 Revolution and even more the 1948 al-Wathba and the 1952 *intifada* – revealed their politicization especially with the expansion of the education system. *Nadi al-Nahda al-Nisa'iyya* ("the Club of Women's Awakening") was the first women's organization, which was founded in 1923 and composed of bourgeois women from the Baghdad urban elite.

The British, along with the Iraqi monarchy they brought to power, created a small class of powerful, semifeudal landlords, marginalized the tribal population, and discriminated against the Shi'a population, giving rise to growing communist and nationalist sentiments. These movements thus found a claim to unite their advocacy for social justice and liberation: the end of British domination. From the 1930s to the 1950s, the anti-British movement had a unifying effect and contributed to the weakening of sectarian and religious divisions (Bashkin 2008; Davis 2005). Following this evolution, women's charities and political groups, both nationalist and communist, became involved in the burgeoning transnational Middle Eastern and Arab nationalist women's networks; such networks advocated for women's political and legal rights alongside the Palestinian and anti-imperialist causes. When the monarchy was overthrown in 1958, Iraqis were more than ready to demonstrate, especially through women and gender issues, that their new revolutionary regime was no less radical than that of their Arab and Muslim neighbors.

Nationalist Feminists and Communist Feminists: Competing and Overlapping Trends

The Iraqi Women's Union (*al-Ittihad al-Nisa'i al-'Iraqi*) was founded in 1945 after the Arab Women's Congress in Cairo. This union was mainly composed of bourgeois women close to male nationalist elites and advocated for women's rights in the Constitution, marriage, and work, as well as the development of girls' and women's education. Simultaneously, women's groups linked to the Communist Party gathered in the League for the Defense of Women's Rights (*Rabitat al-difaʿ ʿan Huquq al-Marʾa*) and advocated for social justice, anti-imperialism, and women's rights. All organizations that made up what was commonly called the "women's movement" organized literacy and charity programs, including in rural areas, as well as civil and political rights campaigns. In the beginning of the 1950s, campaigns were launched by the women's movement demanding that the Iraqi government implement women's social, economic, and political equality; reform legislation on private matters; abolish the TCCDR; and reform the Constitution. Moreover, the leftist secular atmosphere in Iraq – the Communist Party dominated the political scene from the 1940s to the 1970s – helped to somewhat bridge sectarian divisions and spread egalitarian conceptions of citizenship and women's rights.

In the mid-1940s, women's organizations had broadened, strengthened, and to an extent institutionalized. Two trends characterized the women's movement landscape – the nationalist feminist and the communist feminist. While their activists seemed to work together as part of the Women's Union, the government crackdown against left-wing organizations in 1947 shifted their activism (Efrati 2008: 65, 2012: 137–62). The Iraqi Women's Union yielded under this pressure and removed the representatives of the leftist Women's League Society from its directorate. While Iraqi Women's Union received support from the government and royal family and remained a relatively small, elitist organization loyal to the regime, the Women's League acted underground after failed attempts to obtain government permission under the name of the League for the Defense of Women's Rights in 1952. The League was composed of leaders from the lower middle class and very much influenced by the radical anti-imperialist Iraqi Communist Party. Two personalities of the time represent these two trends, sometimes aligned and often in competition, Naziha al-Dulaimi, who remained vocal regarding the repression of the government of leftist activists, and Sabiha al-Shaikh Daʿud, who in contrast stayed silent regarding the shift in women's activism due to governmental pressure.

Naziha al-Dulaimi, in her book, *al-Marʾa al-Iraqiyya* (*Iraqi Woman*) (1952), posed the first and dominant competing narrative on Iraqi women's activism. Here al-Dulaimi puts forward a short study of the conditions of women's lives in Iraq in the 1940s, which uses social class as an analytical framework. Al-Dulaimi was a gynecologist by trade, a prominent figure of the League for the Defense of Women's

Rights,[13] the first Iraqi (and Arab) woman minister,[14] and prominent communist activist; hence her reading and experiences with activism differed greatly from those of the nationalist elite. She considered women in the *al-fallahin* ("peasant") class as the most deprived of rights. She depicted the "double servitude" of these peasant women: they were enslaved and exploited by male domination and tribal rules and by class oppression. When analyzing women of the land-owning, bourgeois and working classes, al-Dulaimi noted that although the conditions of economic oppression varied, women of all classes were oppressed by marriages in which they were considered possessions rather than individuals, as well as social injustice and imperialism. Using a Marxist and early feminist understanding of justice and equality, al-Dulaimi tackled issues of maternal and child protection, marriage, and, indeed, prostitution – a subject on which she did not employ a moralizing analysis of sexuality but rather pushed the boundaries far beyond even that which Iraqi women activists would be able to cross today.

In this book, al-Dulaimi situated *qadiyyat al-mar'a* (the "woman question") as a fundamental part of the struggle for class and national liberation; thus her argumentation was far more radical and challenging of the status quo than that of al-Shaikh Da'ud. Al-Dulaimi and women's activist of the left believed in the line of the leader of the Iraqi Communist Party, Yusuf Salman Yusuf, that Iraq has lost its sovereignty to imperialist forces, who had fortified their position by allying with local reactionaries. Getting rid of the whole system thus was the only way to attain liberation for both men and women. Therefore, feminist activists of the radical left rejected the idea of "gradual modernization" promoted by the pro-British nationalist elite in power and considered that only a radical political change could put Iraq on the road to becoming modern, which meant achieving economic prosperity, technological progress, social justice, rights for women, and political freedom. For al-Dulaimi, women of the bourgeoisie could not escape the lot of their less-privileged sisters because their marriages too had the characteristics of a financial transaction between their fathers and their future husbands which did not allow them any real say about their marriages. The discourse and activism of the women of the League on less-privileged women were characterized by a willingness to address women's everyday and concrete problems.

---

[13] The League for the Defense of Women's Rights became the Iraqi Women's League in 1958.
[14] She was appointed in 1959 at the Ministry of the Municipalities.

Sabiha al-Shaikh Da'ud's landmark book, *Awwal al-Tariq* (1958),[15] represents the second competing trend of feminism in Iraq, the nationalist feminist. Her book was published three months before the Revolution that ended the monarchy and is considered one of the first feminist books in Iraq. It provides interesting insights into the social, economic, and political realities of women under the British Mandate (1920–32) and the monarchy (1932–58). Al-Shaikh Da'ud, the first female lawyer in Iraq, belonged to a prominent Sunni family[16] and provided an Arab nationalist version of Iraqi social and political history[17]; her work overlooks underground, especially communist, women's groups. Nevertheless, her study is the first account detailing the gender dimensions of Iraq's modernization in the decades after the establishment of the Iraqi state, as well as of such modernization's social, economic, and political realities at the turn of the first Republic (July 14, 1958). Al-Shaikh Da'ud's work brings to light the emergence, among urban educated Iraqi women, of a growing nationalist awareness that placed women and gender issues at the core of aspirations for modernization and national liberation. It gives fascinating details about how women's rights issues – such as access to education and the work sphere, veiling, and legal and political rights – structured the emerging nationalist consciousness and the idea of the "new nation" among the elite. The politics and representations of gender issues, along with the evolution of women's realities, illustrate the vision of "the nation" for certain social and political elites. Thus al-Shaikh Da'ud's study poses fundamental considerations about how to approach women and gender in Iraq: to equally consider women and gender's material, ideological, and political dimensions in the colonial and postcolonial context of nation-state building.

Al-Shaikh Da'ud and the Iraqi Women's Union activists were more accommodating to the government's "gradual modernization" discourse that considered that women needed to progress before they could be granted full citizenship rights. As shown by Efrati (2012: 137–62) and expressed clearly in *Awwal al-Tariq*, women of the Union used the

---

[15] *Awwal al-Tariq ila al-Nahda al-Niswiyya fi al-'Iraq (First Steps of Women's Awakening in Iraq)*, al-Rabita, March 1958.

[16] Her father was al-Shaikh Ahmed Da'ud, a Sunni religious figure and nationalist leader, and her mother was Naima Sultan Hamoodeh, one of the founders of *Nadi al-Nahda al-Nisa'iyya* (the "Women's Renaissance Club"), in 1923, the first Iraqi women's group.

[17] The author draws a very elitist, urban, upper-class reading of women's social, economic, and political history; she overlooks rural and underprivileged women's realities, although she does draw a dramatic picture of women of the countryside in her chapter, "*Al-Iraqiyya fi al-Rif*" ("The Iraqi Woman in the Countryside"). Throughout al-Shaikh Da'ud's study, she gives an apologetic view of the monarchal family and the Sunni Arab nationalist elite.

rhetoric of the "new woman" active and assertive and the "modern woman" – educated, professional, patriotic, and capable citizen willing to build the modern state – to promote the expansion of women's legal and political rights. As pointed out by Efrati, these activists from the elite families conducted their struggle in an "orderly manner" through legal and constitutional channels: asking the government to expand education and health services. In order not to be perceived as "too radical," they insisted on the fact that they did not want to "compete with men" in power leadership but "participate in the country's problems," such as poverty and illiteracy, and act as "mothers" demanding their rights to participate in the drafting of laws for their sons and daughters, as a natural extension of their maternal duties that would not threaten the family structure, let alone the political and social order.

Awwal al-Tariq sections dedicated to the contribution of Sunni and Shi'a religious thinkers to the defense of women's rights contrast with Al-Dulaimi's silence about religion. This use of a Muslim feminist rhetoric is very typical of transnational nationalist narratives of the time that relied on the work of Muslim reformers to advocate for an indigenous Muslim modernity. However, Al-Shaikh Da'ud seemed to have been influenced by Al-Dulaimi on the condition of the peasant women as she also evoked in her book the "double servitude" that characterizes her life. This precise issue can be analyzed through the argument of hybridization of the different nationalist narratives – pan-Arab and Iraqi – analyzed by Bashkin (2009: 194–228). The division between the civilized nation – the urban – and the uncivilized – the rural – structured the nationalist narrative as the difference between the capital and the *rif* structures' nationalist visions of the nation. This shows that despite their very different ideologies, agendas, and proposed solutions to change the political order of the time, nationalist and communist narratives also shared common visions regarding the relationship between modernity and nationhood.

In 1954, the government intensified its repression of the opposition, dismantling hundreds of societies and clubs and banning the existence of unions. The Iraqi Women's Union had to be reestablished as a single society rather than as a federation; it would be called the Women's Union Society (*Jam'iyyat al-Ittihad al-Nisa'i*). Members of the Union and the League now, after this repression campaign, explicitly criticized the government gender discourse that constructed women as noncitizens: the TCCDR that symbolized the absence of state intervention in matters of personal status and women's disenfranchisement. This evolution echoes the radicalization of the intelligentsia now dominated by the radical anti-imperialist left; it also prepared the ground for the institution of a legal frame regarding personal matters uniting all Iraqis – rural and urban, Sunnis and Shi'as – the Personal Status Code (PSC).

The New Iraqi Republic (1958–1963): The Foundational Years for Women's Activism, Legal and Political Rights

The Postcolonial State: Toward an Indigenous Modern Nation-State

The military coup (July 14, 1958) that toppled the monarchy and led to the radical regime of 'Abd al-Karim Qasim (1958–63) furthered this evolution, contributing to the consolidation of the middle class and the weakening significance of ethnic and religious belonging. Qasim put oil revenues toward efforts to reduce poverty, build social housing, and institute a welfare-state system. Moreover, the power of tribesmen and the significance of ethnic (Arab/Kurd) and sectarian (Sunni/Shi'a) belongings weakened for several reasons: first, increasing rural to urban migration[18] and Qasim's various land reform policies, which affected the power of tribesmen, the clerical class, and the aristocratic class, and second, the growing sectarian heterogeneity of the middle class due to the gradual incorporation of rural Iraq into the state and the national market. Although oil revenues were weaker in the 1940s and 1950s than in the 1970s, they were still sufficient to develop the state, modernize education, and update essential infrastructures, but the monarchy (1932–58) operated through a clientelist system open only to selected businessmen. The dismantling of the institutions for nation-building, such as Parliament and the Upper House, pushed the new revolutionary regime to rely mainly on the military and popular support for its power. Although Qasim's regime lasted fewer than five years and made no attempt to establish institutions for democratic participation, it did enact openly nationalist and socialist policies that benefited the poorest and contributed to unifying Iraqi society across communal belongings. According to Bashkin (2011), this period was also marked by a certain hybridization of pan-Arab nationalism and Iraqi nationalism, although the latter was predominant at a moment when international anticolonial leftist activism was also present in the vision.

Moreover, the revolutionary regime initiated radical reforms that strengthened the urban, modern middle class, questioning traditional powers, both tribal and religious. Socioeconomic reforms favored the poorest and aimed to narrow the gap between the upper classes and the

---

[18] In 1947, 35 percent of the population was urban; in 1977, that number jumped to 65 percent.

impoverished population. Medinat al-Thawra (actually Medinat al-Sadr) is one of the most commonly referred to of such measures; its aim was to welcome the impoverished population – known as *al-sharagawa*, who hailed originally from the southern tribal regions and were either already living in the slums of Baghdad or were newcomers – into modern urban housing. Three of Qasim's measures symbolized the rupture with traditional aristocratic, tribal, and religious powers. First, the abolition of the TCCDR ended tribesmen's power in rural areas and enhanced the state's power. Second, land reforms consisted of the appropriation and redistribution of land from the clerical and aristocratic classes to the impoverished population, provoking a huge backlash from the classes that had lost some of their privileges. Third, the enactment of the new family law provoked much criticism among the *'ulemas*, both Sunni and Shi'a, who feared the radical questioning of their authority. According to J. Ismael and S. Ismael (2007), through all these reforms, the framework of feudalism and tribalism in Iraq was effectively undermined.

Women Mobilizing in Revolutionary Times

The family law, in the form of the Personal Status Code (PSC),[19] represented a *field of struggle* between different political elites, the women's movement, and the state (Charrad 2011) in the postcolonial Middle East. In Iraq, as Efrati (2005, 2012) points out, the adoption of a PSC in Law No. 188 (promulgated in December of 1959) was not only the product of the revolutionary elite surrounding 'Abd Al- Karim Qasim, which had ended both the monarchy and British colonial domination over the country, but the adoption of an openly egalitarian and unified PSC also marked the questioning of *'ulemas* and tribal leaders' control over private matters; both the *shari'a* courts and the TCCDR were abolished. Very importantly, the PSC also marked the beginning of women activists' inclusion in the process of negotiating for their rights. Many articles of the PSC openly opposed religious – Muslim, Christian, Jewish – jurisprudence (Khayun & Badurzeki 2006). By adopting measures such as putting the intestate inheritance rights for male and female heirs under the Civil Code and thus granting through an indirect mechanism gender equality in that matter in certain cases, severe limitations on polygamy, making eighteen the legal age for marriage, and protecting women from arbitrary divorce (Anderson 1960: 546), the state was sending a clear message of its authority over this new Republic to the *'ulemas* and Shaikhs. Women were also given political

---

[19] More precisely, the PSC addresses issues of marriage, divorce, childbirth, paternity, custody, maintenance, bequests, and succession.

rights, though limited, for the first time: the right to vote and run for office. As mentioned previously, Qasim appointed Naziha al-Dulaimi Minister of Municipalities in 1959, the first woman Iraqi and Arab minister.

Law No. 188 was a text clearly stating its routings within *shari'a* and uniting Sunni and Shi'a jurisprudences, granting the authority to a judge appointed by the state to rule on personal matters without the intercession of *'ulemas*. Moreover, according to Efrati (2012), women activists, such as the Iraqi Women's League (al-Rabita) activist Naziha al-Dulaimi, participated to the drafting of the PSC alongside legal specialists and Sunni and Shi'a *'ulemas* who elaborated it straight after the July 14, 1958 Revolution. Thus the PSC was the result of women activists' demands of and participation in the legislative process. Under Qasim, the political field was open, but sporadic repressions did occur. For example, communist organizations, which dominated the political scene at the time, were authorized and then forbidden a few years later; some communist leaders were also brought to power, and then dismissed shortly after due to Qasim's fear of competition. Nevertheless, women activists were very vocal during this period and advocated to extend women legal rights: forbidding extralegal marriage contracts, outlawing judges from marrying girls under the legal age, reforming articles related divorce and polygamy that privilege men's rights, and extending women's rights to child custody.

Maqbula B., seventy-four, is one of al-Rabita's oldest and most active women activists. Maqbula belongs to an urban Sunni Arab family from 'Ana that emigrated to al-Kerrada, central Baghdad, at the beginning of the 1950s. Born in 1938, she was twenty years old when the Revolution began; at that time, Maqbula was already an active member of the Communist Party, and her mother was a founding member of al-Rabita. Prior to the Revolution, Maqbula was drawn to communist activism by the Palestinian cause. After the Revolution, she dedicated her activism to women's rights and the establishment of the PSC:

After the establishment of the Personal Status Code, I dedicated my struggle to the defense of women's rights. Me and the other activists, we started with the struggle against analphabetism, and with working in the countryside, especially against polygamy. We went to the women of the countryside and informed them of their rights. While peasant women worked as much as men, they ignored most of their rights, like for example her husband was obliged to ask for her permission in order to marry a second wife. We were rejected by some husbands there, because they thought we were bringing disorder to their families. We were telling women that men were not their superiors, and that they were not obliged to obey them, neither to obey their sons. We were telling them that they were equal to men. It was a difficult struggle, and many women did not accept our ideas.

We relied heavily on the fact that the Personal Status Code was elaborated by all the religious schools and the *'ulemas* from all of them. The Personal Status Code was legitimate and popular because of the support of the religious leaders, and because it was not against *shari'a*. The committee that drafted it was composed of jurists and *fuqeha'*. We obtained, in 1959, equal shares in inheritance. This changed in 1963 with the Ba'th and then with Saddam.

Maqbula participated in the formation of the well-known *lejna hal al-mashakel* (the "problems resolution committee"), which were dedicated to mediating in private matters and supporting women within the family sphere. Being from an urban, educated Sunni Arab family, Maqbula had good connections with women of the nationalist elite and mentioned that some al-Rabita's actions were supported by or even conducted in partnership with other women's groups. The effervescence of women's political activism in Iraq following the establishment of the Iraqi Republic was also described by Al-Ali, in her chapter "Living with the Revolution" (2007: 56–108). The women of the same generation interviewed by Al-Ali also spoke to the politically and socially revolutionary atmosphere, as al-Rabita emerged as a prominent women political organization.

Indigenous Secularism: Gender and Nation

This period also signified a time of secularization: traditional religious practices were on the wane, and the adoption of nonreligious ideologies, such as communism, Marxism, and secular ideologies, dominated the political culture. For example, the year after the Revolution, Shi'a participation in communist-led political life was at an unprecedented high, absorbing the energies and attention of vast masses, especially among the middle, lower, and manual, urban, and rural classes (Jabar 2003: 75; Nakash 1994). Thus, in 1959, pilgrimages to Karbala and Najaf – the cornerstones of Shi'a religious rituals – were at their lowest-ever number, clearly indicating that traditional religious practices and rituals were not strong at the time.

Nevertheless, I argue that the symbolic power of religion, especially as it pertains to women and gender issues, did not completely lose its status but instead was reformulated into the nationalist, socialist, and anti-imperialist framework. For example, the way Qasim himself advocated for the PSC, especially the more radical articles, such as the one on inheritance, is very revealing. In March 1960, Qasim gave an interview on the issue in *Al-Thawra*, he insisted on showing his "Muslimness" by indicating that he had "fasted Ramadan since the age of ten" and "knows the Qur'an by heart." In response to "the men of religion's" protest on the issue of inheritance, Qasim developed an argument that would be deemed by many today as Muslim feminist. He directly quoted the verse of the Qur'an related to inheritance, interpreting it as an exhortation (*wisaya*) and not a command. He compared this verse with other verses from the Qur'an – those related to the punishment of thieves and fornication – and pointed out that the verb used in the latter verses clearly indicates a divine "command." He then said:

I repeat: some of my brothers the men of religion have visited me and objected to sections of this code. And I recited to them these noble verses and we argued about them. I said: In so far as the salaries of civil servants are concerned, and our own salaries and even yours, you men of religion, both before and after the Revolution, these are derived from the proceeds of taxation, including the duty on wines. But has one of you refused to receive his salary? So long as our aim in enacting this code is the service of the nation as a whole, there is no doubt that the Creator will always help us and support us. (Anderson 1960: 562–63)

In addition to revealing the symbolic power of religion in the postcolonial period and its use in nationalist terms, the Muslim feminist rhetoric used by Qasim showed how much gender issues were at the core of the "new nation." Questioning the power of the *'ulemas*, as well as affirming the identity of the new nation, was symbolized through reforming gender-related laws and granting women more rights. Here, in the framework of the formulation of the postcolonial state with conflicts between Westernization and cultural authenticity, the link between gender and nation appears very clearly. As shown by Jayawardena (1986) and others, women were represented as "bearers of the nation," their issues and rights symbolizing the progress of the new nation obtained in the framework of anti-imperialist struggles.

Consensual Memory on Revolutionary Times: Women's Liberation and the Unity of the Nation

The oldest women activists I interviewed, who were born either at the end of the 1930s or early 1940s, recalled this period with nostalgia and admiration. It is described as an era characterized by both political openness and women's emancipation and national unity, especially regarding religious and sectarian divisions. My interviewees described this period as foundational to and influential in their political awareness and activism, especially regarding women and gender issues. Rabab H., a leading figure of al-Rabita and active in the postinvasion women's movement, was twelve years old when the Revolution started. She was living with her apolitical Arab Christian family in Basra at the time.

I can say that the 14th July 1958 was a turning point in my life. I considered it as a turning point because the July Revolution introduced us to a new era characterized by an opening for the people, for their participation in social life in general. It was an opening for women's participation, her liberation from the veil and the *'abaya*, and the opening of education to her. It was also the emergence of new social and working movements, such as the Students' Union, the Women's Union, and movements that pushed citizens' participation in social life. I started my involvement very young, in secondary school and then in high school, with the Students' Union.

Haifa F. – a sociologist and professor at Baghdad University and member of al-Rabita – was sixteen years old when the Revolution began. She belongs to a nationalist Baghdadi family with close ties to leftist and communist political groups at the time. She recalled participating in demonstrations for "social justice" in secondary school. Haifa described this period as very culturally and intellectually rich and dominated by leftist ideas: "everyone was reading a lot" and "open minded." She described the Communist Party as having "a civilizing role" for the population, and of the gender norms during this period, she said: "[a]t the time, the veil was internal. People were well mannered. Boys were not harassing girls even when they were not veiled, and no matter what they were wearing."

Nashwa A. – a member of a women's rights organization in Baghdad – was fifteen years old when the Revolution began. She belonged to a prominent Shi'a religious family from Karbala. Her father was one of the leading Shi'a nationalist figures who opposed the British under the monarchy and participated in the 1920 Revolution. Nashwa's family moved to the Medinat al-Huriyya neighborhood in Baghdad after the Revolution. One of her brothers, a communist activist, was jailed under Nuri al-Sa'id. Nashwa recalls that the time of Qasim was a period of great happiness and expressed admiration for the leader: "We were so happy for the revolution; my brother was jailed under Nuri al-Sa'id. I loved 'Abd al-Karim Qasim's personality, and appreciated him very much. After the 14th of July, the houses were open; there was no stealing at all. 'Abd al-Karim was clean."

Whether expressing admiration for the Revolution's leader or its reforms, most of the activists I interviewed – from various political, regional, ethnic, and religious backgrounds – remembered this as a time of national unity. Maha S. – born in 1946 and a prominent women activist in Baghdad – was a teenager during the Qasim period. At the time, she lived in Nasiriyah with her mother, father, and four brothers and sisters. Her family emigrated from a Christian village north of Mosul and settled there until the mid-1970s. Maha's father worked as a merchant, opened a shop, and was a communist activist. She speaks of the Nasiriyah period in her life with great nostalgia and a strong feeling of belonging:

We never experienced any discrimination there, neither religious nor communal, despite the fact that my father was selling alcohol. Nobody ever criticized that, and we were highly respected and loved in Nasiriyah … The atmosphere was very political, and culturally very rich. We were organizing a competition for who could learn popular poetry and *al-mu'alaqat* the best. In high school, we all knew *al-mu 'alaqat* by heart. The atmosphere was towards political readings and debates between boys and girls. I remember that there were no distinctions between us, neither between religions or between boys and girls. This way of thinking, this shared culture was dominant; there was no distinction between Christians and Muslims. Initially, I did not even know that there were *mazahib* ["religious schools"] for either Christians or Muslims.

Maha S. gives a very emotional and tender recollection of her youth Nasiriyah at the end of the 1950s and beginning of the 1960s. She speaks of the fact that despite here being a Christian, the atmosphere of sharing and unity was so strong in the Arab Shi'a–dominated south that she was even invited to participate in Shi'a rituals:

I remember laughing today that I performed 'Arus al-Qasim in the *qraiyyat* [Shi'a religious ceremonies]. I was seen as pretty, and they imagined that 'Arus al-Qasim was very pretty, so they would cover me and make me participate in the *qraiyya* … This city, Nasiriyah, I consider it mine. I never had the idea that I would not belong there.

Although biased due to their grounding in women's subjectivities, these personal and emotional accounts are nevertheless revealing of what the Qasim period meant for many Iraqis, especially women political activists. Al-Ali (2007: 56–108) interviewed diasporic Iraqi women who had experienced that period; they also expressed similar feelings and the sense of a unified nationhood. Their words show how much the idea of national unity overlapped with women's emancipation in the context of communist and nationalist activism. Qasim himself – the son of an Arab Sunni father and a Faili (Shi'a) Kurdish mother – personified national unity. His noncommunal, pro-women, and pro-poor politics marked Iraqi women activists' vision and created a consensual memory. This consensual memory, where both the advancement of women's rights and shared nationhood are perceived as interrelated, forms the basis of what women activists designate as "Iraqi culture." In their attempt to define a unified national memory, women activists did not mention the military nature of the revolutionary regime in their narratives – e.g., the bloody ethnoreligious conflicts of Mosul and Kirkuk – choosing instead to focus on the general atmosphere of political openness and the feeling of unified nationhood. The intense violence that characterized the Ba'th overthrow of Qasim's regime can explain the terms in which this period is narrated.

The Ba'th Coup of 1963 and the 'Arif Brothers Regime (1963–1968): Breaking with the Revolutionary Atmosphere

The first Ba'th coup of February 1963, backed by the CIA, ended the revolutionary regime. The Ba'th campaign of repression, from February to November of 1963, has been described as the most terrible and bloody moment in the post–World War II Middle East (Farouk-Sluglett & Sluglett 1987). The Ba'th blamed the communists for the Mosul and Kirkuk events[20] and claimed that their mission was revenge. The sectarian, anti-Shi'a dimension of the repression of communists was also clear in the Ba'th militias' slogan: *La Shi'i, la Shuyu'i, la Shargawi* ("No Shi'a, No Communist, No Sharagawa").[21] Such militia's purged Baghdad's communist (and predominantly Shi'a) neighborhoods – such as Medinat al-Thawra (actually Medinat al-Sadr) and al-Kazimiyya. At the time, opponents responded, *La za'ym illa Karim* ("No Leader but Karim"), which referred to 'Abd al-Karim Qasim. Stadiums were transformed into huge prisons for political prisoners, communist activists were shot in the streets, and thousands of people were tortured and imprisoned. Summary executions, the torturing of political activists, and the threatening, interrogating, and searching of their families occurred on a massive scale. Political activists were traumatized.

Maqbula B. narrated this very dark and traumatizing period of her life. She was arrested, imprisoned, and tortured along with her husband, a communist activist to whom she had been married for only one year:

Democratic work unveiled the faces of the activists. We became visible after the revolution, which made it possible to repress us in 1963. The Ba'thists began to talk against the communists, against Iraq itself. They started to ally with the US;

[20] In Mosul, in March 1959, conflicts between communists and nationalists who were mostly conservative Sunni Arabs provoked the death of more than 200 people. According to Batatu (1978), the clashes were more sectarian and tribal than political. A few months later, in July, conflicts between Turkmens and Kurds, who were mostly of communist obedience, provoked the death of between thirty-one and seventy-nine people, Turkmens in the majority. The communists were accused of being responsible for these events and of representing a threat to the central state authority.

[21] The *shargawi*, all Shi'as, are a population that emigrated from the southern region such as al-'Amara, and who occupied the slums in Baghdad in the 1950s. After the building of social houses by Qasim, they lived in the popular areas of Baghdad.

they said it themselves. Many acknowledged it: "We came in American trains." It was the radio channel *Sawt America* that guided them to the opposition activists on the ground. 1963 was a terror and surprise for the nationalist forces . . . They promulgated Declaration 13, which stipulated that anyone suspected of being a communist could be killed without judgment. It was savagery; even tribal laws do not do that. Blood was flowing in the streets. Entire families were killed . . . They came to take me from my place of work [she was an employee in the faculty of engineering at the campus of Bab al-Mu'azem]. They gathered us in buses. There were doctors, lawyers, educated women, even pregnant women who then gave birth in prison. When we arrived in the prison, we found it full. There was a part for men and a part for women.

Maqbula narrated crying about the month she spent in prison: the general atmosphere, torture, and the solidarity between the prisoners.

I stayed a month in prison. There were 800 women in my prison, despite the fact that there was only enough space for no more than 50. The cells were named after the detained groups. There was the Ba'quba cell and the Baghdad cell. There was no cell for Najaf, because it was considered a holy place; the women from Najaf were interrogated in Bayt al-Mokhtar. In Najaf they did not jail; the main detention centers were in Baghdad because it was not simple to detain women in the country-side; people would have made an uprising for that. So they took the women, and brought them to Baghdad with their kids, because women could not leave their kids when their husbands were detained as well. Our cells were full of children; babies were even born inside the cells. Al-Rabita was in prison. This is why prison was not so hard in the beginning, because we were all together, supporting one another. I was jailed with Rosa Khaduri, Salima Fakhri, and the actress Nahida al-Ramah. Then they sent us to detention centers; I was in the Kerrada center. There, we heard the men being tortured in the basement. After 24 February, from one o'clock in the morning, they would start hitting iron against the wall; it was deafening. Torture would begin after that. We were left in our underwear, and they plunged us into iced water and threw heaps of garbage on us. In that place, it was like an iced bathroom where we were plunged; we were four women; one had just got married and another one was pregnant. We took turns sitting in the only little corner where one could sit, just to warm up our feet, one after the other. The one who was pregnant gave birth. We stayed a month like that. They interrogated us, tried to force us to speak. I heard about some who spoke.

During the campaign of repression, Maqbula's father was jailed and interrogated, her aunt's husband and one of her close friends were killed, her sister ran away, and her two brothers left the country. Maqbula's father told her about his experience of detention: how he was interrogated and the harsh torture experienced by male political activists, even when very old. He described that he saw "men as old as Shaikh Bahr al-'Ulum[22] hanging from their hands" and tortured to death. Her mother was the

---

[22] Shaikh Bahr al-'Ulum is a prominent Shi'a figure and nationalist activist.

only one left at home and was frequently harassed, interrogated, and searched by security forces who wanted information on her family. Maqbula, after her release from prison, asked everyone she knew for information on her husband's whereabouts and managed to visit him in Qasr al-Nihaya prison:

He was another man, emaciated; his face was not the same anymore. They had ripped the nails from his feet and hands, and extinguished cigarettes on his skin, even on his intimate parts. He was so weakened, and terribly sick. He caught Tetanus and was cured for it. I did not know that human beings could endure so much. I visited him a second time and brought him what he had asked for: a transistor radio, some linens, simple things and some food.

Later, when Maqbula asked to visit her husband again, she was told that he had been moved to another detention center. She thinks that this is when her husband was likely killed because she never saw him again and still does not know what happened. She got mobilized and organized with the help of activists who fled the country and settled abroad, starting an international campaign to release Iraqi political prisoners. These activists also opened the organization to women from the bourgeois nationalist elite who had supported them during the period of political repression. Although most of their activities were underground, the activists managed to restructure al-Rabita:

After that, our activism became more structured and organized, always underground. But we built connections with abroad and we were working very well. We structured al-Rabita, and the house of Rosa Khaduri was our headquarters after we came out from prison. The bourgeois nationalists supported us a lot during that period. This solidarity movement helped us to psychologically overcome this ordeal. We were witnessing the cases of women that were dealing with situations far worse than ours. We carried on until 1968, we set up our High Committee and Naziha al-Dulaimi also came back.

Then, after the second Ba'th coup, Maqbula would again have to endure Ba'th repression because the Ba'th arrested and tortured her elderly mother in 1979. Maqbula fled the country, returning only after the Ba'th regime fell in 2003. Nevertheless, she remained active abroad, representing al-Rabita and dedicating her activism to organizing awareness campaigns against the Ba'th regime and solidarity campaigns with Iraqi political prisoners.

PSC reform – specifically the articles related to inheritance and polygamy – was one of the measures undertaken by the Ba'th regime after the first coup (Anderson 1963).[23] The inheritance article, which had

---

[23] These articles of the PSC were reformed as soon as March 18, 1963, right after the fall of the Qasim regime in February of 1963.

relied on the Civil Code, was replaced with an article that relied on *shari'a* and privileged Ja'fari jurisprudence. The revised article on polygamy, while preserving its limitations, added a clause that allowed for polygamous marriages contracted outside the courts. Thus the new article legitimized the illegal practice of polygamy. Reforming the PSC's most controversial and symbolic articles was clearly aimed at marking the end of the revolutionary atmosphere. Women activists, especially in the communist ranks, were violently repressed: some were jailed and tortured, and many others had no choice but to flee the country.

In November 1963, the 'Arif brothers overthrew the first Ba'th regime via a military coup; their regime ruled the country for the next five years (1963–68),[24] combining military discipline with clan and kinship allegiances, the *jumailat* (Sakai 2003). The 'Arif brothers' reliance on a small Sunni Arab clan exacerbated feelings of sectarian oppression among Shi'a. Despite their opposition to communists, the 'Arif brothers instituted several nationalist measures, such as nationalization of the banks and assurances sectors, foreign trade, and several industries. As long as oil revenues were limited and the political elite divided, income from the oil industry was not completely centralized, and thus the state's despotic potential was restrained. The arrangements for state-elite cohesion proved weak, at times disastrous: four successful, and a dozen more attempted, coup d'états shook the nation during this period, proving the vulnerability of this disciplinary regime.

During this period, leftist and communist organizations resumed their activism semiofficially and mainly underground. Rabab H. – an undergraduate law student at Baghdad University at the time – recalls this period, when she was very active in the General Students' Union affiliated with the Communist Party:

I belonged to the General Students' Union of the Iraqi Republic; I was one of the leading members. We were not officially members of the Communist Party, as most of our activities had been underground since 1963. I remember that during the student elections organized by the Iraqi Government in 1967, we won more than 75% of the seats as the list of the General Students' Union. After obtaining my law degree in 1967, I got involved in the women's movement. It was a semiofficial action, because at the time most of our activities were underground. We were insisting on the link between women's liberation and democratic freedom in the country, in the broader meaning of the term.

---

[24] 'Abd al-Salam 'Arif led the country from 1963 to 1966, and his brother, 'Abd al-Rahman, ran the country from 1966 to 1968. They were both Free Officers.

Perhaps the predominance of the Communist Party and organizations' political culture, as revealed by Rabab's experience, pushed the 'Arif brothers to adopt an openly "Islamic" discourse, Sunni tinted, and present itself as a Muslim power. The "Islamic discourse" combined with kin-based, patriarchal, and patrimonial politics produced conservative political measures, which my interviewees remembered as the "moral police." The regime's security officers went to university campuses to paint women's uncovered legs and prevent "immodest" clothing, such as miniskirts. Haifa F. was, at the time, a young lecturer in sociology at Baghdad University. She recalls a day she wore a knee-length skirt to work:

I was told by one of my colleagues, when I was about to leave the faculty building after class, that I should stay for a while. I asked why and was told that there was a soldier outside holding a bucket of dark paint and a big brush, and that he would paint my legs if I came across him. I decided to go out and talk to him. I told him that I am not a student, that I am a professor here, and that my skirt goes below my knees. After discussing with him for a while, he authorized me to leave the faculty without having my legs painted.

In fact, according to many (Al-Khafaji 1986; Batatu 1978, 1991; Farouk-Sluglett 1991; Farouk-Sluglett & Sluglett 1991, 1987), Iraq's modernization and entrance to the world market were not as developed as those of other Arab countries, such as Egypt. The introduction of modern consumerism and sophisticated communications systems represented a facade of modernity more than the real transformation of a traditional, precapitalist functioning society. Until the 1960s and 1970s, "beneath this facade, patriarchal values, and ties of family, clan, locality, tribe, and sect continue[d] to be reproduced" (Farouk-Sluglett & Sluglett 1991: 1412), and the dictatorial regimes worked against the disintegration of such values and ties. Thus, as described by Jabar (2003), cultural tribalism became an urban phenomenon: migrants from rural areas retained their tribal names, value systems, lifestyles, and solidarity commitments.[25] Social alienation from urban life – with its fragmenting division of labor, commercialized economy, alien lifestyle, and hostile environment – strengthened cultural tribalism. Moreover, this process was reinforced by the authoritarian nature of the post-1963 regimes; as Zubaida (1991: 209) notes: "[t]he 'orientalist' picture of 'Islamic' societies as communalistic, religious and impervious to modern

[25] The most common example is Medinat al-Sadr, built as Medinat at-Thawra by Qasim to contain the slums filled with peasant migrants in Baghdad who fled from the feudal Shaikhs of al-'Amara and Kut in the 1950s. Initially, each avenue or street was numbered in order; in one year, these numbers were displaced by tribal names, usually of the *hamula*.

ideologies has actually been realized as a modern phenomenon under totalitarian regimes in Iraq and elsewhere." According to J. Ismael and S. Ismael (2000), who apply Sharabi's concept of neopatriarchy to the Iraqi context, the first decades after the end of the British Mandate – i.e., the formation of the Iraqi state – represented a "modernization of patriarchy" – the *distortion*, not the replacement, of traditional patriarchy and the *malformation* of the state by integrating a kin-based tribal social dynamic into the public sector.

Conclusion

In colonial Iraq, the formulation and context of the "woman question" were marked by both marginalization from power and the tribalization of the majority of Iraqi society, which was ruled by tribal law in rural areas and by a Sunni elite in the cities. Colonial Iraq was led by a politics of uneven differentiation in terms of legal rights that created a fragmented citizenship and nationhood. From its beginnings, the "new nation" was contested by the majority of the population. This contestation, grounded in class, ethnic, sectarian, and regional (urban/rural) divisions, gave the "woman question" a peculiar shape. The most radical advocacy for women's rights came from secular and leftist political forces as religious authorities were reluctant to relinquish their powers. Thus, unlike other Muslim majority and Arab countries, in Iraq, Fleischmann's (1999) stages – described in the introduction to this chapter – did not emerge until later; in the context of a secularized society with a political culture dominated by the Iraqi Communist Party, these stages also came in the form of nationalist, leftist, political forces.

The new Iraqi Republic contested tribal and religious powers, instead pushing the emerging, modern middle class. The defense of women's rights was central to the new regime's modernist nationalist politics, which were shaped by a sense of shared nationhood and weakening religious, ethnic, and sectarian divisions. Nevertheless, "Islam" remained a key symbol of cultural authenticity, especially among nationalist feminists. Although it included radical measures, the adoption of a PSC within the framework of *shari'a* indicated the postcolonial formulation of the "woman question." The link between a unified nation and women's emancipation was revealed through the adoption of a PSC that both guaranteed progress in women's rights and worked to overcome sectarian divisions between Sunni and Shi'a jurisprudence. This linkage was also expressed by many of the women activists I interviewed. Nevertheless, the exacerbation of ethnic, religious, and sectarian divisions; the new nation-state's lack of legitimacy as a result of colonization; and the military nature of the revolutionary regime resulted in a weak and contested political elite. Then the Ba'th coup that ended the first Iraqi Republic chose bloody and patrimonial authoritarianism to preserve its rule over state and society.

As a result of these political, economic, and social developments, women's issues and gender norms evolved into what Hisham Sharabi terms "neopatriarchy": the old social structures of society were preserved and *distorted* along the lines of the *malformation* of the new state by British colonizers. Although revolutionary times contributed to the progress of women's rights and activism, and also revealed radical political forces within society, the nature of the state and the preservation of old social structures limited changes to gender norms and relations. The bloody authoritarianism that followed these revolutionary times – its repression of radical forces, normalization of political violence, and patrimonial nature – reversed any process of social change and national unity, processes on which women's rights activists had relied for their advocacy.

As for political activism, the last period (1963–68) had the following effects: it changed the political system and the social/ethnic and religious structure of the ruling elites, disturbed national integrative processes, altered the role of the state, and gradually led to the destruction of radical movements on the left and the right, thereby creating an ideological/political vacuum. These mutations broke with democratic and popular social and political movements, opening the door to political movements that favored identity-based modes of activism, as I show in Chapter 2.

2 Women, Gender, Nation, and the Ba'th Authoritarian Regime (1968–2003)

Introduction

On the heels of Chapter 1's analysis, it is interesting to take a closer look at Hisham Sharabi's *Neopatriarchy* (1988). In this book, Sharabi defines neopatriarchy as distinct from traditional patriarchy, a "modernized patriarchy." One of Sharabi's basic assumptions is that over the last 100 years, the patriarchal structures of Arab societies were far from being displaced or truly modernized; rather, these structures have been strengthened and maintained in deformed, "modernized" forms. That is, the nineteenth-century *Nahda* ("Awakening") not only failed to break down inner relations and forms of patriarchy but also paved the way for a new hybrid sort of society/culture, the "neopatriarchal society/culture." Material modernization, the first (surface) manifestation of social change, only served to remodel and reorganize patriarchal structures and relations, reinforcing them through new, "modern" forms and appearances. Neopatriarchy was neither modern nor traditional; it was an *entropic social formation*, highly unstable, and characterized by a transitory nature and specific kinds of underdevelopment and nonmodernity visible in its economy, class structure, and political, social, and cultural organization. Neopatriarchy's concrete historical formation was shaped by both internal and external forces. Arab societies' forced introduction into "dependent capitalism" within a "Western-dominated world market," through colonization, in the nineteenth and twentieth centuries was one of the most essential dimensions of these forces. Thus, for Sharabi, neopatriarchal societies are the outcome of modern Europe's colonization of the patriarchal Arab world – the marriage of imperialism and patriarchy. This phenomenon produced the "neopatriarchal petty bourgeoisie," a hybrid and dominant class. According to Sharabi, modernization in this context is, for the most part, only a mechanism promoting underdevelopment and social entropy that produces and reproduces the hybrid and semirational structures and consciousness typical of neopatriarchy.

Sharabi conceptualizes the nature of the neopatriarchal society and state. He argues that whether conservative or progressive, the central psychosocial feature of such a society is the dominance of the male figure of the father. Significantly, the most advanced and functional aspect of the neopatriarchal state was its internal security apparatus: the *mukhabarat*. It worked as a two-state system: the military-bureaucratic structure and the secret police structure that dominates everything. The neopatriarchal state was, regardless of its legal and political forms and structures, in many ways no more than a modernized version of the traditional patriarchal sultanate; the internal structures remain rooted in the patriarchal values and social relations of kinship, clan, and religious and ethnic groups. Thus patriarchalism resisted the nationalist and secular wave of the 1950s and 1960s and found legitimacy in the claim of a supposed "authentic Islam," a legitimation that represented a form of cultural and identity-grounded resistance to Western imperialism. Moreover, the nature of the neopatriarchal state – authoritarian and kin based – pushed individuals toward "primary social structures," such as family, tribe, ethnic community, and religious sect, instead of letting the individual subject be the basis of citizenship.

In line with Sharabi's neopatriarchy concept but looking more specifically at the formation of modern nation-states, Floya Anthias and Nira Yuval-Davis (1989) show the centrality of women and gender issues in the modernization process. They argue that control over women and their sexuality is at the core of national and ethnic processes. Women are deemed the "mothers of the nation," the bearers and reproducers of ethnic/national groups, and the signifiers of national difference. Thus a "new nation" can produce structures that are just as limiting as traditional tribal or kin groups. Regarding how women deal with neopatriarchal structures, it is interesting to look at Deniz Kandiyoti's "Bargaining with Patriarchy" (1988). Here Kandiyoti argues that analysis of women's strategies and coping mechanisms leads to a "more culturally and temporally grounded understanding of patriarchal systems" than the abstract notion of "patriarchy." Kandiyoti argues against simplistic feminist theories that invoke "patriarchy" as "monolithic male dominance," using it as a blanket term to explain very complex realities. She shows that women strategize within a concrete set of constraints, which she calls "patriarchal bargains." Kandiyoti highlights the various forms of patriarchy and the different contexts in which such forms are deployed, which present women with distinct "rules of the game" and strategies to "maximize security and optimize life options" with varying potentials for active or passive resistance.

Returning to Sharabi, the emergence of Islamism as a movement of political emancipation and cultural revival that opposed Westernization and was critical of the ability of nationalism, communism, and socialism to oppose imperialism was also the product of neopatriarchy. Thus Islamism was related to imperialism in the sense that it sought to oppose it. Islamist movements emerged from an in-between social class strata, the petty commodity producers and distributors, and the proletarianized small bourgeoisie, contesting the petty bourgeoisie class established during the formation of the new nation-state. Although I believe that Sharabi's social class reading of the emergence of Islamism in Arab societies to be limited, I do agree with the fact that he situated Islamism within the European imperialism-imposed process of modernization. On this point, Sharabi concurred with the analysis of Zubaida (1989) and Burgat (1996) of the emergence of Islamism in postcolonial Muslim majority countries. In contrast with essentialist approaches that build a historical continuity between a supposed "Islam" and its political expressions, Zubaida and Burgat situate Islamism within the framework of nation-state formation and the process of modernization imposed by colonization.

Suad Joseph's edited volume *Gender and Citizenship in the Middle East* (2000) follows Kandiyoti's approach bringing new lights to the different ways in which citizenship is gendered. According to Joseph (2000) in the Middle East the enterprise of state-building emerged less as an expression of specific class formations and more in conjunction with the demise of empires, resulting in top-down citizenship. Parallel to these processes have been the on-going enmeshment of state and civil society, state and kinship, kinship and civil society. The fluidity of the boundaries between the governmental, nongovernmental, and kinship has often resulted in continuities in patriarchal practices in a multitude of domain. Women have experienced citizenship differently from men not only because they are women but also because they are women and members of particulars classes, races, ethnicities, and religions – all of which gender them in complex and contradictory was. Thus, if citizenship is mandatory in the modern nation-state, as Zubaida (1989) has argued, then the modern nation-state has mandated a masculine citizen.

In the light of these analyses, I pose the following questions: How relevant is the concept of neopatriarchy to Iraq under the Ba'th regime (1968–2003), and in what ways is it related to the entanglement of gender issues with issues of religion, nationhood, kinship, and the nature of the Ba'th state and political regime? How were women and gender issues posed and used within Ba'th political projects, and how was the Ba'th regime experienced by Iraqi women? What were the gender dimensions of political contestations to the Ba'th regime, particularly of the Shi'a Islamist movement? In other words, what were the terms of and context in which Iraqi women "bargained with patriarchy" and experienced citizenship under the Ba'th regime?

Under the Ba'th Regime (1968–2003): Women, Gender, Nation, Society, and the Authoritarian-Patrimonial State

Authoritarianism prior to 1980

The 'Arif brothers' takeover in November 1963 was merely a short breather before the second Ba'th coup of July 1968. When the Ba'th returned to power, their campaign of repression and terror began again – including imprisonment, torture, intimidation, and executions – but this time targeting a broader political spectrum: communists, Nasserists, pro-Syrian Ba'thists, old ministers and officials, alleged spies, and any other Ba'th opposition groups. Nashwa A., born in 1943, remembered this period with great pain because her family – originally from Karbala – belonged to the renowned Baghdadi clerical class and includes several leading nationalist and communist figures. Two of her brothers were jailed in 1963 for being communist activists, and her brother-in-law, a young pilot and leftist activist, was executed. Nashwa's brothers had fled to Germany, but was caught by the regime's security forces when he returned for a visit in 1968.

In 1968, after the coup, when my brother came back from Germany, they came and took him in front of his wife and son. I was the one who opened the door, and I confronted them. After that, I spent months running around between his prison and people that could help me get him out. I was terrified for him; I was young at the time. I was so active in trying to get him out that he even heard in prison "your sister is running around for you." When he was finally released, he came back completely destroyed; he looked like nothing. He told us how he was tortured, savagely tortured; it was not possible to be tortured that way. They destroyed him. His teeth, they broke his teeth, he had cigarette burns all over his body, from his chest to his feet. He had scars from a whip on his feet that scarred his heels. Our [her brother's name] was so sweet; he was the sweetest of the family. We could not bear to see him scarred like an animal. With time, he came back to himself. He became again the sweet and patient soul he was, and he is until today ... He got treated after prison, because it was obvious that he had been tortured, but he had to hide it from people. After a while, he managed to escape to Germany with his wife and son, and I visited them there, although it was risky.

Such repression was experienced by both men and women activists; there were many reported cases of "violations of women's honor" – i.e., the rape of women political activists in Ba'th prisons (Omar 1994; Zuhdi 2008).

This Ba'th regime, unlike its predecessor, stayed in power; hence the families of political prisoners and missing or executed activists endured harsh discrimination and control by the Ba'th, with some even fleeing the country when possible. In subsequent years, the Ba'th brought the army and security services under its influence, and the Ba'thification of Iraqi state institutions only furthered as Saddam Hussein's power increased over Hasan al-Bakr, the head of state. With much of the power already secured, Saddam Hussein officially became president in 1979. Immediately after, Hussein embarked on a campaign of arrest and torture of political opponents and a violent purge of anyone suspected of opposing his clan's, the Tikritis, hegemony within the party. In 1979, Maqbula B. – the previously quoted al-Rabita activist who was imprisoned and tortured after the 1963 Ba'th coup – was again targeted. Because she was away when the security forces came to her home, Maqbula's elderly mother – a founding member of al-Rabita – was arrested and tortured instead.

They came and took my mother. They took her because my car was registered under her name. They tortured her and interrogated her about me. They hit her and gave her 16 electric shocks on the most sensitive areas of her body: on her chest, and all the sensitive areas, despite the fact that she was over 60 years old!! [She cried] I wish she was here in order to tell you. They circled the house, waiting for me to come back. They were trying to get her to speak, [to] tell them where I was hiding. They continued to harass her until the fall of the regime. They even proposed to pay for her flight ticket to go and get me abroad.

Maqbula did not go home; she escaped, without a single personal item, the same day her mother was caught. After hiding inside the country for a year and having been reported as "missing" in Baghdad, she clandestinely entered Syria. Like many activists who fled during this period, Maqbula received support from Palestinian activists – from the Popular Front for the Liberation of Palestine – in the Damascus and Beirut refugee camps, and the Yemeni government provided her with a fake passport. Later her mother was able to secretly visit her in Syria. During Maqbula's twenty-four years in exile, she lived in Syria, Lebanon, Libya, Russia, Czechoslovakia, and Bulgaria; throughout this time, she remained active in the opposition and al-Rabita. In the mid-1980s, Maqbula even participated – along with leading al-Rabita figure Hanaa Edwar – in the armed struggle of al-Ansar (the armed branch of the Communist Party in Iraqi Kurdistan) against the Ba'th in the Kurdish mountains. After the fall of the regime in 2003, she was finally able to return to Iraq; on her return, Maqbula actively worked to rebuild al-Rabita and participated in civil society organizations in Baghdad.

Emergence of the Shi'a Islamist Movement

In the 1970s, an oppositional political force emerged: the Shi'a Islamist movement led by Muhammed Baqer al-Sader. The first Shi'a groups – such as al-Da'wa al-Islamiyya (Da'wa Party) and Jama'at al-'Ulema' – were founded in the years following the 1958 Revolution, partly in reaction to growing secularization and explicitly opposing the new Personal Status Code (PSC). The opposition of many Shi'a figures to the PSC was perceived as a direct threat to the power of the 'ulemas over family and women's legal rights. The writings of one of its female figures, Bint Al-Huda – sister of Muhammed Baqer Al-Sadr – on women and gender issues shows how much Iraqi Shi'a Islamism is gendered from its very formation (Pursley 2012). Nevertheless, akin to other Islamist groups in the region, their activism became more visible in the 1970s (Batatu 1989; Jabar 2003; Marr 1985; Nakash, 1994), especially after the 1967 Naksa (Burgat 1996). Interestingly, several Islamist women activists I interviewed – born between the mid-1940s and early 1950s – specifically mentioned that the shock of the 1967 defeat was directly linked to their growing interest in Islamist activism. As a result of socioeconomic and political conjunctures, according to Jabar (2003), Shi'a groups evolved from a universalist Islamist ideology that embraced the umma in its general sense to a particularist ideology focused on defending Shi'a identity. Shi'a groups contested both the state-led secularization and reproduction of ethnic, religious, and communal inequalities in terms of political representation and economic benefits. Moreover, there was an "ideocultural clash" between the etatist, pan-Arab, pro-Sunni, social-nationalist ideology (Davis 2005) and the universalist or particularist Shi'a Islamic discourse (Jabar 2003). Finally, relations with Iran, especially during the war, represented an essential point of divergence between the Ba'th and Shi'a movements because the Iraqi Shi'a movement had strong ties with the Iranian (Shi'a) clerical class. Thus the regime's repression of the Shi'a movement was not strictly due to sectarian-oriented patrimonialism; this repression also had sociopolitical, ideocultural, and geopolitical dimensions.

The Da'wa Party and other Shi'a political groups – such as Munazzamat al-Amal al-Islami – became more visible in the 1970s, openly defying the regime in mass street protests. In February 1977, the Marad al-Ras upheaval[1] in Karbala and Najaf, which occurred during the Arba'in

---

[1] Also called Sufar Intifada by Shi'a activists.

procession, marked the first urban-based mass political mobilization. The regime arrested around 2,000 activists, including one of the movement's leading figures, Muhammed Baqer al-Sadr. Shi'a religious rituals, especially 'Ashura and Arba'in, became important points of Shi'a mass mobilization against the regime, despite Ba'th control and limitations (Sassoon 2012; Khoury 2013).[2] The regime intensified its repression, executing prominent Da'wa Party figures and expelling Khomeini from his residence in Najaf in 1978.

The Iranian Revolution of 1979 had a massive impact on the Shi'a movement inside Iraq and the population more generally; even former communist activists were turned to Shi'a Islamist militancy. Since that time, the Shi'a movement and its potential alliance with Iran was deemed a threat to the Ba'th regime. According to the account of a conversation between Saddam Hussein and Egyptian President Hosni Mubarak, Iran was considered by the Iraqi regime even more dangerous than Israel (Jabar 2003: 226). In Shi'a majority neighborhoods, demonstrations of support invoked slogans such as *Bism al-Khomeini wel sadr, al-Islam dawmen intesar* ("In the name of Khomeini and al-Sadr, Islam will always be victorious") (Jabar 2003:230). In March 1980, after several Shi'a revolts, the regime decreed membership in the Da'wa Party to be a capital crime. In April, after the attempted assassination of Tareq 'Aziz, a leading Ba'th figure, Muhammed Baqer al-Sadr and his sister, Bint al-Huda, were arrested, tortured, and executed. It was the first time in the modern history of the Middle East that an ayatollah, the highest religious rank in Shi'a Islam, was executed. This execution showed the Ba'th regime's determination to break the Shi'a movement, as well as the extent to which it felt threatened by it. Since then, Ba'th-Shi'a Islamist relations shifted from limited cultural opposition to bloody confrontation.

Intisar K., born in 1954 in Basra, was exposed to Islamist militancy during her youth. She attended Baghdad University, studying physics, and joined Da'wa activists on the university's campus. She describes the atmosphere at that time, as well as her encounter with and involvement in Islamist activism.

In Basra, I was not wearing the *hijab*; I started wearing it at university. But I was already oriented toward religion. My family was conservative, but not very practicing. My sisters, for example, do not wear the *hijab*. I do not know exactly why I have always been oriented toward religion. I started praying at a very young age and reading the Qur'an. I also loved and defended the motherland a lot. I used to

---

[2] According to Jabar (2003), participation in Shi'a rituals, especially 'Ashura and Arba'in in Najaf and Karbala, increased (without any foreign presence) to more than 2.5 million participants in 1995, representing more than 12 percent of the Iraqi population.

be very interested in the Palestinian cause, the Jihad, the Resistance. I used to search about the Palestinian *feda'iyyat*, Djamila Bouhired, the Algerian *feda'iyya*; I used to be fascinated by her. The people in struggle, the revolutions attracted me. When I arrived in Baghdad, the campus dormitory of Bab al-Mu'azem was life-changing for me. As you know, in the campus dormitory you are away from you family, you are free, on your own; it changes you a lot, positively or negatively … I met there a group of sisters. At the time in 1971–1972, the Communist Party was very powerful on the campus, and they were always debating. They were debating about the existence of God. Who is God? What is the Qur'an? Is the Qur'an true? What proves that Muhammed is really a Prophet and that what he says is true? You know, those kinds of debates. They were arguing with us a lot, and it pushed us to go and read in order to respond to them. We were reading books of philosophy, because they were opening a lot of debates, and we had to reply to them. At our time, there were miniskirts and that kind of thing, but I was guided *al hamdullilah*. We were representing the line of resistance to the regime at the university. The slogan of Muhammed Baqer al-Sadr was *Kela Amrica, kela Isra'il, kela ya sheytan* ["No America, No Israel, No oh Devil"]. *Sheytan* ["Devil"] was Saddam, of course, everyone knew it. We were very active, especially among the female students. We were trying to give them orientations. We had to look after many of them, thanks to God. A lot of them changed; they started to wear the *hijab*, their lives changed. But not only the *hijab*, I mean, their behavior in general. We were giving them advice, telling them that their families trusted them, that they were thinking, that they were sleeping in the dormitories with the other female students. We were saying: "Pay attention to what you do, for yourself, for your family." Some of them listened; some of them did not. Some accepted partially; some refused. The most important is that we were trying to spread the Word of God [*da'wa*] as much as we could. The response is in the hands of God. Even the Prophets cannot do anything if people choose not to believe. We have the *taklif* ["responsibility"] to advise people. With this person you go and watch a film; with the other you go to the cinema and you discuss the film with her, or in the market. You try different methods according to the person, and you do what you can in order to respond to the person's needs.

In addition to showing the emergence of Islamist militancy within a political culture still dominated by leftist ideas, Intisar's words also reveal the gender dimension of her Islamist militancy. How she became involved in "spreading the Word of God" (*da'wa*) on the university campus shows the extent to which the Da'wa Party opposed secularization and the communist political culture. Defending the *hijab* and female morality represented an important dimension of her activism, which aimed to resist both secularization and the authoritarian regime. Such activism shows that Da'wa militancy aimed to both promote Shi'a Islamization and oppose the regime's authoritarianism. Moreover, Intisar's experience reveals how much Shi'a Islamization, with its gender norms (*hijab*, sexual morality) and religious rituals ('Ashura and Arba'in), became a tool to resist the Ba'th.

Intisar married a lecturer in science who worked at Baghdad University and was a Da'wa Party member. In 1980, her husband was arrested and executed by the regime; Intisar had only been married for two years, had one daughter, and was pregnant with her second child. She knew she had to escape but decided to hide inside the country.

I was at work when they took my husband. I left my job and escaped. They assassinated him the 31th October 1980. They took our house in Hay al-Jawadein and took everything we had. I never saw my husband again. I had to escape and hide with my little girl, and I was pregnant with my second one. I did not leave Iraq. I hid for about three years, moving from one house to another. In the beginning, I was even afraid to go to my family's house. Then, little by little, I began to live normally until the events of the 1990s, and the state eroded.

Intisar K. stayed mainly in Najaf. In 2003, after the fall of the regime, she was "called" to participate in the first Da'wa Party Congress. In Najaf, she set up a Shi'a charity and cultural organization and an educational institution dedicated to the memory of Muhammed Baqer al-Sadr; in Baghdad, she set up a Shi'a women's organization in which she is still very active.

Repression of the Kurds in the 1970s and 1980s

Despite the regime's integration of a Mesopotamian narrative into its game of ideological inclusion and exclusion, which included access of non-Arab communities such as the Kurds to its ideal of nationhood, as showed by Wien (2012: 105–18) and Baram (1994), the 1970s and 1980s were also marked by the repression of the Kurdish nationalist movement. Such repression took place in the framework of the regime's Arab nationalist rhetoric and conflict with Iran, which was partially supporting the Kurdish opposition to the Ba'th. The Kurdish population, in addition to losing many men in the armed struggle against the Ba'th, experienced harsh discrimination by the Iraqi state and felt like second-class citizens. Shno P. – a founding member of Asuda, a women's rights organization in Iraqi Kurdistan – remembers this as a difficult period for her family. Shno's father, a Peshmerga, was killed in a clash between Kurdish nationalists and the Iraqi army in 1972.

I am from Sulaymanyah. I was born in 1963, and when I was nine years old, my father, who was a Peshmerga, was killed in Halabja. As a child, I did not understand why he was killed … We were seven siblings, and my mother suffered a lot. She sold her gold and bought a sewing machine. She started to work as a seamstress to be able to provide for us, in addition to looking after us on her own. She encouraged all of us to pursue our studies. I saw how much my mother suffered; it was painful for me. Growing up, I understood why my father died, the reasons why he struggled and was killed. I understood that as Kurdish people, we are marginalized; our national identity is not acknowledged. We experience discrimination because we are Kurds. A sanction was imposed on us, [and] we lacked everything. The more I grew up, the more I was aware of the injustice. My brothers worked very hard to provide for the family. We all managed to study at the end, girls and boys. The more we grew up, the more we experienced discrimination. It was forbidden for us to work in certain sectors, completely forbidden. There were also the bombings of the Ba'th army: villages were destroyed, and inhabitants of cities at the Iranian borders, like Khaneqin, were deported to other regions, forced into exile.

In the name of "Arabization politics" and with the Kurdish-Ba'th clashes and conflict with Iran as its backdrop, the 1970s represented a harsh, discriminatory, and bloody period for the Kurds and the so-called *taba'iyya* populations (Iraqis who are presumed to be of Iranian origin). In the mid-1970s, hundreds of thousands of Kurdish Shi'as (Failis) were displaced to either the Iranian border or other Arab-dominated regions of Iraq. Bushra Z. – now an active member in a Shi'a women's organization in Baghdad – was eight years old when her family was deported from Khaneqin, a city near the Iranian border, to a city in an Arab-dominated area close to Ramadi. She narrates this period with sorrow and anger.

Around 1974, they began to deport people from Khaneqin to another city situated ten kilometers north of Ramadi. You know, my husband is Kurdish, my mother is Kurdish, but my father is Arab from the holy city of Najaf. My mother was hated by the regime for the simple reason that she gave birth to a daughter who was Kurdish and Shi'a. We were detained in a camp for six months. When we finally got out, the people of Ramadi were calling us "Iranians." Our conditions of detention and the conditions of our lives were unbearable. We would reply to them, "May Allah forgive you. We are not Iranians; we are Iraqis as much as you." After that, during the Iraq-Iran war, they were telling us, "Your sons do not want to fight with us!" But how could we fight other Muslims? This war was an unfair war.

During the same period, the Ba'th undertook a campaign of "internal population redistribution," deporting thousands of Yazidis from Sulaymaniyah and Sinjar. From 1975 on, the cultural identity and very existence of the 4 million Iraqi Kurds were under threat: between 250,000 and 300,000 Kurds were deported from Kirkuk to the south in order to "Arabize the population." From the 1970s to the 1990s, the repression of both the Shi'a movement and the Kurdish nationalist movement made the Ba'th regime one of the most violent dictatorship in the world. Under the banners of Arab nationalism and the struggle against Iranian influence, the regime undertook massive campaigns of repression.

Sectarian Patrimonialism, Rentier Economy, and State-Society Relations before the Mid-1980s

Due to its weak base, the elite lived in constant fear of losing power and searched for reliable sources of cohesion. The new Ba'th regime was radically different from both the traditional-liberal monarchy (1932–58) and the modern-populist authoritarian military regimes (1958–68). Sassoon (2012a) argues that Saddam's previous experience, including as vice president (1973–79) to Iraq's fourth president, Ahmed Hassan al Bakr, taught him to weaken the military to prevent a coup d'état and to ensure his survival with a sophisticated bureaucracy that issued rules and regulations covering almost every aspect of life. It produced a totalitarian model with a patrimonial character that combined modern populist politics, state rentierism, and primordial solidarity networks; the single-party and clan systems fused into one with a rentier economy. Most agreed, however, that while tribal law never disappeared from modern Iraq, in the 1970s and 1980s its operation in urban areas was limited. During these decades, the state court system functioned throughout the country, and while in Iraq's more tribal areas traditional dispute resolution continued for problems of all types, the process was often parallel and subservient to state legal proceedings. As Jabar (2003) describes, etatist tribalism went through various phases from 1968 onward, peaking in the late 1980s and early 1990s. This process relied on Arab Sunni clans of the Tikrit region, as well as associated groups, and involved the integration of tribal lineages and symbolic and fictive primordial systems and cultures into the state so as to enhance the political power of the fragile and vulnerable elite. Together with other factors, etatist tribalism contributed to the enhancement of a patrimonial totalitarian state.

More generally, the pyramidal relations established by the regime's patrimonialism contributed to furthering the atomization of the population and prevented the emergence of modern horizontal relations. Thus, instead of being viewed as citizens' rights and the principles of individualized economic relations, the social welfare system and the functioning of the private sector were perceived as favors (*mukarimat*) accorded by the regime. According to Sassoon (2012a) and Yousif (2013), it is precisely this system placing the party and its head, the president, as the core of the *mukarimat* system that ensured its domination over society and not only its use of violence, as has often been argued. There were thus no systems of collective identity to replace ethnic, sectarian, or kin-based (family, clan, tribe ones). The violent repression of political groups, independent associations, and trade unions silenced the expression of political identities and ideologies. Batatu (1989) described how the regime functioned in relation to the social and political groups comprising Iraqi society as *tarhib* or *taghrib* politics: *tarhib* ("intimidation, terrorization") encompassed the violent, bloody repression of any form of contestation; *taghrib* ("rewarding") consisted of offering *mukarimat*, such sending a child abroad for treatment in response to a letter from his or her family, financing the building of a mosque or *Husainiyya* (Shi'a mosque), or allocating social advantages, such as lessening the taxes or raising the salaries of a specific social group.

The regime's popularity within Iraq and the region began to rise with its nationalization of the oil industry in 1972, the most important nationalization to ever occur in Iraq. Nevertheless, nationalization did not mean that Iraq had complete control over its oil resources. Instead, it was the Ba'th that held all the resources. The despotic and patrimonial potential of the regime was strengthened after the rise in oil prices in 1973. Thus, rising oil prices not only led to a substantial rise in national revenues but also strengthened the power of the Ba'th regime. According to Al-Khafaji (1986, 2003), Yousif (2013), and Alnasrawi (1994, 2002), the rentier state's wealth contributed to its transformation into a powerful Leviathan state rather than being a motor of development and modernization.[3] Society became dependent entirely on the state, a state that, for its part, was almost completely independent of society, thanks to enormous oil revenues. The state did not need to tax the population, and its development of the public sector, especially administrative and government related, did not cost anywhere near as much as the development of industry – such as agriculture – would require. During the 1970s and 1980s, the state became both the unique employer of the labor force and the unique generator of a strong currency, leading to its status as the main consumer of goods and services for the private sector it was developing. Nevertheless, the welfare state did enhance the living conditions of the poor and lower middle class, particularly with regard to the civil service, governmental bureaucracy, universities, military, police, security services, and state institutions.

Davis (2005) shows that during the 1970s, no Arab oil state was devoting as much of its resources to the process building up "memories of state." Saddam Hussein's regime used its enormous wealth to strengthen the state, particularly through efforts to appropriate

---

[3] According to Al-Khafaji (1986, 2003), oil revenues represented $6 billion between 1970 and 1971, $8.5 billion in 1976, and $26 billion in 1980.

understandings of the past and cultural production. Davis (2005) provides the example of the "Project for the Rewriting of History" (*Mashru' I'adat Kitabat al-Tarikh*) that used ancient Mesopotamian, Abbassid, and pre-Islamic Arab cultural heritage predominantly, as well as the more recent pan-Arab nationalist imaginary, to build up its memories of state. According to Davis (2005), the Ba'th regime attempted to create an "imagined community" that was essentially anti-Shi'a. Its focus on an Arab Golden Age situated in the Abbassid Empire (750–1258) is intended not only to suggest parallels between past greatness and the greatness of the Ba'th but also to promote distrust among Iraq's main ethnic groups. Davis argues that one strategy to accomplish the latter was to argue implicitly that *al-shu'ubiyyun*, the Arabized Persian Shi'as who formed the core of the Abbassid bureaucracy, worked to undermine the empire from within, causing its downfall. The message sent to the Sunni Arab minority was that the Shi'as were suspect in the modern era. The state's message to the Shi'a was that only by renouncing their cultural heritage could they enjoy the benefits distributed by the state. Thus, according to Davis (2005: 1–29), only Shi'as who made such a renunciation and subscribed to pan-Arabism achieved any political prominence under the Ba'th.

In addition to its exclusivist sectarian and patrimonial national imaginary, according to Al-Khafaji (1986, 2003), the socialist reputation of the Ba'th regime in the 1970s was more myth than reality. In contrast with its Gulf neighbors, who all invested sufficient capital to develop their countries without obstructing the private sector, the Ba'th regime constantly tried to legitimate its politics of development and gain popularity through a nationalist and socialist discourse. In addition to legitimizing the regime, the Ba'th economic policies that both guaranteed public and administrative positions to all its candidates and developed the education, health, and welfare system also perpetuated its role as main provider of goods and services. Instead of developing industry and agriculture, the Ba'th contributed – through a variety of measures, such as reducing taxes and not regulating the prices of even primary goods – to the development of the private sector and a class of private entrepreneurs who counted the regime as their first and main client.

The 1980s process of economic liberalization – called *al-Infitah* – included Ba'th involvement in the private sector and the burgeoning bourgeoisie. This process, according to Farouk-Sluglett (1991), undermined the regime's ideological claims and support – support that had included those who believed in Ba'th advocacy for social justice, such as members of the party, government functionaries, and the urban and rural working classes. The regime compensated for this ideological vacuum and loss of support by instituting a cult of personality and propaganda campaign. The regime created its own workers, youth and women's organizations that promoted and implemented its economic, social and political measures. As for the women's movement, which had flourished under Qasim, most groups were banned and only able to operate underground. In 1968, the Ba'th created the General Federation of Iraqi Women (*Ittihad al-'am li Nisa' al-'Iraq*), which was in charge of implementing and promoting Ba'th politics. The General Federation of Iraqi Women (GFIW) was an essential tool for the regime. Although Rohde (2010) shows that GFIW figures were not merely regime "pawns," because they did make suggestions and participate in the elaboration of gender policies and reforms, the GFIW was still an integral part of the regime's legitimization policies. While some GFIW members did try to improve women's rights, it was always through the argument that belonging to the party's institutions was the only way to improve women's life conditions.

Moreover, despite the control and censorship in which activities within state institutions were framed, some women activists I interviewed were still members of governmental research institutions – such as Bayt al-Hikma. Noor S. – a prominent activist since the fall of the regime in 2003 – obtained a master's degree in political sciences from Baghdad University in the mid-1980s. In our interview, she points out the limits of her subject and the approach allowed during her research; she could never select topics directly related to the Ba'th regime. Nevertheless, Noor S. worked as a researcher for Bayt al-Hikma, benefiting from its intellectual openness and richness.

I worked as a researcher at a governmental institution called Bayt al-Hikma; it was a beautiful institution. I have to say that a lot of my relations and an important part of the building of my thinking came from it. The atmosphere was nice. We were trying to widen our horizons and political views, especially at a time when narrowminded and extreme ideas were emerging. I have to acknowledge that it was a remarkable experience.

Prior to the invasion of Kuwait in 1991, the regime's popularity was high in both the region and socialist countries more broadly. This popularity had an impact on oppositional political organizations outside the country. Rabab H. and Maqbula B. were both very active in al-Rabita outside the country. They represented Iraq (as the opposition) in leftist-oriented international women's conferences and UN congresses. At the time, the GFIW was also a part of the international women's movement, and its members attended UN conferences as the official Iraqi delegation. At such conferences, Rabab H. and Maqbula

B. actively campaigned for solidarity with Iraqi women political prisoners and the denunciation of the Ba'th regime. Despite their fear of
being caught by the Ba'th security services, because they made themselves highly visible in front of GFIW representatives, Rabab H. and
Maqbula B. still attended the gatherings and tried to raise awareness
about the atrocities committed by the Ba'th regime. Such activism was
not always welcomed by the representatives of socialist and Arab
countries because the Ba'th regime played a leading role in the nationalist, socialist postindependence period. Maqbula B. speaks of her
participation in the UN World Conference on Women in 1980.

I remember in 1980, Hanaa Edwar and myself attended the UN Conference on
Women in Copenhagen; al-Ittihad [GFIW] also attended. Saddam had sent
personalities that were supposed to show the good side of the Ba'th regime.
Manal Yunes was there. I was campaigning for the release of Iraqi women political
prisoners. At the time, the regime was very popular among Arab and Muslim
countries. During the conference I was gathering signatures and talking to participants, explaining our situation to them. I wanted to inform all these women
from all over the world. I remember there was this woman from Tanzania who
signed and then, after going back to her group, came back and asked me to
withdraw her signature. She told me she had made a mistake in signing the
petition because her country was in favor of Saddam Hussein. We and
Argentinian women, we were in the same situation. We were supporting one
another at the time. Hanaa and I were going to the committees and groups,
informing them about the nature of Saddam's regime and the situation of political
prisoners. We did not give our real names, [and] we were very vague about our
identities, because the women of the Ba'th were accompanied by the regime's
security services. These men were attending the conference and searching for us.
We agreed with the women's organization in Denmark to remain incognito. They
agreed to host us and keep our anonymity. We stayed in a house with a Danish
translator, who was a communist activist. The place where we stayed was not
communicated to anyone. We stayed around ten days, and the conference lasted
a week. After that, we toured with Argentinian women to gather signatures and
were located by the men of the Ba'th. A man speaking with a Lebanese accent
proposed to accompany me as I was leaving a venue. Luckily, the head of the
Sudanese Women's Union understood straight away what was going on. She
replied for me: "No, we are together, and we are leaving together." The Ba'th
security services and their allies were capable of kidnapping us, just like that.
We informed the Danish Women's Union about this incident, and they gave us
people to contact in case it happened again.

Maqbula's account reveals how much the Ba'th authoritarian state's
propaganda was very powerful in the 1980s both inside and outside the
country. Davis (2005: 148–75) describes the Ba'th state's endeavor to

propagate its positive image inside Iraq and at an international level as the most powerful and effective propaganda campaign in the Middle East.

A Gendered National Development Project (1968–1980)

The years 1968–85 marked the Ba'th nationalist and developmentalist project, as well as economic development and social and cultural growth. During this time, Baghdad was a cultural capital of the Arab world; despite the limits posed by the authoritarian regime, Baghdad's cultural and intellectual life was flourishing. The negative effects of the war with Iran, which began in 1980, were only felt by the state and society after the mid-1980s. Perhaps the most revealing progress that characterized this period was the regime's campaign to better the education system and eradicate illiteracy. Al-Zublef and Said's study (1980) on women's education and literacy from 1920 to 1979 shows that women's and men's educations, at every level (primary, secondary, and higher), had risen substantially from the mid-1960s and doubled since the mid-1970s. At the time, Iraqi women were deemed the most educated in the Arab world. In 1971, Law No. 153 was enacted to combat illiteracy by opening literacy centers across the country; such centers began proliferating from 1973. In 1978, Law No. 97 mandated that all illiterate citizens between the ages of fifteen and forty-five join a literacy center. The GFIW was the main body in charge of implementing this law through its own centers. The literacy campaign was so successful that Saddam Hussein received a UNESCO prize for combating illiteracy.[4]

As pointed out by many (Al-Ali 2007; Farouk-Sluglett 1993; J. Ismael & S. Ismael 2007), the GFIW was central to implementation of the regime's developmentalist campaign placing women at the core of the country's progress. Throughout the 1970s, the party ideological discourse on women was to "focus on equal rights" and "on rejecting the views that put women in a secondary position" associated with "feudal and tribalism views and mentality" (Sassoon 2012a: 254). The GFIW's work during this period was well perceived by many of the women activists I interviewed, especially those who were not politically active during this period and thus did not experience the regime's repression. Iman H. – forty years old and a founding member of one of Baghdad's main women's networks since 2003 – thinks highly of the GFIW's contribution to Iraqi women despite its association with the regime and persisting discriminations.

---

[4] According to Al-Zublef and Said (1980), of the estimated 1,535,937 illiterate women, 778,177 received literacy training in 1978 alone, especially in the countryside.

Despite all the bad sides of the former regime, there was an organization dedicated to women, al-Ittihad [the GFIW]. I did not belong to it because I was too young at the time. They contributed to Iraqi women; they advocated for women's rights. Although their proposals were not always accepted or implemented, they did write in the paper and propose more rights for women. Things like limiting the hours of work for women, child care, and access to consumable goods at accessible prices for women and their children, a lot of things in order to protect women. And of course, the most important was their involvement in women's education. There were discriminations for sure, especially regarding access to higher education, but still, there was something done for women.

In the 1970s, the Ba'th implemented a series of legislative measures aimed at encouraging women's participation in the labor force and the general development of the country. The provision of free child care, equal salaries, and paid maternity leave enhanced women's working conditions on a large scale. In 1978, the Ba'th reformed the PSC on an unprecedented scale, reinforcing women's rights to divorce and child custody, imposing strict limitations on polygamy, and criminalizing forced and extralegal marriages. More important, the language of the PSC was modified and secularized: the religious term *zina* ("adultery") was replaced with *khiyana zawjiyya* ("martial betrayal"). The GFIW's social work, reports, publications, and media campaign, along with Saddam Hussein's numerous declarations of "women's liberation" at GFIW annual meetings, showed women's essential place in the Ba'th modernization and development project.

Rohde (2006, 2010) analyzes the gender discourse of the *al-Thawra* journal and *Alif Ba* cultural magazine, both media that disseminated Ba'th propaganda. Rohde shows that the 1970s media discourse on women and femininity was designed to weaken traditional perceptions of masculinity and femininity by constantly depicting women in professions previously reserved for men. Until the 1980s, the regime often employed the language of "women's liberation" and the modernist discourse in order to marginalize religious conservatives. In *Alif Ba*, images of barely dressed women as well as eroticized pictures of Iraqi women in Western fashion – miniskirts, short sleeves, and bathing suits (including bikinis) – functioned as symbolic markers of the Ba'th Party's secular modernity. However, Rohde also points out that these symbols did not question patriarchal relations: the regime's rhetoric still promoted women's role in the family, caricatured the "depraved" sexuality of the West, and criticized its "lack of family values." Moreover, not all parts of society approved of this fashion, including the educated urban classes. The issue of women's dress was controversial among GFIW activists: some saw Western fashion as reducing women to sexual objects, while others saw it as a dimension of women's sexual liberation. In GFIW publications, there were voices critical of the overemphasis on women's dress, choosing instead to tackle issues such as women's domestic work. However, GFIW demands to raise the age of marriage for women to nineteen or twenty years old, forbid polygamy, and outlaw arranged marriages were touted by the regime as "going too far" and disrespectful of Iraqi culture and a population "not ready" for such changes.

The literature on Ba'th gender policies during this period of economic growth, secular modernity, and socialist development varies according to the weight given to the state's authoritarianism and patrimonialism, as well as to the impact of its rentier economy on society. Such literature offers a spectrum of analysis that ranges from presenting the Ba'th Party as eliminating feudal and tribal structures and assigning women new roles to painting the Ba'th as maintaining and reasserting patriarchal structures and roles, highlighting the effect of its authoritarian nature on society. Al-Sharqi's research (1982) falls into the former category because it asserts that the Ba'th liberated Iraqis from the burdens of tribalism and colonialism, and promoted women's emancipation. Amal Rassam's research (1992, 1982) is more skeptical; it shows how the dilemma between the regime's national progress, secularism, and "cultural authenticity" translated in the private/public division and the PSC. The PSC represented the untouched sphere, where the "authentic" culture remained unsecularized. However, Rassam does not address issues of authoritarianism and patrimonialism; she takes seriously the regime's pretention of "liberating women." Al-Khayyat's research (1990) on Iraqi women, which is based on fieldwork from 1982, is very critical of, in Al-Khayyat's words, "patriarchal Iraqi culture." She argues that Iraqi women are caught between the "bad sides of Westernization" (double workday, fashion) and lost traditional solidarities (support of the extended family). Al-Khayyat further asserts that Iraqi women are hostages of an "ideology of honor and shame," an ideology that paints them as the symbolic markers of moral and cultural purity. The problematics of both Rassam and Al-Khayyat's research lay in their homogenization of Iraqi women, lack of historicization, and assumption of the existence of an "authentic patriarchal culture."

Farouk-Sluglett (1993) radically criticizes the "cultural argument" by pointing out that the preservation of patriarchal Islamic values in the Ba'th nationalist ideology stemmed from reasons other than asserting Arab-Islamic authenticity in the face of change and Western domination. Using the analytical framework developed by scholars working on authoritarian and totalitarian regimes in other parts of the world, she argues:

As well as helping to understand the nature of its fundamental power structures, an analysis of Ba'th politics in terms of its populist patrimonial features also indicates that its policies vis-à-vis women are not merely a reflection of something specific to Islam or to Islamic culture. In other words, while it is true that Arab nationalism "reclaimed many of the most patriarchal values of Islamic traditionalism as integral to Arab culture identity as such" . . . it is in the nature of populist regimes that their ideologies tend to be based on traditional social and cultural norms. (Farouk-Sluglett 1993: 70)

Cobett (1986), J. Ismael and S. Ismael (2000), and Omar (1994) all insist on pointing out the contraction between authoritarianism and "women's emancipation." Their research show that even the promotion of women's education was not due to Ba'th feminist belief. Women were not perceived as individuals who could exercise their right to instruction but instead as mothers whose ideological views held sway over their children. As an example, in an April 1971 speech given at the GFIW, Saddam made this point clearly: "An enlightened mother, educated and liberated, brings to the country a generation of conscious and engaged fighters" (Hussein 1979).

Al-Ali's modern history of Iraqi women (2007) – based on life stories and oral histories – engaged critically with the state's modern and developmental policies of the 1970s, stressing the prevailing norms of femininities and masculinities. Relying on women's narratives from this period, Al-Ali shows the effective impact of the regime's gender policies on women's family and work life, the limited scope of women's political expression allowed by the state's authoritarianism, and the concrete impact of state repression on women's lives. In a similar vein, Kandiyoti (1991) compares Ba'thist Iraq to Kemalist Turkey and Nasserist Egypt, positing that integration into capitalist markets – rather than legislative reforms – was the most decisive factor in changing traditional gender relations in the Middle East. Joseph (1991) shows that from the 1970s to the end of the 1980s, the centralized Iraqi elite, which was unified around the authoritarian Ba'th Party and supported by oil revenues, placed state authority at every level of society, including in community and family matters. Joseph compares the situation of Iraq to that of Lebanon, which was more ethnically and religiously diverse, had a more heterogeneous and factionalized elite supported by fewer resources, and was characterized by a divided and weak state reliant on primordial affiliation rather than national loyalties. The Lebanese noninterventionist state relied on religious institutions when it came to family and women, which explains Lebanon's community-based PSC. According to Joseph (1991), the Ba'th regime attempted to subordinate family to the state by taking over family functions (i.e., children, socialization, healthcare, and social control), thus transforming the family from a unit of production to one of consumption. In addition, until the mid-1980s, the Ba'th subsidized the nuclear family in order to turn allegiances away from tribal and sectarian groups.

All my interviewees born between the 1950s and early 1960s and from middle-class urban families believe they benefited from high-quality education at all levels. All enjoyed their university years and, despite limits posed by the authoritarian regime, still benefited from an advanced level of educational and cultural activities. Their spare time, social life, and family gatherings were often occupied by going to the cinema, theater, and cultural and leisure spaces of Baghdad and others cities. They describe this period as marked by access to state health and family services, a good salary, and a standard of living that allowed them to own a car and, for many, a house. Most of these women got married after graduation (from either university or technical school), had between two and five children, and had careers. None stopped working after having children because they benefited from child care services and maternity leave. They all considered family, domestic life, and work to have structured their everyday lives. However, they all see their husbands as the main breadwinners, even when they had equal salaries. Child care and domestic duties (cooking, cleaning) remained the woman's prerogative. Some of these interviewees belonged to conservative families who, despite encouraging them to study, prevented them from traveling abroad alone. Many complain about this "double working life," but most also consider it to be the best period of their lives. Most of these women speak about how their choice of partner, always done with their family's approval, was "based on his education" rather than "his money." According to my interviewees, this period was marked by a good quality of life, as well as moral and cultural openness.

Naswha A. graduated from a technical school in 1963 and was employed by the Ministry of Irrigation in the mid-1960s. In the 1970s, she was sent to work on al-Haditha Dam in al-Anbar Province, far away from her home in Baghdad. Nashwa A. was the only women sent to do this work; in such a heavily male-dominated sector. In order to manage working in this environment, she had to "behave like a man" and control her behavior.

I was considered like a man, and I had to behave like a man in order to be respected. I think that it is the way a woman behaves that changes everything. All is in our hands. Men would harass me, once, twice, and then because of the way I behaved, they finally respected me. I was never promiscuous, always weighty.

Naswha's words reveal that during this period, women were both advancing in the job market – to the extent that they were entering male-dominated sectors – and yet still compelled to behave in a "morally acceptable" way according to prevailing gender norms.

However, several of my interviewees experienced harsh discrimination and had to quit their jobs because they refused to join the Ba'th Party. Many of these women suffered Ba'th harassment for several years before deciding to leave their jobs or flee the country. Those belonging to political families – especially families with *shuhada'* ("martyrs") killed by the regime – faced difficulties finding a husband. Among the activists I interviewed, almost all of those who never married had been in prison, tortured, exiled, or had a family member (father, brother) detained or killed by the regime.

Women's personal trajectories were affected by the precariousness of political families and by being subject to the regime's discriminatory campaigns. Amel F. – a prominent lawyer and activist since 2003 – belongs to a Faili Kurdish political family. She and her sisters were married at seventeen because of their father's desire to "protect" them. Amel and her sisters could not pursue education because of the precariousness triggered by their family's deportation. When Amel tried to return to her studies years later, she experienced discrimination due to her status as *taba'iyya*.

I was born in Baghdad in 1961 and I grew up there. I was very late in my studies; when I joined university, I was eight years late. Our context was particular; it was the time of the deportation of the Kurds Failis. My father was a communist activist, but we were forced . . . He was forced to marry me and my sisters at the age of seventeen because he was afraid that we might be abused by the security men and army during deportation. He wanted protection for us. I was seventeen years old when I got married, and I was twenty-six the first time I applied to university. After so many hardships, I managed to obtain a BA in law. But when I wanted to register for a masters, my application was rejected because I was deemed an Iranian. I had no possibility to carry on or get a scholarship . . . I had to continue my studies abroad in London. It was extremely difficult. In the morning you study; when you come back, you have to take care of the household, do the domestic job, and raise my son. Then you go to work in the afternoon to provide for the family, and you are supposed to study when you come back in the evening.

Despite these difficulties, Amel became a lawyer and jurist specializing in women's issues. She is a very well-known feminist activist and was also a parliamentary candidate for the Kurdish Alliance in 2005. Her career as a lawyer has been so successful that the last time I met her in Baghdad in 2012, she was thinking of working for the Iraqi Federal Court.

My line of argumentation on the impact of authoritarian-patrimonialism and rentierism on Iraqi society follows arguments developed by Al-Ali, Farouk-Sluglett, J. Ismael and S. Ismael, Joseph, Kandiyoti, and Rohde: there is a clear contradiction between feminism and an authoritarian-patrimonial regime. Moreover, interviews with Iraqi women activists who experienced this period pushed me to also argue that this so-called state feminism was merely a facade; patriarchy and gender norms and relations were never truly questioned. For example, an article in the 1969 Penal Law No. 111 authorizes domestic violence in the framework of *ta'dib al-zawja* ("domesticating the wife"). The adoption of this article, which remains unquestioned, clearly showed that the regime ascribed women an inferior status and considered men to be the head of the family and society. Moreover, in the mid-1970s, Ba'th rhetoric on gender shifted from using a Eurocentric conception of modernism to using an "indigenous" path to modernity (Rohde 2010). This shift reveals that populism – along with concerns about aligning with the political atmosphere in the Arab region – was at the core of Ba'th policies, not a genuine belief in "women's liberation." However, because I also argue that women and gender issues – both conditions of life and representations – cannot be disconnected from social, economic, and political realities, it is clear that the first period of the Ba'th regime (1968–85) was marked by an enhancement of women's life conditions and legal rights. The literacy and education campaigns and women's participation in the labor force, along with the regime's gender discourse marked by the will to break with "traditional" gender roles, all had positive structural impacts on women's lives.

The Iraq-Iran War (1980–1988): Its Major Impact on the State, Society, and Women

Military clashes between the Iraqi and Iranian armies mainly took place at the countries' borders. Even if other regions in Iraq did not directly experience the battles, the border cities were terribly affected by the war. Wazira K. – a teacher and head of the Baghdad branch of a Kurdish women's organization – is originally from Mandali, a city in the Diyalah border province. She was twenty years old when her family was forced to flee Mandali to escape the bombings. Wazira witnessed the destruction of her city, and this memory has marked her life.

During the war with Iran, the city was bombed in the most savage way possible. It destroyed the gardens of our beautiful city of Mandali. All our gardens looked like nothing at all; you could see the burnt palm trees, just like in Basra and other cities close to the Iranian border. These images, this reality, it made me get involved later for women, for human beings, for the protection of human lives.

In order for this tragedy to never happen again so that people could choose their destiny and be protected from violence. We fled Mandali, my family and I, my husband, my kids, my parents, and my brothers and sisters. The bombings were so intense, so violent. On our way from province to province, we saw so many horrors. We left our houses, our belongings, our gardens; we left with our cloths; we had nothing. There were not air strikes, there were tanks strikes. We saw the destroyed houses, the dead bodies of kids and people. In 1986, we finally settled in Baghdad. All the people of Mandali had fled; it became a ghost city.

In addition to the fighting itself, the policy of *tasfiraat* ("displacements and deportation") of *taba'iyya* and the Kurdish population of the northern regions intensified during the war with Iran. At the end of the 1980s, half a million Kurds (Sunnis and Shi'as) were displaced. The regime's fear of Iranian influence in the country took a dramatic shape. *Tasfiraat* was done to hundreds of thousands of Iraqis deemed to be *taba'iyya*. In the 1980s, entire families were taken from their homes and expelled to the Iranian borders. Moreover, several legal measures directly addressing the family – amendments to the PSC – revealed the ideological pressure of the campaign against Iran on Iraqi society. In 1982, an article was passed stipulating that a woman could (should) seek divorce if her husband was accused of "betraying the nation." In 1985, the right to divorce was given to women whose husbands had left the country for more than three years; in 1986, that right to divorce was extended to women whose husbands abandoned their posts at the front. These measures also included men – encouraging them to divorce *taba'iyya* women – with explicit reference to political opposition to the war in the framework of *taba'iyya* persecutions.

Dima M. – a prominent Shi'a Islamist women's activist since 2003 and MP since 2005, who was born in Baghdad in 1955 – remembered this period of her life with pain and sorrow. She belongs to a conservative Shi'a family involved in the Shi'a Islamist movement. She grew up in the al-Kerrada neighborhood in Baghdad and remembered being one of the few young women who wore the *hijab* in both this area and the University of Baghdad, where she studied technical sciences. Dima recalled being mocked by students and discriminated against by teachers because of her *hijab*. Her family was under constant surveillance by the regime due to their closeness to prominent Shi'a political figures. After graduating, Dima worked in the media sector, married a Shi'a activist in 1979, and had a son soon after her marriage. In 1980, her husband refused to go to the front and disappeared. She was living in al-Kazimiyya when the *tasfiraat* of *taba'iyya* families began; Dima was pregnant, on her own, and worried. She describes the fear and tension of that time.

At the beginning of the *tasfiraat*, I went to visit my neighbor one day, knocked on her door, and something terrifying happened. She refused to open the door and started screaming: "Why are you coming here?! Go away! I don't know you!" I did not understand why she reacted like that, and I left. A few days later, she came to see me and apologized. She had thought the regime's security men had come to get me and that I was trying to hide at her home. She said: "I reacted like that because I was afraid for my kids." After that incident, I thought that if people were reacting like that when the security services had not even come for me yet, what would be their attitude if they really came for me?! I was sure that they would be the first ones to give me up. Straight after that, my neighbors were taken by the security men and deported for *taba'iyya*. God knows where they were taken. I decided to flee to Turkey with my little baby in my arms ... It was so hard; I was young, and I did not know anything about life. I did not know how to look after a kid on my own. I fled to Turkey, then to Syria, and finally I arrived in Iran and settled there. I said to myself: "Be patient, it is just an issue of several weeks, and [her husband's name] will join me." Several weeks turned into years. It was nine years before I saw my husband again.

During this period, Dima's brother was killed and her uncle detained and tortured. She tried hard to get news of her husband and finally heard that he had been detained for refusing to go to the front. Dima's husband divorced her in order to obtain his freedom because the law rewarded those who divorced *taba'iyya*. He was finally released from prison in the mid-1980s.

It was when Saddam was giving 2,000 dinars to those who divorce a *taba'iyya* person. At the time, 2,000 dinars was something huge. We earned around 100 dinars per month, so you can imagine how important this amount of money was. Saddam tried to destroy families from the inside, pushing people to betray their own families. My husband obtained his release after he divorced me. He was released in 1984 and I saw him again for the first time in 1991.

During this same time, Muhammed Baqer al-Hakim announced the establishment of the Supreme Assembly of the Islamic Revolution of Iraq (SAIRI) in Tehran. All Shi'a groups transferred their headquarters and the bulk of their human resources to Tehran. Dima was very active in the opposition in Tehran and was involved in many activities regarding displaced women and their families. However, her situation was precarious because she had fled without her documents and thus could not work as a refugee. During the 1991 uprising, Dima clandestinely reentered Iraq; she held a picture of her husband in her hands as proof of their marriage. Dima, like many Shi'a Islamist activists, thought the regime was about to fall and was horribly disappointed when the regime violently put down the uprising. She returned to Iran, and her husband eventually joined her there. Dima found him psychologically unstable and unable to work or live normally. In Iran, they were able to survive thanks to money from her relatives. When she returned to Iraq in 2003, Dima discovered a changed country and realized how much she had lost.

I spent years having this dream of our family house in al-Kerrada; I dreamt that I managed to get to the house just when the regime security men came to take me. I imagined I could never see this house again. Until today, I still have a kind of terror in my heart when I go to see my family house. I always fear that some atrocity will happen after I knock at the door. This fear is always in me. I found my mother so old and weakened. She used to be such a strong woman. I found her so fragile when I came back. It was too late. If we had come back in 1991, everything would have been different, but by 2003, time had passed, and it was too late. We had already lost our families.

Dima's experience can be analyzed through Joseph's (1991, 2000) conceptualization of citizenship in relation to gender, state, and nation-hood. Not only did the state intervene within the family and affect women's rights and conditions, but its intervention also included the definitions of "good" and "bad" citizens that in the 1980s were marked by an anti-Shi'a and anti-Kurd rhetoric. The Ba'th exclusivist ideal of nationhood relegated women like Dima to the bottom of the citizenship ladder, as both a woman and a part of the political minority labeled by the regime's Iraqi Arab anti-Shi'i national narrative as "other." In addition, she was placed in an even more precarious position by being related to the political opposition by kin. As in 1982, the Ministry of Defense issued a directive calling for the arrest of first-degree family members of deserters who fled to Iran to escape military service. This included the wives, children, and parents of deserters. If the deserters joined the insurgents, then punishment extended to second-degree kin as well. The same applied for kin whose male relatives had been executed for desertion. (Khoury 2013 177–78).

Moreover, as argued by Khoury (2013), by mastering and manipulat-ing memory and the war experience, the regime imposed its definition of the ideal citizen: the male soldier. Through its educational, cultural, and media institutions and organizations, the state shaped the public culture with models of heroism and manliness, as well as of death and mourning through war celebrations with commemoration rituals under the purview of neighborhood party officials. The regime drew on the militant libera-tionist ideology of the Ba'thist version of "Third Worldism," with its anti-imperialist rhetoric and emphasis on the need to create "new men and women," and molded this message to convince Iraqis that war with Iran was an extension of the Ba'thist revolution. It also drew on the visual and literary cultural output that had developed around the world wars in Western Europe and the Soviet Union. Khoury argues convincingly that unlike the project to manipulate the historical memory of Iraqis for the purposes of shaping public culture analyzed by Eric Davis (2005), the memory discourse initiative marked an ambitious attempt by the state to regulate the inner emotional self of the Iraqi individual as he or she experienced war. More important, its deployment by institutions of public culture marked the emergence of memory and martyrdom as categories of experience through which individuals or communities could make claims for social and political rights via the construction of difference based on degrees of participation in suffering incurred as a result of war. War dead were promoted and celebrated and elevated within the party hierarchy posthumously or inducted into it when not members. The ideal citizen thus was a member of the Ba'th Party and a loyal combatant and or a family member of a soldiers or martyr.

Not surprisingly, the turning point of the Ba'th politics toward women was the war with Iran. Just one year after the start of the war, the regime started to encourage early marriage, and in 1987, it began to encourage increased fertility through financial rewards given to families who gave birth to a fourth child and bonuses for those who already had four children. Bonuses would be paid for future births (Sassoon 2012a: 253–58). Al-Ali (2007) argues that the rhetoric of the "good Iraqi man and woman, educated and participating in the labor force" changed radically. During the war, the state engaged in a glorification of militarized masculinity and emphasized Iraqi women's reproductive responsibilities. Being a good Iraqi woman became synonymous with being the mother of future soldiers. In several speeches, Saddam Hussein stated: "a woman who does not bring at least five children is a traitor to the nation." The regime pressured women to raise the fertility rate by banning contraception, making abortion illegal, and enhancing maternity benefits, including free infant food. Rohde (2010) shows that in the 1980s, the regime's gender rhetoric took shifted radically toward the reinforcement of normative conceptions of masculinity and femininity. Men were pictured as soldiers: the protectors of the nation's women and children. Because national agency was masculinized and the land was presented as female, a sexual connotation was denoted in poems and propaganda literature. In the war's last stages, sexual representations left room for an Islamic discourse, presenting women as "mothers" (Rohde 2010). Even children's literature was militarized and, in it, Iranians dehumanized. The new masculinity embraced by the government marked a shift from the ideal Iraqi male as worker, peasant, party militant, and committed intellectual to a mixture of the former combination of traits with a tribal archetype. The reification of tribal masculinity was particularly evident in popular songs and war poetry that glorified militarism (Khoury 2013: 182–218).

With regard to patrimonialism, the authoritarian Ba'th regime went from opposing tribal networks (1960s and 1970s), to integrating them (1980s), to opposing them again (end of the 1990s), all while celebrating central patrimonialism (Charrad 2011; Jabar 2003; Sakai 2003). Until the 1960s and 1970s, the regime prohibited the use of a family name that referred to the tribal or regional origin of its bearer (Sakai 2003). The state also moved to directly challenge tribal hierarchy and authority, as party cadres and government agents "assumed roles hitherto traditionally assumed by community notables of the tribal domains" (Jabar 2003: 89). This corresponds to a period when Iraq was at its economic peak, and hence the regime was comforted by enormous oils revenues. In the 1980s, the Ba'th regime promoted temporary military-ideological tribalism confined to specific tribes; Shi'a and Kurdish tribal groups were mobilized to meet an external threat during the Iran-Iraq war (1980–88). During this long and bloody war, the regime mobilized over 1 million soldiers[5] because men were needed to meet the numerical superiority of Iran.

Moreover, it is important to recall that *al-infitah* was an economic failure because it did not contribute to developing sectors of the economy that were key to broadening the country's production and industries. Oil revenues were still the state's central income (98 percent); the private sector and other non-oil-related sectors represented no more than 2 percent of national income. The state economy was structurally weak, and its orientation toward military-related industries – due to the war with Iran – only accentuated this weakness (Yousif 2013; Alnasrawi 1994). The state also failed socially because the etatist tribalism and patrimonialism that favored only certain groups, along with its economic monopoly, quashed the emergence of an independent social class capable of contributing to the country's development.

This important dimension contributes to the debate opened by Efrati in "Productive or Reproductive?" (1999), which investigates the Ba'th regime's conflicting gender policies during the war with Iran. As Efrati argues, women's productive role was emphasized in the war's early years – i.e., women were asked to increase their participation in the labor force – and from 1985 on, their reproductive role was emphasized. Efrati discusses particularly Rassam's "cultural argument" in explaining the contradictory gender politics. Adopting the pragmatic argument, Efrati criticizes the "feminist" pretensions of such an authoritarian regime. Using Kandiyoti's "patriarchal bargain" (1988), Efrati argues

---

[5] In 1979, 220,000 men were mobilized for the war. The percentage of people serving directly in the arm forces grew from 1.7 percent in 1979 to 17 percent in 1987.

that the regime's ambivalent politics during the war was the result of conflicting pragmatic demands: on the one hand, the need to replace male workers sent to the front and, on the other hand, the need to compete with Iran's numerical superiority and provide employment opportunities for former soldiers. We can add to Efrati's analysis Charrad's (2011) conceptual understanding of the relationship between the state and tribal kin grouping as central to understand the evolution of women's legal rights through the reforms of the PSC. The regime's politics in the 1980s were to integrate local patrimonialism and celebrate tribalism as a part of Iraq's essential identity (Charrad 2011), which had an impact on the way it dealt with women's rights.

My interviews echoed Abdul Hussein (2006) and Al-Ali's (2007) accounts of the war's concrete impacts on society and women's lives, resulting in putting the burdens of both family and work on women's shoulder. Many of my interviewees lost male relatives during the Iran-Iraq war, and those whose husbands had gone to the front had to manage their households on their own during this period. Even young unmarried women helped to financially support their households when their fathers and brothers were at the front or wounded and unable to work. Hanaa T. – a founding member of a Chaldean women's organization – was born in 1962 in Baghdad. Because her three brothers were at the front and her father had lost his hand, Hanna had to quit her studies and begin working to provide for her family at the age of eighteen.

I was attending Christian school for girls. I had done my primary and secondary education in Baghdad. Unfortunately, I could not continue my studies because I had to work to help my family. My father lost his hand in an accident, and my brothers were at the front during the Iran-Iraq war. My mother could not work outside the home, so I worked as an employee, and I tried to provide for the family. My brothers, who were soldiers, always needed me to send them money, because their military salaries were not sufficient.

Hanaa worked for many years as an employee to provide for her family. She finally got married at the age of thirty-nine. She had never wanted to give up her studies. Now, at the age of forty-one, Hanaa has applied to study political science and law at a private Shi'a university. Her account echoes the ones collected by J. Ismael and S. Ismael (2008) that show that while before the Iraq-Iran war, in economic terms, the urban household was primarily a unit of consumption, because there was an inflow of goods and services into the household, the situation changed as a result of the war. The flow of income into the household from participation in the formal economy had become insufficient to support household consumption, and participation in the informal economy had increased significantly. In addition to this, the flow of consumer goods into households had been dramatically reduced, and there had been a significant flow of resources out of households. Households in effect were turned into units of primitive accumulation by the state for human as well as financial resources. J. Ismael and S. Ismael (2008) argue that this situation changed patriarchy and women's role in the society: women were more and more segregated socially and geographically as men's role were militarized and the household was feminized.

Finally, Khoury (2013: 70) shows the importance taken by the GFIW in propagating the government's war narrative in its local branches, in providing support to soldiers' families, in encouraging women to participate in the war effort, in training nurses, and even in collecting women's gold and jewelry "donations," as well as in surveillance and reporting dissent. The local branch of the GFIW was the organ through which the families of martyrs addressed their requests for compensation and their complaints. The GFIW played a crucial role as mediator between the cultural, social, and security components of the work of the party at the local level. Its role transformed from serving a developmental and social agenda in the 1970s to one intimately bound to managing the war's social and political repercussions. Its role in the following decade will prove to be no less central.

Post-1980s Iraq: Violence and the Post-1991 "Shadow State"

The end of the 1980s and beginning of the 1990s represented one of the most violent moments in the history of Iraqi society. Between 1988 and 1989, al-Anfal campaign, including the chemical attacks on Halabja, killed more than 180,000 Kurds, mostly civilians (Kutschera 2005). The Ba'th extermination campaign against the Kurds was particularly brutal in the Bahdinan region, which was the bastion of the Kurdish nationalist resistance (Bozarslan 2009). Kadrya W. is a Kurdish feminist activist from Sulaymaniyah; she founded an organization dedicated to supporting the women and families who survived the al-Anfal campaign. Kadrya believes that this campaign aimed to exterminate the entire Kurdish population.

Al-Anfal was planned by the regime, from the day Saddam appointed Ali Hasan al-Majid to be in charge of the Kurdistan region. It was entirely planned. They put a cross over the places of the Peshmerga and the Kurdish nationalist struggle. It was like sentencing all the Kurdish population to the death penalty. Even our nature, our whole environment, was destroyed. It was a violence that you cannot describe. From February 1988 to September 1989, the chemical massacres began. It destroyed everything, entire families, the entire inhabitants, even nature, the animals. It was so terrible. I was in Sulaymaniyah at the time, but I was traumatize by al-Anfal. It was proper terrorism. This is why I have dedicated my whole life to support the victims of al-Anfal, especially the women. I conducted precise research on it in order to show how it impacted Kurdish women and destroyed our people. I spent most of my time supporting the displaced families, helping the ones who lost their families, helping the women survive that as much as I can. I will always remember one of the women I met in one of the villages destroyed during al-Anfal. She told me that she buried more than 1,000 babies and kids with her own hands.

At the end of the 1980s, Iraq was badly in debt. The long, unsuccessful war with Iran (1980–88) had depleted the state's resources, and its attempts to further exploit oil reserves in order to pay off such debts became a source of conflict with other OPEC members, especially Kuwait. Saddam held Kuwait responsible for the drop in oil prices, considering such an action to be a declaration of war (Luizard 2002). Believing that he had US backing, Saddam invaded Kuwait on August 2, 1990.

The next year, Kadrya participated in the 1991 uprising by raising awareness among the population; she supported the Peshmerga struggle by distributing leaflets at the Sulaymaniyah municipality, where she was an employee. The 1991 uprisings of the Kurdish nationalist in the north and the Shi'a in the south took place in the shadow of the Gulf War. The Kurdish uprising gained international attention because the al-Anfal campaign had sensitized the international community to the Iraqi Kurds. The population was still reeling from the terror of al-Anfal, and the Iraqi army's advance to repress the uprising created panic. More than 2 million Kurds fled to the Turkish and Iranian borders. In April 1991, Operation Safe Haven was undertaken in the Kurdish region to protect the population from the Ba'th army. Since that time, the three Kurdish governorates have become almost completely autonomous; the Kurdish nationalist parties have structured Iraqi Kurdistan – both politically and economically – as independent from the rest of Iraq.

The uprising in the southern regions – Shi'a majority regions-, in contrast, did not gain as much attention. Despite the fact that the US-led coalition had pledged its support to the leaders of the opposition, the international community was generally indifferent to the plight of the population in the south; hence the Ba'th regime repressed this uprising using unspeakable violence. Hundreds of thousands were killed or tortured, imprisoned, and declared missing. This was in addition to the more than 100,000 victims of the 1991 coalition bombardment. The southern uprisings marked a moment of sectarian oppression in the Shi'a collective memory, exacerbating

Shi'a-Ba'th relations to the extreme. Moreover, the uprisings represented a key moment of divergence between the Sunni and Shi'a populations: while many Sunnis were exposed to the official Ba'th narratives, which claimed that the uprisings were orchestrated by Iran, many Shi'as described them as popular uprisings against a sectarian and secular dictatorship. Haddad (2010) argues, with regard to sectarian relations, that memories of the 1991 events are the most polarized and contentious of any episode in modern Iraqi history.

Ibtihal I. – an al-Rabita activist and member of the Communist Party in Baghdad – is originally from Najaf. She was eighteen years old when the uprising began. Ibtihal remembers the events as incredibly traumatic and she describes the uprising as a popular "revolution" that was violently repressed.

The American bombings in 1991 were indescribable savagery for sure. But even more horrible was what has happened next, the revolution. I respect the ones who call it a revolution, those who gave their lives for their principles and for our motherland. What happened next was the mass graves. It is from this event that one can understand the violence, the hatred, and the lack of value given to human life that we experience today in Iraq. Everything started from 1991. We tried to hide from the American bombings in the southern villages, because it was safer than the cities. But then, when people talk about the Day of Judgment, I can say that I experienced it in 1991. We were thousands of people heading toward an unknown destination to flee the massacres. We could not even take our personal documents; we escaped like that. We stayed nine days, and then we were told that the massacre in Najaf had ended. We came back home. What did we see when we came back?! I saw corpses lying in the streets; I saw faces with their eyes gouged. I was just eighteen years old, and I saw horror. My little sister was eight; imagine what these kinds of images would do to a child. I saw things worse than that, but I cannot speak of them. People were taken by the regime from their houses and ended up in mass graves. They did not distinguish between men, women, and children. It is from this specific period that values started to be lost, that people changed, that trust between people died. From that time, some families started living in the houses of slaughtered families. This would have never happened in the past. People would refuse to inhabit the house of the deported *taba'iyya*, for example. I am from Najaf, and I know that the prayers of a person who inhabits a stolen place are not accepted. But after 1991, people started to do things like that; the loss of values started from there. We saw everything, animals eating corpses. We experienced war and saw it with our own eyes.

According to all the women I interviewed, the bloody events of the 1990s traumatized the Iraqi population. The Shi'as and Kurds in particular felt threatened after the repression of the 1991 uprising. Noor S. was twenty-seven years old in 1991 and was living in Baghdad. Although she and her family had never been political, Noor felt very vulnerable as a Shi'a after 1991. She narrates the general atmosphere during this period.

We stayed silent at the time, because we were among the people who could not do anything. We saw the repression of 1991. We had this feeling of vulnerability and fear. I am among the people who still have that inside of them. I still feel that I am guarded, that someone is monitoring me. You see, even inside my family house, we did not insult Saddam, under our own roof. Believe me, even when I was inside my car with my brother with the windows closed, if I wanted to make a joke about Saddam, I stopped straight away if we passed in front of a picture of Saddam on the street. The picture itself terrified us. We heard stories about what happened to people. We heard about this neighbor who was arrested not for a joke she had made, but for a joke she had listened to. The army was serving the regime, and we felt that Saddam's security intelligence was everywhere. We knew what happened to that minister that disagreed with him: he was executed the day after he expressed disagreement. We knew what he did to the Minister of Defense, to people of his own clan, how he killed people from his own tribe in the 1970s. We felt we could not; we did not have the strength to oppose that. Even the political opposition abroad could not do anything about it.

The coalition's six-week bombing campaign in January 1991 and the United Nation's imposition of drastic economic sanctions in response to the invasion of Kuwait were the final blows for the Iraqi economy and state. A UN special report from March 1991 indicated that after the bombing campaign, Iraq moved from a modern, highly urbanized, and mechanized economy to a preindustrial one.[6] The US-led military campaign did not distinguish between military and civilian targets.[7] In six weeks, it dropped more than 88,000 tons of explosives on Iraq, more than what was used during the whole Vietnam War.[8] The United Nation's economic sanctions – the most severe imposed on any country – were, as Gordon (2010) argues, an "invisible war" led by the US administration that plunged the majority of the population into poverty, destroyed the middle-class, and deprived the state of its primary source of income – oil revenues. Sanctions destroyed the sectors on which women mainly relied: the public infrastructure and social, educational, and health systems. A UN report from 1998 indicated that more than 20 percent of the Iraqi population was living in extreme poverty; it was estimated that

---

[6] M. Ahtissaari Report to the Secretary-General on Humanitarian Needs in Kuwait and Iraq in the Immediate Post-Crisis Environment, UN Report No. S122366, New York, March 1991.

[7] The coalition forces bombed civilian infrastructure, oil fields, oil pipelines and refineries, power stations, transport and communication networks, water treatment plants and distribution canals, fertilized plants, food plants, food warehouses, iron and steel plants, bridges, hospitals, warehouses, industrial plants, irrigations sites, and civil buildings. An estimated $232 trillion worth of damage was done.

[8] A comparison drawn by Parker Payson, describing the numbers of the Pentagon and the Defense Ministry, appears in "Figure It Out," *The Washington Report on Middle East Affairs*, May–June 1991, p. 37.

between 500,000 and 1 million Iraqis – primarily children[9] – were victims of these UN sanctions. In addition to the estimated 500,000 war widows (UNIFEM 2004), the sanctions caused a devastating humanitarian crisis that altered Iraqi society.[10] The sanctions deprived Iraq of the equipment and parts required to repair the damaged infrastructure from the 1991 US-led bombing. Although existing stocks were used to restore some services, without the replacement parts essential to restore damaged or destroyed facilities, the provision of electrical power, clean water, and sewage treatment to Iraqi households was severely hampered. As a result, waterborne diseases mushroomed, increasing infant and child morbidity and mortality rates.

Many women spoke of their experience of the bombings; it was a traumatic moment that affected both their minds and their bodies. Aziza S. was twenty-six years old and living in Baghdad when the bombardment began. She had just given birth and remembers the fear of that time.

During the 1991 bombings, I had just given birth to my daughter. Today, *al hamdullilah*, she is a university student. The way Iraq was bombed traumatized me. I also had a friend who was seven months pregnant. She already had three girls, and she was pregnant with a boy for the first time. Because of the shock of the bombings, she lost her baby. She miscarried at seven months. Me, I had just given birth to my daughter, but my milk dried from the fear I experienced. I did not have any milk anymore. This terror of 1991 stayed in my mind. Yes, we wanted the regime to fall, but not this way, not in such a violent way.

The Oil for Food Program was established in 1996. This program allowed Iraq to sell oil on the world market in exchange for food, medicine, and Iraqi citizens' other humanitarian needs without allowing Iraq to boost its military capabilities. Although the program did not greatly lessen the humanitarian catastrophe, it did have a positive impact on the Kurdistan region because 13 percent of oil revenues were given to the Kurdish governorates. Regarding the regime itself, the program's implementation was rife with corruption. While a class of "new rich" – corrupt personalities linked to the regime – benefited greatly, the Iraqi population was plunged into misery. Many among the Iraqi elite fled the country for either economic or political reasons because the regime's repression

---

[9] United Nation's Department of Humanitarian Panel.
[10] Halliday and Von Sponeck – heads of the Oil for Food Program in 1999 and 2001, respectively – both resigned in response to the humanitarian catastrophe provoked by the sanctions.

continued. The repayment of the debt to Kuwait represented more than half the oil revenues, even though the country was badly in need of funds to rebuild an infrastructure destroyed by the coalition bombings.

Marr (1985) argues that during this period Saddam allowed the Ba'th Party to deteriorate and relied for support instead on his own extended family and networks of Arab tribes, especially after the 1991 Gulf War. Sassoon (2012a), however, establishes that the party's membership and responsibilities did not diminish, that the party displayed extraordinary flexibility and responsiveness to changing conditions and continued to successfully recruit new members, run party schools and conferences, and sponsor public festivals. However, for Khoury (2013), who analyzes the way the regime dealt with the wars – invasion, US-led bombings, and sanctions – the Ba'th Party of the 1990s was despotic and marked by extreme improvisation. The party drew on tribalism, sectarianism, Ba'thism, and a host of new categories to reward and punish its citizens through a method of rule that oscillated between charity and mercy. The image of the "good" citizen changed to belonging to the nation of "patient ones" who persevered in the face of adversity. This was very noticeable in the commemoration of the dead. The prototypical martyr was no longer the heroic fallen soldier but rather the civilian victim of US bombardment and the UN-imposed sanctions. The state had lost its tenuous monopoly over the national memory discourse because it could no longer finance the institutions that produced it, nor could it stop the other versions circulating within the diaspora.

For Khoury (2013), the hierarchical citizenship was pushed to its extreme in the 1990s with the infantilization of the population and personalization of politics through the exacerbation of the *mukarimat* system. The privatization of social services started as early as October 1991 and left a large section of the salaried population of Iraq vulnerable to malnutrition and black marketeering. This was accompanied by the privatization of the party itself and its violence: its cadres had to compete with other entrepreneurs, security and military figures, religious and tribal leaders, businessmen, and intellectuals, all clamoring for attention from the Office of the Presidency (Khoury 2013:147–48; Al-Rachid 2010: 389–486). The hierarchical and differentiated nature of Iraqi citizens' rights introduced during the war years had a profound impact on Iraqis' practices of citizenship. Rather than associate citizenship with a stable set of legal rights defined by equal status, they came to view it as a relational enterprise in which every individual was connected to his family and to the state in a complex web of privileges and exclusions. As a result, Iraq citizens found that they had to continuously lay claim to their privileges or negotiate exclusion (Khoury 2012).

Women, Gender, and Post-1991 Iraq

The regime undertook austerity measures: it reduced the number of government employees, demobilized thousands of military personnel, and deeply restricted women's work in the public sector. To provide an idea of the impact of the economic sanctions, in 1988, a teacher earned around 75 Iraqi dinar per month (equivalent to US$227 at the time); in 1997, a teacher earned 3,000 Iraqi dinar per month (equivalent to US$1.5). This greatly affected women's involvement in the job market (Al-Jawaheri 2008) and pushed the population into a "survival economy" – e.g., working several jobs, selling personal belongings, and sewing their own clothes. Until the 1980s, Iraq was touted as the country with the most educated women and the most developed and efficient higher education system in the region. By the 2000s, Iraq was listed as having one of the highest rates of female illiteracy and infant mortality.[11] The dismantling of the education system, public sector, and state services was the direct result of sanctions and had a deep impact on women's everyday lives. Al-Jawaheri (2008) shows how such impacts were especially felt by female employees in the public sector, who saw their salaries plummet to such a degree that they could not even afford to pay for weekly transportation. Women could not work alternative jobs; a man, in contrast, could work as an engineer (for example) in the morning and as a taxi driver or store salesman in the afternoon. This limited women's financial contributions to their households and pushed many into domestic life. More generally, women bore the burden of household survival because many men were involved in the military. Many women found alternative, informal ways to provide for their family's basic necessities, such as selling ready-made meals, personal objects, and homemade sweets, giving tutorials for teachers or engaging in nursing or cleaning.

According to J. Ismael and S. Ismael (2008), the transformation of households into a subsistence economy led to the domestication of professional women and resulted in the loss of public identity. Many women I interviewed sewed their own clothes and offered cleaning, cooking, and sewing services in addition to their jobs. Many had to sell their property and live off annuities. Many also quit their jobs because they "could not afford working"; their salaries did not even cover the cost of gasoline or

---

[11] According to a UN-OCHA report from 2006, 55 percent of women between the ages of fifteen and forty-five were illiterate at the end of the 1990s.

a bus pass to get to work. Iman A. was in her twenties at the time, employed in the production sector and married with two kids. She speaks about the fall in her salary, as well as the fact that most of her female friends had quit their jobs. Iman also speaks about how her sector managed to carry on despite the lack of staples.

The sanctions taught us a lot. How to face difficulties, how to be autonomous. I decided to carry on working, although my salary was 6,000 dinars [around US$20], so almost nothing. It was not enough to buy the monthly bus ticket to go to my place of work. I chose to carry on my job despite the fact that all the women around me were quitting their jobs because it was a waste of time for almost no salary. I did not work for the salary; I worked in order to have something to do, to morally and psychologically handle the terrible situation of the 1990s. Most of the women around me who quit their jobs ended up at home; they did not find another job. It morally and psychologically destroyed so many women … In the sector of production where I worked, there was something that we called the "substitution." We learned to reproduce what was made abroad, we were told to reproduce the same products with our own means, and we researched how to do it. We were able to reproduce things like makeup, house objects, all kind of things. We learned a lot during this period.

Al-Jawaheri (2008) points out that in the context of extreme poverty, new forms of patriarchy – marked by conservatism and the idea that women "needed protection" – emerged. In a context where each nuclear group folded into itself in the struggle for survival, family solidarities eroded. Al-Ali (2007) and Al-Jawaheri (2008) demonstrate how values of social prestige shifted during the sanctions and affected women and families. For example, a "good potential husband" would be capable of providing for his household, no matter his age, family background, or education. Thus the criteria for marriage changed drastically; young women from poor backgrounds were more likely to marry men with financial resources, even if they were older, uneducated, or already married. In order to support themselves and their families, some women also looked to marry men living abroad.

Heba I. was twenty-six years old in 1991. Her father had died during the Iran-Iraq war, leaving her uneducated mother to provide for the household. Heba's mother had to sell their house in Karbala and move to Baghdad with her kids. Heba I. recalls how much her mother struggled to provide during the sanctions period and fell into deep depression. Heba also speaks about her experience of the extreme poverty brought on by the sanctions and her decision to move to Yemen and marry an Iraqi man there.

The weight of the sanctions pressured my mother to the point that she ended deeply depressed. She had to manage our life, my brothers, sisters, and I, our survival. She also struggled to protect us from the general corruption provoked by the sanctions. During this period, we had to sell all that we possessed and live in a rented house . . . This situation pushed me to decide to go to Yemen. I married an Iraqi man there. The 1990s were the most difficult years of my life. I think it was even more difficult than today. It was an offense to human beings, to human life. It was hardcore life every single day. I left for Yemen because of this poverty, but I also left for Yemen because of my sadness. Everything was making me angry, everything around me. The misery, the poverty around me drove me crazy and made me insanely angry. I was not myself. I started to be afraid of becoming embittered, full of hatred. I left in 1997; I sent money from my salary in Yemen to my family, and it is thanks to this money that I bought the house in Baghdad where I live today.

According to many of the women I interviewed, the change in marriage criteria affected many families. Among the women who faced difficulties marrying during the sanctions period, the economic situation was the main issue. In addition, for certain women, the fact that they belonged to political families was an additional factor. Shayma N., who belonged to a prominent religious family close to the Da'wa Party, faced such difficulties. Two of her brothers were Da'wa Party members detained in 1980s; one was executed by the regime. Marriage was a very tough issue for Shayma and her sister. Despite the fact that her family was very conservative and religious, her parents and brother – an authority in the family – became less rigid in choosing a partner.

I finally managed to get married in 1999, at the age of thirty-two. The fact that one of my brothers was a *shahid*, executed by the regime, made it difficult for me and my sister to find partners. People were staying away from us. No one wanted to marry us. Opportunities for marriage were very limited. So we started to look for people from abroad. My younger sister had found somebody. But for her it was easier than for me because she was like them, very conservative and very religious. Me, I did not fit. It was more complicated because I disagreed with their vision of religion. They could not bring me someone like them, and it was difficult for me to find somebody among the people I knew because my brother was a *shahid*. The issue of my marriage became a burden for my family. This is why they accepted the man I proposed to them. He was an Iraqi leftist political activist, an atheist, living in Amman that I got in touch with through friends. My brother told me, "This rejection of our beliefs is pushing you to make bad choices." I answered, "Maybe, but I want to try with him." He said, "I would like someone else for you, but it's your choice; you will have to assume the entire responsibility for it." I do not know if he remembers this conversation, but I handled the situation, and I never brought any problems related to my husband to my family. I even had an autistic son, but I always handled everything, and I kept my promises to them.

Betul M. is an important Shi'a Islamist activist from Medinat al-Sadr. She got married during the sanctions period to a man who, after discovering that she could not get pregnant, wanted to take a second wife.

In these very difficult times, Betul was terrified that he might divorce her if she refused. Because she came from a humble family, she was afraid of ending up on the streets. It was a very difficult period in her life, and she was pressured by her in-laws to allow the marriage. Betul felt that she had no choice and decided to choose a second wife for her husband. She chose a young, poor orphan woman to be the second wife, and they ended up getting along very well. Betul thought it was better to choose a "woman in need because God would regard this as an act of charity."

According to Jabar (2003), Al Rachid (2010), and Charrad (2011), a type of social tribalism took root after the imposition of sanctions, signifying a new turn in the development of the totalitarian system; the regime had lost much of its potency and struggled to govern an increasingly restless urbanized society. This social tribalism was partially the result of the resilience of cultural tribalism and not only driven by the state, as Jabar (2003) suggests, criticizing Baram's (1997) strict focus on the state in his analysis of "neotribalism," but also partially manipulated and designed to strengthen the state-society relationship. This devolvement of state authority to extraneous social centers of power was anchored in a new hierarchical power structure, with tribal and clannish groups acting as an extension of the state itself. Contrary to etatist tribalism, this pattern was spread broadly across the communal and ethnic divide. Thus social retribalization was the effect of both the social vacuum that stemmed from the destruction of civil society institutions and the decline of the state as a provider of security and social services. Interestingly, the social retribalization pushed by the regime was Islamic tinted, as the Ba'th Party attempted to align its ideology with the rise of Islamism in the region in order to regain popularity.

The regime launched its *hamla al-Imaniyya* ("Faith Campaign") at the beginning of the 1990s. Saddam recast himself as a Muslim leader, added *Allahu Akbar* to the Iraqi flag, and financed the building of huge mosques and *waqf*. This "tribo-Islamic" campaign had a peculiar gender dimension and affected women's rights. The relatively progressive PSC was reformed through the control of tribalism and Islamic traditionalism. Symbolic measures were taken: a law lightening the sentence for crimes committed in the "name of honor" was passed in 1990; a measure requiring women to have a *mahram* ("male relative") to travel abroad was adopted; and death became the punishment for prostitution, already criminalized in the 1988, in 1994. Dramatically, public beheadings of prostitutes were undertaken in Baghdad.[12]

---

[12] According to Amnesty International, Saddam's son beheaded 300 women accused of prostitution in 2000.

Among the women I interviewed, opinions of the Faith Campaign varied. Some consider it crucial to the process of Islamicizing Iraqi society, through which the *hijab* became widespread among urban women. Others think that the Faith Campaign was just a part of the turn toward religion and conservatism already started as a result of the war and sanctions. Shayma N. was in her late twenties during the launch of the Faith Campaign. She had already been wearing the *hijab* from age eleven, a choice she described as "political." Because her family was close to the Da'wa Party and one of her brothers had been executed by the regime, the *hijab* symbolized to Shayma a "will to oppose the regime's authoritarianism." She gives her own reading of the Faith Campaign and its impact on society.

I believe that, after the 1991 war, when the soldiers came back from the front, the regime needed women to go back to domestic life. It launched the Faith Campaign, instrumentalizing religion to get women back home. I think that it also represented the fall of a system of thinking, due to the loss of wars and the general impoverishment. I think that the regime was responsible for the rise of conservativism in society in the 1990s, because of its political emptiness and its inability to provide anything for society. People became inclined to believe in the invisible. Religious practice is encouraging for people who live in despair. I think women came to the *hijab* for reasons that were, at the beginning, very practical and not really religious. It was difficult during the sanctions to look after our hair. It became more difficult to maintain a good hairstyle and nice clothing. It was a financial charge as well. It became more convenient to wear something over the head.

Interestingly, the argument for wearing of the *hijab* due to economic difficulties rather than piety was put to me several times by the women I interviewed. Nevertheless, many activists did not necessarily see the rise of religiosity as a negative; some even denied the regime's influence on the spread of religious practices in the 1990s, pointing instead to the influence of Islamist underground militancy.

The GFIW was again in charge of implementing the regime's new tribo-Islamic policies. Several of its leaders appeared on television wearing a loose headscarf and using an Islamic discourse. Saddam Hussein's declarations and the GFIW's publications of this period show that the gender rhetoric was focused on denouncing the corruption of the Western world, as well as applying *shari'a* and the "good Islam" to promote women's rights. Qur'an lessons were even organized in Ba'th-affiliated organizations, and the GFIW trained women on Islam and the Qur'an. Nevertheless, according to Rohde (2010), the GFIW kept a remarkably low profile during this period, which reflected the state's general loss of status. In contrast, Khoury (2013) shows that the role of the GFIW was central during this period in propagating the regime's versions of events, managing the concrete impact of the bombings and sanctions, as well as in surveillance of dissent and opposition.

Concerning the participation of the GFIW to the military conflicts themselves, Khoury evokes the dominance of women as witnesses and informants, as well as the participation of what the Ba'th called the *mujahidat* in the 1991 uprising who were hitting the antiregime prisoners with their shoes (Khoury 2012: 245–67) The role of women as informants, fighters, victims, and most important barometers for the morality or immorality of the perpetrators (whether Ba'th or rebels) becomes central to all the narratives of the events that emerged in the 1990s. The other aspect of the reports is the centrality of the Ba'th Party leadership at the provincial and national levels to the collection of information, the planning of responses, and the assessment of damages. Khoury also shows how deeply the GFIW was involved in the regime's surveillance system; local members were sent to participate in the celebration by women of Shi'a religious rituals in Muharram that were perceived by the regime as expression of the Shi'a opposition and places of politicization. The GFIW spread the regime's "modernist" religious narrative in reminding women participating in these processions that the practices of extreme mourning of al-Husain were potentially harmful to their and their children's health and that they should not wear the traditional *'abaya* because this was a sign of "backwardness" (Khoury 2013: 65, 80).

The women activists I interviewed expressed diverse opinions of the GFIW during this period. Some believed that after the events of the 1990s, participating in regime institutions was corrupt and unethical. In her final year at university, Noor S. did a political science internship at the GFIW and noticed the limit of the organization's freedom to work because it was part of the Ba'th authoritarian apparatus. She also comments on the content of GFIW's work and its shift toward an Islamic discourse in the 1990s.

If you asked me if I did feminist activities under the Ba'th, I would answer that I really wished I could. But feminism was reduced to the GFIW, affiliated with the regime. During my fourth year of study, I did an internship at the GFIW. I was happy to deal with women's issues, and at the time, it was the preparations for the Beijing Conference. They screened films showing Algerian and Pakistani women struggling for the rights of women in Islam and using Islam to fight for women's rights. They knew verses of the Qur'an by heart, and they also knew international conventions related to human and women's rights. After seeing this film, I wished we had the same kind of movement in Iraq, and I tried to work around this issue with the GFIW. But I very quickly noted that the involvement had more to do with the Party than with feminism. Its head had absolute authority over everyone and everything. Her office had a scary power. I could not carry on like that. I tried, but I could not. Also, the political climate was very tense in the 1990s, and my family and I were the kind of people who tried to stay away from any contact with politics, any situation or position that would be political in one way or another. We knew that if anything happened, we had no one to protect us. Like we say: "We had no one to carry us." At the time, there were many incidents regarding the violation of people's dignity. The security apparatus of the regime terrified people, and the men in charge of the security apparatus had power over the streets.

Iman A. has a different opinion of the GFIW. She joined the organization in the mid-1990s as a researcher.

I was surprised to find a lot of exceptional women at the GFIW; finally the Ba'th Party devotees were not that numerous. There were even women of communist sensibilities who were publishing papers in the new review: *al-Ittihad al-Gender*. I mean it was a very important organization for women. They contributed to social protection, women's literacy, vaccination campaigns, and women's health issues. Despite the fact that they belonged to the Party, they produced an important amount of research material. I was very surprised to discover some of their research in the 1980s that was very advanced. I found recently, for example, [that] one of their researches was gathering a bibliography of all the published women's press in Iraq since the 1930s. They researched important things. It belongs to our heritage. Their image is very negative among the population; many people think that its head was just a puppet of Saddam Hussein. I found out that she was, in reality, a very strong woman. Manal Yunes wanted to incite a new movement. She welcomed anyone who was eager to work and was serious. There were amazing women, such as Thaera Abdulwahid, a Sabean woman, very active, an exceptional woman. They published and released my work on the women of the *shuhada'*, the war widows. There was also Hanaa Ibrahim; she was a communist, and like me, she was not affiliated with the Ba'th. It was an amazing learning experience for me. I definitely think that the review of Hanaa Ibrahim, *al-Gender*, was a real feminist review, very rich.

Rohde (2010) eloquently analyzed the ambiguity that characterized the 1990s: on the one hand, there was the regime's Faith Campaign and, on the other, the erosion of sexual morals. The latter issue was visible in the spread of prostitution and pornography, the kidnapping of girls, young women marrying – or forced to marry – old wealthy men, a general decrease in marriage due to poverty, and the rise of informal unions ('*urfi* marriages) and temporary marriages (*mut'a* for Shi'as, *misyar* for Sunnis). More generally, Al-Jawaheri (2008) and Al-Ali (2007) discuss the erosion of moral and social values in general, the spread of corruption and individual relations based on economic interest, and the fragmentation of family solidarity in a context where individuals struggled for survival. This period restructured the social and cultural fabric of Iraq, altering the values of sociability and morality. However, J. Ismael and S. Ismael (2008) argue that although the atmosphere of social insecurity fostered mistrust of strangers and competition with outsiders, at the same time it promoted the strengthening of social networks within neighborhoods for the provision of security and mutual support.

Maha S. – a middle-class Baghdadi activist – was in her late twenties during the sanctions. She describes how people's behavior and mentality changed.

The sanctions made our lives difficult at every level. In my family, we noticed many phenomena linked to the sanctions. For example, many students told us that their teachers were accepting money and gifts in exchange for elevating their marks or treating them with privileges at school. Before, this would have been impossible. It became acceptable because the teachers were earning no more than 3,000 dinars, which was equivalent to 10 dollars per month. It was of course not sufficient for their families to live on. It became more and more acceptable to ask for money or gifts in exchange for favors in the workplace. We noticed that the Iraqi being was changing deeply, languishing from the inside. Despite this atmosphere, none of us tried to leave the country. My father used to say that the motherland is not a hotel; you do not leave it if it is not five stars anymore, not clean, not tidy and comfortable. It is your country, and you have to stay in it in order to improve it. I acknowledge that we were more and more rare, the people who thought this way, to follow these principles; we felt more and more isolated. Day after day, like most middle-class families in the 1990s, our life deteriorated, regressed to the point that we reached poverty. It affected all the values of hard work, all these principles about working hard to earn a good living.

Moreover, I noticed during my interviews that the 1990s Ba'th authoritarian regime and its security apparatus and system were always represented through male figures; expressions such as "Saddam's men" and the "security apparatus men" were commonly used. At the time, as rumors and news circulated about the kidnapping of women by "Saddam's men," women felt more vulnerable. Salma A., for example, worked in the media sector and speaks about how she would avoid "powerful men" in order to stave off sexual harassment.

As a woman during a time like the sanctions period, I had to stay away from men who had responsibilities, men of power, or any man close to the regime. In doing so, I avoided sexual harassment. I knew that if anything happened with a man close to the regime, nobody would protect me, and I would have nowhere to complain.

At the end of the 1990s, according to Tripp (2000), the Iraqi regime became a "shadow state" with a "shadow army." The political and economic system relied on *umena'* Saddam (Saddam's supporters): 500,000 individuals linked to the regime by clan, tribe, region, or corrupt economic interests. The Gulf War and sanctions affected the country's infrastructure to such an extent that until the end of the 1990s, the countryside had only sporadic access to electricity and running water. Thus it is not surprising that Ba'th politics shifted toward the tribes in the mid-1990s because the regime feared that local networks had become too autonomous and uncontrollable. Intertribal conflict took extremely dangerous and bloody forms because the tribes had received powerful artillery from the regime throughout the previous decade. As the rise in tribal leaders' power revealed the weakness of the state, in 1997 Saddam outlawed tribal tribunals and brutally killed repressed rebellious tribal leaders, outraging even those most loyal to the regime (Sakai 2003).

The regime continued its repression of society, trying hard to contain the wave of exile – for both economic and political reasons – of political activists, intellectuals, and scientists. Saba S. is forty-two and from an educated Baghdadi family. She obtained a Ph.D. in biology from Baghdad University in the mid-1980s and was the recipient of a very prestigious international prize for female scientists. As a high-profile biologist, Saba worked in the public sector. Like many who attained positions of responsibility, she was exposed to harassment and threats from the regime because she refused to join the Ba'th Party. Saba insists on pointing out that she is from a well-known nonpolitical Sunni family.

My family name is [a well-known Arab Sunni name], and I have never belonged to the Ba'th Party, nor anyone in my family. On the contrary, I was among the people who suffered from the regime, especially after graduating from university. It was a time of the brain drain. Instead, I decided to quit my job in 1999. I experienced harassment to get back to work; then, when they felt I was willing to leave, they put my picture and my name in all the airports of the county and forbid me to leave Iraq. If I tried to leave the country, my family and I would have been punished, jailed. I could not put my family in danger. It was so painful when I received the order from the government. I was so afraid that if I leave, they will make my family suffer, because my parents were not able to leave Iraq. I was forced to go back to work on the condition that I move to another office with the same position. Then I carried on my life. The prohibition on leaving the country was only removed in 2002.

Saba S., who had never been involved in any political movement prior to the fall of the regime, joined the Iraqi Communist Party after 2003. She is now the head of the Women's Promotion Committee at an important ministry.

Conclusion

Ba'th authoritarian patrimonialism – with its use of political violence, bloody repression, kin-based power relations, and a rentier economy – is a good example of Sharabi's neopatriarchal state. If economic, social, and cultural growth due to oil revenues helped to enhance women's life conditions and legal rights during the 1970s, as well as weaken normative gender representations, the nature of the regime itself partly consolidated neopatriarchy. The head of the state was represented as the father, held a monopoly over violence, and exercised great violence against anyone opposing his hegemony. Moreover, the state's discriminatory and repressive politics pushed the atomization of Iraqi society, provoking a shift in the forms of contestation along identity-based lines. Shi'a Islamist militancy – the product of socioeconomic, ideological, political, and sectarian forms of contestation – developed its own gender norms and practices and politicized women's dress codes and morality.

The 1980s were marked by the war with Iran; the militarization of society, which involved the strengthening of normative masculinity and femininity and male-dominated power structures; and the regime's use of political violence. All these factors contributed to loss of gains in women's rights made in the preceding decade. From 1991 on, the significance of ethnic and sectarian belongings has shifted. Cloaked by an Arab nationalist discourse, the regime's violent politics of the 1970s and 1980s against the Kurds, *taba'iyya*, and Shi'a opposition provoked irreversible consequences. After the horrors of the Halabja chemical attack in 1987 and 1988 – considered by many as a genocide – and the terrible repression of the Kurdish and Shi'a uprisings in 1991, the clash between the Ba'th regime and the Kurdish and Shi'a populations was definitive. There was no longer a nationhood to be shared. The safe haven established in April 1991 protected only the Kurdish regions, which would be granted autonomy. The polarized and contentious memory of the 1991 uprisings also divided Shi'as and Sunnis; the latter were exposed to the regime's propaganda claiming that the Shi'a uprising was initiated by Iran. The coalition bombings, the era of sanctions, the ensuing humanitarian crisis, the regime's tribo-Islamic politics, and the erosion of moral and sexual values affected women's everyday life conditions, rights, gender representations, and practices of normative and conservative social values.

The evolution of Ba'th gender politics from 1968 to the 2000s illustrates how women's rights, bodies, and sexuality were at the core of the regime's ideologies and definitions of nation. Such an evolution shows the overlapping of gender issues within the definition of the nation-state discussed by Anthias and Yuval-Davis. It also shows the ways in which women are differently positioned regarding citizenship according to their ethnicity and religion, as argued by Joseph (1991, 2000). In Iraq, the exacerbation of hierarchical citizenship since the beginning of the war with Iran and the normalization of war itself affected women in different ways according to their position vis-à-vis the party, the level of their participation to the war effort, and their ethnic and sectarian belonging. Women as part of the opposition or associated with opposition members by kin occupied the lowest level of citizenship. The exacerbation of sectarian and community-based conflicts through the use of violence, the tribo-Islamic shift in the context of impoverishment, the turn in moral values, and the humanitarian crisis will shape the post-2003 dynamics. However, the changing politics of the party are also all related to the very concrete and devastating impact of the UN sanctions that in themselves deteriorated the Iraqi social fabric and started the very destruction of the state as one of the main social and economic providers on which women relied heavily. The exacerbation of poverty and the humanitarian crisis created by the sanctions brought Iraqi women and the whole society to a survival mechanism that enshrined normative gender norms and relations.

This chapter laid out the underlying ingredients of Iraqi women's "patriarchal bargain" in the period 2003–14: imperialist interference, sectarian politics and conflicts, and exacerbated poverty. All these factors led to one essential phenomenon: violence.

3   Experiencing the Invasion and Occupation and the Women of the New Regime

Introduction: Reaching Medinat al-Sadr

At the entrance to the Medinat al-Sadr checkpoint (Figure 3.1), one of Baghdad's main Shi'a neighborhoods, 'Amu Abu Manal insisted on being very careful. Medinat al-Sadr is well known for both its popular reputation and as one of the first targets of sectarian violence against the Shi'a population because it has become since the occupation the rear base of the "Mahdi army." It is an area where at the time of my fieldwork car bombs exploded on a weekly basis, but despite this, it is still very lively and busy. 'Amu Abu Manal's worries also show how Baghdad's divisions are no longer based solely on the sectarian Sunni–Shi'a divide; violent clashes also occur between political groups and militias of the same sect. In addition, such conflicts also have class dimensions.

Medinat al-Sadr is one of the most populous Shi'a neighborhoods of Baghdad. It was built in the 1960s by 'Abd al-Karim Qasim's revolutionary regime to house the population recently settled in the slums of the city. This population had come from the southern region and was originally rural, Shi'a, and tribal. Originally named Medinat al-Thawra (the Revolution's City), the neighborhood was renamed Medinat Saddam ("Saddam's City") under Saddam and, after the fall of the regime in 2003, was renamed again. Its current name, Medinat al-Sadr ("Sadr's City"), commemorates the Shi'a religious figure executed by the Ba'th regime. Medinat al-Sadr is an impoverished suburb carrying all the associated negative prejudices, even from the point of view of other Shi'as from upper and upper middle-class areas of Baghdad like al-Mansur or al-Kazimiyya. A Baghdadi from another area would not feel safe in Medinat al-Sadr; it is considered both a popular neighborhood where tribalism dominates and the site of internal conflicts between Shi'a political groups.

Due to sectarian and political violence, life in postinvasion Baghdad is very unpredictable; Baghdadis live in a constant state of tension and worry. As a result, when living in Baghdad for my fieldwork, I spent more time on the phone than any other time in my life. I had to contact

Figure 3.1 Al-Shuhada' Square in Baghdad with a missing statue of Saddam Hussein (March 2010).

the people I wanted to meet, call them before leaving home, and then call them after passing their neighborhood's checkpoint. Since many women activists have been the targets of violence, assassinations, and explosions, many organizations do not publicize the location of their offices or hang a sign outside their door. An activist from a well-known women's organization told me that she debates with herself every morning as to whether to hang a sign above the organization's new office. She finally decided against it after receiving death threats during the sectarian war of 2006–7. Thus I had to get in touch with the person I was meeting right after passing the last checkpoint so as to obtain the precise address where the meeting would take place. The offices always looked like any other residential building and were often shared by several organizations.

Despite this difficult context, almost all the numerous meetings I organized for participant observation and interviews took place at the agreed time. If the security situation made a particular meeting complicated, it would be rescheduled. All the people I met gave me their undivided attention during our discussions and often offered to meet again should I require. Similarly, most of the cultural and political events and mobilizations organized by civil society and women's organizations would take place, often with stop and search at the entrance, even the day after a dreadful explosion in the same area. Moreover, I was struck by how the scholars, activists, and individuals I met for this research gave much importance and commitment to our meetings. I was often received very warmly, and my research given a lot of attention despite my young age and whether or not I was related to the person through family, neighborhood, or a personal acquaintance. It became clear that the women I wanted to meet were eager to talk, share their thoughts and ideas, and contribute to the research itself. Many of my interviewees expressed feelings of being "stuck" in and "suffocated" by a city of walls, separations, and checkpoints. I was also told that they were even happier that my research would also be accessible to the "outside world."

I called Fatima A. after passing the checkpoint of Medinat al-Sadr. I was introduced to Fatima through other activists, who described her as engaged and sincere. From the car window, I saw her standing in front of an innocuous middle-class-looking residential house. She was smiling and looked quite elegant. In her midforties and wearing a long brown skirt, purple cardigan, and a short flowery head scarf, Fatima shook my hand and kissed me several times. Because I usually mentioned al-Kazimiyya on the phone when being guided to a meeting location, I was often greeted with remarks such as, "What a brave young woman you are, coming here from al-Kazimiyya to meet us." This comment was often followed by someone else saying, "This is the Iraqi woman." On entering the office, I was welcomed by a young man – the secretary – and several young female activists. Similar to the majority of my first encounters in such offices, I tour the offices, I am introduced to everyone, and then invited to sit in the director's or general secretary's room. Soon after I begin introducing myself and my research, I am served tea, water, and sweets. Often I am asked if the temperature of the room is okay or if the air conditioner should be turned on. In such cases, the cuts to public electricity is always mentioned, as well as the ridiculous prices of private electric companies. During a two-hour conversation, the electricity always cut out at least once, bringing a sort of intimacy and agreeable silence, because the loud and annoying generators can be heard everywhere in the city.

After casual conversation about families, region, neighborhood, the traffic, and insecurity, I always ask permission to record the interview, indicating that doing so allowed me to focus on the discussion rather than on taking notes. Throughout my fieldwork, I noticed that recording is easily accepted, almost naturally, by many activists who had not experienced repression or exile – mostly those of the younger generation (thirties and forties). Older activists would also accept, but with hesitation, because many of them had experienced repression from the previous regime. Fatima –

forty-five years old – accepted being recorded straightaway because she had heard about my research from others I had interviewed previously. She heard that I had come from exile and was working on women's political activism and rights in Iraq. She did not ask for details about me and my family; she considered me to be a colleague and a trustworthy person. As a founding member of the Iraqi Women Network (IWN) and the Baghdad Women's Association, Fatima spoke of her involvement in the women's movement that emerged after the fall of the regime. She mentioned her love for Medinat al-Sadr, where she has lived her whole life, and her role as a representative at the Municipal Council of Baghdad. Fatima described her family background as "conservative and political" and spoke about her experience of discrimination under the previous regime. Because one of her brothers was an active member of the Da'wa Party, she could not get a job in the education sector after completing a BA in biology. She describes the environment of and her involvement in Medinat al-Sadr.

I grew up in Medinat al-Sadr, with all the political changes it has experienced. I think that the situation of this neighborhood is exceptional. It is a particularly conservative area, a tribal environment. It has slowed down our work in the past period, but we are trying to be active despite that.

Despite being from a Da'wa family and growing up in a conservative environment dominated by Islamist Shi'a militancy, Fatima chose to get involved in nonsectarian, nonreligious independent women's groups. She is also a representative in the Medinat al-Sadr Council; she ran as a candidate of one of the main Shi'a political groups – Tayar al-Islah, which includes Islamist and non-Islamist Shi'a political activists – to join this council. What she told me, of course, is as important as what she did not tell me, and the context in which our conversation took place is as important as the discussion itself. After our formal conversation, we met several other times at meetings, gatherings, and conferences. Through these informal encounters, I got to know her better and understand her background, trajectory, and personal story.

I chose to begin this chapter by describing how I made appointments with a prominent woman activist from Medinat al-Sadr because most of these activists are members of the communal and political groups that were marginalized under the previous regime. Medinat al-Sadr, its political culture and marginalized population, has moved from the margins to the center since 2003. I also chose Fatima to illustrate a particular feature of the post-2003 situation: the institutionalization of ethnosectarianism. Despite being an independent woman's rights and civil society activist involved in a nonreligious and nonsectarian activism, Fatima is also a representative of a Shi'a political list that she joined in order to run for the provincial council election because the Iraqi political system since 2003 relies on ethnosectarian quotas. How I conducted my research and the choices I made regarding my identity in relation to the different spaces and individuals with whom I interacted gave me a very concrete sense of the realities of postinvasion Baghdad. It is a context characterized by sectarian violence, powerful Islamist militias roaming the streets, and the legacy of the Ba'th authoritarian regime: decades of war and thirteen years of harsh economic sanctions. This chapter seeks to explore the post-2003 context and the ways in which women activists have experienced postinvasion Iraq, focusing particularly on women representatives. How did women activists experience the fall of the regime and the occupation? What characterizes their lives since 2003? How did they participate, if at all, in the post-2003 regime? How did this context affect their legal rights and political activism within the new Iraqi government and institutions?

The Colonial Invasion and Occupation

Experiencing the Fall of the Ba'th Regime

Iraqi women activists told me that in the months leading up to the US invasion of Iraq. They were very anxious about the war. Even political activists who welcomed the fall of the regime, and those that specifically cheered US intervention, feared another war. The trauma of the US-led bombings in 1991 was still present. Aziza S. – a prominent Shi'a Islamist who conducted underground political activities opposing the Ba'th regime in Baghdad – was traumatized by the 1991 bombings. She describes how the events of 1991 made "her breast milk dry" and how much she feared another US-led military intervention:

The terror of 1991 stayed in my mind . . . Yes, of course we wanted the regime to fall, but not through violence. We were following the news at the time. Despite the fact that satellite dishes were forbidden by the regime, we managed to get some news of what being discussed by the Americans. Sometimes we managed to get recordings of TV programs from people abroad. We did not want to experience the horror of the bombings again. But it did happen, and it did provoke another trauma, once again, inside of us and in our children's memories. Until now I remember it, my house was in al-Mansur neighborhood at the time. Our street was one of the last streets in the neighborhood that the Americans entered: Hay al-'Arabi Street. My son was in the garden and he heard everything. I think that it provoked a real psychological trauma for him. We did not want the Americans to come, we wanted change in another way. But for sure, the fall of the regime was necessary.

A few years after the invasion, Aziza lost her son and sister; they were assassinated in the sectarian violence that followed the fall of the regime.

Noor S. was not politically active before 2003. She was convinced that the regime had become weak and would have fallen without external intervention. She narrates her experience of the invasion.

In 2003, the arrival of the Americans shook me. We were afraid of war. We were people who hated war, we were so tired of war. My parents were from the generation who witnessed the death of the royal family, and they had very sad memories of it: all the blood, pain, and fear. Then, the war with Iran, the missiles, the death, we were tired of all of that. Honestly, when we heard about the war, we first thought that it was another crisis that would pass, that they were just threatening the regime. Also, we were all seeing that the regime was destroying itself; it was weak. We were not people who welcomed the Americans. We were afraid, afraid for our lives. My mother was afraid for her kids and her grandkids . . . After the fall and the American bombings, I was [in] shock, I could not even move, I stayed home. I kept asking myself: "Where is the state we used to know?" Everything fell so fast, in a blow, nothing was left. I did not go out the first weeks after the arrival of the Americans. At the time, there were no mobiles phones; we had only a landline, and it was cut. My mother was so used to wars and crisis that she had already prepared stocks of food. This anxiety was always present.

Noor lost her sister and her brother in the outbreak of sectarian violence in Baghdad. Her sister died in 2004 and her brother in 2007, leaving behind a son and two sons, respectively. As her mother died shortly after "from the shock of losing her children," Noor became the main caretaker for her three nephews.

Like Noor, many of my interviewees felt that war was not the only way to change the regime. Some believed that the regime would have fallen in a way similar to the recent Arab uprisings. Maysoon S. – a Sunni Islamist – expresses this point of view:

Of course, we all wanted this regime to end, but not necessarily in this way. We all have now witnessed what happened in Tunisia and Egypt especially. When people want their regime to fall, then they provoke a revolution and preserve their revolution. In our case, a foreign, Western country came and made the whole country fall, a state with all its institutions. This is not a proper way to act. We know that their objective was to make an entire people fall.

With regard to views of the occupation, there is a noticeable difference between the women I interviewed and the women of the diaspora interviewed by Al-Ali (2007). Exiled women activists were more supportive of the war and hopeful about the fall of the regime; women inside Iraq were more anxious and negative. The differences in their feelings about 2003 are clearly linked to their personal experiences. Iraqis in the diaspora wished to "come back," while those inside Iraq wanted to avoid the worst scenario.

Some of the Iraqi activists I interviewed – all of whom were directly victims of Ba'th authoritarian repression – were in favor of the war. However, even those who favored war expressed their shock and revulsion at the US-led occupation, which was legitimized by UN Security Council Resolution 1483 (adopted May 2003). Naziha A. – a prominent Shi'a activist and MP since the fall of the regime – is such a person. Her brother was executed by the Ba'th regime in 1990.

We were happy for the 2003 war, because we were following news that told us it was a war of liberation. After, we were hurt, because we were already upset by the fact that our army did not liberate us from Saddam. Also, it has to be noted that there was only a very small elite that supported the regime at the end. After the Americans came, we criticized this elite, and we were saying that it was the role of the Iraqi army to liberate us. We should not have needed to ask a foreign army. I can tell you, however, that when the Americans entered, we felt joy and happiness to be finally liberated from this regime. But the blow, the shock we experienced when the UN Security Council Resolution stated that we were "occupied"! This was an occupation. Then, we began to fight. I joined the National Iraqi Association, and I began my political involvement in 2003. Straight after the fall, we were consulting our great *marje'*, the great Ayatollah al-Sistani, and the other *maraje'* around him. I was ready to do all that I could to struggle against the occupiers.

Moreover, most of the Iraqi activists from all backgrounds expressed the opinion that the US administration already held Iraq's destiny in its hands; Iraqis were not free to decide the future of their country. The most common example given was that of the 1991 uprising and the fact that the US-led coalition "decided" not to support Iraqis in *their* attempt to overthrow the regime. Shayma N., who hails from a Shi'a Islamist family that was severely repressed by the regime expressed this opinion.

I had many concerns about the American intervention, because when Iraqis revolted in 1991, when they were at the point of making the regime fall by themselves, the Americans repressed them and let the Ba'th regime massacre them. So, as many, I had totally understood that they are the ones who decide, and that it will be only when they have decided that the regime would fall. Today, there is much research proving that the Iraqi opposition attempted many times to end the Ba'th regime, including attempts by some of the regime's officers. All these attempts failed for one simple reason: the Americans were informing Saddam of these attempts to overthrow his regime. This is why it is only when the Americans decide that the regime will fall, that the regime can fall. It is as simple as that.

The invasion of Iraq, coupled with the bombings and fights that occurred between March and May 2003, led to around 150,000 civilian deaths.[1] Among the activists I interviewed, one lost her husband in the US-led coalition bombings. Most of the activists lost relatives or were the direct targets of violence (explosions and assassination attempts) in the outbreak of sectarian conflict after 2004. After the establishment of the occupation administration through the Coalition Provisional Authority (CPA) and the establishment of governing councils based on communal – ethnic, religious, and sectarian – quotas, Iraqis' daily lives began to be characterized by violence.

Human Rights Abuse and Sexual Violence

The invasion and occupation itself could be considered as a form of human rights abuse; however, despite the opposition of the UN Security Council, it was later given legitimacy by UN resolutions. The United Nations provided administrative support and a frame to the US-led occupation administration. From the very beginning of the occupation, organizations such as Amnesty International, Human Rights Watch, and many observers provided reports on human rights abuses of the population at the hands of the occupying forces. The massive and indiscriminate imprisonment of the opposition to the occupation; the inhuman, brutal, and unspeakable treatment of prisoners that made famous the name of Abu Ghraib prison; and the sexual violence committed by soldiers of the occupying army, including toward children, are all well-known realities today. The normalization of violence, torture, and inhuman treatment on a large scale justified by the war itself and then under the name of the "War on Terror" has altered Iraqi society. It has also paved the way to the new Iraqi regime in its handling of dissent and opposition, as I will show later in this chapter.

As pointed out by a Human Rights Watch report (2003) on sexual violence and the abduction of women and girls in Baghdad, the "climate of fear" and the failure of the occupying power to protect women and girls from violence and redress it when it occurred had both direct and long-term consequences for the safety of women and girls and for their participation in postwar life in Iraq. According to many observers, sexual violence against Iraqi women was widespread and far more extensive than the cells of Abu Ghraib. The proliferation of different forms of

[1] Estimated according to *The Lancet* (2004), Iraq Body Count, available at www .iraqbodycount.org, and Iraq: The Human Cost, available at web.mit.edu/humancostIr aq/.

prostitution and sex trafficking of women and girls within Iraq and in the region has been widely documented.

The Organization of Women's Freedom in Iraq (OWFI) opened its offices at the very beginning of the occupation and worked on sheltering and providing care and assistance to women victims of abuse, sexual violence, and trafficking. The OWFI's report (2010) shows very clearly how much the very invasion and occupation provoked the rise of sex trafficking of women and girls in the country and how much the social chaos and the security vacuum created situations of extreme vulnerability for women and girls. OWFI is still today the only organization that provides shelters for women victim of abuse in Iraq (with the exclusion of Iraqi Kurdistan) because such shelters are still considered illegal by the central government.

Destruction of the State and Imposition of a Fragmented Nationhood

The preparation of the Iraqi National Council – a group of opposition political leaders – and the US administration for the invasion of Iraq, as in the famous London Congress, along with the political process of the Anglo-American occupation exacerbated the implosion of Iraqi society that began in the 1990s. If the wars, the violent and repressive nature of the Ba'th authoritarian regime, and the general impoverishment brought on by UN sanctions had already deeply affected the social and cultural fabric of Iraq, the invasion and occupation only pushed the process of social and political implosion to its extreme. As J. Ismael and T. Ismael (2015) argue, the terrible situation of sectarian violence and political crisis that Iraq is experiencing today has not simply "happened" but were foreseeable consequences of a set of policy choices taken by occupation authorities supported by the new Iraqi elite composed of former exiles that the occupiers have brought to power. As observed by many (Z. Al-Ali 2014; Arato 2009; Dawisha 2009; J. Ismael & T. Ismael 2015), instead of a pretended "state building," the CPA, led by Paul Bremer, and the whole execution and administration of the invasion and occupation itself provoked the very destruction of the Iraqi state and imposed a fragmented version of Iraqi nationhood. The destruction of the state was engineered through the "de-Ba'athification" campaign launched by the CPA and supported by the new elite. The de-Ba'thification policies were both perceived as anti-Sunni and failed to truly expel Ba'th leaders from positions of power. The dissolution of the Iraqi army and administration forced hundreds of thousands qualified staff and soldiers into unemployment (J. Ismael & T. Ismael 2015; Lafourcade 2007). The de-Ba'thification was used by leaders of the new political elite to marginalize many Sunni individuals who formed the social elite of the former regime such as university professors and administrators of the former state (Lafourcade 2012). In addition to being perceived by the Sunni political leadership as a clear tool of discrimination against them, it also deprived the new state of experienced administrators and a skilled social base. In addition to that, the US-led occupation administration integrated the politicized Shi'a Islamist militias in the army, which introduced sectarian elements into it.

At the economic level, Paul Bremer, head of the CPA, put in place aggressive economic policies that infuriated Iraq's business class, some of whom responded by funding the insurgency. His policies kept of the legacy of Saddam's regime only the laws that restricted collective bargaining and trade unions. He introduced a set of laws in September 2003 to bring in transnational corporations, lowering corporate taxes from almost 40 to 15 percent, permitting foreign companies to own 100 percent of Iraqi assets, and entirely exempting corporations working with the CPA from taxation. Foreign companies, especially oil companies, were entitled to leases or contracts that could remain in effect for forty years, and foreign banks were favored with the same terms (J. Ismael & T. Ismael 2015: 13–39).

Arato (2009) describes in details how the occupation itself produced all the ingredients of the failure of the new state from the very elaboration of the Iraqi Transitional Administrative Law, supposed to be an interim Constitution during the provisional governments (Iraqi Governing Council from July 2003 to June 2004 and then the Iraqi Interim Government from June 2005 to May 2005, replaced the same year by the first post-2003 permanent government), to the drafting by the Iraqi Constitution Drafting Committee and then adoption of the new Constitution through referendum in October 2005. As I will illustrate through the example of the direct appointment of a women representative by the CPA, members of the Iraqi Governing Council were chosen by the occupation administration according to a sectarian, limited, and prejudiced vision of the Iraqi people. As shown by Arato (2009: 1–57), the whole process was exclusionary and hierarchical: Iraqis themselves were treated as advisors rather than being the real decision makers, and all the groups that were critical of the invasion were excluded, such as Sunni political groups and the Sadrists. The Constitution-building process was characterized by a neoimperial modality of imposition despite the interventions of Ayatollah Sistani that were aimed at guarantying the indigeneity of the process (Z. Al-Ali 2014: 75–102; Arato 2009, 99–134). In the end, and despite the very marginalization of the opposition, the new Constitution was adopted in 2005 through a referendum.

If for Arato the very process carried all the elements of failure of the state's so-called reconstruction, according to Romano (2014), the Constitution that was adopted provided the essential elements for a functioning state. It is the evisceration, especially by al-Maliki's regime, of key components of the Constitution, such as the decentralization and power sharing that were never respected, that led to the total alienation of Iraq's disparate Sunni Arab populations. As I will illustrate in Chapter 6, dedicated to the issue of women's legal rights and Article 41 of the Constitution and its implications regarding the PSC, the Constitution has a number of ambiguities. However, it generally describes the new Iraqi system as a federal state in which the system of government is republican, representative, parliamentary, and democratic (Article 1). The Constitution recognizes Islam as the official religion of the state and a source of legislation while also guarantying "full religious rights to freedom of religious belief and practice of all individuals such as Christians, Yazidis, and Mandean Sabeans" (Article 2). As pointed out by Romano (2014), Shi'a Islamist parties originally preferred stronger wording of Islam as "the source of legislation" but compromised with secular parties on the issue. Articles 3 and 4 recognize "multiple nationalities, religions and sects" as belonging to the country, which at the same time is "a founding and active member in the Arab League and is committed to its charter, and it [Iraq] is part of the Islamic world." This, too, represented a compromise between Arab and Kurdish negotiators, since the Arabs originally wanted wording recognizing Iraq as an Arab state. Article 4 recognizes Arabic and Kurdish as the two official languages of Iraq but also guarantees other groups such as Turkmens, Assyrians, and Armenians the right to educate their children in their mother tongue in government schools. Very importantly, the Constitution grants equality of all citizens in the Article 14: "Iraqis are equal before the law without discrimination based on gender, race, ethnicity, nationality, origin, color, religion, sect, belief or opinion, or economic or social status." The Constitution makes clear that Iraq's election law will aim to achieve a 25 percent female membership in the Council of Representatives. In addition, the Constitution requires that "violence and abuse in the family, school and society shall be prohibited," as is "trafficking of women and children, and [the] sex trade." The Constitution also lays out civil and political rights of individuals in Iraq comparable to that of any Western state and guaranties economic, social, and cultural liberties that even go farther than those of some Western states, including "the right to health care" and provisions for "the handicapped and those with special needs" (Romano 2014). It also includes injunctions against unlawful detention and torture of any kind and guarantees "freedom of expression using all means" – including "freedom of assembly and peaceful demonstration" – provided that the exercise of these freedoms does not "violate public order or morality."

The issues of federalism and share of the country's oil and gas resources were central to the debates, and tensions between Kurdish and Shiʻa representatives, on the one hand, advocating for federalism and the other political groups, on the other hand, advocating for centralization. As I will show in Chapter 6, federalism was placed over women's rights even by many women activists. Despite stating that oil and gas resources are owned by all the people of Iraq, the Constitution articles related to the way the resources should be managed and the possible autonomy of Iraq's regions are at the core of the political crisis involving the opposition of the central government and the Kurdistan Regional Government (KRG) today. The status of Kirkuk and its oil fields has led to military clashes since the Kurdish referendum in the fall of 2017. According to many, as a result of the central government's mismanagement, corruption, and nepotism, many political groups who initially favored a centralized state, such as Sunni and secular groups, are now pushing for more decentralization.

Very importantly, nothing in the Constitution ever applied ethnosectarian quotas or allocated certain positions (president, prime minister, etc.) to specific ethnosectarian groups. The only quotas included are for non-Muslims and women in the Council of Representatives. The very essential aspect of the post-2003 regime is the institutionalization of communal-based identities – ethnic, religious, and sectarian – and especially ethnosectarian divisions between Arabs and Kurds and Sunnis and Shiʻas. In addition to the effect of the de-Baʻathification, the colonial process that characterized the establishment of the new political regime – government and Constitution – led by the CPA, the very institutionalization of a political system in which communal identities are the core of the state's organization, is what led Iraq to the sectarian war. The Iraqi Governing Council members were selected by the CPA according to ethnic, religious, and sectarian quotas, which corresponds to a rupture with the Iraqi political system that was based – at least in principle – on equal citizenship. Since 2003, following the CPA projection of a fragmented Iraqi identity based on ethnic, sectarian, and religious belonging, the new political system – government, parties, and ministries – is based on communal belongings because seats and positions are distributed to representatives of ethnic, religious, or sectarian communities. According to this communal quota system, the president should be Kurdish, the vice-president should be a Shiʻa and a Sunni, the prime minister should be Shiʻa, the vice prime ministers should be Kurdish and Shiʻa, the president of the Parliament should be Sunni, and the vice-presidents should be Shiʻa and Kurdish, and this principle is applied for all ministries, security apparatus, and institutions. As a result, the electoral law, as well as the whole functioning of the political system – designation of the president and vice-president and the distribution of ministries, political parties, and provincial and parliamentary seats – functions according to *nizam al-muhasasa* – the quota system – based on communal identities.

The US army's repression of uprisings against the occupation – especially in Fallujah, where napalm and poison gas were used, and Najaf – and the rise of political and party-associated militias benefiting from the power vacuum all took a sectarian shape (International Crisis Group 2008a, 2008b). The exacerbation of sectarian conflict reached its extreme during the 2006–7 sectarian war. This civil war, and all the associated events, represented the third turning point in Iraqi sectarian relations, the first being the war with Iran and the second the repression of the 1991 uprisings (Haddad 2010). Since the fall, but even more after the dreadful events of 2006–27, sectarian violence reorganized society and territory. Such is visible in the division of Baghdad into homogeneously Sunni and Shiʻa neighborhoods, each of which is controlled by different militias, divided and fragmented by concrete walls, and by checkpoints of the occupation administration and the new Iraqi army (Damluji 2010; Pieri 2014). Sunnis have been threatened by the rise to power of conservative, competing sectarian militias in the streets, as mentioned previously the integration of sectarian armed groups into the state's security apparatus, and the Shiʻa Islamist parties' consolidation of central power and its associated sectarian and discriminatory policies.

The very nature of the new political elite that came back from decades of exile is also central to the crisis because it was dominated by those who had been at the margins of the previous Iraqi state, Kurds and Shiʻas, and had their own experience and memory of the Iraqi nation. Their claims of victimhood and demands for compensation and reward for being oppressed and marginalized contributed to a redefinition of Iraqi nationhood (Z. Al-Ali 2014; Al-Rachid 2010: 315–45; Tejtel et al. 2012; Harling 2012). As I will show via the mentality of many women's rights activists, the idea of belonging to an ethnosectarian group – Kurd or Shiʻa – that suffered from the repression of the Baʻth regime has been developed as an ideology of *mazlumiyya* – victimhood – and, for some, revanchism. The *mazlumiyya* ideology also characterizes the new state's official narratives, with officials putting forward their own versions of events that marked Iraqi social and political history: the Baʻth regime is depicted as solely driven by bloody communalism – ethnic and sectarian – and the entire Ba'th era was characterized as one of violence and dictatorship. In the post-2003 context, more nuanced points of view and narratives not built around celebration of the Iraqi political opposition to the Ba'th regime are rare among the elite of the new regime. The area that is today Iraqi Kurdistan developed and progressed according to its own political agenda, with narratives of nationhood, symbolism, and memory of 1991. In Arab Iraq, the sectarian divide has been exacerbated. On the one hand, the "Shi'a revival" (Haddad 2010, 2014) – its narratives of victimhood, affirmation of political memory and religious history, and show of force – emerged. The affirmation of memory and history is commemorated ostensibly through Shi'a rituals and symbolism – such as the 'Ashura and Arba'in ceremonies in Najaf and Karbala, visits to the holy shrines, and celebrations associated with the Twelve Imams. On the other hand, the Sunni population has lost its symbolic majority despite the fact that the Ba'th regime only privileged very specific tribes and clans. The nationhood Sunnis related to under the Ba'th regime were fundamentally questioned by the moves from the margins to the center of political power by Kurdish nationalists and Shi'a Islamists.

Most of the welfare measures are directed at families of the *shuhada'* ("martyrs"). Victims of the Ba'th regime are entitled to land and money compensation for their loss and exile, whereas victims of the sectarian conflicts can apply for lower compensation. As pointed out by Khoury (2013: 248), the orders of martyrs and the different levels of citizenship associated with them by the former regime have been totally challenged in post-2003 Iraq. The new political elite that came from exile decided that the first order of *shuhada'* is composed of those connected with the ruling Shi'a elite who died in the Iranian territories fighting in the Badr Brigade, whereas those who died in Iraqi prisons under the Ba'th regime are of second order. In contrast to the situation under the Ba'th regime, those who died or had been imprisoned during the Iran-Iraq War or the First Gulf War are excluded from privileges. Thus the new regime created its own hierarchical citizenship according to its own vision – tinted by ethnosectarianism – of who is a good and a bad citizen.

For Kurdish women activists, especially those affiliated with either of the two main Kurdish nationalist parties, the Kurdistan Democratic Party (KDP) and the Patriotic Union of Kurdistan (PUK), the fall of the regime and the US-led invasion were not even a subject of conversation. Iraqi Kurdistan acquired its autonomy through the "Safe Haven" operation in 1991, which aimed to protect the Kurdish population from Saddam's military and chemical attacks. US and international nongovernmental organization (NGO) funds were welcomed by the Kurdish political elite and not debated among most activists. Some are indeed apologetic regarding the invasion that allowed the Kurdish region to become almost completely independent from the rest of the country. Kurdish women activists' enthusiasm is as strong as their experience of repression and violence under the former regime.

Among the communities targeted by the Ba'th regime, Faili Kurds were certainly the most vulnerable. Both Kurds and Shi'as, this community experienced displacement and deportation from the north of the country to the center and south as part of the regime's 1970s and 1980s policy of "Arabization." Bushra Z., quoted earlier, experienced this displacement. She is an active member of a Shi'a women's organization in Baghdad affiliated with the Islamic Supreme Council of Iraq. Bushra wants to set up a civil society organization that does not have any religious affiliation and is focused solely on the defense of women's rights.

Americans were our saviors! Until today. Unfortunately, some of our Shi'a brothers are now opposed to them, we [Faili Kurds] think that it is an expression of contempt toward us. Who else saved us from the oppression we were living? We were waiting to be rescued. According to us, the one who is against Americans is a Ba'thi, because he does not care about our suffering … How come could we refuse the help of the Americans! My family and I experienced an oppression that Allah only knows, just because we are Shi'as. If countries are sensitive to our cause and offer their help and financial support, I am honored to work with them. So, it is an honor for me, because America is a powerful country. If I am able to help, even just one member of our community, I will be very satisfied.

Bushra's point of view was common among the Kurdish activists I met; very few Arab activists speak of the US intervention in such a positive way. Bushra's words reveal the impact of suffering and a desire to be acknowledged as victims of the previous regime. Opening a new page in Iraq's history cannot be done without recognizing the pain and suffering experienced in the previous era. Bushra's words also reveal the feeling of vulnerability of the groups targeted by Saddam's regime. The Ba'th's victims, political exiles, and many other Iraqis expressed their fear of a return to the Ba'th age. The feeling of being threatened by a potential return of the Ba'thists is very strong among activists, especially those who have a record of opposition and repression. For many, this fear explains both their collaboration with the occupation administration and their near acceptance of the political situation. When I mentioned the CPA's de-Ba'athification measures, most activists who had experienced repression and exile replied, "Do you really believe that we got rid of the Ba'thists?" or "Ba'thists are still around, and some are still in power." Certainly, a desire to be recognized as victims and fear of the old regime's return characterized the transition to the new era; these feelings are at the core of understanding the political realities of post-2003 Iraq.

Postinvasion Iraq: Sectarian Violence, Conservatism, and the New Iraqi Regime

Sectarian Violence, Conservatism, Weakness, and Dysfunction of the New State

The invasion put an end to the United Nation's economic sanctions and thus had a considerable impact on Iraqis' average income. Nevertheless, the push for liberalization, privatization, and foreign investment (J. Ismael & T. Ismael 2015), especially favoring US economic interests, is a feature of the post-2003 context. Bremer felt that Iraq was still a rentier state, and the deterioration of its oil fields during the war, as well as OPEC policies, ensured that it took the country some time to be able to fully exploit its oil revenues (Bayt al-Hikma 2009). Moreover, in order for Iraq to overcome the dramatic impact of the sanctions and wars on its infrastructure, education, health, and state services, a well-managed plan of reconstruction and development would be required, a plan that had not yet been put forth because of the mismanagement and corruption[2] of its political elite (Z. Al-Ali 2014; J. Ismael & T. Ismael 2015: 13–39). Considered to be the biggest corruption scandal in history, the money for "reconstruction" – provided by the United States and the UN Programs for Development and Habitat in the first years of the occupation – had evaporated from the country (Lafourcade 2007). The money cannot be found in the city streets, buildings, and infrastructure or in the country's education, health, and welfare sectors. As pointed out by Zaid Al-Ali (2014: 103–24), corruption in its institutional form and through nepotism constitutes a major cause of political and sectarian violence in Iraq.

I argue in line with Yousif (2016) that Iraq's economic situation since 2003 has to be read as a continuation of the sanctions period. Postinvasion Iraq has pursued the path that started in the 1990s, characterized by continued deterioration of its infrastructures and state services, and this despite the end of the economic sanctions in 2003. Both Yousif (2010) and Sassoon (2016) pointed out the very "political economy" of sectarianism in Iraq and its devastating impact on the functioning of state services and vital institutions. Corruption is deeply rooted in the ethnosectarian political system that creates new forms of nepotism based on communal belongings. Iraq's rentier economy relies on its oil resources managed by the state; thus a political system characterized by ethnosectarian corruption has proven to be totally dysfunctional. Therefore, instead of addressing the

---

[2] In 2014, Iraq ranked among the ten most corrupted countries in the world.

economic and social crisis in which the country has been plunged since 1990s, the postinvasion era has pursued the crisis, giving it an ethnosectarian nature.

Moreover, the new regime seems to be following in the footsteps of the previous regime in terms of armament and security spending. The sectarian conflicts and military operation against the Islamic State organization (IS) in the north of the country explain the new regime's spending in those fields, but there seems to be no indication of an end to the cycle of violence started in 2003. Since the sanctions, poverty and illiteracy have become the main features of Iraqi society, and unemployment has reached 30 percent. There is a housing crisis and lack of basic services – such as access to running water and electricity, especially in the countryside. This is the situation more than a decade after the fall of the regime. In 2007, over half the Iraqi population lived on less than one dollar a day. Acute malnutrition has more than doubled since 2003, affecting no less than 43 percent of all children between the age of six months and five years by the summer of 2007. Forty-three percent of all households have been deprived of healthy sanitation facilities. There is a critical lack of drugs and medical equipment, and more than 15,000 doctors have been killed, kidnapped, or fled the country. Even in Baghdad, the state provides a maximum of five hours of electricity per day (Z. Al-Ali 2014; Dawisha 2009). In addition, the lack of control and stability since 2003, as well as the privatization and liberalization of the economy, provoked a drastic increase in the prices of staple goods and necessities. As a result, most Iraqis are poor while living in a rich country. No major plan or policies have been undertaken by the new regime to deal with these issues. The state, already weakened by more than a decade of sanctions, appears to be absent in its role as a social and economic provider

Between 2006 and 2007, the sectarian civil war claimed an average of 1,000 lives per week, mostly civilian, and both internally and externally displaced around 2.5 million according to the United Nations High Commissioner for Refugees (UNHCR). The weekly (if not daily) explosions and assassinations still persist today. The invasion by IS of Mosul in June 2014 and parts of northern Iraq exacerbated sectarian tensions and plunged the country again into a cycle of war and militarization.

Heba I. witnessed the rise of sectarianism, even among educated and urban intellectuals, when she returned to Iraq in 2004. She also noticed the atmosphere of chaos and lawlessness in the country.

Coming back from Yemen, I was anxious to see American soldiers walking in our streets. I wondered how I would react to it, and I was afraid of suffering too much because of it. But in fact, what hurt me very deeply was not that. When I crossed the border, I found a country whose borders were not controlled by anyone; left in surrender. I carried with me many books from Yemen, as there was nobody to control my possessions. The driver laughed when he saw my surprise at the fact that my passport was not even checked. This broke me. I don't like talking about that. But like we say, the personal is political. And everything I just said is political. I believe in that … The first thing I did when I came back was to go to al-Mutannabi to see my friends. I was shocked by the mentality I found there. People with whom I grew up experienced the wars and sanctions, all these people that I used to know for so many years were beginning to think in a very different way from how they used to think. I was thinking: "do we need a dictatorship to feel that we are all Iraqis?" Now, everyone agrees upon a way of thinking that is so far removed from how we used to think. We talk based on identity words, we categorize: "the one who opposes the war is a Ba'thi; this one is from that community, and this one is from the other." The way of thinking changed so much. It hurt me so much when I came back.

Sectarian violence impacted women's activists' everyday lives. Among the activists I interviewed, most experienced the violence of postinvasion Iraq directly through the death of a spouse, brother, sister, cousin, or neighbor. Explosives are the number one cause of women's mortality in Iraq, as well as the leading cause of damage to the healthcare infrastructure (WILPF 2014). Both women and men adapt to make their way around Baghdad; the most common strategy is to avoid crossing sectarian boundaries, staying within one's own neighborhood. In this context, a representative or public figure is exposed to violence in a peculiar way. Wafa F., for example, was married to a representative in the Fallujah Provincial Council. Her husband, a Shi'a Islamist, was killed in front of Wafa and her three kids at the front door of their house by armed men emptying by force the area of Shi'as. After the execution of her husband, Wafa was warned that she had to leave the city if she wanted to stay alive. She left with her kids and settled in a popular Shi'a neighborhood of Baghdad. A housewife for almost a decade, Wafa had to turn over a new leaf and look for a job to provide for her family; she got involved in the Al-Fazila Party, a Shi'a Islamist party, that offered her protection and support. Most of the women activists I interviewed, especially public and media figures, have received death threats or been directly targeted by violence – e.g., car bomb attacks in front of their offices or homes. Some had to flee the country or live in the Green Zone of Baghdad, but many remain in Baghdad. Some moved into areas controlled by their sects because their neighborhoods were attacked by sectarian militias.

Ibtihal I., age thirty-nine, a very active women's rights activist of al-Rabita narrated how, in an attempt to kill her, a group of men placed explosives in front of her house and made it explode in 2007. The event occurred after she had received several death threats from conservative Islamist militias in the form of phone calls and messages. Fortunately, no one was in the house at the time. Ibtihal speaks of the police incompetence and lack of will to help her find the perpetrators of the attack and provide her protection. She describes the atmosphere of Baghdad in 2006–7 and her feelings about it.

You know, in 2006 and 2007, after 2 PM, the streets of Baghdad were empty. There was no life in Baghdad. The next day, everything opened at 8 AM. But people were scared to go out very early or later than 2 PM. Violence was everywhere. Armed groups, death threats, militias – the everyday reality was terrible, frightful. Until today, you know, the value of life is lost in Iraq. Any disagreement between political leaders ends up with violence in the streets. We face death every single day; every Iraqi who goes out of his house is not certain that he will come back alive. Iraq transformed into a scene of death. Even when we have moments of joy, we feel that we are stealing those moments, and we then refrain ourselves saying *Allah yesterna* ["May God protect us"]. The worse is that we do not even have a state, a government from whom we could seek protection or complain.

The new class of politicians, selected according to ethnosectarian lines, built political support through appeals to tribe or sect rather than constructive visions of national reconstruction and Iraqi nationhood. Thus the sectarian dimension of the social retribalization observed by many that started under the Ba'th regime was pushed even further in the chaos that followed the invasion. If the retribalization carries its conservative dimensions especially in terms of women and gender issues as rightly noted by J. Ismael and S. Ismael (2008, 2007), it has also been analyzed in terms of the society's retrieval of its indigenous functioning in a climate dominated by armed Islamist militias. As observed by more recent research, such as that by Carroll (2011) and Hamoudi, Al-Sharaa, and Al-Dahhan (2015), far from resenting state law, Iraq's tribes, often embrace Iraq's state law and regard tribal law as being in cooperation with the state in maintaining order within their respective social field. Tribal Shaikhs in Baghdad (Carroll 2011) and in southern Iraq (Hamoudi, Al-Sharaa, & Al-Dahhan 2015) all expressed longing for a just, functioning state legal system and resentment that they had to take on so many roles that should have been handled by the state. In addition to this, this recent research also points out that in the current climate of lawlessness and absence of a functioning and transparent judicial system away from corruption and sectarian conflict, the tribal modes of reconciliation, being cross-sectarian in their very nature because tribes are composed of both sects, have been more efficient than the state in dealing with extremely violent sectarian conflicts. Shaikhs are concerned by the repartition of their territories according to sectarian lines as a result of conflicts of the new competing forces represented by armed militias. Moreover, because armed militias are related to the government, individuals who do not have any relation to the new political elite would turn to their local Shaikhs to administrate their issues or resolve conflicts. As rightly pointed out by Carroll (2011), during the widespread and terrible political and sectarian violence of 2006–7 and beyond, it was difficult to settle on the conflict because violence was generalized and sometimes anonymous, and only the tribal system created forgiveness and communal cross-sectarian reconciliation.

In addition to the overall insecurity that led to the death of many Iraqi women activists, most of the women I interviewed noticed how the rise of conservative gender norms affected their dress and ability to move freely in specific neighborhoods of Baghdad. Because many neighborhoods are controlled by militias and armed groups backed by conservative sectarian Islamist parties, many women have witnessed or experienced incidents regarding clothing or behavior when crossing checkpoints. Even Christian women activists prefer to wear a loose shawl over their head when moving between the capital's different neighborhoods. More generally, in Sunni-dominated cities, women often wear a *jubba* [*hijab* and long overcoat]; in Shi'a-dominated cities, such as in the southern region, women often wear a black *'abaya* over their *hijab* and cover their feet with black socks. Many of the women I interviewed described incidents such as the closing of hair salons and car bomb attacks to forbid women from driving.

In addition to sectarian violence committed by conservative Islamist militias, women political activists have also been subject to violence for being part of the opposition to the new regime. Infiltration of hooded armed men and saboteurs in the demonstration against the government is now a feature of the Iraqi political scene. More generally, an overwhelming sense of tension has been created by the violence, checkpoints, T-walls, ethnic, religious and sectarian fragmentation of Baghdad, and the dominance of competing armed militias in the streets. This feeling was expressed repeatedly to me: "Before we had one Saddam; today we have a Saddam at every street corner." Many forms of human rights abuse and indiscriminate arrests and imprisonment of civil society activists by government forces have been reported. During my interviews, I was told by many women's rights activists that the repression of political mobilization against the new regime exposes women to a double sentence: because torture and imprisonments are also synonymous with sexual violence. More generally, the case of both men and women victims of rape and different forms of torture in Iraqi prisons illustrates the failure of the new political regime to provide basic rights to its citizens. Stories of violence and repression at the hands of government forces affect the structure and challenges of Iraqi civil society mobilizations in postinvasion Iraq.

As mentioned in the Introduction of this chapter describing Medinat Al-Sadr, the generalized violence in which Iraq has been plunged since 2003 goes beyond sectarian violence opposing Sunni and Shi'a political militias. As shown by Harling (2012), the intra-Shi'a conflict has class dimensions opposing social outsiders represented by the Sadr current and other similar formations and coalitions of conservatives formed of Iraq's Shi'a middle class, the commercial elite living off the pilgrimage industry and tribes that historically enjoy close ties with the sanctuaries of Najaf, Karbala and al-Kazimiyya. In addition to this political-classist violence, there is also a very peculiar form of criminality of armed groups profiting from the very weakness of the state and the situation of lawlessness associated with it, especially in the first years after the invasion with assassinations and kidnapping for ransom. The Sunni and Shi'a armed groups targeted representatives of Iraq's modern and cosmopolitan middle class, such as doctors, professors, engineers, and lawyers living in the mixed areas of Baghdad and representing what was left of a mixed, progressive, and technically skilled population that was both the product and the basis of the modern state. For example, the Iraqi Lawyers Association declared in 2007 that since 2003, the number of lawyers decreased by 40 percent because 210 lawyers and judges had been killed since the fall (Sassoon 2012b).

The new state's weakness – its inability to provide security and respond to basic needs (such as access to running water, electricity, housing, and employment) – mismanagement, and corruption pushed Iraqis to rely on alternative sources of protection and service (Dodge 2005). In addition, according to many activists I interviewed, in line with reports of human rights abuses in Iraq conducted by Amnesty International in 2011 and 2013 regarding the abuse and neglect of detainees, the lack of respect for basic human rights by the army and security forces is common. The violent repression of the al-Anbar Sunni movement and more generally of all movements of protest against the new regime is also common (International Crisis Group 2013; Dodge 2013). Interestingly, Ala Ali's recent work (2014) on women's involvement in the al-Anbar conflict shows that women of al-Anbar expressed their attachment to the "state," positioning themselves outside sectarian belonging. For example, these women asked for the state to intervene against al-Qaeda groups rather than relying on local tribal leadership. In Sunni-dominated provinces, as Ali observes, women remain attached to the "unified state" as the protector of their lives and interests.

In a context characterized by violence and a weak state, where individuals are pushed to rely on alternative sources of protection and security, tribal leadership gained significance. It is not surprising, therefore, that a large number of tribesmen and political leaders chose to join IS in June 2014, during its capture of Mosul. After this shocking event, Grand Ayatollah Sistani – the most important *marje'* in Iraq – called for a "*jihad* to preserve Iraq," which incited thousands of civilians to join the military operations against IS. The fragmentation of Iraq along communal lines – Kurds in the north, Sunnis in the West, and Shi'as in the south – appears irreversible.

Insiders, Outsiders: A Contested New Political Elite

As the country was under occupation and directly run by the American administration through the CPA, it was clearly impossible for anyone trying to organize a group or activity inside the country to avoid dealing with the occupation administration or the new political elite. It was inevitable for Iraqis inside the country, as well as for political exiles trying to return to Iraq. Some exiled women's rights activists decided not to return because of their opposition to the occupation and refusal to deal with such conditions. Some activists did return for two or three years, wanting to contribute to the "new Iraq" but left the country again out of anger about the occupation, disappointment in the new political elite, or fear for their lives as insecurity grew and living conditions became too hard to bear – e.g., electricity cuts, lack of running water, difficulty in moving around due to checkpoints, and so on. Most political exiles who returned to the country after the fall of the Ba'th regime had obtained citizenship in their host countries, whereas Iraqi women activists "from the inside" do not enjoy such a privilege. Many political activists left the country after the explosion of violence in 2006–7, when more than 1,000 Iraqis were killed every week in explosions, assassinations, or kidnappings; some of them did settle in Iraq, especially in the Green Zone, but had their children and families stay abroad. Again, non exiled Iraqi activists could not leave the country when the situation became unbearable, even when they received death threats from militias. Moreover, most of the new political leadership that came to power after 2003 settled in the Green Zone of Baghdad with the foreign embassies and the US-led administration. The rest of the population of Baghdad, including most women's rights activists, live amid thousands of checkpoints, concrete T-walls, and barriers that divide the city according to sectarian lines.

Sarah H., an activist of al-Rafidain Women's Coalition, believes that most Iraqis were afraid of political activism itself at the time; therefore, it was only natural that political activists from abroad were the first to participate in the political process after the fall. Nevertheless, she deplores the fact that the state formation process was undertaken by an elite that had been in exile for a long time and that "Iraqis from the inside" were not represented by the new political elite. Sarah also criticizes the new elite for its sectarianism and considers its politics to be a failure.

The change was difficult to take for us Iraqis. At the beginning, we did not even realize that the regime had fallen. We were afraid to get involved, because our memory of political activism was executions and repression, and not only of activists, but also of all their families. We were still afraid of Saddam. I tell you honestly, I was among these people who could hardly believe that Saddam's time was over. We did not even believe at first that he was dead. We thought he was about to come back. Thus, even among those who had political, nationalist awareness, people were scared to get involved in politics after the fall. The people who came back from exile, they came specifically for that. They came back from exile in order to get involved and, for some of them, to serve their own interest. The Governing Council was set up very far away from the people. It was so far away from us [that] there was only the political opposition from abroad who sat around the table, with the exception of very few political figures from the inside. There was Aqila al-Hashemi who was from the inside. She got killed shortly after she was appointed to the Governing Council because she was considered to be a figure of the previous regime, this is why. Other members of the Governing Council came from Kurdistan, people who were disconnected from Iraq for decades. It is true that they came with ideas and a will to implement the transition to a new regime, from a society ruled by one party to another, more pluralistic one. But they did it by adopting the wrong behavior, a sectarian way of being. They did not succeed at all. They failed.

Clearly, an activist's view of the political elite brought to power by the coalition forces relied heavily on the nature of the activist's relations with the opposition in exile. The more they were connected, through family or personal relations, to the new elite, the lower the level of their criticism. Nevertheless, after several years in power and the formation of several governments, the new elite received harsh criticism even from those who first welcomed their arrival. Corruption and mismanagement, as well as a sectarian managing of power, were (and are still) the main criticisms of the post-2003 political leadership. Shayma N., age forty-three, is a feminist activist member of the IWN and academic at Baghdad University. She worked at the Iraqiyat Studies Center on research on women and gender from a feminist perspective. As mentioned earlier, Shayma is from a family close to the Da'wa Party. Two of her brothers were sentenced to life in prison for their Da'wa Party membership and were detained in Abu Ghraib prison; one was executed by the regime. Like many Iraqis who suffered under the Ba'th regime, especially those who belonged to opposition organizations, Shayma welcomed the fall of the regime, and despite her concerns, she was not opposed to the US-led intervention. According to her, Iraqis had no other choice because their uprisings had been repressed and silenced. Regarding the new political elite, including individuals close to her family, she explains:

If we think that people who struggled will come back occupying the position of simple advisor, we are living in Plato's Republic. I cannot understand the harshness toward people who have suffered so much. The first generation suffered enormously from the regime; maybe the second generation is now more at ease. When I used to hear about them and told about their activism, I was really proud. I wished some of them could be in power, but they did not have the opportunity to reach power or, when they came, their discourse changed into a sectarian and self-interested stand. I understand that some elements are stronger than them, [and] regional and international agendas were imposed onto them. Since the London Congress,[3] the Unites States faced divisions inside the opposition ... I did not have any opposition to their arrival to power; on the contrary, I am the daughter of a Da'wa family. These people from the political opposition undertook a dignified struggle and suffered a lot. They experienced the destruction of their families and exile; they have martyrs ... maybe my judgment toward them is influenced by the fact that I was among the people who did suffer under the regime. But you can notice that I am paying the price for a thought that I do not belong to. This is why I am paying for my identity while I disagree with them and write articles criticizing them.

Shayma has lived in Baghdad under very difficult conditions for almost her entire life. However, despite the religious and political orientation of her family, she chose to get involved in a secular mode. Shayma does not agree with political Islam, but she also does not condemn it; she does not consider religious parties' rise to power as illegitimate in itself but has criticized the new elite for its mismanagement and corruption.

Corruption was widespread under Saddam, and it was very difficult to get rid of this phenomenon. Those who came to power acted as if corruption was legitimate. These incredibly exorbitant salaries for their work convinced the population that corruption is normal. These religious parties are guilty of a great fault. It is not illegitimate that religious parties access power, as well as all the groups that struggled ... But, if you see the Parliament today, if you look at their diplomas and their level of culture and education, they are not representative of Iraqis ... Administrative corruption became legitimate when people saw incompetent individuals coming to power, people who are only following the lines of their parties and not doing anything else. People wait for their wishes to be realized, martyrs

---

[3] One of several congresses organized by the US administration and Iraqi political opposition to prepare the invasion prior 2003.

families wait for compensations … competent individuals are waiting for their turn to participate. What happened is the destruction of a dream that Iraqis believed in.

Like many women's rights activists, Shayma participates in demonstrations and gatherings denouncing corruption, mismanagement, and sectarianism and demanding democratic and transparent elections. Again, these civil society dynamics were not easy to set up because widespread insecurity did not facilitate the organization of any political action. Some activists also considered that power should have been shared between "insider" and "outsider" political opposition and pointed out that people who left Iraq for decades were disconnected from the on-the-ground realities and thus incapable of running the country.

Maha S., like many activists who never left Iraq, thinks the issue should not be about insiders or outsiders but about who cares for Iraq and will serve the country's interest rather than their own personal, political, or sectarian interests.

It became normal for these people, just because they were involved in the political opposition, to think that they deserve access to the government, even when they don't have the competence, experience, or capacity. To be from the inside or the outside is not an issue for me. When somebody has struggled so much, why doesn't he want to share with the people of Iraq what he learned abroad? Democracy, cleanliness of public spaces, public health – why not implement them here? Why don't they want the best for our children? Export what is good abroad, for example, the peaceful power transition. We are paying the price of that. I know very well that the government members, who receive exorbitant salaries, all have a second passport, a second residence abroad, and children who do not live inside Iraq. If tomorrow the situation becomes too dangerous for them, they will leave Iraq and go back to their homes abroad. They would all run away from the country. Every day I am scared; I feel the absence of security. They do not put a foot on Iraqi streets; they move around with tinted windows, escorted by dozen of cars protecting them in the front and back.

Maha points out the privileges enjoyed by the new political elite, which represent a fundamental difference between Iraqis from the inside and those from the diaspora. She criticizes the lack of interest in and knowledge about the concrete needs and realities of Iraqis. Many activists express the distance they feel between themselves – who have lived in Iraq all their lives and experienced wars, uprisings, and the sanctions period – and activists who have built their lives abroad under very different conditions. Certainly, the image of the political elite and its fancy life abroad is a fantasy of many "insider" Iraqis; many exiles and their families had far from comfortable lives in the countries in which they settled. Some women activists had lived in very difficult conditions, settling in three or four different countries and never holding a European or American passport. Some former exiles benefited from grassroots support, whether as prominent religious leaders or as "simple" activists involved right after 2003 who managed to build themselves a reputation of integrity and transparency.

Between Gender and Sectarian Quotas: The Politics of Representation and the Women of the New Regime

In Iraq as in Afghanistan, international political actors and the new political leaders insisted on women's visibility in the political sphere (Kandiyoti 2007; Khattak 2002). Under the pressure of international nongovernmental organizations (NGOs), UN-Women, and the American occupation administration, an enormous focus was placed on "women's visibility" and "political participation." As a result of this international pressure and in addition to the mobilization of women's rights activists, Iraqi politicians were urged to appoint women at decisional positions. On the ground, what I heard and observed was that women were often chosen by male political leaders to fill the quotas for each party, the government, or the Parliament. In the first years after the invasion, women's nominations for government, Parliament, provincial, and municipal councils were mainly based on family and personal relationships.

The first period (2003–5) was characterized by the presence of women who were themselves either former exiles or personally related to the families of exiled anti-Ba'th leaders. However, because the communal quota system established by the occupying powers allocates a certain number of positions and seats to each community (Shi'a, Sunni, Kurd, etc.), women of the new regime represented both their gender and their communal groups. In line with the overarching politics of the invasion's first years, competence was less important than representativeness in choosing the new political leadership.

Aziza is a forty-five-year-old former dentist from an educated middle-class Baghdadi family. Aziza's young cousin was close to the anti-Ba'th Shi'a movement and was executed by the regime in 1978. Before the fall of the regime, Aziza attended underground religious gatherings and was close to important Shi'a Islamist figures of the opposition. After the fall, she immediately joined the meetings organized by the newly returned Shi'a political leaders. Aziza organized many meetings and activities for women – primarily lectures on issues related the women's everyday lives but in the framework of Shi'a political Islam – that she called the "School of Shahid al-Sadr." As a member of the Iraqi National Association, a Shi'a political group, Aziza was appointed to the first Iraqi Governing

Council and the first Iraqi Parliament. I meet her at her home in Baghdad's Green Zone. At our meeting, Aziza tells me me that her appointment to the Iraqi Governing Council stemmed from the assassination a Shi'a women political leader.

> After she was killed – may Allah have mercy on her soul – they needed a personality, a woman, Shi'a, educated, who spoke English. As most of my studies were in English, I was eligible to join the Council. The Americans asked me to pass an English test, and after I got 7/10 on the test, they chose me out of twenty women to become a member of the Council.

Aziza also says that the US administration was at first reluctant that she joined the Governing Council because of her 'abaya. According to Aziza, many US policymakers disregarded women political leaders who wore the headscarf or 'abaya.

> The big issue I have encountered with the Americans is that they take issue with my 'abaya. I was coming to the Council in my 'abaya; I signed the Administration Treaty of Power in Iraq in 'abaya. For them [the Americans], the 'abaya refers to Iran. I have never seen Iran before; I have no link at all with Iran. The first time I went to Iran was in 2005. They [the Americans] were telling me that I was wearing the Iranian chador. I tried to explain that it is not the case. There were also these Western women that came with the Americans and were advisors in the ministries; they also disregarded us, we veiled Iraqi women, and considered us backward. I tried to explain to them that we were not that.

Aziza's narrative is interesting on many levels because it reveals the concrete interactions and the nature of the relations between Iraqis and the occupying administration. The insistence on English proficiency as a requirement for admission to the Governing Council shows that Iraqis were supposed to make the effort to communicate with the occupying forces. Iraqis had to be English speakers; the Americans did not have to learn a word of Arabic, even though they were establishing, and putting into power, the new political elite of Iraq. The reaction to the 'abaya – and confusion with the Iranian chador – reflects the US administration's total ignorance of Iraqi culture, as well as its desire to form a leadership based on its political interests and criteria of Iraqiness. The CPA needed a Shi'a Arab woman to achieve its sectarian representation of Iraqi identity, as well as fulfill its women's quota. This desired "Iraqiness" had to adhere to the CPA's criteria: not pro-Iranian and not too "backward." Their ignorance of and contempt for such a typical Iraqi garment reveals a lot about the occupying power's approach to Iraq and Iraqis. It is also interesting to note that Aziza does not always wear the 'abaya; hijab is her everyday garment because she considers the 'abaya to be impractical when lecturing at Baghdad University or seeing patients at the medical clinic. Aziza explains that she wears the *'abaya* only on "special occasions," such as religious and political events and gatherings. In Aziza's opinion, representing Iraq is a religious duty. Hence she wore the *'abaya* at the Iraqi Governing Council because it is an important symbol of Iraqi culture and a reminder – like a uniform or a religious garment – to perform her role as both a political and religious leader. The English language and garment criteria are two examples among many that show the nature of the interaction between the occupying administration and Iraqis – a clear cultural and political domination typical of colonial power relations.

Aziza became a very well-known political activist in Iraq, and as mentioned previously, she lost her son and sister in the sectarian violence. The sectarian feature of post-2003 Iraqi politics created lot of victims among the ranks of women political activists. However, not only was the violent aftermath of sectarian politics a real problem for women's activism, but it also had a direct impact on the work of Iraqi representatives in state institutions. Many government, Parliament, Baghdad municipality, and provincial council representatives told me that the distribution of committees and sectors according to sectarian belonging constituted a real problem for their work. The ministerial, parliamentary, and provincial committees are distributed in advance according to ethno/religious/political group of belonging. Thus a political leader does not choose his or her sphere of work according to competence and merit; the sphere of work is chosen according to his or her political affiliation, which corresponds to his or her ethno/religious/political belonging. Thus many representatives were appointed to positions that have nothing to do with their spheres of knowledge or competence. This situation led to dysfuntion and inefficiency within state institutions and contributed to the political and administrative chaos that dominates the Iraqi political scene.

Betul M. – a prominent Shi'a Islamist representative – believes that the ethnosectarian quota system is the root of state and government dysfunction. She represents Tayar al-Islah, a Shi'a political group founded by Ibrahim al-Ja'fari, at the Baghdad Provincial Council and faces much difficulty.

We face a lot of problems at the Baghdad Provincial Council. The greater problem, in reality, is the communal quota system. Democracy is still immature in Iraq, still at its beginnings. It is like a newborn that is disabled; it needs a lot of time and care to make it walk properly. Because of the communal quota system, the allocation of seats and committees in the council are not related to the representatives' skills or competence. I had to struggle to get on the Committee of Civil Society Organizations, because I felt that as a civil society and women's activist, it was my place to be on this committee. But once I joined this committee, I faced a lot of conflicts with the head of the committee. This man, once he became the head of a committee, thought he became the King of Baghdad. We are both elected representatives; he has his position, and I have mine. I proposed him to divide Baghdad into different zones in order to operate more efficiently. He imposed the areas where he wanted to work, and he refused to work in certain areas. Let's be honest here, the problem is sectarianism. He told me: "You take al-Sadr, al-Kazimiyya, al-Istiqlal, al-Kerrada etc. [all Shi'a areas], and I take Abu Ghraib, Tarmiyya, Mayadin and al-A'zamiyya etc. [all Sunni areas]." I finally told him that I agreed, because I cannot go to these places with my ID card and my *'abaya*. The *'abaya* is the most visible sign, as you know. And at the time, after 2005, it was dangerous. But even today, I do not know these areas or trust going there. Anyway, I cannot access these areas ... Before the fall, didn't we live all together, Sunnis and Shi'as, all neighbors? I am a Shi'a from Medinat al-Sadr, and the wife of my maternal uncle is Sunni. Before, it was normal. When the militias began to expel Sunnis from Medinat al-Sadr, my family and I we did not give any names, not one Sunni name. We also gave a *ta'ahed* ["protection contract"] to our Sunnis neighbors, in order to take these Sunni families under our protection. But this was not the case for everyone. Some people were under pressure; they felt pressure from foreign agendas, but I do not consider these people Iraqis, or even Muslims. Islam is innocent of all that. Islam made us "peoples and tribes" [quote from the Qur'an]; it teaches us respect and tolerance.

The government, cautious to show its efforts at encouraging women's participation and improving their conditions, created a Ministry of Women's Affairs in June 2004. Nermin Othman, from the Patriotic Union of Kurdistan, was appointed as a state's office minister. This ministry was framed and sponsored by UN-Women (previously UNIFEM) and other international organizations, which financed most of its activities, just as they would any other organization or civil society association. The ministry itself does not have any allocated budget and is still, according to two ministers with whom I spoke, an office inside the general secretary of the prime minister's building. The ministry has only a dozen managerial staff.

The second period (2005–10) was marked by the drafting of and referendum for the new Iraqi Constitution, as well as the legislative election that followed. Although there were very few women involved in the process of drafting the Constitution, the new Iraqi Electoral Law instituted a quota of 25 percent for women (30 percent in the Kurdish governorate) in representative assemblies.[4] While controversy surrounded Article 41, there was a general consensus on the adoption of

---

[4] According to Article 49.4 of the Constitution and according to Election Law no. 16 of 2005 as amended by no. 17, candidate's certification, 2009, paragraph 1/C, the proportion of women in the candidate lists cannot be less than 25 percent.

a women's quota; many activists see this adoption to be the result of their mobilizations, despite the fact that most women's organizations advocated for at least 40 percent. However, for many activists and analysts (Al-Nadawi 2010; Jameel Rashid 2006, 2010; Mekki Hamadi 2010), the quota brought to power "women of parties" rather than women's rights activists. In addition, the participation and "performance" of such "women of parties" in the assemblies has been very weak and mostly limited to "women's issues" (Al-Nadawi, 2010; Mekki Hamadi, 2010). Many parliamentarians and members of provincial councils, as well as candidates and members of electoral lists that I interviewed, noted that male political leaders "chose" women in order to fulfill their party quotas but had no real intention of opening space for women's concrete participation, especially when it came to important decisions. According to some activists, the idea that women were "politically incompetent" was reinforced by this quota system because women's presence in assemblies was seen as solely due to the quota, not political competence and experience. However, most activists also acknowledged that without the quota system, very few women would have been elected to the Parliament or provincial councils (Jameel Rashid 2006, 2010).

For example, the scholar-activist Ilham Mekki Hamadi pointed out in her qualitative study, "The Political Culture of Iraqi Women Parliamentarians" (2010), that 64.3 percent of the parliamentarians she interviewed refuted the idea that women's entry into Parliament has had any "impact on their traditional roles, which consist of being mothers and looking after their family." Khadija A. is a forty-year-old mathematician who directs a department in the Ministry of Sciences and Technology. In 2012, Khadija ran for Parliament on the Iraqi List of the Ayad 'Alawi, a non-Islamist and nonsectarian political group, and did not win. She spoke of her experience with this political group.

I wish we didn't need the quota to take our place, that men were not privileged, but the mentalities consider women to be incompetent. You cannot find a woman in a decision-making position. I am a leader in the Iraqi List, but I didn't attend any meetings where important decisions were discussed. I am invited only to the meetings where we are informed of the decisions that have already been made. It is the same for all the women of the List. The political leaders that we had, they obtained their position through the quota, not because of their competence. Look at our ministry, among our twelve offices, we don't have a single woman director of office, although we have many competent women. Also, if we look at our parliamentarians, they come only to occupy the number of seats required and the thirty body guards that are provisioned. The last parliament [2005–10] didn't serve women, including in the writing of the constitution.

Furthermore, Nahla al-Nadawi pointed out in her study, "Iraqi Women's Parliamentary Performance" (2010), that the interest in women's visibility did not translate into political concern for women's issues; among the 400 laws voted on between 2005 and 2010 in the Iraqi Parliament, only one directly concerned women's issues. Moreover, the focus on women's visibility has decreased as Iraq has become a less central issue for international policymakers. During the formation of the Iraqi Interim Government between June 2004 and May 2005, five women[5] were appointed as ministers; after the January 2005 legislative elections, there were only six women[6] among thirty-two ministers; and after the December 2005 legislative elections, there were only four women[7] ministers.

Since 2010, only two women ministers retained positions: Ibtihal al-Zaidy, the Minister of State in Charge of Women's Affairs, who is a forty-eight-year-old Ph.D. (Arabic Literature) and member of the Da'wa Party, and Bushra al-Zuwaidy, from the Shi'a Islamist Party al-Fazila, who is in charge of the office dealing with victims of terrorism in the Ministry of Social Affairs. The reduced number of women ministers indicates a lessening concern for women's participation in the political sphere and reveals how this "concern" was always more of a showcase than a real interest. In addition, conservative Shi'a Islamists won the majority of seats in the new Iraqi Parliament, and many activists believe that the power held by such Islamists does not serve women's rights activism. Islamist women, even if individually supportive of women's rights, have to toe their political group's line even if such implies voting for conservative measures regarding women.

After the parliamentary election of 2014, it has been difficult to follow the appointment of Iraqi representatives because the country has faced a deep political crisis caused by the invasion of IS of parts of western and northern Iraq in June 2014. With great difficulty, but thanks to the popular and Sadrist pressure, Haider al-'Abadi replaced Nuri al-

---

[5] These five ministers were Mishkat al-Moumin, Minister of the Environment; Nesreen Berwari, Minister of Public Works; Pascal Esho Warda, Minister of Immigration and Refugees; Nermin Othman, Minister of State in Charge of Women's Affairs; Leila Abdul-Latfi, Minister of Work and Social Affairs.

[6] These six ministers were Nesreen Perwari, Minister of Public Works; Nermin Othman, Minister of the Environment; Bassima Yusuf Butrus, Minister of Sciences and Technologies; Jwan Maasum, Minister of Communications; Suhayla Abdel Jaafar, Minister of Displacements and Migrations; Azhar Abdel Karim al-Shaikhly, Minister of State in charge of Women's Affairs.

[7] These four ministers were Nermin Othman, Minister of the Environment; Wijdan Mikhael, Minister of Human Rights; Bayan Diza'i, Minister of Housing and Construction; Fatin Rahman Mahmoud Shaikhli, Minister of State in Charge of Women's Affairs.

Maliki, and the government was partly reappointed through the principle of hiring "technocrats" instead of politicians. A Kurdish Islamist, Bayan Nuri, was appointed as the new Minister of Women's Affairs, and he pointed out the same issues already mentioned by former ministers: the absence of proper funding and governmental support.

Politicized Islam and Sectarianism at the Core of Women's Representatives Divide

Several measures and declarations of the Islamist Minister of State in Charge of Women's Affairs, Ibtihal al-Zaidy, provoked controversy in the Iraqi media and among women rights activists, who painted the new minister as a fundamentalist opposed to women's rights. I interviewed al-Zaidy in her office at the General Secretariat of the Prime Minister in May 2012 and discussed the controversies surrounding her. At the time, she opposed the opening of women's shelters and recommended that "women employees wear appropriate attire" in governmental offices. She explained that, on a personal level, she was not against opening shelters for women victims of abuse, such as the ones in Kurdistan. Al-Zaidy spoke about the huge number of cases she received every day and related the story of one particular woman. This woman was about to be released from prison, and al-Zaidy was helping her start her life again by finding a house and job for her. According to al-Zaidy, there was no social and political will for such projects in Iraq today; the reality of running the Ministry of Women's Affairs, which itself relies on other ministries to set up any project, made all her initiatives dependent on the will of male political leaders.

We have to convince political leaders. The opening of shelters for women must not be carried out by organizations, but put under the responsibility of the Ministry of Work so that it is under the ministry's protection. I want it to be a "State house." Just like "the house of orphans" and the "house of elderly people," it would be a "house for women without shelter" protected by the Interior Ministry. For that, I have to convince the Ministry of Work and the society. In Kurdistan, they have worked on this since the 1990s, and they have only just managed to open it. We need time for that, even if I acknowledge that it is a real necessity. You know it existed in the Abbasid period; they called it the "house of angry women." We will try not to name it like that, because this will scare men. We will call it a "house for women without a shelter" because we have women that live on the streets and don't have anywhere to go, even very young girls. We want a "house of the state" that would give them training, support them in their studies, and help them find a job and get married. If I had a budget, I could do all that, but I am actually dependent on the other ministries, and I have to convince them.

The minister also pointed out the reality, highlighted by many activists as well, at the core of her ministry's inability to truly function: the ministry was created to be merely an "advisory office" of the prime minister's office. Most women activists consider this ministry to be just a facade for the new regime to show its concern for women; there was never any intention of allocating a proper budget or giving it the same status as other ministries. The lack of funds and state support caused Nawal al-Samara'i, the former minister, to resign after six months in protest.

I entered al-Zaidy's office after several old women left; the women were visibly from a very poor background and had come to ask the minister for help. Very often, between electricity cuts, the minister receives groups of women in need. With the help of her team, the minister tries to help such women by offering financial support or helping them find housing and a job. The ministry does not have offices in the provinces, its work is concentrated in Baghdad, and only occasional trips are made to the provinces. On its website, the ministry asks women running small professional and social projects to submit a form in order to see whether the ministry can find a way to support the project. Indeed, the Ministry of Women's Affairs works as any other civil society organization; the only difference is that the ministry is headed by a woman with ministerial status and a security escort. Of course, this reality did not prevent Ibtihal az-Zaidy from morally supporting the project of women's shelters. Her insistence on the limitations of Iraqi society and political leaders sought to excuse the fact that she did not want to cross the line of conservative gender politics and be associated with liberal women's rights activism. In a very normative climate regarding women's clothes, her insistence on "appropriate women's attire" revealed her desire to perform alignment with Islamist politics.

In a context where all the Ministry of Women's Affairs' measures follow the agenda of UN-Women, requiring "appropriate attire" is a very symbolic affirmation of an Islamist agenda. According to the minister herself, all her projects and strategies – e.g. "opposing violence against women", "women's promotion" and the "gender mainstreaming campaign" – are "elaborated, written and evaluated" by UN-women; "translation into Arabic" is the ministry's role. However, Ibtihal al-Zaidy was also in agreement with most Iraqi women activists in terms of the need to preserve the PSC. In addition, she supports the reform of the discriminatory articles in the PSC and Punishment Law according to "a modern perspective that breaks the old ideas and traditions, and follows the example of other modern countries." She also expressed a desire to establish gender training programs in all state institutions and require male political leaders to attend such trainings. When I asked if the ministry was planning to follow the KRG example – i.e., partnering with the Ministry of Religious Affairs and the Union of the 'Ulema to give campaigns religious legitimacy – al-Zaidy said she never considered such an approach. Therefore, despite symbolic measures typical of Islamist politics, such as "appropriate women's attire," the ministry's politics are secular; al-Zaidy never considered including religious institutions or scholars in the ministry's initiatives.

Azhar al-Shaikhly – a fifty-five-year-old human and women's rights activist and professor of constitutional law – was the Minister in Charge of Women Affairs between May 2005 and May 2006. We discussed her experience at her parliamentary office in al-Kerrada in May 2012. She explained that unlike many women activists, she did not consider the new minister's Islamist background, in and of itself, to be a barrier to defending women's rights because *shari'a* is and has always been a main source of legislation. According to al-Shaikhly, Ibtihal az-Zaidy's lack of experience in women's rights and disconnection from women's rights activism in Iraq is the problematic point. Al-Shaikhly believed that it would be far more useful to close this "fake ministry" and create an entity that follows the KRG model of the High Council of Women's Affairs. She also said that the PSC should be preserved and discriminatory legislations should be reformed.

I am not for a specific group; I am for the respect of the law. The *shari'a* is part of the law and I am against opposition to the law. Now, there are some articles and measures related to past conditions that are now obsoletes and have to be reformed. I am for individual freedom within the limits of what is possible in our oriental culture. I also defend the Personal Status Code that is until now, apart from Tunisia and Morocco, the best guarantor of women's rights in the Arab world.

Despite their ideological differences, these two ministers are in agreement with regard to the PSC. Al-Shaikhly is from a liberal, educated Sunni family and lived all her life in Baghdad's mixed al-Kerrada neighborhood. Al-Zaidy is from an educated Shi'a family and grew up in Mosul; her father was a university professor, and most of her friends and neighbors in Mosul were Christians and Sunnis. Both al-Shaikhly and al-Zaidy emphasized the importance of respecting Iraq's "Muslim culture," considering their culture to be "specific" and "different from the West," especially with regard to women's morality and respectability. They both come from a generation that despite awareness of discrimination related to communal belonging was not structured around sectarianism and believed in a unified Iraqi "nationhood." Their divergences relate to politically oriented issues associated with the sectarian politics of post-2003 Iraq.

As Haifa Zangana points out, Baghdad turned into a "city of widows" (2007) in a country in political and economic chaos, where official estimates count 1.5 million female-headed households (mostly widows and divorced women).[8] Female representatives receive an enormous number of grievances and demands. However, despite the conservative environment that dominates Iraqi politics, the lessening interest in women's visibility and international actors' support for women's presence in the political sphere, many activists feel that the women elected in 2010 were more representative of women's concerns and less linked to the opposition's political leaders. According to many, the emergence of independent women political leaders helped to compete with party-backed women who privileged their parties' line over women's rights concerns. Several attempts were made, especially through the initiative of independent women parliamentarians, to set up a women's parliamentary caucus to unite women of different political orientations around essential women's rights claims. The latest initiative – the Parliamentary Coalition in Support of Women – was launched in March 2012; it is primarily composed of independent parliamentarians who wish to transcend the divisions in Iraqi politics – especially the Islamist/secular, sectarian and ethnic divides – around women's rights issues.

Conclusion: Women Representatives Acting between a Weak State and a Fragmented Nationhood

As pointed out by J. Ismael and T. Ismael (2015), the United States failed to achieve many of its aims in Iraq. If it removed the regime of Saddam Hussein and improved the position of Western oil companies in the Iraqi oil market, the political elite that it put in power in Iraq is not the pro-American regime it had envisioned but a regime that is inclined toward Iran. The engineering of a fragmented ethno-sectarian Iraqi state, while beneficial in the short term to the United States in the realm of oil, has important consequences in terms of regional politics and the rise of sectarianism in the Middle East and beyond. History seems to replay itself: like the British occupation of

---

[8] Although there are no precise data due to a lack of statistic research on the Iraqi population because of political reasons, this was an estimation given to me in May 2012 by the Ministry of Women's Affairs, the Committee for Women, Children and Family, and the Ministry of Planning.

Iraq in 1917, the United States aligned itself with conservative forces.

Postinvasion Iraq has been marked by the rise of sectarian violence, political chaos, and the rise of conservative Islamist forces. The CPA's institutionalization of a communal ethnosectarian political system, the coming to power of the Ba'th opposition's political elite dominated by Kurdish nationalists and conservative Shi'a Islamists with their *mazlu-miyya* ideology, and the different policies undertaken by the CPA and the new regime have exacerbated social and political tensions and plunged Iraq into unspeakable violence. The new state imposes a fragmented nationhood and grants different levels of citizenship according to its own sectarian and *mazlumiyya* version of Iraq's history. The very destruction of the state as a unifying entity, a social and economic provider, deeply impacted Iraqis social and economic life. The new regime's endemic corruption and use of violence as a tool of repression of the opposition exacerbate sectarian and political violence. As a result, women activists are working in a context where the state is weak and unreliable: it is incapable of providing basic rights for its citizens – such as security and access to basic services (water, electricity, healthcare) – and implementing a *state of law*. The overall climate of insecurity and political crisis, along with the competing powers of militias on the streets and conservative parties in power, have a great impact on women's everyday lives and shape the limits and possibilities for women's rights advocacy.

The new Iraqi regime emphasizes women's political participation in the framework of the communal system; as such, women involved in state institutions act as communal "representatives" rather than as independent activists. The women's quota and emphasis on political participation seem to stand at odds with women's current social, economic, and political realities. These policies did, however, bring women into the governmental sphere: they allowed women representatives – mainly from Shi'a Islamist and Kurdish nationalist parties – to enter government, Parliament, and provincial councils. Thus it can be argued that the gender politics of postinvasion Iraq are marked by "representativeness" rather than addressing economic and social inequalities. This brief description of the context that shapes Iraqi women's realities shows how they are caught between, in Deniz Kandiyoti's words, "the hammer and the anvil": "they have to fight both for their formal *de jure* rights that are under constant threat from conservative social forces and for their substantive rights to security and human dignity that have become the casualties of endemic lawlessness and impunity in their societies" (2007a).

4   The Emergence of Women's Groups and Networks
After the Fall of the Ba'th Regime

Introduction: A Sense of Postinvasion Baghdad University

Ehna nisa' muthaqefat ("We are women of education and culture") was a sentence I heard thousands of times throughout my fieldwork in Baghdad, during which I spent a considerable amount of time observing several university campuses: Baghdad University's main campus in al-Jadrya and Bab al-Mua'zem (Figure 4.1) and al-Mustansiriyah campuses. The huge central campus of Baghdad University in al-Jadrya, which began construction under 'Abd al-Karim Qasim and finally opened under Saddam, reveals the importance of education to postindependence regimes. The campus is so big that to visit its various departments, one must use the buses that travel from one department to another throughout the morning and afternoon. The university's degradation is visible: inside, the sanitary spaces are almost all out of order, the classrooms are in need of serious repair, and most of the desks and chairs need replacement. Such scenes illustrate a vanished past.

At Baghdad University, I immediately noticed two types of signs either plastered on the university's walls or hanging from signposts: pictures of *shuhada'* students (Figure 4.2) and signs intimating female modesty (Figures 4.3 and 4.4). The *shuhada'* signs consist of students' pictures and names and are ornamented with religious invocations or verses from the Qur'an.[1] Such signs are also visible across Baghdad – in shop entrances, on office desks, and plastered on walls surrounding houses – and suggest an atmosphere of mourning and morbidity. The signs relating to female modesty are large posters or placards with text and, occasionally, illustrations of a woman's body. The text often begins with verses from the Qur'an on female and male modesty. The illustrations often show a woman wearing "correct *hijab*," with long clothes covering her body, and a woman wearing "wrong *hijab*" or no *hijab* in high-heels and a knee-length shirt. The text also refers to "the temptations of the Devil" when pointing to

---

[1] Such verses include "Do not consider dead the ones killed in the path of God [*al-shuhada'*]; they are alive and will receive their reward from God."

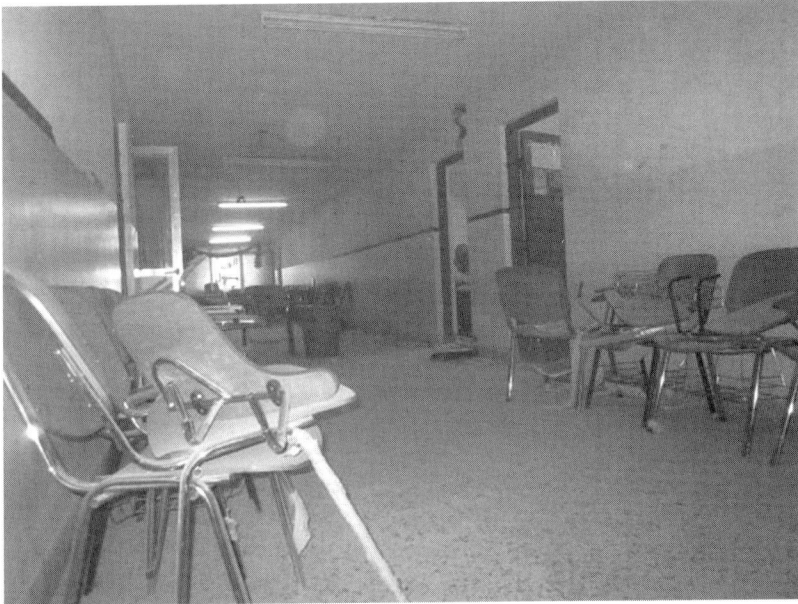

Figure 4.1 Exam day in the Department of Sociology, Bab al-Mu'azem College (May 2012).

makeup and "unacceptable gender promiscuity" between male and female students. Interestingly, some placards are also dedicated to young men, recalling a *hadith*[2] condemning likeness in men's and women's clothing and pointing specifically to skinny jeans and the "emo" controversy.[3]

Indeed, most young female students at Baghdad University cover their heads with flowery and colorful scarves and dress elegantly: large and skinny trousers, long and semilong skirts, flats or high-heels, and makeup. Their appearance is often more attuned to attending a party than a university course. Young male students' cologne can be smelled from a distance, their hair shines with gel, and their elegant shirts and trousers make them look as if they are attending a cocktail reception rather than a classroom. The matrimonial business on university campuses is common in Iraqi society because such campuses are the main spaces where young people

---

[2] The words, stories, and behaviors attributed to the Prophet of Islam.
[3] In 2012, several young men were reportedly killed by Islamist conservative militias for wearing "emo" hairstyles and tight clothes. The skinny jeans fashion adopted by many young Iraqis provoked controversy in the media and society because it was associated with homosexuality.

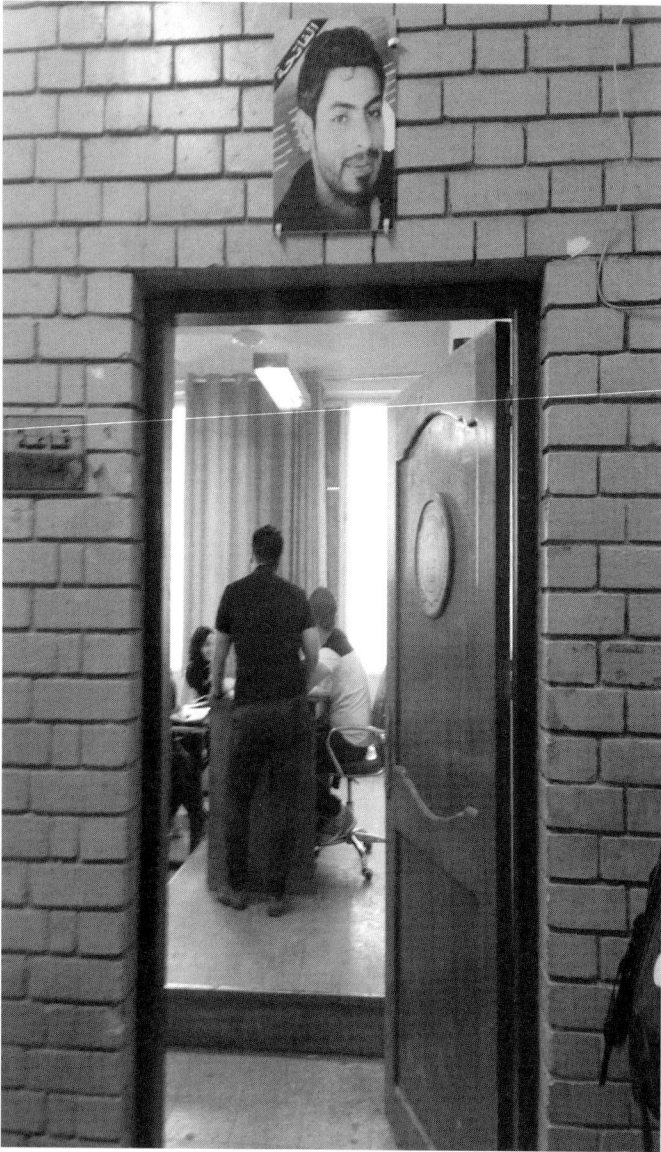

Figure 4.2 Entrance of a classroom at Baghdad University with a picture of a *shahid* hanging above the door (May 2017).

Figure 4.3 At the entrance of al-Mustansiriyah University, there are two signs commemorating *shuhada'* students. On the ground to the left, a third sign is addressed to female students, reading: "You are beautiful like the beauty and delicacy of a flower, BUT, do not be easily accessible" (May 2012).

can meet future spouses outside family supervision. I was told by family and relatives that even religious and conservative families tolerate certain styles of dressing and behaviors between female and male students that would be considered "loose" in other contexts because university constitutes the best place for young women and men to meet and eventually get married.

Almost all the women activists I met are educated; they all pursued additional education after secondary school, whether a professional course or BA, and many have done postgraduate studies. The importance of education is central to their discourse about their life trajectory and activism. Up to the present, the Iraqi education system has been centralized, and the course a student undertakes is determined by baccalaureate examination grades, not personal choice.[4] Thus many activists pursued studies based on their baccalaureate results, not on their desire for or affinity to a certain field. Work in the public sector, the main sector occupied by women, is also centralized and linked to examination grades. For these middle-class women, being educated is more important than

[4] Those with the highest grades are offered places in the faculties of medicine, engineering, pharmacy, and other natural sciences; those with lower grades have the option of social sciences, arts, and humanities.

Figure 4.4 Sign reading: "Dear female students, a woman's decency and real awareness are central to building an awakened society. Declaration of al-Mustansiriyah University" (May 2012).

pursuing a professional career; it is a social criterion that defines how they value themselves and others. Education is not directly linked to the professional position one occupies after obtaining a degree, nor is position always directly linked to the content of one's studies. Instead, university matriculation and postsecondary training are tokens of social and relational respect and consideration. There is an important generational gap between the women born between the 1950s and 1960s, who benefited from good-quality education, and women born in the 1970s, who attended university during the sanctions period and spoke of the degradation of the education system.

Today, according to UNESCO, about 23 percent of the Iraqi population is illiterate, and the situation at Iraqi universities is dramatic. Many women academics I met complained of the chaotic education system and the lack of means to teach and elaborate lectures properly. I conducted many interviews with Iraqi women academics at their offices at Baghdad University and was shocked to hear of the conditions under which they work. Because the upper levels of many university buildings are "out of order" due to electricity cuts, there is no access to functioning elevators. Thus five or six academics often share one office. It is hard to find a functioning printer, and most academics bring their own materials and internet devices.

The women academics I met often complained about the anarchic change of programs decided by their department heads, as well as power struggles between colleagues and generalized corruption that affects their administrative work. Jawad and Al-Assaf (2014) describe the functioning of the university as marked by corruption, nepotism, and chaotic administration. They note that the de-Ba'thification campaign also affected the university, resulting in the firing of 300 members of the academic staff. De-Ba'thification was followed by threats and a wave of assassinations that hit Iraqi scientists and university staff. A fair number of non-Ba'thists scientists were also assassinated or kidnapped. This phenomenon started with the assassination of the president of Baghdad University, Dr. Mohammed A. Al-Rawi in May 2003 and other members of different Iraqi universities, mainly those who voiced their opposition to the occupation, as shown by other research (Al-Ali et al. 2012; Jawad and Al-Assaf 2014). Although both female and male academics share the same overall situation of violence and corruption, women also spoke in addition of gender-specific burdens related to "prevailing cultural attitudes, social norms, and practices that are being reinforced by a general social climate of social conservatism toward women as well as widespread nepotism."

I attended several seminars and conferences organized by the Department of Sociology at Baghdad University, where I listened to Master's and Ph.D. students present their research on various subjects and professors speak of their latest academic publications. Presentations and subsequent discussions with the audience occurred as in any other university in the world, with debates and exchanges of ideas about the subjects presented. Nevertheless, a common theme of these gatherings related to the difficulty of conducting fieldwork, accessing new academic and bibliographic resources, and an overall sense of fatigue and exhaustion. One young Baghdad University lecturer made a particularly memorable remark. After listening to a well-known woman activist and sociologist's presentation on the theoretical perspectives of research in social sciences in Iraq, the young lecturer stood up during the question-and-answer session and said:

My dear Professor, what perspectives are you talking about? Look at me, I am one of your colleagues; look at my suit and shirt; look at my trousers and shoes; look at the way I am sweating. We are all sweating this way because of the heat in this venue, because there is not enough electricity to provide air conditioning! What perspectives can we pretend to talk about when we do not even earn enough to buy ourselves suitable clothes, sit in air-conditioned rooms, or come to our campus without fear. What are you talking about? Let's speak about our real issues here! Then we can speak theories and concepts.

The young lecturer's face was red with anger and sweat; his clothes were smart and elegant but visibly old and overused, especially his shoes. The audience remained silent for a few seconds, and many nodded in agreement with his words. After the session chair thanked him, the young scholar sat down, and it was someone else's turn to speak. Then the discussion around the theoretical perspectives of the social sciences in Iraq continued.

Because unemployment has reached 30 percent, the lack of interest in a university education among young people is not very surprising. Academic staff expressed despair and exhaustion with regard to the general situation of the education system and considered their "educational mission" compromised by the climate of insecurity and the new Iraqi regime's lack of provision for higher education. Because travel in Baghdad is chaotic and insecure, many lecturers expressed to me their difficulties in dealing with students' punctuality and attendance. Only upper-class people in Baghdad have a driver who takes them to work or university in the morning and picks them up in the afternoon. Most students at Baghdad University use *khat*, a taxi driver from their neighborhood, who takes them to and from campus. Neighborhood drivers pick up several students from the same area. Such drivers are often neighbors known by the local families who agree to a monthly price for the service. The farther the place of work or study is from a person's residence, the more common it is to use *khat*. People, especially women, in Baghdad would only take taxis on their own from the street in an emergency, and such rides usually entail travel within the neighborhood or very well-known journeys. As a result of general insecurity, as well as the employment crisis, it feels like most men in Baghdad have become *khat* drivers and transport has become a main component of Baghdadis' budgets.

After six months of fieldwork, I began to use public transport for both finances and research reasons; I only asked for 'Amu Abu Manal to drive me when traveling to areas of Baghdad I did not know very well. Very quickly I felt comfortable taking any taxi and using the little buses known as *keiyyat* (in reference to the car brand Kia), which are ten times cheaper. Basically, low-income people can afford only *keiyyat*; middle-class Baghdadis use *khat*, *keiyyat*, and the occasional taxi; and upper-class people have their own drivers. Some working women also drive their own cars. However, the traffic jams and the rise in car bombs have pushed many Baghdadis to prefer *khat* or public transport over the use of their own cars.

The circulation in a city fragmented by walls dividing its population according to ethnic, religious and sectarian belongings, where a checkpoint guarded by young and middle-aged armed men, soldiers, and police officers can be found at every intersection, transformed Baghdad into a city of men. Baghdadis are obliged to negotiate and anticipate their circulation according to sectarian belonging, reducing the possibilities in moving around the city. Women's circulation is surrounded by the presence of armed men. When a woman drives in Baghdad, she has to pass dozens of checkpoints on her way to work; at each checkpoint, she must roll down her window and salute the male soldiers. The infiltration of the Interior Ministry and several security forces by Islamist conservative militias, close to the main parties in power, adds to this reality a scrutiny of women's dress that has become completely normalized since 2003.

This introduction of Iraqi women's political activism since 2003 by means of a description of the situation at Baghdad University and circulation in the capital is essential to contextualizing my subject. Most Iraqi women activists are educated middle-class women, and their political discourses and mobilizations are both the product and mirror of these realities. The degradation of the Iraqi education system has affected their cultural and professional training and thus the development and nature of their political discourse. The overall situation of violence and chaos, the division of Baghdad along sectarian lines, and hegemonic conservative gender discourses shape Iraqi women activist's everyday lives. Their context of activism shapes both the possibilities and impossibilities of their activism and the conditions in which it is expressed. More important, the context stands between the personal – linked to class, communal belonging, or place of residence – and the political. My questions in this chapter are: How has Iraqi women's political activism emerged, developed, and organized since 2003? What are the main issues at stake for Iraqi women activists in relation to the new Iraqi regime? What are the different trends and dynamics that characterize women's political activism in postinvasion Iraq? In other words, what are the different forms of feminism in post-2003 Iraq?

Thinking Women's Rights Activism in Post-2003 Iraq between Local and Global Agendas

Women, Gender, and "Muslim" Civil Societies

In "Does Feminism Need a Conception of Civil Society," Anne Phillips (2002) shows how, historically, civil society has been central for women's rights advocacy and highlights Carol Pateman's emphasis on the differentiation between the domestic sphere and the "public world" of civil society. Pateman and colleagues note that focusing on the difference between civil society and the private sphere could lessen attention to the difference between the state and civil society. Feminist scholars' discussions on political obligation, freedom, and feminism insist on the importance of the context in which women's engagement in the public and private sphere should be understood (Pateman, Hirschmann, & Powell 1992). Regarding women's participation in the public sphere, Molyneux (1985) uses the notion of "practical gender interests" in the context of women's activism in Latin America, particularly Nicaragua. By means of this concept, Molyneux explains that women enter the public sphere from a social position distinctive from men's – a position shaped by the sexual division of labor. Practical gender interests arise from the concrete conditions of women's positioning within the gender division of labor and represent a response to an immediate perceived need. The notion of practical gender interests does not generally entail a strategic goal, such as women's emancipation or gender equality. Instead, "it has been argued that by virtue of their place within the sexual division of labor as those primarily responsible for their household's daily welfare, women have a special interest in domestic provision and public welfare" (Molyneux 1985). Thus, when governments fail to provide these basic needs and the livelihood of families is threatened, women become bread rioters, demonstrators, and petitioners. This notion is interesting to explore in the context of post-2003 Iraq, which is characterized by political, economic, and social crises, as well as a general state of sectarian violence.

In the Middle East more generally, the promotion of "civil society" and "gender" became buzzwords for international and transnational policy-makers in the 1990s. From UN institutions, such as UN Women and the United Nations Development Programme (UNDP), to the US administration, World Bank, and International Monetary Fund (IMF), encouraging "civil society" and "empowering women" are main features of "democratization" in the Middle East (Greenberg & Zuckerman 2006; Metcalfe 2008; Norton 1993; Rehn & Johnson Sirleaf 2002; UNDP 2001). As Islah Jad (2007) points out, the growing number of Arab nongovernmental organizations (NGOs) in general and women's NGOs in particular must be seen in the context of a broader development trend that views NGOs as vital vehicles for social change and democratization in the region. Thus most NGOs promote economic empowerment based on the neoliberal funds and politics of the IMF and World Bank. Droz-Vincent (2008) argues that under nondemocratic regimes, civil society activism in the Middle East also became a lucrative activity for educated youth searching for spaces to implement their vision of human rights and democracy in tolerable, socioeducative, and therefore not directly political spaces.

More generally, Deniz Kandiyoti (2007) notes a significant shift in the way gender issues are raised in "postconflict" contexts. As women's rights issues were framed as an integral part of national consolidation and development within the process of postcolonial nation-building in Muslim majority countries, political contestations around women's rights issues primarily took place among "internal constituencies" against the influence of former Western colonial powers. In postconflict situations, however, Kandiyoti notes that there is an internationalization of state-building under new forms of tutelage. International policymakers and their donor-led institutions propose a set of steps to building a new state, such as the drafting of a new constitution and the organization of general elections with quotas for women representatives.

The investment of the United Nations and international NGOs in women's issues has been important in the Middle East since the Beijing World Conference in 1995, adoption of the Convention on the Elimination of All Forms of Discrimination against Women (CEDAW), and Security Council Resolution 1325 on Women, Peace and Security adopted in October 2000. Jad (2003) describes the "NGOization" of women's activism in Palestine and many Arab countries; other research has analyzed this phenomenon in Jordan (Latte Abdallah 2009; Pietrobelli 2013) and Egypt (Abdelrahman 2007). According to Jad and other researchers on the Palestinian context, the post-Oslo period was marked by the multiplication of NGOs funded by the United Nations and international and European donors that significantly changed the shape of women's activism on the ground (Abdel Hadi 1998; Hasso 1998; Jad 2003, 2007; Richter-Devroe 2008, 2009). According to these studies, this new form of work led to a depoliticization and "careerization" of women's rights as "small-project logic" was carried by new professional elite women attracted to an industry of funding and projects developed around issues related to democracy, peace building, and women's rights. According to Jad (2003, 2007), the rights-based agenda of women's NGOs had a negative impact on the mobilizing potential of mass-based women's organizations and created a space for right-wing and conservative groups to stand as powerful forces in Palestinian civil society. Furthermore, Jad, Richter-Devroe (2009), and Hasso (1998) argue that NGOs promote a depoliticized activism – an activism that does not address the core Palestinian issue of the Israeli occupation and is hence perceived as irrelevant to most of the population, who therefore turn to Islamist groups.

Abu-Lughod, in her latest work (2013), provides a similar critique of women's rights activists who use an "Islamic framework." Describing women activists involved in right-based agendas as belonging to educated urban elites who "spend a good deal of energy studying, thinking, drafting position statements, applying for funds, and presenting Islam to the West (and the East) as something not incompatible with gender equality," Abu-Lughod questioned their relationship to "those in whose name and on whose behalf they work." According to Abu-Lughod (2013: 173–200), there is a profound disconnect between the lives of "grass-roots" women and the terms in which they are being "imagined" in the field of rights, including in Islamic feminist versions.

Iraqi "Civil Society" and Women's Groups

Regarding Iraq, Barakat (2005) and Al-Ali and Pratt (2009) eloquently question this politics of "rebuilding" in situations where foreign military intervention has created a state of chaos, destroyed a functioning state, and imposed a "prefabricated nation" after overthrowing a regime. The state of chaos and weakness of a regime brought to power through foreign military intervention affects both basic human rights and the concrete context in which civil society activism can be deployed. One can draw a comparison with the situation of Palestinian women activists in the 1994 formation of the Palestinian Authority, which developed a governing body resembling the formal bureaucracy of a nation-state but remained economically, politically, and geographically dependent on Israel. Thus, as Abdo (1999) argue, the absence of sovereignty and geographic cohesion result in the absence of an independent, functioning governing body and civil society, as well as a rise in general conservatism. This reality affects women's lives and women's rights activism more generally. Similar analyses have been provided on the situations in Afghanistan and Iraq because the notion of citizenship is questionable when civil society is marked by sectarian violence, the rise of conservative powers, and general impoverishment (Al-Ali & Pratt 2009; Barakat & Wardell 2002; Kamp 2009; Kandiyoti 2007; Khattak 2002).

Some research argue that, like many African countries, the post-2003 emergence of civil society in Iraq has been characterized by political quagmire and juridical anarchy; as such, civil society does not represent an entity that is autonomous from the state. Civil society organizations are infiltrated by the same sectarian divisions that characterize the state's politics and institutions (Droz-Vincent 2008; Lafourcade 2007;

Mofarah 2008). Thus these studies note the confusion between NGOs, political groups, and the government as political or politicoreligious parties, militias, and private security companies funded their own NGOs. Lafourcade (2007) also points out the widespread confusion between civil society, political parties, charitable associations, lobbyists, and business groups in Iraq since the invasion.

Regarding civil society women's groups, Al-Ali and Pratt (2009) show that the US administration put a special emphasis on women's issues in its rhetoric justifying the invasion, as well as in its political discourse justifying the occupation. Al-Ali and Pratt argue that organizations and networks dealing with women's rights and issues represented a prolific and profitable space within governmental and nongovernmental spheres. Iraqi women activists have quite a large and open space of engagement for women's issues and rights, and they represent a very important part of the new Iraqi civil society. Al-Ali and Pratt also note the "careerization," the politics or "representativeness," and the "competition for funding" that characterized some women activists' networks. Mojab (2007) is also very critical of the US-led coalition's influence on women's organizations in Iraq; she argues that it is important to distinguish NGOs from "grassroots" organizations. On a very different note, Henrizi's research (2015) on women's agency in Iraqi NGOs, which criticizes peace and conflict studies that limit so-called local agency to resist global agendas and poses binaries between local and international spaces, argues that external intervention has also created spaces for Iraqi women activists to exercise different forms of agency. Seeking to outline a concept of gendered agency that integrates a "relational conceptualization of space," Henrizi tries to show how a relational theory of space contributes to grasping "hybrid realities and notions of agency on the ground."

Sense of Freedom and Effervescence

As shown in Chapter 2, under the Ba'th regime, there were no civil society activism or pluralistic spaces for public political engagement. The General Federation of Iraqi Women (GFIW), which had been affiliated with the Ba'th regime since its creation in the 1960s, was the main space dealing with women's issues and rights. The GFIW was used as an organ of the state in that it implemented and advocated the regime's reforms regarding women and family issues. Since civil society activism was not permitted under Saddam Hussein, the notion of political activism took on a new meaning for Iraqis after the fall of the regime. Indeed, there is a "before" and "after" 2003 for Iraqi women's rights activists and political activism in Iraq more generally. The fall of Saddam Hussein's authoritarian regime paved the way for the emergence of civil society because it enabled pluralist and large political and social engagement. The formation of the first political and civil society organizations after the fall of the Ba'th regime reflected the climate of the invasion's early years: many Iraqis affected by the terrible economic sanctions and decades of political repression welcomed *al-taghir* ("the change") and hoped for a brighter future.

Most of the activists I interviewed expressed a sense of hope after the fall of the regime despite the fact that it was provoked by a US-led military intervention. I was often told, "We could only hope for better, because nothing worse than what we had experienced under the Ba'th could happen to us." Even those who were critical of the US-led occupation of Iraq saw the fall of the regime and the new political possibilities after 2003 in a positive light. For example, Rabab H. – an important feminist and communist activist, former exile who represented al-Rabita abroad, and major figure of the al-Amel and the IWN – says:

It is true, women's organizations have developed across Iraq; the new situation that ended the isolation we have been through is a considerable input. There wasn't the possibility to travel before; today we are in contact with the outside world. The use of modern technology is a huge step forward for us ... But I think that the most important point is the inner liberation of human beings from terror and fear. There still might be some effects of it among Iraqis, but there is an opening, an understanding of the facts that doesn't fall under the central and dominant authority. There is an opening, a horizon in the way problems are dealt with ... I want to insist on the fact that woman has been liberated in her thought. The woman being and, more broadly since the fall of the regime, the Iraqi being begins to liberate himself in his relation to others. Previously [under Saddam], the Iraqi was afraid to think, he was afraid to occur outside the framework established by the state. Many tragic events occurred due to public expressions of political ideas. The achievement will come when we know how to get out of obedience, submission, control, and privation. This was allowed by the conditions that followed the US occupation; for example, the Constitution grants freedom of expression and institutes it by right. Once it is a part of the right ... although the security apparatus weakens the practice of these rights. However, what we have won is the feeling for woman to be and participate in social life, her attempt to participate and criticize the injustices she suffers.

As will be discussed later in this chapter, Rabab is one of the few activists who categorically refused to work directly with the occupying forces and refused any form of direct US financial support for her civil society activities.

Despite harsh criticism of the post-2003 context, especially regarding the new political elite and outbreak of sectarian violence, the idea that this "new era" ended the country's isolation and opened spaces for freedom and positive change was widespread among civil society organizations and women's rights activists. This feeling was not only expressed by former exiles or Kurds and Islamists who came to power after 2003 but also by most of the activists I met from various political, religious, and ethnic backgrounds. Former exiles found their place in the new regime after decades of forced exile. More generally, according to many activists, Iraqis were "discovering" political and social activism after almost three decades of harsh authoritarianism.

There was an overall climate of effervescence in the first months after the fall of the Ba'th regime. Many activists speak of this period with excitement and hope: "everyone wanted to contribute to the new Iraq and find their place within it." Lamia I. is a fifty-six-year-old lawyer from the al-Sha'b neighborhood of Baghdad, where she has lived all her life. She is one of the founding members of the Women for the Sake of Women Organization and al-Rafidain Women's Coalition. Lamia speaks of her organization's formation in July 2003, as well as how she became an activist after the fall of the regime.

At the beginning, we didn't have a civil society culture. We opened the door to a space that was completely unknown for us. I began with my law office in al-Sha'b. During the first meeting we organized, forty-six people came: six men and forty women from our neighborhood in Baghdad. There were several of my former clients, women lawyers, and friends. My office was completely full; people were sitting in the outside stairs. We discussed how we were going to form our organization, membership, who would be active members, who would be ready to come for additional support, who would be the board members. This was the first meeting, and it had the ambiance of a wedding, as we distributed appetizers and refreshments, and some brought sweets. We drew the basic outline of the organization, and they asked me to be the first president, and I accepted. It was in July 2003, just after the fall.

She carries on, explaining how she learned to organize and set up activities in the spaces provided by the US-led occupying administration, the United Nations, and international NGOs.

Every Wednesday in the Congress of Associations [in the Green Zone], all the newly formed civil society organizations were gathering. I was going there with another member to listen to what was said. We learned the outline of demands, what we should do, what was to do. During these meetings, we met with national and international organizations, and then we attended trainings inside and outside Iraq on how to write a project, set it up, and launch a campaign to advocate for a cause. There was so much motivation and goodwill but no experience and no knowledge in that field. All this was in 2003.

During this period, supported by the United States, the United Nations, and international actors, many Iraqi activists started getting involved in women's rights organizations, and as the first interlocutors with international actors and the new political leaders, many former exiles were founding members of the first organizations. Furthermore, the first important women's groups and networks – such as the National Council of Women, the Iraqi Women's Higher Council, the Iraqi Independent Women's Group, and the Society for Iraqi Women for the Future – were set up by people linked to the Iraqi National Congress, which was formed after the 1991 war and works to gather a wide range of Iraqi groups from the political opposition. Many activists told me that "as they were coming from abroad" and "had the experience of democracy," former exiles knew civil society activism and funded or framed the first groups. Wafa S. is a fifty-year-old engineer, feminist, and parliamentarian; she was also among the wave of communist students to leave the country in 1979 due to regime repression. While in exile, Wafa represented al-Rabita in her European host country. She returned to Iraq after the fall of the regime and became a well-known civil society activist and figure of the IWN. She explains her role as a former exile in the new era.

If you remember well, the first demonstration in Iraq after the fall of the regime was a women's demonstration. The demands [of this demonstration] related to women's participation and presence in decision-making spheres. I got involved because I felt that Iraqi women wanted to benefit from this change and obtain their rights. Unfortunately, the regime left a legacy of twenty years of authoritarianism, where there was no civil society, no apparatus that allowed connections with international organizations and peace-building work. Iraqi society was very far away from that kind of thing. I dedicated all my time to support women's initiatives. We had reached a point that, in 2003, Iraqis didn't know how to manage a simple meeting. They didn't know how to speak or how to organize a meeting where everyone wanted to speak, everyone wanted to do something. So, thanks to the experience I got abroad, I helped set up women's associations and supported their work. I taught them how to start an organization, how to carry a project, because I knew how to deal with all these issues.

Former exiles, whether interlocutors with the US-led occupying administration or political activists played an important role in the post-2003 political life, including women's activism. Some – such as the Women's Alliance for a Democratic Iraq (WAFDI), which actively supported the invasion – even received training before the fall, during the months of preparation preceding the invasion. Nevertheless, despite the fact that Iraqi women's groups and networks were framed by former exiles, the situation evolved significantly after 2006. The explosion of sectarian and political violence in 2006–7 forced many Iraqis to again leave the country, especially political activists, who were the first targets of this overall context of violence. Moreover, according to many activists, a significant number of former exiles – those either targeted by sectarian violence or who did not get positions in the new Iraqi regime – returned to their country of exile because many had obtained dual nationality. Thus civil society and political organizations on the ground have become more and more composed of Iraqis "from the inside" since 2006 as they gained experience in civil society activism and the groups linked to the diaspora were decreasing. The outbreak of sectarian violence, despite its direct impact on activists' lives, facilitated the emergence of local and nonaffiliated NGOs. Many activists expressed their desire to be separate from party-backed organizations targeted by militia violence.

Nevertheless, according to many women activists, the activism of women's groups and networks was weakened by the overall situation of violence and division provoked by sectarianism after 2006. Ibtihal I., a prominent al-Rabita activist, comments on the impact of violence and sectarianism on the evolution of what she called the "women's movement."

The women's movement was stronger before the sectarian war, before 2006, than it is today in 2012. Now the movement itself is divided. There has been an explosion of civil society; there are now three times more civil society and political organizations. In fact, we have reached 6,500 civil society groups! I was talking to my father the other day and said: "In other countries, like democratic countries, when 6,500 people go out on a demonstration, there is a reaction from the state, the regime. Our problem is that we have 6,500 groups who are divided, mostly because of sectarianism, and a state that does not care or does not have the power to do anything about it. The state does not support us despite the fact that we have been working so hard to make democracy and civil society work in Iraq since 2003. The state itself is sectarian.

Ibtihal's words reveal the concrete impact of both the sectarianization of the Iraqi political system since 2003 and the weakness and dysfunction of the state described in Chapter 3.

Although some campaigns and mobilizations gathered women activists from all over Iraq, women's activism in Kurdistan can be analyzed separately because the Kurdistan Regional Government (KRG), which governs the Erbil, Dohuk, and Sulaymaniyah provinces, gained autonomy after 1991. International NGOs have been active in Iraqi Kurdistan since the 1990s, but still, activities and mobilizations in the region significantly improved after 2003. The impact of state institutions and government on the campaigns and mobilizations for women's rights, as well as the different historical, economic, and cultural realities of Kurdish women's activism, necessitate a separate analysis despite some attempts by Arab or Kurdish women to build partnerships. As it will be discussed in Chapter 5, some

Kurdish women activists – for example, those who were members of the IWN in the first years after the invasion – decided to leave national networks because they either felt that the "specificities" of Kurdish women were not being considered sufficiently or preferred to focus on their own issues and realities. Clearly, Kurdish women's activism evolved autonomously from that in the rest of Iraq and had its own priorities and agendas.

Dealing with Funding, the Occupying Administration, and the New Regime

As shown by Al-Ali and Pratt (2009), the US administration put a special emphasis on women's issues in its rhetoric justifying the invasion and occupation. The Coalition Provisional Authority (CPA) set up an Office of Women's Affairs because women were considered to spearhead the project of "bringing democracy" to the country. Linked to the US government and dedicated to the so-called reconstruction of Iraq, the Special Inspector General for Iraq Reconstruction (SIGIR)[5] was created after the dissolution of the CPA in June 2004. SIGIR, the United States Agency for International Development (USAID), the US Institute for Peace, the National Endowment for Democracy (NED), the International Republican Institute (IRI), and the British Department for International Development (DFID), along with other US, British, and European organizations, funded women's empower-ment, democracy, and peace-building programs in Iraq. Several funds allocated to Iraqi women's organizations dealt with democracy training programs focused on participation in elections and women's empower-ment trainings on political leadership and entrepreneurship. These donors, along with the important deployment of the United Nations Assistance Mission for Iraq (UNAMI), UN-Women (previously UNIFEM), UNDP, UN-Habitat, and international NGOs such as Global Fund for Women, Oxfam, and other European NGOs, somehow echoed the US justification to invade Iraq through the plea for "democracy" and "women's empowerment."

Regarding the different funding available (international, United Nations, United States, European, and Arab) and ways of dealing with the occupying administration and the new political elite, I also noticed – like Al-Ali and Pratt (2009) – that women's rights activists deployed strategies characterized by pragmatism. Very few people and

---

[5] It dedicated a budget of US$52 billion to the reconstruction process; see www.sigir.mil /index.html.

organizations refused direct US funding; most took "what was possible to have" in order to fund their offices, activities, and projects. Few activists were critical of the origins of funding and partnerships with the US, European, and international NGOs, even when they opposed the occupation. The different stands on the issue revolved around the idea of building a new era and bargaining a space within it. Very often I was told that refusing money had no meaning in a situation where "everything is held by the Americans." Many of the most critical of the US-led invasion argued: "'dealing with' does not mean 'collaborating with.'"

Interestingly, and in contrast to what was widely reported in most Arab and international media, none of the women activists I interviewed – even the most radical, who refused any fund that was linked to the occupying administration and were critical of any participation in the post-2003 governments – were supportive of the "armed resistance." As I began my fieldwork in 2010, militia and armed group violence marked the everyday lives of Iraqis, especially in Baghdad, where I conducted most of my interviews and participant observations. The 2006–7 sectarian conflicts and the situation of chaotic and ongoing violence were (and still are) the context in which the activists lived and worked. If I had conducted this research prior to 2006 or directly after the beginning of the occupation in 2003, it might have been possible that some activists would support the "armed resistance" to the occupation. A few activists (both Sunnis and Shi'as) told me that they were supportive of the "armed resistance" at first, as an anti-imperialist resistance. However, as soon as the violence took a sectarian shape and became mostly characterized by civilian deaths, organized crime–style crimes (kidnappings for ransom and intergang violence), and politicoreligious militias, most civil society activists denounced the violence as terrorism or organized criminality.

The organizations that were most critical of the invasion and opposed to the new regime are the Organization of Women's Freedom in Iraq (OWFI), the Iraqi Women's Will (headed by Hanaa Ibrahim), and al-Amel (headed by IWN activist Hanaa Edwar). The president of OWFI, Yanar Mohammed, is a feminist, leftist, and anti-imperialist activist. OWFI is also the organization that can be considered the most radical within the field of women's activism. Through its discourse, the *al-Musawat* journal, and the "Iza'at al-Musawat" radio program, OWFI is one of the women's rights organizations that is most critical of the new regime, especially of the conservative Islamists brought to power in 2003. OWFI's and al-Amel's main offices are situated in central Baghdad, in an area that is often targeted by militias and sectarian violence, where explosions are sadly a common reality. Despite this situation, OWFI carries on its activities and keeps its offices open to visitors and women in need of help or support. OWFI members are very political and critical. Huda A. is one such example. In her early twenties, Huda is a very active and outspoken member of OWFI, as well as a member of the Worker-Communist Party. She is very unsatisfied with the political elite in power and pointed out that the government is not willing to fund OWFI because of its liberal orientation. Her critique is focused on the religious turn in Iraqi political life; Huda believes that Islamists' power is the biggest problem the country is facing and the most important challenge to women's rights. Like most women's rights organizations that emerged in 2003, OWFI is mainly funded by international NGOs, the United Nations (especially UN-Women), and Western countries' embassies.

Rabab H., sixty-four, is as previously mentioned one of the very few activists who categorically refused to collaborate with the occupying forces and any form of direct US financial support in her civil society activities. Forced to leave Iraq in her early thirties due to communist political activism, she came back after the fall of the regime in 2003 and is now a leading figure of al-Amel, an organization she founded in 1992 in the Kurdish region, and the IWN. She was part of a leftist network of political exiles that opposed the US-led war, describing it an imperialist invasion and occupation.

We [al-Amel] are not a political organization, and we refuse the war and the use of violence as a principled position. A regime must be overthrown by its internal forces and not by foreign interferences. But despite that, we were [prior to 2003] preparing ourselves for the fall of the regime because we understood that ending the regime was in US interests, although we did not participate in any meeting or forum with the Americans. We worked as independent activists, as Iraqis, not affiliated to any party, we decided to get ready for the eventual fall of the regime. We refused to collaborate with the US army because we knew that there would be an occupation and we decided then to boycott any activity linked to the army or any US funding titled "freedom of Iraq." Until very recently, our position was to not receive anything, neither from the army nor directly from US programs. Until today, we have refused any direct support from the Americans. But now we receive funding from organizations that are US based, like the Institute of International Education, but no direct support from the United States.

The views expressed by OWFI and al-Amel activists are quite marginal within the Iraqi civil society spectrum because most organizations accepted direct US funding – such as USAID, the National Democratic Institute,[6] and the Iraqi Women's Democracy Initiative. Again, this reality is the result of a significant evolution in Iraqi political life since 2003, which followed the uprisings in the west (mainly the al-Anbar

---

[6] Founded by the Democratic Party, this institute set up important programs aimed at "promoting democracy" in Iraq.

region) and the south led by Moqtada as-Sadr. Repressed very violently by the US and Iraqi armies – a repression that is certainly at the core of the current situation of the rise of IS in the country – most of the leaders, religious and tribal, finally joined formal politics, especially the Sadrists, and became part of the new government. The Sadrist movement is today an important and heavily political trend in the Iraqi government and Parliament.

The post-2003 Iraqi political scene was mainly open to anti-Ba'thists, and priority was given to people who suffered under the former regime and political exiles and their families, people who experienced repression and torture whether inside or outside the country. Relatives and families of political exiles or people involved in anti-Ba'thist underground activities or networks inside the country had a wide scene open to them. While, as mentioned previously, political exiles founded most of the first organizations after the fall, some organizations were established by Iraqis from inside, mostly by women with connections to the opposition through family or personal relations. The leadership was often given to a woman who had a "record of opposition." Most Iraqi women who did not belong to the opposition were selected and introduced to the political arena through an exile figure, who wanted their participation due to their competence and professional experience, such as lawyers or scholars, prior to the fall.

Originally from a nonpolitical Baghdadi middle-class family with no relation to the opposition abroad, Noor S., forty-six, is a prominent women's rights activists in Iraq. Noor was introduced to women's rights groups by a formerly exiled member of the Iraqi Governing Council who was assassinated in 2004. Noor runs the 2003-founded Women's Leadership Institute (WLI), an important women's rights organization that focuses on training women graduates, political activists, and representatives and supports female education in Iraq. This is how she approaches the issue of funding:

We used to receive American funding, but we stopped our collaboration with them. To be honest, we really insist on partnership, and we think that partners are also partners in vision. If we feel that a partner wishes to make us work according to its own agenda and place its priorities above ours, we put an end to our collaboration – without any hesitation. We think that we have our own vision. We work with the Norwegians and the Swedish. I am among the people who are satisfied to work with the United Nations, although we have sometimes concerns about the bureaucratic dimension of its action, but generally, we are satisfied.

The WLI is mainly funded by the UNDP and UN-Habitat and works with several organizations and groups across the political spectrum.

We have a training program for women inside political parties, the "Women's Committees," including women from Islamist parties. I have no fundamental opposition to Islamist ideology; what I want is to nurture this ideology with a gender perspective. We want to say: "You women, you are important, do not wait for opportunities to come to you, create opportunities for yourself." We encourage them to join the decision-making process and attain powerful positions in the parties.

Noor, like most activists who never lived outside the country, has been very pragmatic regarding the occupation and the different political groups that came to power, especially the Islamists. WLI was eager to build partnerships and receive support from diverse people, as long as it enabled the group to "be active" and "serve the Iraqi people."

For the political groups that supported and prepared the invasion with the US administration and came to power after 2003 – mainly Shi'a conservative Islamists and Kurdish nationalists but also some Sunni Islamists and communists – collaboration was a necessity, not a question. However, collaboration did not exclude criticism; on the contrary, the occupation administration, especially the United States, was strongly criticized by Iraqi political leaders who came to power because some considered the occupation after the invasion to be a betrayal of their collaboration. This situation created great ambiguity, if not schizophrenia, among the new political elite: on the one hand, they were directed and supervised by the CPA and had to deal with the US administration for every political decision and, on the other hand, they were criticizing the West and its imperialist agenda in their political discourse.

Bayan A., sixty-six, is a prominent religious and political figure from a well-known religious family originally from Najaf. She counts several of the most prominent Shi'a clerics in the country among her family and was a member of Parliament in 2005; she also runs a charity organization for women and children. Her family, like most Shi'a clerical families, opposed Saddam's regime and endured violent repression under the Ba'th, including torture, prison, and assassination. Her son, accused of trying to kill one of Saddam's sons, Uday, was detained and tortured in Abu Ghraib prison, where most of the regime's opponents were held. Bayan spoke of being forced to stop working as a pharmacist due to receiving threats after her refusal to join the Ba'th Party. Despite that, Bayan never left the country and decided to dedicate her life to religious knowledge and activities; she organized underground religious gathering at her house or in *husainiyyat* in Baghdad. Living in a predominantly Sunni area of Baghdad, she faced danger when militias began to clear her neighborhood of its Shi'a population during the sectarian violence of 2006–7. Nevertheless, she decided to stay in her neighborhood and dealt with the US army and Iraqi security forces to ensure the security of her house and neighborhood. Bayan describes her mixed feelings about the occupying forces.

I refused to attend the congress for women organized by Bremer in al-Rashid Palace because I considered that it would be recognizing the occupation. But regarding the issue of sectarian violence, I had to work with the Americans because it was at that time impossible to undertake anything without the Americans. They were present everywhere; they imposed themselves on you in whatever project you wanted to set up. Listen, there is not one point of view on this; there is no mistake or fault, right or wrong; there is what happened; and there was no other choice than this. This is what happened. The Prophet – May Allah honor him and grant him and his family peace – did many things that appeared wrong but ended up being right in their result. Was Siffin a good thing for Imam Ali? He acted on a logic that I am not capable of understanding because it is beyond my understanding … The mistake of the Americans was to introduce the idea of occupation; this was a great mistake … You were obliged to work with them; they were coming to the meetings even if we wanted to organize them without them. One time, there was a Sunni leader that the Americans wanted to put forward. The Sunnis of my neighborhood refused to work in the presence of this person. I said to the Americans that I will not let that person enter our meetings because the Sunnis do not want him. Do you know what happened? This person entered the meeting escorted by them [the Americans]; he imposed himself using their support. But I had to carry on the job with them, bring back the displaced and ensure the security of my neighborhood.

Women's Groups, Actions, and Mobilizations

Women Activists' Profile: Urban, Educated, Middle Class

From the hundreds of women activists I met in Baghdad, Erbil, and Sulaymaniyah, eighty of which I interviewed, there were three main "types" who ran organizations. First were educated middle-class women with a record of political activism and experience of repression before the fall, mainly leftists, Islamists, or Kurds, many of whom returned from at least two decades of exile. Second were educated middle-class women with familial or personal links to the new political elite with or without particular activities or concerns for women's issues. Third were educated middle-class women who sometimes approach women's civil society organizations or women's political groups as entry points to a civil society "career." There is no distinct "profile" for activists not in organizational leadership positions because such activists came from incredibly diverse backgrounds and grassroots bases from the very poor to the lower middle class. However, the first and second categories are the most common characteristics of those in leadership positions within civil society organizations.

Many women found work opportunities in civil society organizations; those involved in parties even used such opportunities as a springboard to a political career. The women activists are aware that they occupy their actual positions as MPs and members of a provincial council or an executive position within their political groups mainly as "women representatives" or as leader of a women's group or organization. Thus it was first as a representative of a communal and a gender identity that most Iraqi women activists accessed the political arena after 2003. The post-2003 era opened new horizons and possibilities for a certain class of people: the most educated, and those who opposed the regime. Many women I interviewed traveled outside Iraq for the first time after 2003 in order to attend workshops, meetings, or conferences for their organizations or political parties. This reality created a feeling of elitism among Iraqis because political activists were seen as enjoying special privileges. It is, of course, difficult to talk about the point of view of the "Iraqi street," but throughout my time in the country, my family members, friends, and acquaintances voice many harsh criticisms of certain organizations and personalities. I hear accusations that such organizations or individuals follow their own personal interest, search for money and privileges, or are corrupted – accusations that seem not altogether unfounded. Such instances illustrate both the mind-set of many Iraqis, who greatly distrusted the new political leadership, and the reality of widespread corruption, which affects women's civil society organizations as in any other sphere.

It is not easy to identify or classify organizations according to labels such as "grassroots" and "elite," as suggested by Mojab (2003, 2004, 2009) in her research on Kurdish women groups. Mojab draws a clear line between the two types of organizations: the independent grassroots organizations are political and more feminist oriented, and the affiliated organizations are depoliticized and "small project" oriented. As pointed out earlier, the post-2003 political and civil society spaces were invaded by US, UN, and NGO funds and programs. The situation of political chaos and widespread insecurity left most activists with little space for action and very pragmatic strategies. If "grassroots" means the poor and lower- and middle-class masses, then only Islamist organizations and tribal leaders can pretend to have a large grassroots base. Most civil society and independent women's organizations have a limited audience and space of action because Iraq's everyday political life is marked by sectarian, tribal, and social divisions.

Women's Groups, Networks, and Organizations

The difficulty in determining the number of women's organizations reveals one of the main features of the current situation: chaotic state institutions and public administration. It is difficult to obtain precise data regarding the number of civil society organizations formed since 2003. Between 2003 and 2010, there were 4,807 NGOs registered with the Ministry of Planning, at least 203 of which were exclusively dedicated to women's issues.[7] In the context of general corruption, where many political leaders were accused of setting up fictitious organizations, diverting international aid, and laundering money, Law No. 12 was passed in 2010. This law attempts to allow greater scrutiny of organizations by forcing them to provide proof of an independent office and activities on the ground. Iraq's administrations, which are just as chaotic as its overall political context, have made it very difficult for organizations to obtain authorizations because there is a prohibitive amount of paperwork that must be submitted. This has led to the reality that many important and well-known organizations are still awaiting their authorization. Moreover, training and workshops on how to obtain authorization were still being organized in Baghdad by Iraqi activists in 2012. I attended a workshop for civil society activists on the new law in Baghdad in April 2012 and was struck by the fact that even the organization hosting the training, the al-Rafidain Women's Coalition, had not yet managed to get authorization.

According to the Iraqi Committee of NGOs, between 2010 and June 2012,[8] there were 665 registered organizations (sixteen registered since January 2012), including forty women's organizations. Many activists I interviewed considered the current legislation to be a burden on civil society organizations because they now had to dedicate time to dealing with administrative procedures. In addition, it is important to point out that NGO does not necessarily mean civil society organization because many NGOs are in fact party-backed organizations. This situation is very revealing of the evolution of the Iraqi political context and its main features; there was real civil society and political effervescence after the fall of the Ba'th regime, but it was accompanied by widespread corruption linked to the chaotic and uncontrollable environment. After its establishment, the government's attempts to control and organize

---

[7] According to the Office of Registrations of Non-Governmental Organizations affiliated with the Ministry of Planning, which I visited in June 2012, and the head of the Committee of Non-Governmental Organizations in Baghdad, whom I interviewed, this number excludes Iraqi Kurdistan. According to the UNIFEM (2007) report, "The Women's Movement in Iraq," 120 women's organizations in Iraqi Kurdistan were excluded.

[8] This corresponds to the last time I visited the Office of Registration of Non-Governmental Organizations in the Ministry of Planning.

public and political life have been tumultuous and emblematic of both its inability to fulfill a relevant legislative framework and its disorganized, corrupt institutions.

Having met and interviewed eighty women activists in Baghdad (primarily), Erbil, and Sulaymaniyah who are active in more than forty organizations,[9] groups, and networks dealing with women issues in Iraq, I can classify these diverse women's groups into five categories: secular and not politically affiliated groups, secular party-affiliated groups, Islamist groups, ethnic and ethnoreligious-oriented groups, and women of the new regime.

Secular and Not Politically Affiliated Groups   Although the frontier between civil society and government or political parties is very blurry in post-2003 Iraq, there are many organizations, groups, and networks of women that formed independently of political parties, religious groups, or the new government. Their founding members may have a clear political affiliation, but the activities and membership are not linked to a specific political or politicoreligious group or orientation. These types of groups constitute a significant part of Iraqi women's activism and civil society; indeed, these networks and groups form what many activists consider the Iraqi women's movement. The most important network that represents this category is the IWN. Although many of its members are party-affiliated political activists, IWN itself is not affiliated with a specific political group. Some of the other organizations that fall into this category do not deal exclusively with women's issues, such as the al-Amel Association or the Tamuz Organization for Social Development. Some of the most important and active women's organizations in this category include the Baghdad Women's Association, the al-Rafidain Women's Coalition, OWFI, the Women's Leadership Institute (WLI), the Women Empowerment Organization based in Erbil, and Asuda based in Sulaymaniyah. Other organizations are more specific in their advocacy, such as the Iraqi Women Journalist's Forum (IWJF), which works for women in the media sphere but also on broad women's rights issues such as sexual harassment and the PSC. Most of these organizations have branches in several cities in Iraq. There is also the Iraqiyat Studies Center, which was active until 2010 and had publications and research from Iraqi women scholar-activists. Many of the members of these groups also interact with other Arab women's networks and organizations – such as the Arab Women's Tribunal, the Arab Women

---

[9] All the organizations, groups, and networks that constitute my sample are listed in the beginning of this book.

Lawyers Network, and the al-Roaa Network – but their activities within these networks are specifically focused on Iraq and the Iraqi context

Secular Party-Affiliated Groups   This category is mostly composed of Kurdish women's organizations, which are associated with the two main Kurdish parties: the Kurdistan Women's Union, which is linked to the Kurdistan Democratic Party (KDP, headed by Mas 'ud Barzani) and based in Erbil, and the Kurdistan Women's Union (Zhinan), which is linked to the Patriotic Union of Kurdistan (PUK, headed by Jalal Talabani) and based in Sulaymaniyah. Al-Rabita can also be considered a party-affiliated organization because most of its members belong to or gravitate around the Iraqi Communist Party. The same is true for the Kurdistan Iraqi Women's League. Still, the reality of al-Rabita's current activities and modalities of actions on the ground brings it very close to that of any other independent civil society organization.

Islamists Groups   Most of the groups that fall into this category are communal-political groups, such as Sunni and Shi'a Islamist women's groups linked to Islamist political parties or movements. Cross-sectarian Islamist groups do not exist in Iraq. Groups in this category include women's branches of political parties, since every Islamist party has a women's branches, and organizations linked to a party or movement. Such groups are very important in terms of their quantity, activities, and visibility. Hawa'una (the Muslim Women's Organization in Iraq) and the Muslim Women's League in Iraq, which are affiliated with the Islamic Supreme Council of Iraq and the Da'wa Party, respectively, have branches in the south of the country (the majority Shi'a area of Iraq). By contrast, the Islamic Women's League in Iraq, a Sunni Islamist women's organization, has its main branches in the west of the country (the majority Sunni region) and is a member of the International Islamic Forum for Family and Women, a transnational Muslim network. Similarly, in the Kurdish region, there are many important Islamist Kurdish women's groups, such as the Kurdistan Islamic Sisters Union linked to the Kurdistan Islamic Union.

Ethnic and Ethnoreligious-Oriented Groups This category includes groups such as the Assyrian Women's Union and the Association of Chaldean Women. Most of these groups are also members of secular women's groups and networks, such as the al-Rafidain Women's Coalition or the IWN.

Women of the New Regime This category includes political leaders, parliamentarians, women with governmental positions, and members of party or institutional women's committees such as the Iraqi Parliament, provincial councils, or municipalities. Most of these individuals set up their own organizations or are members of women's groups and networks; they are the main links between the government and civil society or NGOs.

Actions and Mobilizations of Iraqi Women's Groups and Networks

Whether women political activists got involved in women's groups or social and humanitarian organizations, their initiatives and campaigns cover a wide range of activities that I have broken down into three categories: democracy and human rights mainstreaming; humanitarian, health, social, and educational work; and political lobbying and civil society mobilizations.

Democracy and Human Rights Mainstreaming The activities, campaigns, and initiatives framed by US and international funds – such as Colin Powell's Iraqi Women's Democracy Initiative launched on March 8, 2004 – were widespread within Iraqi women's groups and networks. Iraqi women political activists also work on initiatives aimed at *taw'iyya* ("awareness raising") and *tathqif* ("culture raising") around democracy and human rights, which include references to CEDAW and Security Council Resolution 1325 and trainings on gender mainstreaming, the media, and organizational and leadership skills. Many meetings and conferences were organized during the drafting of the new Iraqi Constitution to explain the basic elements of democratic institutions, elections and constitutional rights. Iraqi women were at the forefront of campaigns promoting participation in both the elections and the referendum on the new constitution.

Humanitarian, Health, Social, and Educational Work NGOs and civil society organizations act as real substitutes for the state's social and welfare institutions. These activities are very diverse and cover different types of needs, such as distributing allocations to poor families, widows, and the disabled; help with housing, electricity, and running water; opening nurseries, orphanages, and free health clinics; training in literacy, sewing, and computers; educational campaigns on hygiene, breast cancer, and maternity needs; and legal aid services for abused women. Most such activities are implemented in partnership with the relevant ministry despite the fact that most of the funding is international aid. Women's rights activists also have launched several educational campaigns related to child marriage and what is commonly known as *zawaj al-Sayyid*, consisting in unions contracted outside the civil court by a religious or tribal figure. Activists have been instrumental in promoting marriage in the frame of the PSC that guarantees legal protection for women and forbids child marriage.

This category also includes initiatives funded by the United States, international organizations, and private foreign companies under the rubric "women's empowerment," such as small-business projects and microcredits. These initiatives considered entrepreneurship as a pillar of democracy and worked in partnership with women's groups dedicated to professional and business work.

Institutional weakness and the state's failure to guarantee basic public services forced women's groups and organizations to mainly rely on international funds, even when dealing with very basic issues such as access to running water and electricity. I was very surprised to discover that even Members of Parliament and the Provincial Councils of Baghdad rely on NGO funds rather than public services. Betul M., fifty-two, is a representative in the Baghdad Provincial Council of Medinat al-Sadr, where she grew up. She is also the head of the Iraqi Women's Organization, which is associated with her political group. She is very well known within Iraqi women's networks for being active, helpful, and "close to the people." I met Betul several times – once at a meeting organized by the al-Rafidain Women's Coalition on the implementation of UN Resolution 1325, where she gave a speech; another at a gathering of al-Rabita, which was celebrating International Women's Day in Ferdaws Square; and once at her office at the Baghdad Provincial Council. Sitting in the living room of her apartment, which is situated just above the offices of the Iraqi Women's Organization in the al-Kerrada neighborhood, we talked at length about her activism and work.

My work is exhausting, you know; there are many responsibilities. It is very hard because people need so many things. If I had these responsibilities in a context of stability, when basic needs are fulfilled, if life was simple and agreeable, nobody would care about me. However, in the context where the state is so weak, when people are in such need, it is normal that the citizen turns to its representatives to complain, or even hurt them sometimes. It is because people don't see anything from politicians – no security, no services, no stability – nothing "has fed them from hunger and protected them from fear."[10] Today, there is no protection from hunger or fear … It is easier now to work and ask for funds from NGOs than the

---

[10] This is a quote from Verse 4 of Surat Quraich (106).

government. If I want to deal with basic services in a neighborhood, it is easier for me to ask for funding from an NGO than from the government because the administrative process and control make it take years to obtain anything. It will be so complicated and so long, and I need to fix some very urgent problems. It is a pragmatic approach. We have so many emergency issues: water, electricity, and basic needs. We cannot wait until the government builds social housing; we have to find concrete solutions.

Betul also mentioned the difficult conditions in which she works and the insecurity that obliges her to lie about where she lives and have constant protection, because she was almost killed by a group of armed men during a visit to families of explosion victims. Betul's account is one of several I heard from women representatives in Baghdad. Many women representatives spend their time dealing with very basic issues: degraded sidewalks, flooding due to neglected infrastructure, electricity, water, housing, domestic violence, and family conflicts.

This dependence of women's groups on international funds, mostly UN and NGO funds, is very revealing of the blurry line between civil society groups and political and governmental organizations. In addition, any group linked to a political party is supported by its own networks. This is especially true for Islamist or religious-oriented organizations, which have their own financial support in addition to international funds. There was a clear competition for funding between women's organizations, especially after 2005. After the Iraqi general elections of 2005, there was a weakening of international funds and support because the United Nations and international actors considered that Iraqi institutions and government were now responsible for fulfilling the needs of its population. Most of these activities were implemented in partnership with relevant ministries, such as the Ministry of Labor and Social Affairs and the Ministry of the Displaced and Migration.

In addition to activities that run alongside those of other women's organizations, Islamists women's groups are also involved in a variety of activities that cover almost all aspects of women's lives. Shi'a and Sunni Islamists, in their own respective neighborhoods and regions, provide welfare and social and cultural services within their specific framework of Islam and using their own funding and support. In addition to their humanitarian, health, and social assistance – especially dedicated to orphans, widows, and elders – Islamists offer a wide range of free services: traditional religious trainings (fiqh and Qur'an); training in computers, sewing, and hairdressing; marriage counseling; and grants for the marriages of young couples.

Political Lobbying and Civil Society Mobilizations   When I began my fieldwork in 2010, ending the occupation and the departure of foreign troops were no longer at the core of women's mobilizations. In November 2008, an agreement was ratified by the Parliament that fixed the progressive withdrawal of coalition troops for the end of 2011 and set up parliamentary elections in which Sunnis would have more representation. This political agreement and organization of elections gave the general impression of regained sovereignty, and thus mobilizations against US troops lost strength despite the atmosphere of uprisings in the region in late 2010. Some activists I interviewed participated in demonstrations celebrating the departure of troops at the end of 2010. Thus women activists concentrated their mobilizations on women's legal status in the Constitution and in the PSC, as well as issues of sectarian politics and violence, public and welfare services, and denouncing state dysfunction and political corruption.

Since the fall, Iraqi women's activism has revolved around two main issues related to women's political representation and legal status: lobbying around the quota system and the PSC in reaction to Decree 137 (reformulated as Article 41 of the Constitution). As shown in Chapter 3, lobbying on the quota system gathered Iraqi women political activists from across the political spectrum (from liberal leftists to conservative Islamists); some groups even proposed a women's quota of 40 percent in representative assemblies instead of the 25 percent ratified. Most independent groups and personalities opposed the questioning of the PSC on sectarian bases. Secular activists, but also Sunni Islamist and Christian women activists, believed that Article 41 threatened women's rights and weakened the unified PSC. Shi'a Islamist women supported the article, arguing that Iraqis must be free to choose their *mazhab* ("juridical religious school") when dealing with family and private matters. The IWN demanded an abrogation of the article and proposed a draft PSC and Penal Code that would reform the articles, instructions, and laws that still discriminate against women.

Since at least 2008, the adoption of legislation that would protect victims of "gender-based violence" and constitute a legal basis for the struggle against domestic and sexual violence has been an essential project for women activists in Iraq. A law "combating domestic violence" was adopted in 2011 in Iraqi Kurdistan that encompass a wide meaning of gender-based violence that includes "any act, speech or threat that may harm an individual of the household physically, sexually and psychologically and deprives him/her [of] freedom and liberties." The law implies a criminalization of forced or precarious marriages, female genital mutilation, and many forms of what is commonly defined as violence against women. A special court and a general directorate specially in charge of "combating violence against women" working in conjunction with the Ministry of Health in coordination of the Ministry of Labor and Social Affairs as well as the Ministry of Interior ensures both the implementation of the law through penalties and/or imprisonment and the protection of victims with the appropriate support, such as shelters and health and social services. The adoption of this law was the produce of the activism of women's rights and civil society organizations, as well as the participation of media networks, prominent politicians, and a significant part of the Iraqi Kurdish government in conjunction with NGOs and UN-Women.

In the rest of Iraq, such law does not exist, and women's rights activists have drafted several versions of a law comparable with the one in Iraqi Kurdistan in an attempt to submit it to a vote in the Iraqi Parliament in vain. As mentioned in Chapter 3, the debate around the legalization of shelters for women victims of abuse emerged several times in Iraqi public and media discourse. The most recent attempt to legalize shelters was launched in the context of the invasion of IS at a time when shocking images of Yazidis women enslaved by the terrorist group were spread across the media. Launched by the OWFI in late 2016 with the support of MADRE and despite involving a very wide range of women's rights and civil society organizations and being supported by prominent NGOs, the campaign did not receive any positive answer from the Iraqi central government.[11] OWFI is the only organization that has opened shelters for women victims of abuse because they are still illegal in Arab Iraq despite being sponsored by the government in Iraqi Kurdistan. Since the invasion of Mosul, OWFI has also open shelters for women and children victims of violence and sexual abuse in the hands of IS soldiers.

Since 2016, women and civil society organizations have renewed their attempts to propose legislation to "combat gender-based violence" using the invasion of IS and its systematic use of sexual violence as a legitimating frame of advocacy. For them, it is urgent to provide shelters and legal protection for women victims of "religious terrorism." Their

---

[11] See the letter and signatories at www.madre.org/press-publications/human-rights-report /open-letter-un-security-council-government-iraq percentE2 percent80 percent99s-ngo -shelter.

former attempt was in 2015, and the proposed law stayed in the Iraqi Parliament without ever being submitted to vote. Conservative Islamist parties that came to power through the US-led invasion and occupation of Iraq opposed any attempt to adopt such legislation, considering it as "against religion" and a threat to the "integrity of the family." Bushra Al-Aubadi, a prominent lawyer and member of the IWN, explained in a meeting organized by the Iraqi Women Journalist's Forum in May 2017 that some leaders of political parties objected during their meetings with women's rights activists that such a law would not only be against religion but also would question the Iraqi Penal Code, which allows *ta'dib al-zawja* ("correction of the wife"). Men of the leading Islamist political parties insist on privileging of *al-sulh* ("reconciliation of spouse") before any separation and on naming shelters *dur amina* ("houses of protection"), intending to Islamize the terms of the campaign that they perceive as too secular. However, most religious authorities were less reluctant than the Islamist parties in power, and as is often the case, Ayatollah Sistani expressed his will not to interfere, considering that in a civil state such matters should be agreed on by the people.

In the Kurdish region, most organizations were formed in the 1990s; their agenda and activities differ quite a bit from those in the rest of Iraq. Some organizations based in Baghdad have branches in the Kurdish governorate and some Iraqi Kurdistan based organizations have branches in Baghdad, but they all work independently. Since the Kurdish governorate has its own parliament, and government, Kurdish women activists mobilized differently, and many are not concerned with or involved in women's rights activism in the rest of Iraq. As I show in Chapter 5, the Kurdish government and the region's political realities have led to a situation where most women's initiatives are linked to the government and international NGOs' decisions and campaigns. The significant mobilization of women's rights activists around the issue of honor killings and female genital mutilation (FGM), which culminated in a national campaign against violence against women, ended with the 2011 adoption of a law that criminalizes excision and all forms of domestic violence against women.

Along with mobilizations around the Constitution and women's legal rights, women civil society activists were at the forefront of mobilizations for welfare and social protection laws, against corruption, advocating freedom of expression, and criticizing governmental salaries and "institutionalized corruption." Most of the independent women civil society activists I met participated in the "Civil Initiative to Preserve the Constitution," which was launched in 2010 to apply pressure on the government, as well as mobilizations denouncing "terrorism," sectarianism, and state incompetence in providing basic public services. The IWN took a strong stand with regard to Iraq's independence from foreign interference; it supported federalism and denounced human rights abuses in Iraq. Activists also raised the issue of the disappeared and prisoners of the antiterrorism campaign who are still detained without judgment, as well as the police and security forces' use of violence during demonstrations.

The impact of the Arab uprisings was at first more visible in the Kurdish region, especially in Sulaymaniyah, where the Maidani Azadi movement mirrored its Tunisian and Egyptian counterparts in components and claims. Independent women activists in Sulaymaniyah participated in several demonstrations demanding transparency and more democratic state functioning, pointing particularly to the autocratic hegemony of the two main Kurdish parties in power. Mainly, Islamist women rights activists, independent women intellectuals, academics, and individuals from nonaffiliated groups supported the Maidani Azadi mobilizations, although some were angered by the movement's "twisting" by Islamist groups.

As pointed out by Zaid Al-Ali (2014:125–60) and in line of my own observations (Ali 2016, 2017), under Maliki's first term (2006–10), there were no mass protests in Iraq because the population was plunged in a sectarian war, and the opposition to the new political system was an armed opposition. During Maliki's second term (2010–14), the Arab uprisings reached Iraq, and protests started. February 25, 2011, was called the "Day of Rage." Thousands took the streets despite the fact that Baghdad was declared a "no-drive zone." The security forces killed twenty demonstrators, but a 100-day deadline was set under the pressure of the Sadrist and the demonstrators. More recently, in the context of the invasion of IS, ordinary citizens, civil society, and women's rights activists launched a strong grassroots movement on July 31, 2015 (Ali 2016, 2017). From Basra and Baghdad's Tahrir Square across Iraq, this movement has expressed citizens' general exasperation at the corruption and mismanagement of the post-2003 government – corruption and mismanagement epitomized by electricity cuts and a lack of public services. These protests quickly turned into a massive popular movement – supported even by the prominent religious figure Ayatollah Sistani – vilifying Iraq's postinvasion regime and demanding radical reforms. Every Friday since, demonstrators have gathered in the main public squares of Iraq's big cities, including Najaf, Nasiriyah, and Basra, and echoed the slogans of the protestors in central Baghdad: *Bi-ism il-din baguna al-haramiyya* ("In the name of religion we have been robbed by looters") and *Khubz, Huriyya, Dawla Medeniyya* ("Bread,

Freedom, and a Civil State"). Demonstrators consider the new regime's corruption and sectarian politics to be directly responsible for the formation and spread of IS.

The protest was launched by ordinary citizens not affiliated to any political party, civil society activists and part of the Iraqi left, especially the Iraqi Communist Party whose leader Jassim Alhelfi became a figure of the movement. The Shi'a Islamist Sadrist movement joined the protest, and its leader, Moqtada al-Sadr, joined the sit-in – that started on March 18, 2016 – in front of the concrete T-walls of the Green Zone in the capital. If many civil society and women's rights activists are critical of the involvement and possible hijacking of the popular movement by the Sadrists, others were far more nuanced. Hanaa Edwar, head of the al-Amal Association and a prominent figure in the IWN, was very hopeful regarding the developments of the popular protests when I met her in the Al-Amel offices in al-Kerrada, central Baghdad, on March 22, 2016, the day she visited the sit-ins with a delegation of IWN activists. Despite remaining critical of the Sadrists' populism and conservatism, especially regarding gender matters, Edwar expressed her support for the protesters and a positive view of the Sadrists' involvement. She believes that Moqtada al-Sadr's presence pushed the Sadrists' wide grassroots proletarian base into the streets in a show of unified nationhood and citizenship, especially at a stage when after weeks of mobilizations some protesters, tired of being in the streets every Friday, were starting to go home. Many women's rights activists who participated actively in this movement of protest emphasized the importance of linking gender equality advocacy with the struggles for religious and class equality. The IWN activists insist on the preservation of equal citizenship for Iraqis from all ethnic and religious backgrounds as a cornerstone of the preservation of women's legal rights. Pro-government thugs with sticks and knives attacked protesters regularly, resulting in a demonstration on February 12, 2017, organized by civil society groups gathered around *Tahalef al-Islahiyun* – the Coalition of the Reformers – that led to the death of ten people, including one policeman, and hundreds of wounded. In addition to the abolition of the ethnosectarian quota system and the denunciation of corruption, the demonstrators were calling for a reform of the Electoral Law in order for it to include nonsectarian, small, and secular parties.

Conclusion: Post-2003 Iraqi Women's Activism – Between the Local and the Global

Whether involved in women's groups or social/humanitarian organiza-tions, women's initiatives and campaigns cover a wide range of activities mainly aimed at substituting the state's (lack of) welfare and social func-tions. In such a context, women activists operated with great pragmatism with regard to funding. Within the broader political and sectarian crises, the general corruption and weakness of the Iraqi state have pushed many activists to rely on foreign rather than state funding. Since women's groups and networks were mainly funded by US, UN, European, and international donors, their activism, programs, campaigns, activities, and even vocabulary were deeply influenced and shaped by the financial support they received. Similar programs, campaigns, and activities could be found across women's organizations, from liberal feminists to conservative Islamists. Thus, going back to Molyneux's (1985) notion of practical gender interests, I argue that Iraqi women entered the public sphere from a social position distinctive from that of men, a position shaped by the sexual division of labor. Their practical gender interests arise from the concrete conditions of life and represent a response to an immediate perceived need: security, healthcare, poverty, the education system crisis, and diverse forms of social constrains such as religious conservatism. However, as clearly shown in this chapter, given the dys-function of the state, their reliance on foreign funds, NGOs, and UN programs also shaped their activities according to neoliberal views of women's "empowerment" and "agency." Thus their practical gender interests are imbricated to global agendas, disconnected from their con-crete realities, but opening spaces for them to exist politically.

The US-led occupation's instrumentalization of women's rights under the banner of "democratization," followed by the UN and NGOs, opened a space for women to enter the social, political, and civil society spheres. Thus it can be argued that the space to be a politically or socially active woman and advocate for women's empowerment within liberal, leftist, or Islamist frameworks opened right after the fall of the regime, along with career, work, or social possibilities for many women. Clearly, the unifor-mity of activities and the "careerization" of professional women's rights organizations constitute an important feature of women's activism in Iraq since 2003, as with many countries in the region (e.g., Egypt, Jordan, and Palestine). Democracy, human rights, and gender mainstreaming cam-paigns were implemented across civil society, as well as across the political spectrum. Iraqi women activists all worked on similar initiatives: *taw'iyya* ("awareness raising') and *tathqif* ("culture raising") around democracy, human rights, and gender, which included references to the Convention on the Elimination of All Forms of Discriminations against Women (CEDAW) and Security Council Resolution 1325, as well as training on gender mainstreaming, media, and organizational and leadership skills. Many meetings and conferences were organized during the drafting of the new Iraqi Constitution in order to explain the basic elements of democratic institutions, elections, and constitutional rights to Iraqis. Iraqi women activists were at the forefront of campaigns promoting participation in the elections and the referendum on the new Constitution. Thus, in the context of the US-led occupation, the "NGOization" of Iraqi women's activism contributed to blurring the lines between secular and Islamist activism in terms of the activities and initiatives implemented and the repertoires of rights used, because many invoked human rights, "culture," and "Islamic" rights. Neither the secular nor the Islamist activists involved in these platforms question the middle-class neoliberal feminist discourse of empowerment and gender mainstreaming carried out by NGOs and UN programs. In fact, the disconnect between the lives of "grassroots" women and the terms in which they are being "imagined" in the field of rights, including in Islamic feminism versions described by Abu-Lughod (2013: 173–200), is indeed very present in Iraq. However, Islamist women activists supported by their political parties developed a wide welfare and social support network for impoverished "grassroots" women in addition to their political and legal Islamic lobbying. In this sense, the Islamists' audience is clearly wider than the IWN, for example. However, "Islamic" charity-oriented activism, although addressed to a wider audience, is not necessarily more adapted to the realities of impoverished and nonurban, non-middle-class, noneducated women.

Returning to Henrizi's depiction of the "hybrid agency" of Iraqi women's activism – as not simply implementing the programs given by the networks of funding but also not acting as entirely independent actors – my own observations and interviews lead me to question this conceptualization. However "hybrid" Iraqi women activists' relationship with global donors has been in their spaces of interaction since 2003, it is grounded in a context that defined the terms and deployment of their activities and initiatives. This context is marked by the devastating effects of the invasion and occupation on Iraq social and political life. Thus, although I find Henrizi's attempt to complicate the activist-donor relationship interesting, I think looking only at donor-activist interactions within specific spaces is too limited to really understand the nature of the relationship between local activists and global donors. Following the

Figure 4.5 Office of the Organization of Women's Freedom in Iraq in central Baghdad (March 2012).

Figure 4.6 Meeting organized by the Women's Leadership Institute in Nadi al-'Alwiyya on female education (April 2012).

Figure 4.7 Meeting organized by the Iraqi Women Journalist's Forum in Nadi al-Nafet (May 2017).

Figure 4.8 Delegation of the Iraqi Women's Network joining the sit-in with demonstrators gathered in the capital Green Zone (March 2016). (*Photo credit:* Iraqi Women Network. All rights reserved.)

theoretical framework of my research, I believe that looking at the relationships between donors and local activists is only looking at one of many dimensions of Iraqi women's activism to investigate. Moreover, the fact that global donors propose, or impose, programs on "women's empowerment" and "women's political participation" that stand at odds with women activists' concrete realities is also a characteristic of the activist-donor relationship. In addition, the same actors who propose these programs, mainly US-led donors, bear responsibility for the main obstacles that women activists face: economic crisis, sectarian chaos, and the rise of conservative forces.

Thus post-2003 Iraqi women's activism is characterized by pragmatism in relation to a political context marked by occupation and sectarian violence, "NGOization," and a blurred division between civil society and party-backed or governmental institutions. In this state of political crisis, women activists became involved primarily as "women" because the political terms set by the US-led occupation and new political elite highlighted "women's empowerment and political participation" within a democracy mainstreaming rhetoric. However, independent women's groups and personalities managed to develop their work at the grassroots and participate in nonsectarian civil society mobilizations that pressured various Iraqi governments to implement welfare and social support and struggle against corruption. The work of independent and nonaffiliated women's groups and networks, as well as women of the Sadrist movement in line with the growing opposition to the new regime, questions the very nature of the post-2003 political system. Since 2011 at least, Iraq's women movement has been divided in terms that are comparable with the divisions that characterize women's rights activism in the 1940s, as described in Chapter 1: on the one hand, women affiliated with the elite in power, mostly conservative, both secular and Islamist, demand social and political reforms; on the other hand, the women's rights groups involved in the more radical political opposition, both secular and Islamists (mostly Sadrists), demand a full questioning of the post-2003 regime (Figures 4.5 through 4.8).

Kurdish activism was not extensively covered in this chapter because its specific context requires separate analysis; even my fieldwork among Kurdish women activists in Erbil and Sulaymaniyah differed greatly from my experience in Baghdad. Chapter 5 deals specifically with women's activism in Iraqi Kurdistan and focuses on the relationship between Kurdish women's groups and the Kurdish Regional Government (KRG).

5 Kurdish Women's Activism in Iraqi Kurdistan

Introduction: A Sense of My Fieldwork Experience in Erbil and Sulaymaniyah

My fieldwork in Erbil (*Hawler* in Kurdish) and Sulaymaniyah differed greatly from my experience in Baghdad. My fieldwork in Iraqi Kurdistan was more limited due to its length, three months total, and the fact that I did not master the Kurdish language.[1] I conducted my interviews in Arabic. In addition, I did not live with a Kurdish family, and I am not related to any Kurdish person. My main two entries points to Iraqi Kurdistan were the French IFPO branch in Erbil and a Kurdish family friend. Sayyid Jamal was a close friend of my departed uncle (husband of my maternal aunt Lamya), 'Amu Abu Heba, because they had served together during the Iran-Iraq War. Sayyid Jamal used to say that not only 'Amu Abu Heba look very Kurdish, with his blue eyes and fair skin and hair, but he is considered a member of Sayyid Jamal's family. Indeed, I was welcomed and looked after by Sayyid Jamal and his wife and daughter in Erbil. They helped me with a family inheritance issue I had and in getting to know the Iraqi Kurdish context. The IFPO provided me with a home in Erbil and, through them and the French Cultural Center, I managed to get some very useful contacts in Erbil and Sulaymaniyah(Figure 5.1).

One of my first concrete encounters with the context of Iraqi Kurdistan involved my mother's shares in an old hotel in Shaqlawah (north of Erbil) and its Kurdish owner. Tensions were high between this Kurdish hotel owner and my mother and I because we were two Arab women coming after more than two decades to reclaim a little piece of property. The hotel shares were originally bought by my grandfather, Jedu Musa Shaaban, and the family used to holiday there over the summers in the 1970s. However, my uncles and aunts had sold their shares in the 1980s and 1990s because they worried that the roads in the Kurdish region would be cut and were in a difficult economic situation due to sanctions.

---

[1] Sorani and Kurmanji are the main Kurdish dialects spoken in Iraqi Kurdistan.

Figure 5.1 Nowruz celebrations in front of Sulaymaniyah town hall (March 21, 2012).

My mother was the only one to retain her part because she was in exile in France at the time. The hotel had been sold at least three times since, and the Kurdish owners never thought that the Arab owner of this tiny part would ever return to claim ownership. With the help of Sayyid Jamal, who represented my mother during the price negotiations that took place in Kurdish, my mother's part was finally sold. I was struck by the tensions between ourselves and the Kurdish owner, his wife, the state employees dealing with property, and every other Kurdish individual we dealt with in this process. It made me realize how deep Arab-Kurdish tensions ran. In every interaction, my mother and I insisted on the fact that we were opponents of the Ba'th regime and political exiles.

In Sulaymaniyah, my "Arabness" also yielded some negative experiences. I knew it would be too difficult to rent a flat on my own there as a young, single Arab woman. Such would have been possible if I was perceived as a Western woman, because a French (white) colleague managed to get a flat on her own. I was thus obliged to be accompanied by my mother in the very long and tiring administrative process of obtaining a residency card that would allow me to rent a flat. The administrative process looked exactly like my experience in Syria, although in Damascus I did not need a family member and was able to rent a flat on my own. Just as in Damascus, the security apparatus of the Kurdish authorities was present at every step of the process. I had to register as a "foreigner" at the police station, where I was interrogated at length about my personal life, my reasons for staying in Sulaymaniyah, and my intention not to "stay for good." In state office waiting rooms, I sat with hundreds of other Arab Iraqis who were fleeing the sectarian violence in Baghdad or other cities. It made sense that Arab Iraqis, especially men, were considered with suspicion by the Kurdish authorities because they wanted to protect Iraqi Kurdistan from the violence that has ravaged post-2003 Arab Iraq. Many Kurds I met randomly criticized me for not speaking Kurdish and openly expressed their exasperation at being "invaded" by so many Arabs.

These experiences in Erbil and Sulaymaniyah led me to understand that it was far more convenient for me to use the "exile in France" dimension of my identity rather than my "Iraqi Arab" one in approaching many Kurdish women activists. However, many signs of Iraqi folklore were visible in Erbil and Sulaymaniyah; for example, in Kurdish cafés and restaurants, Nazem al-Ghazali was the most common singer played, and people seemed to know his lyrics by heart. Most Kurdish individuals over the age of forty master Iraqi Arabic. However, the young generation does not speak Arabic. To my surprise, most of the youth who did attend Arabic classes at Erbil and Sulaymaniyah Universities or the French Cultural Center were learning Levantine dialect, not Iraqi dialect (Figure 5.2). Thus, in my attempt to build a degree of trust, I chose to highlight my situation of political exile in France at most interactions with Kurdish women activists, making it clear that I belonged to the side that opposed the Ba'th regime. The fact that I belong to a family of the political opposition made a huge difference to the people I approached and allowed me to build a good relationship with some Kurdish women activists, especially those who had been in exile in Europe. Interestingly, I got along very well with Islamist Kurdish women activists because they were eager to know more about my life "as a *hijabi* Muslim" in France; for them, my "Muslimness" seemed to go beyond my "Arabness."

Erbil and Sulaymaniyah are two very different cities. Erbil is the economic capital, the place where the neoliberal economic growth of Iraqi Kurdistan is most obvious. Apart from the beautiful Salaheddin Citadel and the old souk in the city center, most of its buildings are new. In addition, traveling in the city requires a car, because most of its recent roads are wide avenues. Big and newly built hotels are visible almost everywhere, revealing the circulation of money, business, and investment companies. Malls are the main sites of socializing in Erbil; both Sayyid Jamal and several women's activists I got to know brought me to a mall on

Figure 5.2 Psychology Department at Sulaymaniyah University (April 2012).

several occasions for eating and shopping. One can find all the symbols of the neoliberal consumerist economy there, from Levi jeans to the Carrefour supermarket and fast-food restaurants. Since the explosion of violence in the rest of Iraq, Erbil has become the main city for international NGOs, where all international events and activities are held. Many Iraqi women's organizations based in Baghdad set up international workshops and meetings in Erbil because the capital is considered too dangerous for foreigners. Erbil and its province are dominated by the Kurdistan Democratic Party (KDP) of Barzani. It is also the Kurdistan Regional Government (KRG) capital and the place where the Kurdish nationalist parties' hegemony can be most felt. Erbil is where political correctness and allegiance to the two main Kurdish nationalist parties are most perceptible. Most of the political activists I met there were predominantly pro-government; they were the least critical of the Iraqi Kurdistan authorities and the most politically correct. Interestingly, I was also told by many that Erbil's population is the most "conservative" of Iraqi Kurdistan. Sulaymaniyah, by contrast, is considered the most "open-minded" city.

Sulaymaniyah is indeed very different from Erbil. It a mountainous city where very few foreigners or international events are seen. To use a normative word, it could be described as very "authentic" in the same sense that I found Damascus. There are still very few malls and supermarkets; most of the places for shopping are little stores owned and managed by local families. The city has several green spaces, beautiful old souks, and restaurants that predominantly serve local food – all much cheaper than in Erbil. Interestingly, although Sulaymaniyah is the strong-hold of the Patriotic Union of Kurdistan (PUK) Party of Talabani, it is also where the most pluralistic political groups and opinions can be found. I met many activists of the opposition there, and even members of the main nationalist parties who reside there were more critical of KRG politics. In Erbil, the demonstrations of Maidani Azadi were almost taboo or not taken seriously by most activists; in Sulaymaniyah, by contrast, many women activists participated in the Maidani Azadi demonstrations. Many of them considered it the "Kurdish Spring," in reference to the Arab uprisings, and were very outspoken in demanding a more transparent and democratic political system.

In terms of the religious and cultural atmosphere, both Erbil and Sulaymaniyah are visibly Islamized cities; mosques, small and large, can be found in each of their neighborhoods. The *hijab* is worn mostly by middle-aged and older women in the "Kurdish style" – a loosely wrapped shawl with some hair uncovered, which can be tossed back over the head when it slinks to the shoulder. Some women, both young and older, wear a *hijab* similarly to the rest of Iraq, covering all the hair and worn with either long, large clothes or fashionable, tight clothes and visible makeup. Very few women wear the "Islamist type" of *hijab*, which consists of a *hijab* and a long robe of similar color covering the whole body. Young men were likely to wear Western-style clothes, mostly jeans and t-shirts, whereas middle-aged and older men wear traditional Kurdish clothes: a *serwal*, shirt, jacket, and a keffiyeh wrapped around the head. Women would wear traditional Kurdish clothes, such as those shown in Figure 5.1, for special occasions. The few Friday prayers I attended in both Erbil and Sulaymaniyah, in different mosques in the cities' centers, were only attended by a small number of mostly older women. I could understand some words in the imams' sermons – such as *al-Anfal*, *Saddam al-la'in* ("Saddam the cursed"), and *shuhada'* – after which all men and women were crying. I was marked by the way in which memories of victimhood from the al-Anfal campaign are still very vibrant in the Kurdish cultural atmosphere. The trauma of the Ba'th regime's ethnic cleansing campaign is very present in the religious and political dis-courses, as well as in personal conversations among people.

As I did in Baghdad, I spent time observing university campuses, women's organizations' offices and centers, and places where women activists gathered and organized their activities. I also conducted interviews with leading members of Kurdish state institutions related to women's issues, mainly the General Office in Charge of Women's Affairs, local offices in charge of the struggle against gender-based violence, and several women's shelters. My first observation was that there are numerous institutions dedicated to women's issues, "women's committees" are given importance within most political parties, and there is a plethora of events and campaigns related to women's issues. The campaigns around female genital mutilation (FGM), honor killings, and gender-based violence were supported by the Kurdish authorities; the support and funding provided by the authorities were visible in the several governmental institutions dedicated to women. In most of the events I attended, "women's dignity" was advocated in the "name of the Kurdish culture," and women's rights issues were always invoked within nationalist rhetoric. In this frame, Islamists and official religious authorities seemed to agree and work in partnership.

This chapter explores the main issues at stake for women's activism in Iraqi Kurdistan. In particular, I explore the relationship between gender issues and Kurdish nationalism in Iraqi Kurdistan. I try to answer the following questions: How do Kurdish women activists situate their struggle for women's rights within the Kurdistan Regional Government (KRG) framework? What are the different trends that characterize Kurdish women activists? Are there alternative voices outside formal women's organizations that propose their own agendas regarding women's issues?

Women's Rights Activism in Iraqi Kurdistan

Women, Society, and the "State" in Iraqi Kurdistan

Since the 1960s, the region that constitutes today's Iraqi Kurdistan – the provinces of Dohuk, Erbil, and Sulaymaniyah – has been shaken by political and military conflicts involving Kurdish opposition to the Iraqi central government. As shown in the first part of this book, the Kurdish nationalist leadership and the Kurdish population suffered from harsh repression under the Ba'th regime, which reached the stage of ethnic cleansing at the end of the 1980s with the al-Anfal campaign. All the Kurdish women activists I met and interviewed from across the political (nationalist, communist, Islamist), religious (Muslims, Christians), and sectarian (Sunni and Failis) spectrum were involved in the nationalist struggle in one way or another. They all recalled their experiences of discrimination and oppression under the Ba'th regime, as well as the meaning of nationalist struggle. As Shro A., a woman activist from Sulaymaniyah, explained:

What we had to struggle against, in addition to other forms of discrimination, was Arab chauvinism; not Arab people, but chauvinist ideas. I can say that the Kurdish movement was a part of our everyday lives; we were struggling on everyday issues. Being a Kurdish activist was the direct response to the oppression we were experiencing as Kurds.

The repression of the Kurdish uprising of 1991 – called *raparin* among Kurds – in the backdrop of the Gulf War, ended up with the coalition imposition of a no-fly zone, "safe haven." The three provinces' separation from the rest of Iraq since 1991 pushed the region's autonomy even further, and the region became almost completely independent from the central government. Since the establishment of the KRG, commonly called the "Kurdish state," the region's political, social, and economic dynamics evolved autonomously from the rest of the country. Most of the Kurdish activists I interviewed drew a clear line demarcating before and after *raparin*, which is very similar to the way Arab Iraqi women activists described before and after 2003. The post-*raparin* period was characterized by the opening of Iraqi Kurdistan to the "outside world": nongovernmental organization investment in civil society, especially for women's activism, and the building of the "Kurdish state" after the first general election in 1992. Nevertheless, this process was accelerated in 2003 due to the end of UN sanctions and the intensification of NGO and foreign presence in the country. The "internationalization" of post-2003 state-building expanded the region's autonomy, which materialized in the establishment of federalism in the Iraqi Constitution of 2005.

More generally, according to Bozarslan (2009), the Kurdish population and elite of Iraqi Kurdistan experienced significant changes over the past two decades. The population is now predominantly urbanized, and the Ba'th-imposed retribalization of the 1990s did not take place in the Kurdish region because it was outside Ba'th political power. Moreover, the Kurdish leadership has moved from a kin-based, traditionally religious-oriented (Sufi, especially Naqshabandyah and Qadiriyah) form of political leadership to a more youth, educated, urbanized, individualist intelligentsia (Bozarslan 2009: 21). However, the changes described by Bozarslan can be nuanced by the impacts of the decades of war, military conflict, economic sanctions, and 1990s political clashes between the two hegemonic nationalist movements – the KDP and the PUK – on Kurdish society and the KRG. The most common evidence is the status of education and literacy: the region's seven universities were only established after 1991, and according to the Iraqi Family Health Survey of 2006–7, more than 43.3 percent of women are still illiterate in the region. Recent research on kinship, households, and communities in Iraqi Kurdistan, such as that by King (2014), shows how much Kurdish society is dominated by tribal kinship; the male figure of the father is still considered to be the head of the household, the tribe, and, by extension, the society. King also demonstrated how control over female sexuality through the notion of honor, which is built around the symbolic value of the intact hymen, is still an essential feature of gender representations and practices. In line with Fischer-Tahir's (2009) ethnography on gender representations and symbolic violence in Sulaymaniyah, King's research also shows how ideas of purity and honor are associated with women's behavior and considered an essential dimension of gender relations and practices. Despite the changes described by both Fischer-Tahir and King – shifting gender norms and relations as consequences of urbanization, globalization, changing labor markets, and wider access to education – their ethnographies show that patriarchal gender relations and norms are still prevailing features of Kurdish society. Women mainly carry the responsibility of family honor and are considered the "bearers of Kurdish culture."

Several studies have investigated the notion of honor and "honor crimes" in Iraqi Kurdistan. Mojab (2004) and Begikhani (2012, 2005) both adopted a feminist approach that engaged with the intersections of gender and nation, feminism and nationalism. Mojab's very critical analysis of the Kurdish nationalist leadership, which she considers to be patriarchal and authoritarian, also shows the importance of class and political economy in "honor-based crimes." Begikhani stresses the impact of militarization and tribalism of Kurdish society on gender norms and representations. She also mentions the rise in "religious fundamentalism," which she interpreted as a backlash against Western influence in the region. Alinia's research (2013) on gender-based violence is the most recent and well documented; she chose to call such actions "crimes in the name of honor." Based on a qualitative study conducted in Erbil, Sulaymaniyah, and various small towns and villages in 2007 and 2008, Alinia's study looks at victims of "crimes in the name of honor," the responses of women activists and social workers in women's shelters, and the crimes' perpetrators. Alinia argues that violence and murder in the name of honor are characterized by theirs focus on controlling female sexuality. However, using an intersectional feminist approach, she also argues that such crimes cannot be seen as a problem entirely related to gender and sexuality; they are not isolated from the "oppressive structures of ethnicity and class." According to Alinia (2013), this violence is also strongly connected to collective identity construction, boundary-making, and community maintenance, as well as tribal social organizations and the drawing of boundaries based on national, ethnic, and sectarian beliefs and conflicts. In Iraqi Kurdistan, such violence has to be related to the formation of the nation-state and foreign interference, as well as the context of a century of war, ethnic oppression, displacement, militarization, state violence, dictatorship, national oppression, widespread illiteracy, and socioeconomic marginalization. Thus, according to Alinia, these processes must also be seen in relation to political structures – i.e., the nature of the state, political system, Kurdish nationalism, the Kurdish movement, and these actors' gender politics.

I concur with Alinia's complex intersectional approach to gender-based violence in Iraqi Kurdistan. As shown by Yuval-Davis (1997), experiences of gender-based violence and oppression have been subordinated, in many postcolonial contexts, to those of ethnicity and nation. Moreover, in line with Alinia, I also show in this book that demands on women's bodies and sexuality and the consequent violation of their individual rights and freedoms become more politicized and brutal in situations of war, militarization, occupation, and ethnic and sectarian conflict. Thus, gendered representations of the nation and the collective become especially important.

The legislation regarding honor crimes corresponded to Articles 128 and 130 to 132 of the Iraqi Penal Code of 1969, which originally reduced the sentence for crimes involving "honor" motives (Begikhani 2012). After the establishment of the no-fly zone in the early 1990s, the first Kurdish Parliament refused to repeal these laws, allowing killing in the name of honor to persist (Begikhani 2005). Ten years later, killing in the name of honor was criminalized in all parts of Iraqi Kurdistan by the PUK and the KDP administrations. Other legislative measures regarding gender-based violence were undertaken by the KRG under pressure from Kurdish women's organizations. The law prohibiting violence against women is one such example; passed in 2011, this law specifically mentions FGM, a practice still widespread in the countryside, and domestic violence. The KRG also adopted legislation imposing a women's quota of 30 percent in representative assemblies; Arab Iraq adopted a women's quota of only 25 percent. The pressure of women's rights groups was instrumental in passing all such legal reforms, and all – including nationalists, Islamists, and communists – consider these reforms to be important steps in the struggle against women's oppression. For example, Tory Hawbesh is a network of more than twenty women's groups and organizations founded in Sulaymaniyah in 2005. It is composed of a very diverse political spectrum: the Union of Women of Kurdistan, which is affiliated with the KDP; Zhinan (the National Union of Women of Kurdistan), which is affiliated with the PUK; local women's groups, such as the New Life Organization for Anfal's Women; and Islamists women's groups, such as the Kurdistan Islamic Sisters League (affiliated with the Islamic Union Party) and the Sisters' Organization of Kurdistan (affiliated with the Islamic Group Party). All these organizations initiated and/or supported the various campaigns that were launched with the support of the KRG and international NGOs, especially the gender mainstreaming and gender-based violence campaigns. Nevertheless, as I explore in the next sections, opinions vary on the efficiency of these legal measures, as well as definitions of women's rights activism more generally.

However, questions of sexual violence and the memory of the specificity of women's experience of al-Anfal campaign are still selective and fragmented, as shown by Choman Hardi (2011) and Karin Mlodoch (2012: 205–26). In addition to the striking lack of response to the immediate needs of victims and survivors of past crimes, the experience of sexual violence was still very much a taboo. However, after the fall of the Ba'th regime in 2003 and the establishment of Supreme Iraqi Criminal Tribunal on the Anfal campaign as part of the prosecution of the former regime, sexual violence committed by the Iraqi army was revealed, and the memory of rapes started to emerge, although in a limited and selective way, in the political and media discourse (Mlodoch 2012: 205–26).

Women's Rights Activists and the KRG

All research on women's activism in Iraqi Kurdistan concurs on the fact that the post-1991 era represented a turning point for women's activism (Al-Ali & Pratt 2008, 2009, 2011; Alinia 2013: 83–108; Begikhani 2005, 2012; Mojab, 2004, 2007, 2009). However, the nature of this turning point is debatable among scholars analyzing Kurdish women's activism. Mojab's research (2003, 2007, 2009) is very critical of Kurdish women activists' attempt to associate nationalism with the defense of women's rights. According to Mojab, Kurdish nationalism in Iraq has historically been, and remains, patriarchal and overshadowed the women's rights agenda. Although Iraqi Kurdish women have been involved in the struggle for Kurdish rights for many decades, Mojab posits that until 1991, their struggle was mainly focused on gaining national rights for the Kurdish people, not on the pursuit of gender-specific agendas. Mojab (2007, 2009) is very critical of both the "NGOization" of Kurdish women's activism, especially through US funding, and the hegemony of the two main Kurdish nationalist parties, especially their agendas and initiatives since 1991. Mojab also argues that Kurdish Islamist-nationalist movements and Kurdish secular nationalism both stand in the way of transformative gender politics and hinder a feminist analysis of and struggle against gender-based violence and inequalities.

The critique of Al-Ali and Pratt (2011, 2008) of the Kurdish women's movement in Iraqi Kurdistan are more nuanced than Mojab's analysis. They argue that despite the two main parties' political hegemony and women's organizations' lack of independence, post-1991 Iraqi Kurdistan has been an appropriate framework for women's rights activism. For Al-Ali and Pratt, it is women's groups and organizations' lack of political independence that is problematic, not the fact that they support Kurdish nationalism. Al-Ali and Pratt (2011, 2008) argue that it is not nationalism per se that is an obstacle to women's rights in Iraqi Kurdistan; instead, it is women activists' inability to engage with the disjuncture between nation and state that poses significant limitations to their struggle.

I concur with Al-Ali and Pratt because their analysis does not try to conceptualize nationalism and feminism as compatible or conflicting but rather looks at the evolution of women's rights activism and Kurdish nationalism within the peculiar context of post-2003 Iraqi Kurdistan. Thus nationalism per se does not represent an obstacle to Kurdish women activists. Moreover, as in many postcolonial contexts, nationalism and women's rights activism overlap. Most Kurdish women activists I interviewed – whether nationalists, communists, or Islamists – articulated their women's rights advocacy within the struggle for the defense of Kurdish culture and the Kurdish nation. Shawbo S. – a member of the Women's League of Kurdistan[2] and a prominent communist activist in her late fifties – expresses very clearly her women's rights and Kurdish nationalist activism.

We were working underground as the Kurdistan branch of the Iraqi Women's League before 1991. We directly linked women's issues to the issue of the liberation of the Kurdish people. Our oppression existed on many levels: the occupation and abuse of Kurdistan by the Ba'th regime, as well as the overall male-dominated mentality that oppressed women. Our struggle was against all that together at the same time, like one general struggle; there was no possibility to distinguish between the liberation of the Kurdish people and Kurdish women. We were organizing literacy campaigns in the countryside [and] social and welfare support for women and families. This was in the 1970s. We were working to educate [and] provide health and support to women. At the same time, we were supporting the Peshmerga in their struggle. Men were the first targets of war, but women, they were the ones who carried the society and the family when men were at the front or dead. Women also participated in transporting weapons and rations, as well as

---

[2] The Women's League of Kurdistan (*Rabitat al-mar'a al-kurdistaniyya*) was a branch of al-Rabita until 1991, when it became autonomous.

news and letters to the Peshmerga. Women participated in the nationalist struggle in all ways possible.

As in Arab Iraq, Kurdish women activists' advocacy for women's rights has been shaped by the network of US, NGO, and international funds they receive. Thus Islamist, communist, nationalist, and governmental women's groups have implemented very similar campaigns, such as lobbying for a women's quota, gender mainstreaming, UN Security Council Resolution 1325, the CEDAW, and the campaign against gender-based violence. All these campaigns were supported by the KRG and implemented through its institutions dedicated to women's rights, such as the General Office in Charge of Women's Affairs (equivalent of the Ministry of Women in Arab Iraq) and local offices in charge of the struggle against gender-based violence. Unlike in Arab Iraq, where women's shelters are still a subject of debate, women's shelters in Iraqi Kurdistan and the organizations and social workers involved in the protection of women victims of violence all benefit from the protection of the Interior Ministry. Women's shelters and organizations dealing directly with the protection of victims of abuse are secured by the police or Peshmerga. The KRG also adopted legislation that imposes a 30 percent women's quota in representative assemblies.

Nevertheless, Shawbo S. – like many women activists in Sulaymaniyah – talked very openly about the "cultural" and "political" limits of women's rights advocacy in Iraqi Kurdistan. The cultural-barrier argument is widespread within Kurdish women's rights organizations and many activists consider the "Kurdish/Muslim patriarchal context" as a barrier to the achievement of full women's rights. Across the political spectrum, however, those who make this argument define "women's rights" and the limits of advocacy for "emancipation" in very different terms. The example most often given by activists is the opposition of many nationalist and Islamist activists to the proposed abolition of polygamy in the Personal Status Code (PSC) of Iraqi Kurdistan. When the proposition was made in 2011, debates among Kurdish political leaders were very tense; Islamist parties especially felt that the proposal was an affront to religion itself. The reform of the PSC set limits on men's ability to marry more than one woman, especially through the introduction of marriage outside the court, but polygamy itself is not forbidden. This was considered a fair compromise by most Kurdish women activists, including most Islamists. As in Arab Iraq, Kurdish women activists were mainly involved in lobbying for legal reforms, as well as in *taw'iyya* ("awareness raising") and *tathqif* ("culture raising") campaigns about women's constitutional rights and the PSC.

Among them, very few women actually contested the "Muslim culture" argument or questioned patriarchy itself from any perspective, whether Islamist feminist or radical Marxist.

However, the "political barrier" argument is most common in Sulaymaniyah, especially among Islamists and women's organizations not affiliated with the KDP or PUK. In Erbil, women activists were generally less critical of the KRG, and many considered its political framework to be unquestionable. Criticizing the KRG was equal to, for many of them, criticizing the very existence of the "Kurdish state"; many women activists in Erbil depicted the political opposition to the KRG as either "conservative Islamists" or "agents of hidden foreign agenda." Snowber J., thirty-eight, is a KDP-affiliated parliamentarian, head of a development and human rights organization, and prominent woman activist in Erbil. She shares her views on the evolution of women's issues in Iraqi Kurdistan.

In Kurdistan, the two main political parties in power made things evolve very positively, and they impacted people's mentality regarding gender issues. They influenced even religious leaders, pressuring them not to say in their sermons and discourses that women should stay at home. It was a real policy conducted by our nationalist parties to promote women's political participation and women's work. Representations of and ideas about women also evolved thanks to the investment of NGOs since 1991, as well as governmental and media discourses favorable to women. The government's policy of positive discrimination has had a very good impact on women. They encouraged girls' education; they facilitated the entry of girls into the male-dominated sphere of universities and lowered the average marks [mu'adel] for women and girls who seek to enter specific areas of studies. In the military domain, there are trainings for both sexes [and] girls and boys are encouraged to get involved in the military in the same way. Women are also invested in the security domain as well ... Also, I have to say that there is the influence of families who were abroad and returned with their mentality from abroad. Many of them have graduated from foreign universities and have come back with new skills that positively affected the mentalities here and the way we work. It is sad that it was not the case for the rest of Iraq, because of violence and poverty.

Like most members of the KRG, Snowber depicts the Maidani Azadi movement in Sulaymaniyah in negative terms.

The mobilizations of Sulaymaniyah were only demanding the improvement of services. There is no democratic problem in Kurdistan. The opposition is very free. It is about foreign agendas and Islamist groups. We have to be aware of foreign implications and agendas. I think it is better to limit the right to demonstrate in order to avoid violence. We have many enemies that do not want Kurdistan to succeed. We have to preserve what we have gained through our suffering.

Snowber's words are more nuanced than those of many of the KDP or PUK women political activists I interviewed. Such activists depicted the Maidani Azadi movement as guided by *salafis* funded by "foreign countries" aimed at destabilizing Iraqi Kurdistan and the "Muslim" region as a whole.

Most activists of the Union of Women of Kurdistan (affiliated with the KDP) and Zhinan (affiliated with the PUK) were, like Snowber, very apologetic toward the Kurdish nationalist elite and expressed their disagreement with the political opposition and the mobilizations of Maidani Azadi. These demonstrations, which were organized by the political opposition and youth movements, demanded the end of corruption and censorship and the implementation of a more democratic and transparent political system in Iraqi Kurdistan. In their form and demands, the mobilizations of Maidani Azadi echoed the uprisings in the region with their demand for dignity, freedom, and their spectacular collective prayers in the streets. In Sulaymaniyah, even women representatives of the main nationalist parties were more critical of the lack of independence of women's groups and organizations, as well as the lack of political freedom in their advocacy for women's rights. In Erbil, the Maidani Azadi movement was perceived as a threat to "social peace," and most women activists I interviewed described these demonstrations as either an "Islamist movement" or one guided by foreign forces trying to destabilize Iraqi Kurdistan.

Most women activists in Sulaymaniyah – those involved in independent women's groups, intellectuals, academics, and Islamists – participated in the Maidani Azadi demonstrations. Bikhal K., forty-two, teaches psychology at the University of Sulaymaniyah, where she founded a research group on gender-based violence. She is also a prominent woman activist member of the Tory Hawbesh network. Bikhal describes participating, along with other women activists, in the Maidani Azadi demonstrations.

We, the women's rights activists, have been very active in this movement of Maidani Azadi, especially in demanding the end of violence between demonstrators and the Kurdish authorities. They are our children, our brothers. We organized an initiative called "The Motherhood Garden." We demanded, as mothers, that violence must be avoided. We are against violence. Many women were present during these demonstrations. I believe it had a feminist nature. I remember that when it was the time of the Friday prayer, women were praying. I also remember that they were nonveiled women, like me, and veiled women. Here, for example, most of the women of the faculty participated in the demonstrations. It had a positive impact, because the government was pressured to take measures to prevent corruption and the intermediary system [*wastah*]. Here in Sulaymaniyah, we are freer than in Erbil; we can tackle every subject. It is also linked to our history;

we have been this way since the 1960s. It is not possible to impose on the people of Sulaymaniyah what has been imposed on the people of Erbil.

Bikhal's words are very common among women civil society activists in Sulaymaniyah. Like most independent women activists, Bikhal partici- pated in the demonstrations in Sulaymaniyah as a "woman" and a "mother," highlighting women's role in spreading peace and cohesion within society as "mothers of the Kurdish nation." Her words reveal the political role she gives to women activists, because she positioned herself outside KRG and Islamist political rhetoric, emphasizing her symbolic motherhood role rather than employing nationalist or Islamist arguments.

Thus, because I noticed a uniformity in women's advocacy agendas, I concur with Mojab's depiction (2007, 2009) of the uniformity of Kurdish women's activism. However, I also noticed a significant con- textual difference. In Erbil, the uniformity of activism and the link between defending the nation and the state are common among women activists. As noted by Al-Ali and Pratt (2011, 2008), most activists in Erbil support the KRG political system and consider it the unquestionable framework of action for women's rights advocacy. The women activists in Sulaymaniyah, by contrast, offered a more mixed picture, since women representatives of the two hegemonic parties defend this hegemony for the sake of preserving "social peace" while, at the same time, other women demonstrated in Maidani Azadi asking for political freedom and transparency. Interestingly, most women activists were far more critical and nuanced regarding the KRG in Sulaymaniyah in general, and most insisted on the need to build an independent, non- party affiliated women's movement. The Islamists, as part of the opposi- tion, were the most outspoken. Finally, the Maidani Azadi movement took the shape of the Goran movement and entered the Kurdish Parliament and political arena as an opposition group. The actual sig- nificance of this movement is debated among women activists. Nevertheless, I also noticed that tensions around Maidani Azadi mainly divided women of the two main political parties from those working in civil society organizations.

"Unlike Arabs": The Politics of Distinction

Among the women activists I interviewed, few were positive about their belonging to the Iraqi state. Most were very pragmatic about the issue of federalism, considering it a "transitional stage" before reaching a truly independent Kurdish state. Very few activists expressed their sense of belonging to Iraq. Qadam S., in her late fifties, is one of the rare activists who did not advocate for the total autonomy of Iraqi Kurdistan and expressed a strong sense of belonging to Iraq. As a communist and women's rights activist, Qadam married an Arab communist activist from Basra; they lived in exile together for more than twenty years. However, some Kurdish activists, especially those based in Baghdad, got involved with the IWN in the demonstrations and campaigns about the quota and the PSC; there are some activists interested in mobilizations outside the Kurdish region. Nevertheless, a large number of Kurdish women activists stated that they were not concerned with the mobilizations around the PSC launched by Arab women activists in Baghdad, choosing to focus instead on ensuring women's rights in the Iraqi Kurdistan Constitution. Moreover, the fact that most Kurdish women's rights activists work within a secular framework and reject political Islam represents an important element of distinction between Kurdish and Arab women's activism, as in Arab Iraq Islamist political parties and movements play a significant role.

Interestingly, activists of very different backgrounds would, over and over again, express a desire to distinguish between Kurdish and Arab women. Many Kurdish activists use the dichotomy Kurdish/Arab in defending the legitimacy of their work for women's rights; in this dichotomy, Kurdish culture is situated as more in favor of women's rights (Al-Ali and Pratt 2011; Fischer-Tahir 2010). It is thus in the name of "authentic" Kurdish culture, through a willing distinction with Arab culture, that some activists define their defense of women's rights. Kurdish women's rights activists insist on the specificity of the experience of the Kurdish population and culture, especially the experience of Saddam's violent repression and the organization of a Kurdish nationalist resistance that includes women fighters. Shro S., thirty-seven, is a leading member of the KDP-linked Kurdistan Women's Union in Erbil.

The mentality of the Kurdish individual is very positive regarding women; the Kurdish woman is used to carrying weapons. We suffered genocide, chemical attacks, deportation, the worst experiences, and this is why Kurds have accepted that women should bear arms in order to defend Kurdish identity and its oppressed people. Regarding the question of honor, this is linked to traditions and customs, but the mentalities are good, and there is a positive evolution.

Because the Kurdish region is nearly autonomous and has its own government, elections, and legislation, Kurdish women's activism is distinct from that of the rest of Iraq. Kurdish activists have endeavored to work on Kurdish legislation related to women's issues, such as legislation that tolerates "honor crimes" and the practice of FGM, which is widespread in several Kurdish provinces.

It is also revealing that some Kurdish activists who did get involved in mobilizations along with non-Kurdish activists, especially through the IWN, left the mobilization in order to focus on their own issues. Amira W., sixty-six, is a prominent Kurdish feminist and nationalist intellectual, from a family of several martyrs, including two brothers who were Peshmerga. Since 2004, Amira has headed an organization supporting women victims of the al-Anfal campaign based in Sulaymaniyah, where she has lived all her life. Although she defends the total autonomy of the Kurdish region and favors the formation of an independent Kurdistan, she speaks good Arabic and feels close to Baghdad, like many Kurds of her generation. Amira got involved in the IWN in 2003 and 2004 but then decided to leave the network.

We were involved with Maysoon al-Damluji, Safia Suhail, and Hanaa Edwar to demand the institution of a High Council for Women, but we, the Kurdish women, were considered representatives of an Iraqi province, among others. We refused that because we considered ourselves representing the Kurdish state. We refused to be deemed as merely a province among the other Iraqi provinces. Just as in the past, we were a branch of Ittihad al-Nisa' [Union of Iraqi Women] of Manal Yunus; we refused that. We are not just a part of them; our situation, our experience, is different. Most of them were abroad and do not even know what happened here. They need our experience and knowledge about the reality here. But, to be honest, they are racists. I do not accept this situation. I am not a branch of al-Itihad al-Nisa'. I stayed a year in the IWN, and then I decided to leave.

Amira's words reveal how much the experience of repression under the Ba'th regime – its interdiction of any kind of women's activism outside the GFIW to its denial of the very existence of Kurdish nationhood within Iraq – has affected Kurdish women activists' lives and mind-sets. Not accepting to be seen as a branch of an Iraqi organization is, for Amira, refusing to accommodate a framework where Kurdish nationhood and autonomous determination are not fully acknowledged. However, prominent members of the IWN are very close to Kurdish nationalist leaders and have been supporting Kurdish nationalism for decades. Thus Amira's stand toward the Iraqi Arab women's movement reveals the realities of the tensions between Arab and Kurdish women activists in post-2003 Iraq.

Crossing Ideologies and Stands: Religious Women's Activism in Iraqi Kurdistan

There is actually no research dedicated to Islamist Kurdish women activists; most of the scholarship on women's activism in Iraqi Kurdistan focuses on its secular forms. Hence part of this chapter is dedicated to the nonsecular forms of women's activism in Kurdistan, focusing on the relationship between Islamist women's activism toward the KRG and the Kurdish women's movement as a whole.

Islamist Women and the Women's Movement in Iraqi Kurdistan

Kurdish Islamist women's rights activists are largely in opposition to the main political parties, which are increasingly perceived as corrupt and disconnected from the grassroots. Mojab (2007, 2009) and Alinia (2013) concur in their depictions of nationalist and Islamist political parties as essentially conservative and Islamist gender rhetoric as fundamentally antiprogressive. Al-Ali and Pratt (2011) note that Islamist women activists situate their activism within the framework of the Kurdish state while also representing the main political opposition and taking part in the women's movement. Interestingly, I find Islamist activists' discourses and activism in Iraqi Kurdistan comparable with that of Muslim organizations in Europe because they both address a "secular state" and seek to show their allegiance to both secularism and democracy. Many Islamist women activists I met in Iraqi Kurdistan have developed a gender rhetoric similar to that designated as Muslim/Islamic feminist in European and North American contexts. Interestingly, all the women activists I met in Sulaymaniyah directed me to Samya A., the main scholar-activist providing gender training to civil society and political activists from all backgrounds. Samya is a sociologist and teacher at Sulaymanyah University, specializing in gender and development; she is also a leading member of the (Muslim Brotherhood–affiliated) Islamic Union of Kurdistan, which she joined at a very young age. Her trajectory in both Islamism and women's rights advocacy reflects a remarkable evolution in both Islamist and women's activism in the Kurdish region and in Iraq in general.

Originally from Halabja, Samya and her family fled to the Iranian and Turkish borders during the al-Anfal campaign, like most of the population of the region. Her eyes were affected by the chemicals, and she stayed several months in refugee camps with her family. There she was exposed to the Muslim Brotherhood's Islamist discourse and got involved in helping families in their everyday needs and providing a religious framework for the women of the camps. Later, at the University of Baghdad, where she was studying engineering, she became a *da'iyya* ("preacher of Islam") and active member of the women's branch of the Kurdish Islamic Union, which was underground at that time.

On the university campus, we stayed with Kurdish sisters; we did not really care about the Arab sisters. I was given the name of a girl, and I would approach her, sometimes coming to her class, and introduce myself and ask her if she needed anything. We started by helping her in her practical needs, such as accommodation and so on, and then I introduced her to Islam and to the ideas of the Muslim Brotherhood; this was when I began the preaching work. It was at the al-Jadrya campus [in Baghdad]. We recognized each other through our *hijab*; we recognized our sisters through their regular prayers, especially in the prayer room. We knew how to distinguish the ones who were practicing only culturally from the ones who were practicing religion with conviction.

In the 1990s, when the Kurdish region became autonomous and the Islamist parties authorized, Samya helped found the Kurdish Islamic Party. At that time, she and her husband, also an active party member, benefited from both their Islamist movement's network and the support of NGOs. Samya obtained a scholarship from an NGO, which gave her the opportunity to go to Sudan for a Master's degree in development studies. Then this mother of four went to Egypt, accompanied by her whole family, for a Ph.D. in gender and development. There Samya attended classes in human rights and was exposed to the UN and NGO human rights vocabulary and tools. This is the way she described the evolution of her stand:

When I came back from Egypt, I worked in a different way, a way that was more academic, focusing on the development of thought and ideas. Now I have reached a point where my thinking is neither Islamist nor secular but humanistist. I work for the development of critical thinking, of the mind, for human development. Despite this, I have decided to stay in a leadership position in my Islamist party.

The way Samya approaches courses on gender is very interesting, because she considers the academic setting and puts aside the politics of her belonging to an Islamist party. Gender, for Samya, is synonymous with equality, equal participation, and women's empowerment. Just like her "secular" counterparts in the field of women's rights, she distinguishes between the private sphere and the public sphere. Full equality is for the public sphere, whereas the private sphere is governed by religion. Interestingly, where most non-Islamist women activists limit their advocacy for equality, Samya relies on her Islamist legitimacy to ask for equality within the private sphere, articulating what can be called a "Muslim feminist standpoint." She highlights the importance of considering the differences between men and women. "Equality does not mean similarity," she argues, but difference should not be synonymous with hierarchy and male domination over women. Samya considers herself a feminist scholar and activist.

Everyone can listen to me; my discourse is academic. There is no difference between working with seculars and Islamists; I work in the same way with everybody. I am the only person specializing in gender in Kurdistan; I provide training to all type of organizations. My approach is not Islamist, not strictly sociological, but clearly feminist. Very often people are shocked when I arrive to a training session because of the way I am dressed [she wears a veil and a long overcoat that covers her body, except for her face and her hands]. As soon as they listen to what I have to say, they realize that my approach is not religious but feminist. I think that we have to give everyone tools of reflection; I do not care if my students believe in God or not. What is important is that I give them what is necessary for them to think by themselves and then make their own choices. Essentially, what I say is that taking man as a reference is not a good thing. Say, for example, that we want women to work just because men do; it is not good. In the same way, religion has to be an independent referential; it is betraying religion to leave it to men's monopoly in its reading and interpretation. Religion becomes masculine oriented. If that pleases Islamists or not, this is the reality. We need a women's movement in order to establish the independence of religion from men and to withdraw it from men's monopoly.

Samya has a critical view of the reality of the women's movement in the Kurdish region and argues for an independent women's movement that is not linked to nationalist, Islamist, or any political party's agenda.

In Kurdistan, the women's movement has never been independent of the nationalist cause, as in the West. It has always been assigned to the national cause and defined by it. The oppression for women was double: authoritarian and patriarchal. After the liberation of Kurdistan, who took the power? Men! The oppression of the Ba'thist state is not anymore, but there is still men's oppression. Until today, the women's movement is affiliated with political parties and is not independent but partisan. Political parties, whether secular or Islamist, put their own priorities in front and leave women's rights as a secondary issue. No political party, whether secular or Islamist, is on the side of women; they do not really consider women's causes. Today we have reached a point where we have two separated worlds inside the parties: the world of women and the world of men. We, in the Muslim Brotherhood movement, have the world of sisters and the world of brothers. We are reaching exhaustion regarding that question. We need a new reading of the relationship between political activism and women's rights activism. If we do not work on that, the marginalization of women will carry on, and these two worlds will continue to evolve separate from each other.

Many of the Islamists I met throughout the country are developing a similar posture; their trajectories have followed that same evolution: from an Islamist activist path, they develop a human rights and gender-equality discourse and engage themselves in the religious debate using their legitimacy as Islamists to advocate for equality within the family. Their Islamist belonging – based on their conviction of the importance of preserving and defending the spiritual, moral, and ethical values of Islam – has been marked by a communal experience of Ba'th repression, from discrimination due to wearing the veil to the deportation, imprisonment, exile, or execution of a close family member. Their discourse is the product of a translational circulation of ideas and thoughts: the modernist, reformist Islam that dedicates an important space to women carried out by translational Islamist and Muslim-oriented movements in Muslim majority countries, on the one hand, and the human rights vocabulary with its gender mainstreaming focus developed by NGOs and UN actors in the region since the 1990s, on the other.

Furthermore, many Islamist women's rights activists are very aware of the complexity of their position as women advocating for equality within a conservative political framework but consider themselves agents of change from within. Samya A. goes as far as saying, with irony: "I think that without the secular activists, the Islamists would have transformed this country into another Afghanistan!"

At the same time, however, these activists also insist on the important role played by Islamists in integrating women within their political parties. Such is indeed the case in the KRG and the rest of Iraq, where Islamist women hold decision-making positions in their parties and where Islamists have been encouraging women to be politically active, respectively. It is according to this political awareness that Islamist women activists build alliances with non-Islamists and non-communal-oriented activists from NGOs and civil society. These alliances, based on the defense of a women's rights agenda expressed in both human rights and religious terms – such as the Tory Hawbesh network in Sulaymaniyah, which gathers women and civil society activists from across the political spectrum, and similar formal and informal gatherings in Baghdad – constitute important spaces outside communal, sectarian, and political party lines.

Jula S., forty-one, is the head of a women's rights organization in Erbil and a KDP representative; she describes herself as secular and liberal. She spoke about the divisive debates caused by international NGOs' introduction of "gender" into the civil society and political spheres of Iraqi Kurdistan. Jula believes that the KRG's arbitration successfully brought together Islamist and non-Islamist women activists, as well as introducing religious authorities into debates around gender issues.

In Kurdistan, conflicts between seculars and Islamists are not as important as they are in the rest of Iraq because positions and political responsibilities were distributed by the government in a way that allowed everyone to have their seat. For example, in the General Office in Charge of Women's Affairs, Islamist women are also part of it. Me, I am secular, liberal, and I belong to the democratic trend. It is possible that an Islamist woman defines herself as democrat like me, but she won't define herself as secular because here to define oneself as secular is often misunderstood. To be secular is interpreted as being atheist. I am not an atheist; I believe in God, and I respect all religions. Atheism and secularism are two very different things. One can be secular and a practicing Muslim. For example, the word "gender," yes, it is a Western word, but it relates to equal rights and duties of men and women. Islamists think that it means homosexuality and libertinism. Kurdish intellectuals and activists have to explain and demonstrate that it is not about that. Islamists did not have an essential problem with equality; they had a problem with the word "gender." So we put the word "gender" in brackets, and we used other words instead. The role of the government in gathering us at the same table and getting religious authorities and parties to agree on common goals and campaigns was essential. We managed to work together on all the campaigns for women's rights that were launched.

From Religious to Social and Women's Rights Activism: Islamist and Christian Kurdish Women Activists

More generally, I noticed a development within women's religious organizations in Iraqi Kurdistan linked to both their "NGOization" and participation in the KRG institutions related to women's issues. Many spoke of an evolution in their "women's rights awareness" that started from the defense of their ethnic or religious identity and turned into social and women's rights–oriented activism. Khochi Q. is a leading Islamist activist in Sulaymaniyah. She is a member of both the Islamic Sisters Organization and the Islamic Group, an Islamist movement with a military branch during the former regime but turned to a civilian political organization after the fall. Khochi is from a very religious family that suffered repression and serious discrimination under the Ba'th regime, including the banning of the veil, which forbid her from pursuing her studies. This mother of six went back to university in her early forties, obtaining a degree in Islamic studies in Mosul (in northern Iraq). Khochi has been involved in women's charity activities since her twenties and an active member of the Islamic Sisters Organization in Sulaymanyah since its foundation in 1992. Her depiction of her trajectory as an Islamist woman activist is, as was that of Samya A., very revealing of the evolution of women's activism in the Kurdish region. Before the semiautonomy of the region in 1991, most political activities were underground and concentrated in Kurdistan's mountainous region. After 1991, many Islamist groups were allowed to set up civil society and political organizations; they began to get involved and to openly organize. Some of their civil society activities were financed by NGOs in the Kurdish region since 1991. After 2003, many organizations became institutionalized, and Islamists became more and more accustomed to the vocabulary and mode of development of human rights NGOs and UN actors, including their women's empowerment agenda.

Very interestingly, Khochi describes the current work of the Islamic Sisters Organization as mainly charitable, social, human, and women's rights oriented, considering their work in the field of *da'wa* ("Islamic preaching") as secondary.

The religious training represents only a small part of our activities, which could be, for example, teaching women their rights in Islam and providing some Qur'anic classes. But, for several years now, we do not really focus on that. There are religious schools, Islamic universities, centers dedicated to preaching Islam. Since 2004, we've worked on women's political participation, on women's development, on their participation in social life. We also want to show that Islam does not oppress women like some people believe; we want to show that Islam is on the side of women. For example, recently we had a book exhibition where we pushed women writers and writings about women. We organized seminars and training on health, human development, education, and family.

Khochi's words reflect a clear shift in Islamist women's political activism and in political activism in Iraqi Kurdistan more generally. The nationalist or Islamist nationalist agendas have become increasingly human rights and development focused since 1991 – and especially since a large number of NGOs and UN actors were on the ground in 2003, women's groups have become increasingly empowerment/gender oriented.

Khanem I. is a founding member of the Assyrian Women's Union in Erbil. She is an upper-middle-class journalist and activist in her fifties who has long advocated for the Assyrian and Christian communities in Iraq. Khanem and I met in the Christian nursery she runs with a group of women from her organization. She explains how her activism and thinking have evolved from the defense of national and community rights to the defense of women's rights.

Before, I didn't have a feminist awareness; my political awareness was Assyrian nationalist. It was after I got involved on the ground that my women's rights awareness was shaped. I realized that our fundamental rights were violated and that, as Christian women, we had rights to defend. After the fall of the regime, all the groups, all the communities of society, began to be open. It is clearly the Kurdish state that has, straight after the fall of the regime, supported and advocated for women's rights. Our state in Kurdistan is seeking to align itself with other democratic countries. Although our activities here stay quite traditional and the "woman question" is covered by the media, we can feel the support of the state [the KRG].

The activities of the Assyrian groups in the Kurdish area were, like those of all other groups opposed to the former regime, underground and concentrated in the mountainous region until 1991. The Assyrian Women's Union was founded in 1992 and provides services and support to Christian women, children, and families throughout the country. Unlike Islamist groups, the organization considers "the state" – the KRG government – an ally and shares a common political narrative with the two main parties in power. Indeed, the main women's organizations in the region – the women's groups affiliated with the two main parties, the KDP-linked Kurdistan Women's Union and the PUK-linked Zhinan (the National Union of Women of Kurdistan) – both insist on the role of nationalist parties of the "Kurdish state" in promoting women's rights. Most women activists in the Kurdish region consider the "Kurdish state" as their main ally in the defense of women's rights. Some independent women's groups and personalities are exceptions, especially in Sulaymaniyah, where the political opposition is concentrated.

Opposing NGOs, a Woman at Odds: The Women-Only Café Initiative

In Erbil, I heard about a woman hairdresser who started an original initiative: opening a women-only café. I asked several women activists about her and sensed their discomfort; many seemed to dislike her. I easily got her salon's address and decided to go and meet her. Kazhal C., forty-one, welcomed me very warmly and proposed that we speak about her initiative over a cup of tea. A hairdresser from the age of thirteen, she was taught by her mother, who was also a hairdresser. Originally from Sulaymanyiah, Kazhal and her family moved several times due to her father, a KDP member, and his nationalist activism; they lived in Baghdad for more than five years. Kazhal never received a secondary education due to this constant displacement. She spoke about the fact that her family did not allow her to marry a man she loved because a member of his family was Ba'th. At the age of twenty, Kazhal was pressured to marry her neighbor's son, who belonged to a prominent nationalist family. Despite the fact that she witnessed several of his infidelities during the time of their engagement, she was not allowed to call off the wedding and ended up married to him. Even with the three children they had together, she describes her marriage to this man as the darkest period of her life.

The political situation in the region pushed Kazhal and her family to move several times, including settling in Turkey and Iran for several years. Kazhal speaks about the massive displacement of Kurds in 1991, when she fled to the Iranian borders. She gave birth to one of her daughters in between two cars with her mother's help. Kazhal recalls this experience as a deep physical and psychological trauma. Because her husband refused to take any job not suited to his education, she carried her household financially, working two or three jobs at a time. The extent of her poverty, the instability of her life, the seemingly constant moving due to military clashes, the lack of support from her family, and life with her in-laws and her resigning husband drove her mad. She cries while telling me that she had reached a stage of tiredness and pain that pushed her, at the age of twenty-four, to attempt self-immolation. After this incident, Kazhal was hospitalized for a week and obtained financial support from some family members.

Despite her nonreligious background, Kazhal turned to religion in her late twenties. Her family was angered by her religious practice, especially her husband.

In 1998, when we came back from Turkey, I wore a veil over my head. My husband went crazy. He took it off my head and screamed that he would divorce me three times if I chose to wear the headscarf. He would mock me when I was praying. My family, you know, they believe in God, but they do not like religious practice.

After obtaining a separation from her husband in 2010, Kazhal started praying and wearing the *hijab*. Her turn toward religious practice materialized in her move toward a new life, especially after obtaining a divorce in 2011.

I decided to wear the *hijab* during Ramadan. I was looking at myself in the mirror after reading the Qur'an with a *hijab* over my head, and I thought that with it, I am very beautiful; it makes me look and feel beautiful. The *hijab* gives me this pure and innocent face that I love. I fear God, and I love the Qur'an. Now I am financially independent, my kids have grown up, [and] I can make my own choices independently from my husband, my family, or any man. I wanted to wear the *hijab* for so long, but everyone forbade it. Now I finally can do it. I do not like religious parties, or any political parties; my Islam is different from all of them. I have nothing in common with them.

If Kazhal's turn toward religious practice reveals the Islamization of Kurdish society in the context of the 1990s' rise of Islamist militancy, it also reveals how seeking to oppose her family's secular political frame led her to dealing with her life and body in her own way.

After several meetings, Kazhal and I got along very well, and we decided to "do something" together for her initiative. At the time I visited her, the women-only café was closed due to financial difficulties. She explains that her idea of a women-only café stemmed from the fact that coffee and teahouses in Erbil, and most public spaces in general, are occupied by men. She wants to create a "safe" space for women to gather, talk outside their domestic spaces and away from male gazes. She plans to organize talks and discussions about women's issues, especially about body, sexuality, marriage, and divorce. Kazhal also wants to set up a support group for divorced women, like herself, and open the café to young boys and girls for awareness raising discussion groups about sexuality and marriage.

Khazhal believes that many perceived her initiative as "indecent"; several women's activists I spoke with described it as "wrong." She complains about the fact that she did not get much support from women's organizations in Erbil. In fact, when Kazhal proposed her project to such organizations, she received a lot of criticism. "It is a project against men. Why do you need a women-only café?" was a typical response. After organizing a French Cultural Center screening of a short film about her women-only café, I sensed many activists' animosity toward her. In a venue comprised mainly of women's organizations and NGO representatives, Kazhal addressed the audience after the film and criticized women's NGOs for their activities, pointing out that such activities did not address ordinary women's needs.

Kurdish women need to talk, to express their issues between each other, to talk about their bodies, and to address inequalities and discriminations directly. The presence of party-backed women in the Parliament and across NGOs does not serve women's issues directly. You only talk about representation in the parties; you never talk about real issues. I want to have a space for us to talk about intimate issues, to help women to gain self-confidence, and nobody supported me. I want to talk about divorce, dysfunctional marriage, and concrete issues, not only about being politically active for this or that group, organization, or party.

Some prominent women's organization representatives took the microphone and expressed their anger toward Kazhal, saying that her project was "individualistic" and "business oriented," unlike NGOs that aimed to serve society as a whole. The debate shifted around women's need to claim gender-segregated spaces and the way in which they should formulate such demands.

Because I organized this event with Kazhal, I lost credit in the eyes of several women activists with whom I had built good relationships. At the same time, it forced me to realize the realities and limits of interactions between "ordinary women" – like Kazhal, who refused to join any formal organization – and NGO women in Iraqi Kurdistan. I realized the extent to which political correctness is the norm in Erbil and that ordinary women would be heard and supported by women's rights organizations only if their demands followed the appropriate frame and vocabulary – e.g., "political representation" and "legal rights."

Conclusion: Kurdish Women Activists – Between Nation and State

Clearly, women have taken significant strides in terms of legal rights and political representation in the Kurdish region since 1991. The role of the "Kurdish state," the KRG, has been essential in encouraging and executing legal reforms and campaigns in favor of women's rights. Indeed, even controversies around the status of Islam and the PSC, which occurred in the rest of Iraq, did not have an equivalent in Kurdistan. The "Kurdish state" played the arbitrator between religious authorities, such as the Union of Muslim Scholars, and Islamist parties in debates around the PSC and the law on gender-based violence, which was adopted in 2011 and sanctions domestic violence and FGM. Moreover, Islamist parties and religious institutions stand alongside the "Kurdish state" as partners in the national struggle and the reinforcement of the autonomy of Iraqi Kurdistan. It seems that the Kurdish nationalist cause is common ground for most political parties: the preservation and extension of the autonomous Kurdish state, as well as a will to promote a modern and open "Kurdish culture" that also preserves traditions (or folklore) in building an essential distinction with Arab Iraq. The will to protect the "Kurdish nation" against all threats and dangers – a feeling expressed by all the political groups that compose the KRG – has a direct impact on gender issues; gender, or women's rights, issues, and representations, is an essential piece of the puzzle that defines Kurdish nationalism.

Since 1991, different trends have emerged among Kurdish women activists. In Erbil, there is a more consensual trend, since women's organizations and groups consider the KRG to be the essential framework for activism. In Sulaymaniyah, by contrast, many civil society activists believe in building an independent, nonaffiliated women's movement. Apart from women involved in the two main parties and government, most women civil society activists in Sulaymaniyah participated in the popular Maidani Azadi demonstrations, using "motherhood" as an alternative role and discourse amid the nationalist and Islamist rhetoric dominating the opposition scene. Islamist women occupy a specific position, as both women activists and members of the political opposition. Some have appropriated human rights, development, and gender discourses received from NGOs and are very active in building gender-specific agendas.

My encounter with Kazhal, a "nonorganized" woman activist, opened my eyes to other horizons and gave me a sense of the relationship between women activists and representatives and their supposed "grassroots." Kazhal's initiative and the reaction of women's organizations in Erbil highlighted the extent to which women's activism is framed by a discourse of representation and legal rights. Women's organizations' focus on certain issues – such as FGM, honor crimes, and legal reforms on gender-based violence – has made many other areas and types of engagement, such as Kazhal's initiative, appear politically incorrect. Thus, although women's political activism in Iraqi Kurdistan involves a diverse spectrum, the "NGOization" and the KRG affiliation of most activism have clearly marginalized other forms of women's engagement, rights, and enhancement of their life conditions.

Compared with women's activism in the rest of Iraq, Kurdish women's activism has benefited from a more stable social, political, and economic situation; the KRG, despite its limits and allegations of authoritarianism and corruption, plays its role as a state and provides security and basic services for the population. In addition, civil society in Iraqi Kurdistan has benefited from international and NGO donors and support for a decade longer than Arab Iraq. Thus Kurdish women's rights activism is more structured and institutionalized than that in the rest of the country and has benefited from the support of the KRG. Moreover, women's activism's frame of struggle in Iraqi Kurdistan is aided by the fact that the two main nationalist parties are both secular and use a similar, and generally favorable, gender discourse, as well as the fact that the political sphere in Iraqi Kurdistan is quite united around the defense of Kurdish nationalism. In Arab Iraq, by contrast, women activists do not benefit from the support of a strong state and are everyday plunged into a situation of violence and lack of basic services. The sectarian divide has crossed civil society; despite wide support from NGOs and international donors, civil society is still evolving and trying to find its place in a context of political chaos and widespread corruption. In addition, the political parties that came to power after the fall of the regime are mainly Shi'a Islamist political parties, whose gender discourse is framed by both religious conservatism and the sectarian divide. The political, economic, and social dynamics of the two contexts are continuously evolving in different directions, leading to the conclusion that Arab and Kurdish women's activism in Iraq are two distinct entities that pursue different, if not conflicting, agendas.

The sphere of women's legal rights is essential to both Kurdish and Arab women's activism in Iraq. However, as I show in Chapter 6, women's legal rights in Arab Iraq are questioned in a way that reveals the post-2003 context of social, political, and sectarian crisis. Although Kurdish women's rights activists managed to obtain a positive reform of the PSC, Arab women's rights activists are dealing with a very different situation; they face a near-constant sectarian questioning of the unifying framework for women's legal rights.

6   Mobilizing for Women's Legal Rights
Gender and Sectarianism in Post-2003 Iraq

Introduction: Celebrating the "Iraqi Woman"

As for women's rights activists elsewhere, International Women's Day in Iraq is an occasion for women's rights activists to organize meetings, hold events, and raise awareness around sexism and gender-based violence (Figure 6.1). It is an opportunity for every organization and group to express their vision of and agenda for women's issues and rights. In March 2012, a meeting of representatives of women's rights organizations was held at the Iraqi Parliament. Hanaa Edwar – a leading figure of the IWN – delivered a speech to MPs, political leaders, and journalists on the difficult realities faced by women in postinvasion Iraq. I decided not to attend this meeting. At the time, after a year and a half of fieldwork in Baghdad, I no longer had the energy to wait for hours in the sun just to enter the Green Zone. Instead, I attended an al-Rabita gathering in Ferdaws Square. Al-Rabita, or the Iraqi Women's League, is one of the oldest women's rights organizations in Iraq that historically has been affiliated with the Iraqi Communist Party.

Reaching Ferdaws Square, in the city center, was not too difficult that day. I left my house in al-Kazimiyya, took the first taxi I saw, and reached the square in about forty-five minutes. Although I had to pass multiple checkpoints on my way into town, traffic was not bad for a Saturday afternoon. The gathering in Ferdaws Square was not large: 100 people at the most. The square was surrounded by heavily armed Iraqi soldiers, police officers, and an army tank posted at the entrance. Soldiers were managing the circulation of the cars and stopping and checking the belongings of everyone entering the square. I walked toward the al-Rabita activists; they were handing out flyers – entitled "Social Justice" – and offering small bottles of water and sweets. The speakers stood on a small podium next to the empty pillar where Saddam's statue used to stand, and white plastic chairs had been set up in front for the audience. The beautiful Arba'ta'ech Ramadan mosque, with its blue mosaic dome, was to the left of the gathering. In the middle of the

Figure 6.1 Gathering of the Iraqi Women's League in Ferdaws Square to celebrate Women's Day (March 2012).

event, which included women's rights activists, unionists, parliamentarians, and poets, the afternoon call to prayer imposed a moment of silence on the group. Between each speech, middle-aged ladies danced wearing the traditional black *'abaya*. They stood and sang slogans such as "Let her practice her rights" and "Where is our portion of the oil, listen oh Hajji?." We all laughed and sang with the performers and were moved by the recitation of poetry about the glory of Baghdad and the unity of the Iraqi people.

Seated next to me was a well-dressed woman in her late thirties; she wore a beige cotton *hijab* and brown jacket and trousers. While waiting for the next speaker, we began talking. She spoke about how al-Rabita had helped after the death of her husband in the sectarian violence of 2006. She had been unemployed, so the state allocation for widows – about 150,000 Iraqi dinars (less than US$100) – had been her only income; she and her three children were nearly starving. She said: "Really, the government is doing nothing for women like me, for millions of Iraqi women like me. But today, we came to celebrate Iraqi women, all Iraqi women."

Iraqi soldiers stood near the podium brandishing their weapons, acting as the speakers' bodyguards. The presence of armed men was completely normalized, as if they decorated the square with their green, black, and brown uniforms. They were a necessary part of the setting and a reminder that this moment of hope, emotion, and joy was fragile and temporary. Despite our attempt to fully enjoy that moment, violence still surrounds us.

Two months later, I attended a gathering for Iraqi Women's Day, which falls on the birthday of Fatima al-Zahra', who was the daughter of the Prophet Muhammed, wife of al-Imam 'Ali, and mother of the two holy Imams al-Hasan and al-Husain. The gathering took place at the headquarters of the Islamic Supreme Council of Iraq, one of the main Shi'a a Islamist parties brought to power by US-led coalition forces in 2003. The meeting was huge; there were about a thousand women waiting outside one of the barricaded entrances to the Green Zone. When I entered the venue, it was filled with women of all stripes: young, middle aged, and old; party activists from women's branches in Baghdad and the southern regions; and supporters and women who benefited from the party's charity and welfare support. Most of these women wore either a black 'abaya or long overcoat. After being closely checked by a team of women security guards at the entrance, they entered the venue happily. In the front row, on red velvet VIP seats, sat activists from every Iraqi women's rights organization – Islamists, leftists, Kurds, and Christian nuns – and representatives of different religious communities.

In the back, away from the fancy VIP seats, sat women whose travel to the event had been sponsored by the Islamic Supreme Council of Iraq; most came from the impoverished southern areas of the country. The atmosphere was festive, with juice, water, and sweets being distributed to everyone. Ibtihal al-Zaidy, a member of the Da'wa Party and Minister in Charge of Women's Affairs at the time, gave a speech about "the Iraqi woman" since 2003. She advised all Iraqi women to follow the paths of Fatima al-Zahra' and Bint al-Huda, the sister of the tortured and executed Shahid al-Sadr. Al-Zaidy emphasized the importance of women's political involvement in the "new Iraq." Ammar al-Hakim, the head of the party, gave a long and romantic lecture about the "glorious status of woman in Islam," as represented by al-Zahra'. He distributed prizes to those whom he described as the "honor of Iraq, the courageous and strong Iraqi women." Most of these prizes were given to women's rights activists from both secular and religious women's organizations, as well as widows in charge of their households.

After singing songs glorifying Iraq and highlighting the unity of the Iraqi people, a youth group performed a short play about the life of orphans and widows forced to beg in the streets for their survival. A wave of emotion filled the immense venue; weeping could be heard throughout the audience, and tears were even visible in the eyes of prominent political leaders. A renowned female Iraqi poet recited poems mocking sectarian divisions and politics in the name of Iraq's diversity. Between religious preaching, political speeches, and moments of great emotion, reminders of the "unity of the Iraqi people" and the glory of "Iraqi woman" were always present. The continuous emphasis on al-Zahra', as both a political leader and a pious saint, also hinted at the gathering's additional meaning: affirming Iraq's Shi'a identity.

This brief description of my participant observation with Iraqi women's groups and networks paints a picture of the postinvasion context in which women and gender issues are raised. Furthermore, this account reveals the concrete environment in which Iraqi women activists live and undertake their activities: general impoverishment, widespread sectarian violence, militarization, and a capital always supervised by armed men at every corner. In addition, this anecdote also shows how different groups use women and gender issues for their respective ideologies and agendas. Such begs the question: what terms do women activists use to advocate for women's legal rights in such a context?

Fragmentation of Women's Legal Rights in Postinvasion Iraq

In December 2003, a few months after the fall of the Ba'th regime, Abdel Aziz al-Hakim – the leader of the Islamic Supreme Council of Iraq and temporary president of the Iraqi Governing Council – proposed Decree 137. Adopted by a majority vote and with the premise of advocating "freedom of belief," Decree 137 abolished the unified Personal Status Code (PSC) linked to Law No. 188 (1959) and established a new law based on "Islamic *shari'a.*" As a result, the religiously based PSC that applied to all Muslim Iraqis would be transformed into a set of community-based codes modeled on Lebanese family law.[1] Definitively, Decree 137 proposed a return to a legal system emblematic of the monarchic period,

---

[1] Text of Decree 188: "1. The provisions of the Islamic *Shari'a* shall be implemented with respect to cases concerning marriage, engagement, marriage contract, legal competence, testimonial proof of marriage, marriages prohibited according to Islam, marriage to Christian and Jewish women, marital rights – including dowry, alimony, divorce, legal separation, *idda*, relationships by marriage, wills, bequeathals, *waqf*, and inheritance. This law shall be implemented in all religious courts in line with the provisions of the schools of Islamic thought. 2. All laws, decisions, instructions, statements, and clauses of articles that contradict Clause 1 of this law shall be abolished. 3. This law will go into effect as of its date of issue."

where there was no set of laws regarding private matters that unified Iraqis. Many activists of the IWN and most of the country's independent women's groups firmly opposed the decree. According to them, such a proposition from a conservative Shi'a Islamist political leader brought the very notion of a PSC into question on both religiously conservative and sectarian grounds. Many civil society activists expressed fears about the adoption of a system based on a regressive and conservative reading of Muslim jurisprudence given the conservative Islamist parties in power since 2003, as well as the "sectarianization" of issues relating to women and the family. The Sunni Islamists I interviewed also opposed the decree, instead desiring a unified code that facilitates intercommunal marriage and unites all Iraqis. Conversely, many Shi'a Islamist women activists supported the decree, considering it an affirmation of the freedom to practice Shi'a Islam after decades of political repression. Ultimately, the decree was not enacted because women activists' mobilization took on an international dimension that convinced Paul Bremer, head of the Coalition Provisional Authority (CPA) in charge of Iraq not to sign it.

Later, in the context of the drafting and adoption of the new Iraqi Constitution in 2005, Decree 137 was reintroduced at the behest of Shi'a Islamist political leaders as Article 41 of the Constitution. Again, the article purported to support freedom of belief and liberties: "Iraqis are free in their commitment to their personal status according to their religions, sects, beliefs, or choices, and this shall be regulated by law."[2] This time however, Law No. 188 and its corresponding PSC would not be abolished; it remained as one option among other family laws. Despite the controversies surrounding the article, the draft Constitution was adopted by referendum. As mentioned in Chapter 3, the Constitution was mainly welcomed by Kurdish and Shi'a political leaders willing to push the institution of a new regime seen as especially supportive of state federalism. Federalism and the recognition of different Iraqi communities and languages were crucial issues,[3] particularly in terms of the distribution of oil located in the north (near the Kurdish region) and south (a majority Shi'a region). For Kurdish leaders, as well as for Kurdish women activists, this proved an essential point because it guaranteed the

---

[2] This appears in Chapter 2 of the Constitution, dedicated to liberties under Section 2, "Rights and Liberties."

[3] Article 1 of the Constitution states that Iraq is a federal state in which the system of government is republican, representative, parliamentary, and democratic. Article 4 states: "The Arabic language and the Kurdish language are the two official languages of Iraq. The right of Iraqis to educate their children in their mother tongue, such as Turkmen, Syriac, and Armenian, shall be guaranteed in government educational institutions in accordance with educational guidelines, or in any other language in private educational institutions."

autonomy of the Kurdish region. For Shiʻa political leaders, federalism strengthened their hold on power: they would be able to run the country from Baghdad and manage the Shiʻa-dominated south. Sunni political leaders, including Sunni Islamists, were latterly integrated into the process; at the time, they were supportive of a unified state. Already discriminated against by the de-Baʻthification policies and marginalized by the Shiʻa and Kurdish elites recently brought to power, Sunni political groups felt threatened by federalism at the time. They opposed the draft Constitution, calling for people to vote against the referendum. Some political groups – Shiʻa and Sunni, tribal and religious, and opponents of the occupation – simply boycotted the referendum, declaring the new regime illegitimate.

For many women activists critical of Article 41, it became clear that women's issues – highlighted by the US-led administration and new political elite as a symbol of the "New Iraq" – had become secondary to supposedly "more crucial" political matters. Due to the significant international mobilization of women's groups and organizations, as well as the lack of consensus among the various political parties, the implementation of Article 41 was suspended, and Law No. 188 remains in place. Moreover, the suspension took place despite the fact that very few women participated in drafting the new Constitution. Sarah H., forty-two, a prominent women activist, and member of the al-Rafidain Women Coalition, mobilized against the Article 41. She talks about how US representatives dealt with the issue at the time and her feelings about it.

The Decree 137 came back in the form of the Article 41 of the Constitution drafted and adopted in 2005. Fortunately, the implementation of Article 41 has been suspended. It is anyway impossible to implement such a thing in Iraqi society. I remember very well a woman, an American lawyer who was taking part in the drafting of the Constitution with us. She said to us: "But isn't it in the interests of women that each group could have its own law?" I really think that these foreigners did not know anything about Iraqi society and about our context and realities. Perhaps, there, in America, their society is divided into communities, and each community does not mix with the other community and has its own laws. Here, in our society, it is different. We are a fusion of cultures, a Muslim marries a Christian, we get married between different communities, Sunnis and Shiʻas. Such a law will divide our families, our people. We are eighteen communities; we do not want to be like Lebanon.

Sarah H. herself is a Baghdadi Sunni married to a Shiʻa man who was killed during the 2003 US-led bombings. She expresses her exacerbation toward the US administration's simplistic and communal-based representation of Iraqi society, which she perceives and experiences as plural and mixed.

However, Article 41 aside, many women activists still consider the new Constitution to broadly favor human and women's rights. As mentioned previously, Article 14, for instance, states that equality between citizens includes gender equality,[4] and Article 18 allows both women and men to pass Iraqi citizenship to their children.[5] The debate around whether Islam is "a source" or "the main source" has also been controversial. After debates among different political groups, Article 2 of the Constitution identified Islam as "a foundational source of law," but also indicated that laws must respect freedom, democracy, and religious diversity.[6] Many women activists see this as a good compromise. However, the state of lawlessness that dominated Iraqi political life, in addition to the rise of conservatism, make the "good" provisions of the Constitution inapplicable until now; the *ta'limat* – instructions sanctioning the application of a law – of many of the articles have not been set. Thus, for example, as a result of the Ba'th regime's conservative legal reforms regarding women, women of all ages need the presence of her *wali* – male legal guardian – and his approval to receive a passport and permission to travel. The law regarding passport acquisition changed in 2015 as a result of women activists' mobilizations and now allows women to obtain a passport without the consent of a *wali*.[7] However, the law has not been implemented, and it is still concretely impossible for a woman to obtain a passport without the consent of a *wali* because no *ta'limat* have been set to accommodate it. It is the same situation that characterizes the implementation of the Article 14 regarding gender equality and Article 18 regarding the rights for both men and women to grant citizenship to their children.

---

[4] Article 14: "Iraqis are equal before the law without discrimination based on gender, race, ethnicity, nationality, origin, color, religion, sect, belief or opinion, or economic or social status."

[5] Article 18: "First: Iraqi citizenship is a right for every Iraqi and is the basis of his nationality. Second: Anyone who is born to an Iraqi father or to an Iraqi mother shall be considered an Iraqi. This shall be regulated by law."

[6] Article 2: "First: Islam is the official religion of the State and is a foundation source of legislation: A. No law may be enacted that contradicts the established provisions of Islam B. No law may be enacted that contradicts the principles of democracy. C. No law may be enacted that contradicts the rights and basic freedoms stipulated in this Constitution. Second: This Constitution guarantees the Islamic identity of the majority of the Iraqi people and guarantees the full religious rights to freedom of religious belief and practice of all individuals such as Christians, Yazidis, and Mandean Sabeans."

[7] Iraqi Passpot Law reform; see www.ilo.org/dyn/natlex/docs/ELECTRONIC/102984/12 4756/F1073654773/4381.pdf.

More recently, in the context of parliamentary elections of 2014, the Iraqi Justice Minister, Hasan al-Shemmari, a member of Ayatollah Muhammed al-Yaqoobi's al-Fazila Party, declared that he is preparing a *shari'a*-based PSC based on the main Shi'a *mazhab* in Iraq, the *Ja'fari mazhab*. Again, the main argument for this change revolves around freedom of belief, highlighting the freedom of the Shi'a community to practice its faith. On February 25, the Iraqi Council of Ministers approved what is now commonly called the "Ja'fari Law." If the Ja'fari Law is implemented, it will mean a very essential questioning of the PSC on issues such as the legal age of marriage set to eighteen for both sexes and the restriction of polygamy and marriage outside the civil court. The Ja'fari Law, in line with the Ja'fari Shi'a *mazhab*, sets the legal age of marriage for women as nine years old and for men as fifteen and allows unconditional polygamy as well as precarious forms of marriage with no legal protection for women (such as *mut'a* marriages). The race for power between the different Shi'a political parties is being played on gender and family matters because it is clear that al-Fazila wants to put its mark on Iraqi political life and establish itself as a Shi'a *mazhabi* party at a time of division between competitive Shi'a political groups. For the Shi'a Islamist political leadership, the PSC is certainly a site to demonstrate revival and strength, as well as affirm power of their identity in a communal-based political system. In the line with my own observations, according to a survey conducted by a women's organization in southern Iraq, even the majority of the Shi'a population (70 percent) considered Article 41 to threaten the unity of Iraq (Bint al-Rafidain/UNIFEM 2006). Most Shi'a clerics also opposed the Ja'fari Law. For example, Husain al-Sadr – a prominent Shi'a cleric – stated that it was better for the state to adopt civil legislation in line with international conventions and leave issues of *shari'a* to the clerics. He said: "We want Iraq to be a civilian [*madani*] and civilized [*mutahadar*] state."[8] This is revealing in that it is not religion or the religious practice of a certain sect that is at stake in this debate but a politicized/religious sectarianism. Shi'a Islamists' play of women's rights on identity politics is not shared by the Iraqi Shi'a population, nor on parts of its religious institution, such as the *hawza*. This shows that the fragmentation of women's legal rights in postinvasion Iraq is an issue of politicized sectarianism and not religious sectarianism.

---

[8] *Al-hewar al-mutamaden*, March 2, 2014.

Al-Ali and Pratt (2009) show how much gender issues are politicized in contexts where armed intervention is used for imperialist and geopolitical agendas under the guise of "democratization." They point out that increased conservatism, especially related to gender issues, can be seen as a backlash against neocolonial politics and the occupation itself – a reaction in "Islamic terms," driven by sectarianism, opposing what is perceived as a Western invasion. However, the fact that it is precisely the political group that came to power through the US-led invasion and occupation that is today questioning the PSC on conservative and sectarian grounds shows that the issue is even more complex than a binary conservative "Islamic" backlash/Western invasion.

Since the invasion and occupation of Iraq in 2003, the PSC has once again taken a central role in debates between women activists and the Iraqi political elite, which are now dominated by Shi'a Islamist parties and Kurdish nationalists. The questioning of the unified PSC on both sectarian and conservative grounds constitutes the main point of divergence between Shi'a Islamists and other Iraqi political forces in Arab Iraq. As shown in Chapter 1, the text of Law No. 188 is clearly inspired by different schools of *fiqh* and operated within *shari'a*, thus eliminating the differential treatment of Sunnis and Shi'as and allowing state-trained and appointed judges to rule on personal matters without consulting the *'ulemas*. The new PSC, gathering both Sunni and Shi'a jurisprudences, provides a legal framework applicable equally to all Muslim Iraqis. This makes Law No. 188 a symbol of both the new nation's unity beyond ethnosectarian lines and the inclusion of women's rights activists' demands through their participation in the legislative process itself. This shows the strong relationship between issues of nationhood and gender in postcolonial Iraq: at a time when the political culture was marked by the left, especially the Iraqi Communist Party, both ethnosectarian unity and pro–women's rights aspirations were linked to one another. It is precisely this legacy that is questioned by the Shi'a Islamist conservative elite in power since 2003. As I have shown, the emergence of a Shi'a Islamist movement in the 1960s was partly a reaction against the PSC and, more generally, the secularization of society. The revolutionary legacy represented by the PSC has been highly altered by the changing Ba'thist project oscillating first between Arab-socialist nationalism during a period of economic development and then its questioning through a conservative gender discourse tinted by an Islamic tribalism after its engagement in successive wars and the terrible impact of the sanctions. Through the discourses of the Shi'a women activists I interviewed and the Shi'a political leaders, the PSC is associated with both a form secularization and the Ba'th regime itself, all together perceived as oppressive to the Shi'a population.

What Stands Behind the Polarized Discourses?

Sunni and Shi'a Islamist Women's Positions on the Debates on the PSC

In July 2005 in Ferdaws Square, the IWN organized a sit-in demanding the abrogation of Article 41, the preservation of the PSC, and the safety of women's rights activism, which was seen as under threat by both religious conservatisms and sectarian politics. Across from the gathering, a group of women waved signs denouncing "full equality" and defending Islam and the Qur'an. These were Shi'a Islamist women; they were defending Article 41 in the name of freedom of belief and denouncing any potential secularism because they felt that secularism was partially responsible for their suffering under the previous regime.

Naziha A. – fifty-five years old, holding a Ph.D. in administration and economy from Bagdad University, and a former Shi'a Islamist MP – was one of these counterdemonstrators. Naziha has lived in Baghdad all her life, and her brother was executed by the Ba'th regime in 1990. She firmly supports Article 41.

The Personal Status Code has its good and bad sides. It is a complex law, and it does not cover all areas of life. It is not about demanding the full abrogation of the Personal Status Code; it is about keeping what is suitable for Iraqi women along the lines of *shari'a*, because we are a Muslim society and we have to remove what opposes *shari'a*. The Constitution mentions that no laws that oppose Islamic *shari'a* can be passed in Iraq. What is contradictory to Islam, we have to abrogate or change ... If authentic Islam was practiced, Iraqi women would be the best off in the world.

According to Naziha, *shari'a* is synonymous with justice, and the PSC should guarantee the respect of Islam. She does not perceive Article 41 as sectarian; she sees it as a way to ensure that everyone has the right to live according to their religious beliefs. Interestingly, Naziha does not perceive Article 41 as at all related to women's rights or gender. Instead, she relates secularism to authoritarianism and to the repression of her religious practice, she sees the article as strictly related to religion. Many Shi'a Islamist women I spoke with followed Naziha's line: they do not link Article 41 with women's rights; for them, this article represents the affirmation of their Shi'a *mazhab* and religious freedom. In contrast to the IWN activists, who know every detail of the PSC and work in detail on its reform, most Shi'a Islamist women are not very aware of or involved in the issue. In addition, they perceive opposition to Article 41 as opposition to their religious Shi'a identity.

Naziha believes this new era should mark a radical rupture from the mentality of the former regime, a regime she describes as dominated by a secular view of private/public matters and marginalized the Shiʻa population, especially the most religious. Thus the new era should break with the secular itself, and Article 41 and the debates around Islam and the Constitution are markers of such change. Decree 137 and Article 41 can be analyzed in line with the increase in Shiʻa visibility since the fall of the Baʻth regime. Similarly, the commemoration ceremonies for the Twelve Imams, which are held nearly every month in Baghdad, and the Shiʻa religious signs (e.g., green flags, pictures of al-Husain, and drawings of the Battle of Karbala) that cover the city's walls[9] show the strength of Shiʻa politicoreligious power in post-2003 Iraq.

This is very clear in the way women Shiʻa Islamists perceive and describe their post-2003 activism. Bushra Z., a Shiʻa woman activist, gives the following description:

How should we tell women and inform them about who is back [mentioning the Shiʻa political opposition]? Because young people grew up, thirty-five years of Baʻthism is a lot, really a lot. Children grew up without their religion. Saddam made us forget about al-Husain and our slogans. When I do the *hawza* [Shiʻa religious training] for young girls, some of them tell me: "I feel closer to communism than to Shiʻaism!" Such a girl is speaking the language of Saddam without even knowing it. He taught her "Union, Freedom, and Socialism," and she is not even aware of it. He knew neither union nor freedom nor socialism; he knew nothing. All these slogans, they repeat them without understanding. How should we teach that to women; some of them forgot about their own oppression. How do we transform this girl into a strong woman who knows her rights and duties. We begin with issues of *fiqh* ["Muslim jurisprudence"], even though she doesn't accept it. She became *Saddami*. She lives for eating, drinking, getting married, and that's all.

As mentioned previously, Bushra Z. was a child when the Baʻth regime deported all the Faili Kurds of Khaneqin to a city in central Iraq as part of its "Arabization" policies. She strongly believes in the new political elite and considers the new era to be full of hope for the victims of the Baʻth regime.

Naziha and Bushra had an alternative view of the tribo-Islamic turn of the Baʻth regime in the 1990s – i.e., the period of the Faith Campaign. In their eyes, this campaign was purely strategic; it had no true impact on society. In addition, for them, the campaign represented further proof of the regime's sectarian politics because only Sunni Islam was promoted.

---

[9] This does not include Sunni neighborhoods, which have their own aesthetic forms; for example, pictures of al-Medina Mosque, where the Prophet Muhammed is buried, or green and yellow *Muhammed Qudwatana* ("Muhammed is Our Model") signs.

Here it is their perception and interpretation of this period with regard to their political and religious ideas that is important, not the historical accuracy of their reading.

More interestingly, none of the Shiʻa Islamist women activists with whom I spoke opposed Law No. 188. Although many were ignorant of the law's articles, the fact that this law gathers Sunni and Jaʻfari jurisprudence was viewed very positively. I asked: "If you agree that the law is fair and does not oppose *shariʻa*, why are you willing to change it and have a separate family law?" They responded with reference to their freedom to be governed by their own law, independent of "Sunni and secular authorities".

Sunni Islamist women approached this debate completely differently. All the Sunni Islamist women with whom I spoke were firmly against Article 41 because they perceived it as a way to divide Iraqis along sectarian lines. They defended the PSC's current form, explaining that it was the result of an agreement between Iraqis of various backgrounds; it is a unifying law. Maysoon S., forty-two, is the head of one of the main Sunni Islamist women's organizations in Baghdad. She was in complete agreement with Naziha on the importance of governing by *shariʻa* but also considered the PSC to follow this line of thought. Thus Maysoon favors preserving the PSC.

I am against any questioning of the Personal Status Code because I consider that it is a fair and good law and that it is suitable for us. The new laws are sectarian and do not serve our interests; they serve the interests of one community above others. I defend one law for everyone, especially because the actual law is good and suitable. It is something from the former regime that we have to keep; everything that comes from it [the former regime] is not necessarily bad.

Maysoon also expresses a positive view of the Faith Campaign and the last period of the former regime. In her opinion, the Faith Campaign was a positive contribution to Iraqi society.

In the 1970s, the *hijab* was not accepted; people mocked it and veiled women, calling them *Um Luksha* and *Khema*. Later, the *hijab* became the norm, all types of *hijab*, but it is still *hijab*. The Faith Campaign was Saddam's attempt to initiate bonds with Islamists in Iraq. I believe this campaign was a success, because people came back to the mosques, and the *hijab* was more and more visible. It [the campaign] was supported by the Sunni *waqf*. Every issue was well covered by the media; when good money is spent, it is always a success. This campaign was a good thing for Iraqis.

Furthermore, Maysoon does not perceive the former regime to be especially opposed to religion and religious practice. Instead, she feels that religious activists in post-2003 Iraq experienced great opposition from the occupying US-led administration. According to Maysoon, the occupying powers privilege secular political leadership over Islamists.

I do not believe that we [Islamists] are more free today. I believe that we had obstacles of a certain kind before, and now the obstacles are of another kind. Iraqi society is not at peace; there is discrimination, racism, division, fear of religion, and an attack on religion. This fear of religion comes from two places. First, a legitimate fear of terrorism, this idea that religion brings terrorism. Second, secularism does not allow religion to participate in political life and the state, which is a mistake of course. Also, foreign politics has a great role here because it limits the number of religious people in the political sphere.

When asked about some women's rights activists' demands to reform discriminatory articles in the actual PSC, both Naziha and Maysoon firmly disagree. They both believe that the family should be governed by Muslim laws and that demands for equality – e.g., in inheritance, marriage, and divorce – are too extreme and oppose religion. Despite the fact that they share similar views on women's rights and on the importance of religion in both private and political life, they disagree on Article 41. Naziha perceives the article to be an affirmation of her *mazhab*, whereas Maysoon sees it as a threat to her identity. Comparing these women's views on equality, women's issues, and religion shows very clearly that their "political-sectarian stand" is at the core of this debate, not their religious-sectarian views. For the Shi'a Islamist, unified legislation under the previous regime entailed discrimination against her Shi'a political and religious identity; her desire for a community-based law is based on her politicoreligious identity and freedom. For the Sunni Islamist, a unified law signifies equal treatment for Sunnis, who have become a political minority since the fall of the Ba'th regime.

Naziha comes from a very educated, but conservative, background. She grew up in a Shi'a majority city north of Baghdad, and her father was close to the National Democratic Party. Her brother – a high-profile agricultural engineer – was imprisoned and executed by the regime in 1990. She obtained her Ph.D. in 1987 and began teaching at Baghdad University. Naziha pointed out that she was one of the few Shi'a women not affiliated with the Ba'th Party to hold a high academic position at the university. Due to her excellent results, she was even selected for training trips abroad; according to her, this was extremely rare for someone external to the Ba'th Party. Even though she greatly wished to attend such trainings because her research was of central importance to her, her conservative family and husband would not allow it. Like most of the women I interviewed, the sanctions period brought Naziha back to domestic life because her salary in the mid-1990s became too low to even cover weekly travel cost.

Maysoon grew up in a Sunni majority area of Baghdad; her mother was a school teacher and her father a police officer. She describes her family as apolitical and very conservative. She married a soldier from her neighborhood and had four children. Maysoon obtained her BA in administration and economy in 1989. However, even if she had been willing to work, the low salaries during the sanctions period convinced her to stay home. Because Maysoon considered being a housewife as "archaic," she decided to get involved in religious gatherings and her local mosque's charitable activities in the mid-1990s.

As two women involved as "women activists" within their respective Islamist political groups, a comparison of their different stands and trajectories reveals what they actually share. Their perception of the PSC as generally balanced and favorable to both women's rights and *shari'a* shows that their shared view corresponds to an urban middle-class family model: women are supposed to carry the responsibility of family and domestic life, as well as be professionally and socially active, whereas men remain the main breadwinners. Both Naziha and Maysoon believe that demands for "full equality" are akin to questioning Islam. They also shared a normative view – although general and imprecise – of what Islam and *shari'a* should be. In addition, they both caricature "secular women activists" as those who "ask for too much" and are "against religion." For example, although both Naziha and Maysoon believed that polygamy oppresses women and belongs to a "mind-set that is not compatible with modern times," they also saw outlawing it as against the law of God. They paint "secular women activists" as demanding the "right for women to have four husbands." Interestingly, many women critical of "extremist women activists," including some involved in secular activities, brought up this unfounded example; no woman activist in Iraq ever demanded a woman's right to four husbands. This example reveals many women's fear of demands that radically question social and gender norms, which form the core of the neopatriarchal, nuclear, middle-class family.

Fragmented Citizenship and Gender: Sectarianism and Competing Nationalisms

The polarized discourses and political mobilizations around the PSC reveal the entanglement of sectarianism and gender in post-2003 Iraq. The PSC is the essential and symbolic field of struggle between divergent national and political imaginaries, which are entangled with Islam and gender. As Naziha's and Maysoon's stances indicate, the "sectarianization" of Iraqi citizenship – between communalism and ethnicity – contributed to subcategorizing women's political identity (Colp Rubin 2008; Fischer-Tahir 2010; Kamp 2009). Naziha and Maysoon are not simply Islamist women activists; they are a Shi'a woman activist and a Sunni woman activist. Furthermore, the mobilization of Shi'a Islamists can be understood as a show of force, a Shi'a politicoreligious affirmation, in post-2003 Iraq. This show of force is ambiguous; it uses gender issues without being directly perceived by Shi'a women activists as a proper women's rights issue. In this sense, Shi'a Islamist women's mobilization around the PSC is comparable with Salime's description of the Islamist march of Casablanca in 2000, when Islamist women activists demonstrated en masse against the secularization of the Moroccan *mudawana* demanded by the Moroccan feminist movement's march of Rabat. Thus, without directly opposing progressive reform of Moroccan family law or the Rabat march, the well-known Moroccan Islamist activist Nadia Yassine (2011) demonstrated, saying: "I walked in Casablanca with the heart turned to the women marching in Rabat." Salime analyzes the Casablanca march as an Islamist show of force in Morocco. She explains the visibly opposing stand through a theorization of the "movement moment," as represented by the mobilization around women's legal rights in Morocco. The movement moment in 2000 contributed to a feminization of Islamist women's activism and the Islamization of women's rights activists. According to Salime, such a feminization entailed Islamist women activists' incorporation of feminist narratives and rhetoric, whereas the Islamization of women's rights activists entailed the Moroccan feminist movement's incorporation of Islamic references. Salime also situates this movement moment in Morocco within the broader context of the Moroccan government's liberalization, democratization, and adoption of US-friendly economic and political reforms in the 2000s.

Although the Iraqi context is far more complex than the Moroccan one, Salime's theorization of the movement moment is relevant. Post-2003, mobilizations for women's legal rights in Iraq are also movement moments. Such mobilizations are situated in the broader context of global gender discourses and mobilizations through the involvement of UN programs and international NGOs, which use the rhetoric of democratization, and transnational Islamic modernist discourses through Islamist movements in the region. The mobilizations around the PSC are also situated within an ambivalent legacy of gender politics undertaken by the former regime oscillating between secular "state feminism" and "Islamo-tribalism." As a result, Islamist and non-Islamist women activists carry the legacy of the neopatriarchal women's rights framework, Islamic modernist references, and the UN's regime of rights. The sectarianization of Iraqi political identity – exacerbated and institutionalized since 2003 – represents the core of the PSC field of struggle. Thus it is Shi'a Islamist political power that is affirmed through the questioning of the unified PSC, not Islamism per se. Similarly, Islamist women activists mobilized in support of Article 41 are organized as Shi'a Islamists, not women activists.

As shown in earlier chapters through the exploration of Luizard's historical research (1991) on Iraqi Shi'as and Haddad's more recent research (2010, 2014) on sectarianism, it can be argued that Sunnis and Shi'as have not shared a unified national narrative, symbolism, or ideology. Their competing narratives have taken a sectarian dimension, particularly after the brutal putdown of the 1991 uprisings and in a post-2003 era characterized by openly divisive Sunni and Shi'a narratives and self-identifications. As pointed out by Zubaida (2002, 1991), neither Sunnis, Shi'as, nor Kurds represented homogeneous groups because class, kin-based positions, regional belongings, and political affiliations (nationalists, communists, etc.) were also important dimensions of their identities. Hence, in Iraq, women's political identities are not only located in their encounters with modernity and Islam, as well as how articulations of "feminisms," "modernness," agency, and rights are shaped by global discourses and regulatory regimes, but also within competing local and regional nationalist narratives dominating in Iraq since 1991 by the Shi'a/Sunni divide exacerbated by the post-2003 political contexts of invasion and occupation. As Haddad points out, identity politics covered the fluidity, contextuality, and complexity of identity-oriented stands. The Shi'a/Sunni divide itself is also complex; here I present an analysis of the Islamist Shi'a and Islamist Sunni polarization with regard to the PSC. The articulation of gender and nation (Yuval-Davis 1997) is also articulated to communal and religious belongings. This already complex articulation takes place in the context of the circulation and encounters of local (Iraqi) and global (UN and US-led) gender discourses and politics within the frame of the internationalization of the so-called state-building process.

Analyses that posit Islamist political power as a "systematic," conservative backlash against and opposition to Western domination miss the more complex reality: there is a plurality of Islamism(s) – e.g., the Sunni and Shi'a versions have taken opposing stances in post-2003 Iraq – and their arrival to power has been the product of collaboration with Western military intervention. In the context of Iraq, Islamism or Muslim-oriented movements – often defined as an anti-Western and anti-modern and promoted by groups using their own understanding of gender issues rooted in a politics of piety – are far more complex and, to some extent, ambivalent. Islamist Shi'a political groups came to power in Iraq through their collaboration and partnership with the US administration. At the same time, however, these groups are also those questioning the PSC unifying framework on the grounds of "freedom of belief," a very liberal argument. Sunni Islamists, by contrast, are trying to preserve the current regime of rights that guarantees their inclusion. Here, using gender as a battleground, a competitive and antagonistic nation and national imaginary are at stake: unified citizenship versus communal-based belonging. The violent, authoritarian, minority-ruling experience of a unified secular state has resulted in Shi'a Islamists' desire to break with the centralized and secular.

Beyond Secular/Islamist Women's Rights Activism

I explored Islamist women's points of view on the PSC, showing how their political-sectarian positions take precedence over their religious-sectarian belonging and pointing out the commonalities, shared legacies, and imaginaries between Sunni and Shi'a Islamist women activists. I now explore the ways in which non-Islamist activists define women's rights – e.g., equality or equity – and how they have translated and appropriated the gender training sessions that many have attended since 2003. Following the analysis of Abu-Lughod (1998), Hatem (1993, 1994, 1998, 2005), and Salime (2011) and in light of the sociohistorical and political background outlined earlier, it is clear that the overlapping and mixing of terms in which women's legal rights have been advocated in post-2003 Iraq overcome the simplistic secular/Islamist boundary. Here I focus on how Iraqi women activists perceive and define the notions of women's rights and equality. I spent much time discussing and debating these notions with women activists and observed how they talk about and use such notions in their advocacy.

Amel F., forty-nine years old, is a well-known women's rights activist, lawyer specializing in family issues, and former MP of the first post-2003 Iraqi government. She was an advisor for the Ministry in Charge of Women's Affairs and participated in many civil society and governmental committees during the drafting of the new Iraqi Constitution, notably around Article 41. She published several articles and books on the PSC in which she proposed reforming it in a way that respects both women's rights and the Islamic legal tradition. I met her at al-Mansur Hunting Club, where she and her brother are regulars. Amel's son and husband were killed during the sectarian conflict of 2006–7. Amel is from a Faili Kurdish and communist family from Baghdad; she defines herself as simultaneously "secular" and a "practicing Muslim." Despite the fact that she does not wear the veil and is stylishly dressed, she emphasizes that she is closer to many Islamists than "secular" activists. She considers herself a bridge between seculars and Islamists because she approaches the question of the PSC via an "Islamic framework." Amel firmly advocates against Article 41 and defends the Convention on the Elimination of All Forms of Discrimination against Women (CEDAW) as a tool to improve women's rights while simultaneously insisting on respect for "Islamic rules, customs, and traditions." On the notion of equality, she says:

I am against total equality; it doesn't exist. Our society is Islamic; woman are governed by customs and traditions, as well as the limits given by *shari'a*. It is impossible for a woman to have sexual freedom like a man. She could not be free in her sexuality like a man outside the framework of marriage.

I ask if this was her personal view or a statement of Iraq's social and cultural reality. She answers:

I advocate equality in the right to think, the freedom of opinion, the right to work, to create ... Advocating women's rights is not asking to be like men. As he divorces me, I divorce him; as she cheats on me, I cheat on him. Unfortunately, the majority of women have a wrong awareness, and most women activists are this type of woman.

During our discussion, Amel firmly expressed her disagreement with many activists, whom she described as secular, for not respecting the "limits of *shari'a*" and thus harming the cause of women's rights.

Liza T., fifty-one, is from a Chaldean Christian family originally from Dohuk, but she was born and raised in Baghdad's al-Kerrada neighborhood. She is the director of the Chaldean Women's Society, executive director of the al-Rafidain Women's Coalition, and member of the IWN. I met her once at the al-Rafidain office in al-Kerrada and several other times at her organization's meetings. She works hard to preserve her Chaldean Christian identity and the Syriac language; she is also aware of and deeply influenced by Islamic legal traditions. Liza's organization set up gender mainstreaming training sessions and campaigned for CEDAW and Security Council Resolution 1325. In relation to how she defines and perceives the notion of gender, she says:

The concept of gender is equality in the sense of equal access to positions of responsibilities with men. But it doesn't mean that my freedom is like his freedom. We are Orientals; many things are not acceptable for us; this doesn't mean that we are going to advocate for things that could not be accepted by our society. What we want is for equal competence, equal jobs, and equal salaries ... It is true that there is something in the physical constitution of men that is different, and the

Qur'an says, "Men have a preeminence over women." But nobody finishes the verse, "in what they spend for them" [Qur'anic verse], which means that men have to be breadwinners.

Like Amel, Liza quoted the Qur'an, *hadith*, and famous religious figures – such as Imam 'Ali – several times during out discussion. She uses the terms of current Muslim reformist debates around men's and women's different rights and duties within the family.

The examples of Amel and Liza – the former an activist from a communist background who is involved in a secular mode and the latter an activist who advocates for Christians' and women's rights – show the hegemony of Islamic references in Iraqi public discourses since the 1990s. The Islamization of political life was enhanced with the coming to power of Islamist parties in 2003; at that time, Islamist discourses became hegemonic and deeply affected women activists' representations and discourses. Advocating for women's rights using both the UN and human rights frameworks while keeping the private sphere intact through Islamic legitimization highlights the overall context of post-2003 Iraq, as well as the complex debates around the quest for "authenticity" in gender issues in postcolonial Middle Eastern contexts. Amel's and Liza's rejection of women's sexual freedom outside the framework of marriage, along with their distinction between male and female sexual freedoms, reveals the hegemony of the politics of morality and female respectability in post-2003 (perhaps even post-1991) Iraqi society.

The undefined "specificities" evoked by many nonreligious activists or those involved in a secular mode were often justified using arguments of "culture." Rabab H. – a prominent activist and figure in the IWN – explains her definition of the concept gender.

I defend the concept of gender, but I don't accept everything in that concept. Even in France and Europe, there are families that have their own values regarding women. But in these countries, there is a common law because they are secular, and then everybody can define his or her own limits. We in Iraq, we have signed the CEDAW convention, but with some objections, because we consider that we are in a primary stage of women's liberation. We demand that women and men have the same rights in access to education, the job market, and spheres of power, as well as traveling alone and the ability to marry a non-Iraqi and pass nationality to their children. There are many things that we advocate for that have nothing to do with honor and the sacred things of religion.

Rabab believes that Iraq's current "culture" is what makes it not ready for total equality. Even if her discourse relies on contextual and practical legitimizations rather than religious legitimizations and stays open to the possibility of struggling for "total equality," in practice, her stance is to avoid dealing with "private" issues.

Some women who use the human rights framework and are involved in nonreligious groups but define themselves as practicing Muslims think that "religious limits" could be challenged by working within the religious framework. Such women are taking an Islamic feminist stance (Mir-Hosseini 1999) because they consider religious norms reformable and want to debate within the confines of Muslim orthodoxy. Fatima A. mentioned earlier, forty-five and from a Da'wa family, is a women's rights activists from Medinat al-Sadr. After the fall of the regime, Fatima became a member of the Medinat al-Sadr Municipal Council; she is also a founding member of the Baghdad Women's Association and vice president of the Center for Women's Progress. She believes that using "true Islam" is essential to the defense of gender equality, even in the private sphere. Her words go clearly beyond the Western/Islam dichotomy used by many activists: "Feminism is Western to what degree? If we consider the level of rights, no religion has given more rights to women than Islam. Human rights are originally Islamic."

We discuss concrete examples of inequalities in the dominant Muslim jurisprudence (inheritance, polygamy, etc.) and talk about the Muslim feminist standpoint.

We really need that. We need other readings, other interpretations of our religious texts, modern readings, because our religion is universal and valid for all time. The historical context has influenced our religious texts, and political mistakes and personal problems have been added to our religious corpus. It has been a thousand years that our religious reading has not changed, and our readings stay the ones of men impregnated by their culture. We need to renew Muslim thought.

Despite the limits of such a discourse, especially its definition of Islam itself, Fatima's Muslim feminist standpoint is a clear attempt to go beyond dichotomies – such as Western/Oriental – and proposes reforms even in the sphere of the family, which is a sphere deemed untouchable by many activists.

While some women choose to put aside religious references and others choose to Islamize their defense of women's rights for either pragmatic reasons or because of personal beliefs, most activists take an overlapping stance: defending social equality within the limits of cultural or religious specificities. Although the dominant discourse reproduces the West/Arab-Muslim dichotomy by claiming to defend women's rights in an "essentially different" way from the West, a minority of women seek to go beyond the dichotomy by using Islam as a way to claim the indigenous nature and authenticity of their stance. Thus women activists' positions in Iraq are complex and multifaceted: they define themselves differently, or choose not to define themselves at all, within the secular/Islamist, non-religious/religious binaries. This overlapping stance is comparable with women's rights activism in the region more generally, which is the product of modernist, nationalist, and developmentalist rhetoric in contexts where political Islam represents the hegemonic discourse (Abu-Lughod 1998; Charrad 2011; Hatem 2005, 1994). The complexity of sectarianism and the knock-on effect of adding other notions of identity politics to this overlap of references are specific to the Iraqi context.

Beyond the Categories: Islamic, Islamist, and Secular "Feminists"

In her study of pious Muslim women in Turkey, Göle (1993) explains how a modern Muslim gender discourse is revealed by the notion of "modern *mahrem*." Through this notion, Göle shows how practices of piety, which involve alternative temporality and representation of the self, are intertwined with a modern way of life. Her refusal to categorize and define the women she describes as "Muslim feminists" or to use a feminist lexicon more generally left open the discussion and analysis of certain discourses and practices related to Islam, gender, and modernity. Göle's refusal to label is a strong and original stance, which greatly affected my thinking on feminism, Islam, and Islamism. As I showed in my own research on Muslim feminisms, terminologies are political: the development of the Islamic/Muslim feminist concept over the past twenty years is an important statement within feminism and Islam scholarship (Ali 2012). Along the lines of Black and Third World feminisms, Muslim feminisms question radically ethnocentric and Orientalist representations of feminism and Islam, enabling the questioning of normative definitions and the articulation of overlapping forms of gender mobilization within Muslim and Islamist movements. Within scholarship dealing with Islam, Muslim feminisms bring new insight and contribute to situating women and gender issues, or a feminist perspective, at the core of the study of religiosity and contemporary Muslim political and social movements. There is a need to create new categories of analysis because new concepts are often revealing of new realities and their associated power struggles. I situate my work within the endeavor to allow concepts and theories to emerge from social and political realities. Nevertheless, it is important to be able to see what lies in between conceptualized realities and thus not be constrained by categorizations.

To be able to read, analyze, and reveal the complexity of the Iraqi context, I am approaching it through a category "in-betweenness"[10] rather than through the categories of Islamic, Islamist, or secular feminisms. As mentioned earlier, the intersections between local and global discourses and practices are central to understanding Iraqi women activists' overlapping stances, in addition to the evolution of gender politics over the past fifty years as a direct result of political, economic, and social realities that transformed Iraqi society. The "NGOization" of women's groups contributed to a homogenization of their activism, as focused on *tathqif* ("culture raising") and *taw'iyya* ("awareness raising"), as I described in Chapter 4. The hegemony of Islamic references within society is not limited to its Gramscian meaning, as a "cultural framework" that does not need to exercise force or coercion. The weakness of the state and the power of conservative Islamist militias in certain neighborhoods of Baghdad and across the streets of Iraq constitute essential dimensions of women activists' concrete realities. Many mentioned that even though the new Constitution provides a good framework of rights, the rule of law is absent in a context of overall insecurity; hence citizens' basic rights are not in any way ensured. As an example of a positive step, many activists pointed to women's right to pass Iraqi citizenship to their children. However, even though this right exists on paper in the Constitution, concrete implementation is lacking. One activist commented: "[t]he top of the government is so conservative and the state is so weak, so who is going to implement this article?" In terms of legal rights, even the Minister in Charge of Women's Affairs pointed out that the actual laws are not the problem for Iraqi women because they are generally good; the problems arise from the *ta'limaat* that accompany the laws, which reflect the conservative mentality of the political groups in power. In this very conservative and sensitive climate, no political leader – including the Minister in Charge of Women's Affairs – is pushing for this right to be implemented.

The spectrum of Iraqi women's rights activists' swings from extremely "secular feminists" to, on the other end, "Islamist feminists." "Extreme seculars" include organizations such as the OWFI and some members of the IWN, who advocate for radical reform of the PSC toward full equality; very few demand complete secularization of the PSC. "Islamist feminists," by contrast, want the PSC to be preserved in its current form,

[10] For the notion of "in-betweenness," I am very grateful to the organizers and participants in the workshop "Islamic Feminists, Islamist Women, and the Women Between" held in Paris in January 2013 and supervised by Lila Abu-Lughod, Katherine Ewing, and Anupama Rao as part of the project *Gender, Religion and Law in Muslim Societies*, Centre for the Study of Social Difference, Columbia University.

whereas most Shiʻa Islamist women activists call for a specific regime of rights. In between these poles, pragmatic or ideological "Muslim feminists" – including certain Islamist personalities and many activists involved in a secular mode who are personally religious – advocate for the preservation of the PSC and moderate reforms guaranteeing as many women's rights as possible with respect to *shariʻa*. Such "Muslim feminists" call for *ijtihad* on several PSC articles and reform toward more rights for women. What unites this spectrum of activists is their promotion of a specific type of "Iraqi woman": the urban, educated, professionally active, and "strong" Iraqi woman who, in the past, was marked by her intellectual and political contribution to Iraqi culture. In addition, another common thread across the spectrum is the use of the United Nation's regime of rights, the "NGOization" of activism, and the use of Islamic/Iraqi culture as a justification for demands.

Thus, in the line of the analysis of Abu Lughod (1998) and Hatem (1994, 2005), I have come to the conclusion that – in terms of social background (urban, educated, and middle and upper class), agenda, grassroots work, and representations of and discourses on women's rights – there is no fundamental difference between secular-oriented and Islamist women's rights activists in Iraq. Many Islamists have appropriated modernist conceptualizations of women's roles in society, marriage relations, and the family, thereby competing with both conservative modernists and progressive political activists over these issues. In a context of exacerbated identity politics, most "seculars" and "Islamists" engage in the postcolonial "authenticity" debate; only a minority of activists strives to go beyond it. At the crossroads of local and global discourses, the hegemony of religious conservatism and the "NGOization" of activism constitute the framework for advocating women's legal rights. Thus no stance is strictly Islamist, Muslim, or secular feminist because most activists are simultaneously invoking notions of respectability, moral references (justified by Islam or culture), and international human rights.

Conclusion: Contextualizing the "Religious" and the "Secular"

Following the removal of an authoritarian regime that represented and dominated both the state and the nation for almost four decades, post-2003 Iraq is a milieu of "imposed nation-building" by imperialist powers. The year 2003 also marked the coming to power of previously marginalized political groups: Shiʻas and Kurds. Women's issues were used by both the US-led occupational powers and the newly installed political elite in such a way as to partially replay the postcolonial "woman question." In the context of imposed nation-building, imperialist and international political agents – along with the Shi'a Islamist and Kurdish nationalist – enforced a self-serving and self-sustaining definition of Iraq's identity. The sectarian and fragmented vision of Iraq became institutionalized, and this "implanted Iraqiness" imposed a selective rupture with the supposed legacy of the Ba'th regime and, more generally, to the "secular" legacy of the Iraqi state that the PSC supposedly represents and that Shi'a political groups have always perceived as marginalizing. Post-2003 Iraq replayed the postcolonial "woman question" in a sectarian guise, where conservative Shi'a Islamists proposed a national imaginary in which gender issues occupy an essential tool for their identity politics marked by the affirmation of their political Shi'a identity. Once again, as was the case in the colonial period, the "new nation" implies a "new woman." The link between nation-state and gender is defined by a context in which imperialist military intervention imposed a new political elite and self-serving version of Iraqi nationhood. The sectarian questioning of Iraqi citizenship reduces women's status to a subcategory of an already fragmented identity. Here it is clearly not the divide religious/secular that is at stake but politicized sectarianism that questions the supposed legacy of "secularism" of the Iraqi state and the religious sectarianism carried by the majority of the population that accommodates very well the current state of unified legislation. I show that what is perceived as a gender issue – such as the debate around the PSC – is in reality a sectarian gender issue involving an understanding of the secular and religious that is defined through the experience of divergent national imaginaries. In such a context, interestingly, although the PSC is inspired by *shari'a*, it is interpreted as secular by Iraqis because the state remains the arbitrator regarding religious matters. Thus the "secular" PSC has taken on multiple meanings: some translate it as "unifying," as a means to counter politicized sectarianism – and not religious sectarianism – which is the case for the Sunnis and the majority of the population, whereas the Shi'a Islamists see it as synonymous with the marginalization of their political sectarian identity.

I also show that looking at Iraqi women's rights advocacy through both its local and global dimensions with the involvement of international women's rights discourse helps one to understand women activists' overlapping gender discourses and thus break with the simplistic categorization of secular/Islamist. Iraqi women activists are struggling in a context where the state is weak and the political culture is conservative: it is unable to implement the rule of law or provide basic rights for its citizens – such as provide security or access to basic services (water, electricity, and healthcare) – and it imposes constrains on the implementation of positive laws regarding gender issues. The climate of insecurity and the political crisis, in which conservative militias compete for power on the streets, affects women's everyday lives and shapes the limits and possibilities of women's rights advocacy.

As Asad (2003) argues, many scholars and activists consider religion to be dogmatic and secular practices as essentially more liberal. Ironically, Shi'a Islamist political activists are using the liberal principle of freedom of belief – i.e., the right for all communities to be governed according to their own beliefs – to defend Article 41 of the Constitution and the Ja'fari Law. The very liberal and secular intention of democratization was also used as the justification for the US-led invasion of Iraq, which provoked a deep and unspeakable crisis of state and political identity. Women activists also advocate for preservation of the PSC in the name of Islam (or Iraqi culture). So nothing is essentially religious or secular, and the boundaries between are porous, fluid, and impossible to understand outside their context of expression and deployment. The concrete realities that women activists face in Iraq, which go beyond political or religious affiliation, include the institutionalization of sectarian politics by the US-led occupation; the destruction of Iraq's educational, social, and political systems since the 1990s, with the rise of conservatism provoked by successive wars and militarization; and the politicization of gender issues under the banner of democratization since 2003.

Meanwhile, in the areas occupied by IS, women are deemed minors or inferiors and lack the very basis of their legal rights. It is clear that the situation women are facing in Iraq today is not the simple product of a misreading of "Islam" but is rather the direct consequences of a series of wars and invasions that have led to social and political fragmentation coupled with the rise of conservative forces, the foremost victims of which have been Iraqi women.

7   Iraqi Feminisms
Searching for Common Grounds

Introduction: Reclaiming the Past, Negotiating the Present

In all the events, meetings, and gatherings I attended in my two years of fieldwork, I noticed a similarity in activists' discourses and ideas around the advocacy for women's rights. All, regardless of political orientation or ethnic/religious background, would begin their presentations, talks, and conferences about "the Iraqi woman" by presenting her as highly educated; politically, professionally, and socially active; and strong (Figure 7.1). Political groups repressed by the previous regime often mentioned examples of women who were imprisoned and tortured by the Ba'th, such as Bint al-Huda,[1] the sister of Muhammad Baqer al-Sadr. Everyone agrees on figures such as Sabiha al-Shaikh Da'ud, the first female lawyer; Nazik al-Mala'ika, the great poet and intellectual[2]; and Naziha al-Dulaimi, the first Iraqi (and Arab) female minister. Bint al-Huda was a figure of the Shi'a Islamist movement of the 1960s and 1970s, as mentioned previously. The citing of this mixture of personalities to demonstrate the greatness of "the Iraqi woman" by all kinds of activists – Islamists and non-Islamists, Shi'a and Sunnis, leftists and nationalists – appears remarkable to me. Even the older generation of Kurdish women activists brought up such examples, with the addition of famous Kurdish women activists, such as Zakia Isma'il Haqi.[3]

In meetings organized by different women's groups and coalitions in Baghdad, several women representatives would be invited to present their vision of women and gender issues. At such meetings, women activists and representatives from different backgrounds would often gather around a table. Several meetings and workshops organized by women's rights organizations bore variations of the title, "For the Promotion of the

---

[1] Her name is Aminah Hayder al-Sadr. The surname Bint al-Huda means "Daughter of the Right Path..

[2] Nazik al-Mala'ika contributed to the existentialist intellectual trend in Iraq in the 1950s and 1960s.

[3] Zakia Isma'il Haqi was the first female judge in Iraq and the Arab world. She was a very famous Kurdish women's rights activist in the 1960s and 1970s.

Figure 7.1 Meeting organized by the Iraqi Women Network in Baghdad (March 2012).

Iraqi Woman," and those invited often included several well-known women activists and government, Parliament, and Provincial Council representatives. The women activists seated around the table represented very diverse backgrounds – Sunni and Shi'a Islamists, leftists, Kurds, and Christians – and coalitions. The audience would usually be composed of journalists, intellectuals, young and old civil society activists, and supporters or beneficiaries of one of the invited organizations.

Such meetings had a warm and agreeable atmosphere: visit cards would be exchanged, pictures taken, and sweets, water, and juice distributed among the participants and audience. The discussion often followed a presentation on "the great history of the Iraqi woman," Security Council Resolution 1325, or the Convention on the Elimination of All Forms of Discrimination against Women (CEDAW). A representative of the IWN, would insist on "preserving the gains of the past" and remaining faithful to the "legacy of the Iraqi women's movement." An activist from a local women's organization would recall the fact that these gains comply with Islam and were agreed upon by Sunni and Shi'a religious scholars in the Personal Status Code's (PSC's) 1959 elaboration. A representative from al-Rafidain Women's Coalition would then add that these gains are part of "Iraqi culture." An Islamist woman representative, Sunni or Shi'a, would firmly agree and give a short speech about "the greatness of woman's status in *shari'a* and Islam." Everyone, including the Christian activists, would nod affirmatively, and there would be outbreaks of applause from the audience. The discussions would then carry on to how to "educate" women and Iraqi society about women's rights and to "teach them" how to advocate. Often an audience member would request the microphone and say: "If women knew their religion properly, they would know that all these rights are their God-given rights." Everyone would vigorously applaud in response. In any meeting, on any subject, the audience would voice grievances and complaints to the women representatives in attendance. At one workshop, a young woman said: "And you, parliamentarians, what do you do to help the Iraqi people other than sitting around tables, talking, eating, and receiving your astronomical wages?" Women representatives often replied to this type of criticism by saying: "Nobody listens to us" or "Our powers are very limited."

At these meetings, most Islamist activists wore black *'abaya*, headscarves, and long dresses covering everything but the face and hands, but some Islamists wore colorful clothes, visible makeup, and high heels. Some activists involved in secular groups would also dress in long clothes and headscarves covering their whole body. Many young women in the audience wore colorful *hijab*, skinny jeans, and heavy makeup; such women would be involved in secular organizations or Islamist groups or even belong to well-known religious families. Many heads were not covered, and long-standing older activists often would have their hair cut short and would wear a top and knee-length skirt. In addition, some activists wore *hijab* with a knee-length skirt and high heels. There would also usually be several older women with their heads symbolically covered by a loose shawl that showed half of their hair; the shawl would often fall to their shoulders and be elegantly restored onto their head. More important, the Muslimness of Iraqi culture is visibly shared by everyone. Moreover, in their attachment to the model of the modern, educated, professionally and socially active Iraqi woman and her legal gains, it is clearly impossible to distinguish between Islamists and non-Islamists, veiled and nonveiled, half veiled and non–half veiled, the ones in knee-length skirts and short haircuts and those in knee-length skirts and *hijab*.

Such meetings would take place in the seminar rooms of cultural centers, most often in al-Kerrada in central Baghdad. Representatives and activists who live in distant areas of Baghdad often arrive late, apologize, and describe the terrible traffic or checkpoint delays. Women representatives of the government, Provincial Councils, or Parliament always get most of the audience's attention and grievances. Such representatives are always surrounded by activists asking for support at the end of meetings and bombarded by requests from male and female audience members for private meetings to discuss personal issues or help in administrative difficulties.

Among the urban, middle-class women of the post-2003 Iraqi women's movement, an idea of Iraq, of "Iraqiness," through the image of "the Iraqi woman" is expressed, claimed, and performed. According to the women activists, the 1959 PSC gathered the best of Sunni and Shi'a legal traditions at the time and, more important, was elaborated with the agreement of both society and religious scholars. This model is evoked more strongly by the most educated, as well as the older generation. What seems essential is not the factual or historical accuracy of this model and references to the past but the way in which these structure the activists' advocacy for women's rights.[4] Presenting these "gains of the past" as part of "Iraqi culture" and "Islam" is an essential dimension of their advocacy for women's rights. It shows that Iraqi women activists from very diverse political, communal, and religious backgrounds, although mostly educated and middle class, do share a common imaginary that bridges the gains of the past and the struggles of the present. If the Ba'th legacy is not claimed as such in a context where the political discourse is dominated by the *mazlumiyya* ideology and that the Ba'th party itself is banned and demonized, it is clear that the importance given to the centrality of the state as the social and economic provider and guarantor of citizenship rights constitutes a legacy of the Ba'th regime. As pointed out by Ferguson (2015) in the case of Syria, "right talks" in Iraq are dominated by statism, as well as a mix of human rights discourse and the more local discourse around the PSC that merge "Islam" with statism.

Most women activists who were involved in women's groups such as al-Rabita or women's branches of Islamists organizations suffered repression under the Ba'th regime; many returned from exile to re-form their political groups after 2003. Apart from women who had done previous gender-specific activities and built some kind a feminist or women's rights awareness from political activism, other women mostly got involved "as women," without any previous experience of political activism. Thus members of Iraq's post-2003 women's organizations have different levels of political and gender awareness – from those highly involved in political and women's issues to those who encounter activism "as women." Women of the latter category have joined political and civil society groups

---

[4] As I showed in Chapter 1, the political and social process through which the Personal Status Code was actually adopted on December 30, 1959, is more complex than activists chose to present. It was a source of disagreement for the 'ulemas who tried to forbid any appropriation of the realm of *mujtahid* authority. See for further details Anderson (1963, 1968), Sabiha al-Shaikh Da'ud (1958).

for various reasons, ranging from a genuine interest in women's rights issues to career aspirations.

This chapter explores Iraqi women activists' representations and practices of gender norms and relations and women's rights activism. Here I am interested in their views, experiences, and feelings about gender issues, as well as how they define and think about activism for women's rights. In other words, what different feminisms exist among women activists in postinvasion Iraq?

Approaching Iraqi Women Activists' Feminisms

Gender and Conservatism

It is difficult to define the word "conservatism." In most of this research, I rely on a generic understanding that depicts the word as pejorative, indicating a kind of refusal to openness, change, and progress, especially when it comes to women and gender issues. In Iraq, I noticed that the word *muhafez* carried different meanings according to my interlocutor. Although the word was always used in relation to religious conservatism, it did not carry a negative connotation for Islamists and women who presented themselves as religious. Conservatism was, by contrast, understood as pejorative by most of the women who defined themselves as liberals, as well as by some who described themselves as religious. During my interviews, when I asked women activists to describe their family background and upbringing, I deliberately chose to ask: "Was your family background *muhafez*?" Very few women replied "no" to this question; on the contrary, most replied "yes." "Yes, of course" or "Yes, *al hamdulilah*." The reaction to my use of this word at the beginning of an interview often gave me an idea of how our discussion on women and gender issues might progress. The activists who expressed the most egalitarian views on women and gender issues considered "conservatism" to be a pejorative word. They also equated "tribalism" and "tribal mentality" with women's oppression. Interestingly, Iraqi women activists often chose to use the word *taqlidi* ("traditional") to balance the depiction of their background as *muhafez*. Some would describe their upbringing as such: "My family was conservative, but they were mostly traditional" or "My upbringing was quite conservative, but not entirely; let's say it was traditional." Bashaer is an independent parliamentarian and women rights activist in her midforties and originally from Najaf. Her response to my question was: "My family was conservative, but they were influenced by the liberal ideas widespread in Najaf in the 1970s."

Although most Islamist women activists embraced their conservative upbringing, many women activists involved in secular organizations also claimed their conservative backgrounds. Among the women who saw "conservatism" in a pejorative light, only some described themselves as nonreligious, whereas many insisted on their attachment to religious practice. Those who described themselves as religious insisted on their attachment to ritual prayer, as well as to regular reading of the Qur'an and religious invocations. Some of these women wore the *hijab* with long clothes; others wore a short and loose *hijab* with a knee-length shirt; others wore long and large clothes but did not cover their heads; and still others wore a knee-length shirt and skinny jeans. The "anticonservatives" are also diverse in terms of their relationship with religiosity, but they all consider the restrictions imposed on women's dress and bodies negatively. However, most women activists described religious conservatism as the fabric of "Arab culture" – the essential dimension distinguishing it from "the West" and a dimension to challenge or preserved.

Very interestingly, the fact that the word "traditional" was used positively shows that what is considered "Iraqi culture" is not seen as essentially opposed to progressive gender views. On the contrary, "religious traditionalism" is perceived as less harmful to women's rights than "religious conservatism." All the women activists considered "Iraqi culture" as generally favorable to women's rights and designated women's oppression as "foreign" and "external" to their "authentic culture." If "Iraqi culture" or "traditions" are patriarchal, "hardcore oppression" was always designated as belonging to the "other" – e.g., "tribal people" or "politicoreligious conservatives" imported from Iran or Saudi Arabia.

More generally speaking, if one defines "conservatism" as "to conserve or preserve the status quo, the dominant way of life, the hegemonic way of thinking and doing," this implies that conservatism changes and relies entirely on its context of deployment. In the context of a certain religious power's hegemony, the conservatives would be those willing to maintain the religious authority. By contrast, in a context dominated by antireligious ideology and practices, the conservatives would be the antireligious, often called the "seculars" or "liberals." Theoretically, the equation is simple, but the concrete social and political realities are far from this duality. One can be conservative in terms of religious matters but anticonservative in terms of political matters. Social, cultural, political, and religious conservatisms often contradict one another. Moreover, those deemed as liberals in their opposition to the rule of religion over public matters can be conservative in private matters. As shown in Chapter 6, some Iraqi women activists define themselves as "liberals," oppose the rule of religion over public matters and politics, and advocate for individual freedom and rights; however, when it comes to private matters, they defend the preservation of the *shari'a*-based PSC. Such activists' advocacy for preserving *shari'a* could be motivated by personal beliefs or by a political strategy, but their stands show the complexity of the multiple shapes and contextual dimensions of conservatism and thus of "progressivism."

Talal Asad's critique and questioning of the religious/secular dichotomy in his seminal work, *Formations of the Secular* (2003), can be applied to the conservative/progressive dichotomy. It is possible to show the complexity of the conservative/progressive dichotomy first because its meaning relies on the context in which it emerges and second because it obeys different dimensions that are porous as well as ambivalent. I want to expand this complex approach to conservatisms in line with the conclusions drawn in the preceding chapters, where I showed that social and religious conservatisms have been widespread since at least the 1990s due to the retribalization politics of Saddam Hussein and the accompanying Faith Campaign. These politics, coupled with the direct effects of militarization and economic sanctions, ended up eroding moral and sexual values and raising new forms of patriarchy and control over women's dress and bodies. Islamist militants' politicization of women's dress in the 1980s was accentuated by the social, political, and economic situation of the 1990s. Thus, after 2003, as conservative Shi'a parties came to power and conservative, party-backed Islamist militias dominated many urban public spaces, especially in Baghdad, the focus on women's dress code and behavior became widespread and gained legitimacy. Moreover, since 2003, the politicization of gender norms and relations has taken place within the context of the overall "sectarianization" of Iraqi political and social life. Thus sectarianism also represents a form of social conservatism, along with tribalism and kin-based relations, which characterizes Iraqi society today. Earlier I also showed how sectarianism in postinvasion Iraq contributed to a reorganization of women's legal rights and concretely affected women's lives and activism.

Thus I argue that social (kin-based and tribal), political (sectarianism), and religious conservatisms represent hegemonic forces that link to one another and have an impact on the definition of gender norms, relations, and practices. Significantly, I argue that social, political, and religious conservatisms have affected the controlling of women's dress code and behavior, enhanced patriarchal gender norms and relations, and recomposed and politicized women's issues within a sectarian framework. Returning to my comparison of Asad's questioning of the religious/

secular dichotomy applied to notions of conservatism and progress, I argue that social, political, and religious conservatisms – in other words, tribalism and kin-based powers, sectarianism, and normative views invoked in the name of Islam – overlap in a complex and unsystematic way. As discussed previously, Sunni and Shi'a Islamist conservatisms, although convergent in their readings of gender norms, diverge in their political and legal implementations. Within a context of rising Shi'a power, Sunni Islamists felt marginalized and hence defended the unifying legal framework of the PSC; Shi'a Islamists, by contrast, advocated for fragmentation of the PSC and its reconfiguration according to their specific reading of Muslim jurisprudence. This example shows how social, political, and religious conservatisms are context specific and shift according to competing definitions of nationhood, statehood, trends, and transnational gender discourses within different religious groups.

On Piety, Morality, and Respectability

After highlighting the importance of the complexity and multiple layers of conservatisms in relation to gender issues, I show the importance of the variable reading, experience, and understanding of religion, piety, and morality itself.[5] Saba Mahmood's *Politics of Piety* (2005) explores a women's pietist movement within Cairo mosques and proposes a rethinking of normative liberal accounts of politics. Mahmood seeks to understand how women's adherence to the patriarchal norms at the core of such movements challenges assumptions within liberal feminist theory about freedom and agency. Through considering the embodiment of religious rituals among Islamist or Muslim pietist movements, she explores the conceptual relationship between bodily form and political imaginaries. Despite a groundbreaking critique of Western liberal feminism and normative liberal accounts of politics, on a theoretical and political level, Mahmood's research does not historicize, contextualize, or look at the plural and intersectional aspects of the realities of the women she observed. Mahmood's account can give the impression that these pious women live outside society, as if they built a radical alternative way of life completely outside wider Egyptian society. If I had followed an acontextual and ahistorical analysis, I could have shown the same type of discourses and reached the same conclusions –

---

[5] For this section, I would like to thank the organizers and participants of the workshop "Gendering Faith: Islamist Women Activism," supervised by Muwatin, The Palestinian Institute for the Study of Democracy and the Chris. Michelsen Institute (CMI).

i.e., Islamist Iraqi women develop an alternative definition of equality and femininity. However, since I take an intersectional look at Iraqi women activists' concrete realities – their practices and everyday conditions – and do not limit my gaze and analysis to their discourses on faith and gender, I reach very different conclusions. I show in this chapter that certain aspects of Mahmood's "politics of piety" are expressed by many women – interestingly, among both Islamist and "secular" women activists. This "politics of piety" is articulated with other regimes of reference, such as state laws and human rights, and is linked to different religious and national imaginaries. This "alternative" way of articulating notions of women's rights and equality is informed by both the "politics of piety" and the concrete realities in which these politics are deployed. Such realities have been characterized, since 2003 (if not 1991), by hegemonic social, political, and religious conservatisms competing for divergent national imaginaries.

It is interesting to draw a comparison between Islamist Iraqi women's discourses on piety, gender, and modernity and Lara Deeb's exploration (2006) of gender and "public piety" among pious Shi'a women loosely affiliated with Hizbullah in al-Dahiyya (southern Beirut). The comparison with Deeb's research is relevant because of both its theoretical approach and the closeness of the Lebanese context with regard to issues of sectarianism and gender. Deeb considers the definition of modernity to be an unproductive question, arguing that it is far more interesting to explore how pious Shi'a Muslims understand "being modern," as well as how they deploy and engage various discourses and ideas about modernness. In maintaining an ethnographic focus on the ways notions of modernness and piety are lived, debated, and shaped by "everyday Islamists," Deeb demonstrates the complexity and underscored the inseparability of religion and politics in the lives of pious Muslims. Like Mahmood (2005), Deeb rejects approaches that consider Muslim-oriented, or Islamist, engagements to be simply a strategy for coping with or resisting Westernization; she argues, instead, that not only is faith a facade hiding what is "really" going on, but also, in fact, faith *is* what is going on. She shows that the core of this enchanted modern approach is a dual emphasis on both material and spiritual progress as necessary to modernness. Spiritual progress, in particular, is viewed by pious Shi'as as a necessary component of a viable alternative to the perceived emptiness of modernity, as manifested in the West. Deeb suggests that when religiosity is incorporated into modernness in this way, the stakes of being pious change. The dualistic notion of progress and the global political context in which it has emerged has consequences for faith and morality on the personal level, on people's quotidian expressions and experiences of piety. In al-Dahiyya, women's public piety has been incorporated as both necessary to and evidence of the enchanted modern. Deeb argues that looking at these complex daily enmeshments of piety and politics allows one to show that Islam is not in the service of politics, nor are politics determined solely by Islam. She argues that it is only by holding both in view, and thus undoing their separation, that a more complete understanding of the pious modern can be grasped.

I concur with Deeb's approach to piety, which is grounded in the context of local and global political, social, and economic dynamics. I am also very much convinced of the importance of considering faith in and of itself and not reducing it to a political anti-Western reaction or means of contestation, although I do also consider its inherent political dimension. Thus I argue that Iraqi women's pietism, either Islamist or not, is guided by its own dynamics of faith that are imbricated with notions of politics, either anti-Western or anti-secularist, and an antinormative definition of the nation. The complex analysis at the core of this thesis shows how gender dynamics overlap with the state, nation, and dynamics of faith within a postcolonial and contextual understanding of Islam. Interestingly, still exploring al-Dahiyya, Deeb and Harb (2013) also analyze the relationship between leisure, morality, and geography, enriching their analysis in a way that is very relevant to my research. By using the concept of "multiple moral rubrics," they extended their critique of Mahmood's views. Using Schielke's (2009) analysis of Muslim youth in Egypt, Deeb and Harb argue that Mahmood's privileging of piety as a "primary motivator" is problematic. Mahmood's focus on religious piety does not do justice to the complex and often contradictory nature of everyday experiences and can oversimplify the complexities of daily negotiations of moral practices. Following Schielke's analysis, Deeb and Harb (2013) consider that ethical subjectivities are based on the coexistence of various motivations, aims, and identities that can and often do conflict but are not exclusive opposites. Thus they define the concept of "multiple moral rubrics" as the overlapping of the "social rubric" (i.e., manners, values of social obligation, hierarchies shared across society), the "political-sectarian rubric" (i.e., reflecting the conflation of sectarian identity and different moralities associated with politicosectarian communities), and the "religious rubric" (i.e., ideas of piety and religious commitments).

The concept of "multiple moral rubrics" is very relevant to my approach; in the Iraqi context, the "social rubric" consists of kin-based and tribal affiliations, as well as all the behaviors and duties considered part of what is commonly "done" and "approved" by society – that which is moral and respectable – which are the products of complex legacies and imaginaries. The "political-sectarian rubric" is constituted by both local and global political dynamics that ended up in the "sectarianization" of Iraqi political life and society, as well as the legacies of competitive national imaginaries. The "religious rubric" is composed of the different dynamics of faith and religious practices, which obey their own rules and normative ideas and practices. Thus Iraqi women's notions of what is pious, moral, and respectable are built on the overlapping of social, politicosectarian, and religious dynamics. Moreover, the fact that Islamist women's discourses invoke the "religious rubric" as a primary motive for their actions and representations around women's issues does not mean that I should be limited to this rubric in my analysis of gender norms and practices. On the contrary, I argue that the exclusive attention to "discourses" is misleading; it is far more interesting to look, first, at the way discourses and practices are grounded in their contexts – read historically and through a complex lens. Second, I draw attention to the way women activists' discourses are concretely lived and experienced, which often led to analyzing the gap between discourses about gender and their actual implementation.

On Muslimness, Islam, and Feminisms

In her book, *Paradise Beneath Her Feet*, Isabel Coleman (2010) explores "how women are transforming the Middle East" and champions the "gender *jihad*" of "Islamic feminism" as the main voice challenging patriarchy in the Middle East. In her chapter dedicated to Iraq, entitled, "Daughters of Zaynab" (2010: 241–67), she presents the divergence between "secular feminists" and "Islamist women activists" in dichotomous terms, especially around the PSC debate. Since the author chose to present the realities of women's activism in contexts as diverse as Iraq, Afghanistan, Iran, and Pakistan in one volume, it can be argued that this approach risks falling into generalization. Moreover, even if I am seduced by the idea of highlighting the dynamics of feminisms using the religious framework as a main medium for advocating women's rights, I do not see how the argument of "Islamic feminism" as the "right path" is applicable to such different contexts. The very noble intention of challenging Oriental and essential visions of Islam and Muslim women easily falls into simplistic explanations and generalizations. The fact that Coleman met a group of Iraqi women activists in a meeting organized in July 2006 at the US State Department in Washington, DC, is not sufficient for drawing any kind of general theoretical conclusions on feminism in Iraq.

However, I do consider the effort to challenge dichotomist views of Islam and feminism. The Western/Muslim-Oriental representations and the practices and discourses they imply are still important to analyze; and the choice for women activists in the Middle East between "betrayal and betrayal" described by Ahmed (1982, 1992) is still relevant to a certain extent. The emergence of the "woman question" in postindependence contexts – as reflecting both the symbol of the progressive aspirations of a Westernized elite and the expression of "authentic" Islamic culture – has been analyzed in many studies (Ahmed 1992; Esposito & Haddad 1998; Sabbagh 1996). Indeed, feminist/women's movements in the Middle East emerged within nationalist and anti-imperialist struggles (Badran 1995; Jayawardena 1986). Later, the rise of political Islam and its use of the "woman question" in religious terms can also be read through this postcolonial approach. Since the 1980s, a wide range of research has focused on Islamist discourses on women and crossing between feminist aspirations and Islamism (mostly on Egypt and Iran). On that matter, there was a special focus on the unveiling and veiling processes, a focus that is still very prolific today (see Ahmed 2011). Implicit in many of these studies is the representation of the "Islamic feminist" point of view as the "right path" for feminism in the Middle East because it adjusts the Western/Muslim dilemma by developing an "endogenous" feminism (Mir-Hosseini 1999).

This approach broke the modern/tradition conceptual framework and placed the rise of political Islam inside processes of modernization (Gole 1993; Mir-Hosseini 1999), along with other studies on Islamism (Burgat 1996, 2005). However, I also consider Zubaida's critique (2011) of the use of the "Islamic" adjective, which highlighted the fact that its simplistic use essentializes both "Islam" and the "West." I concur with Zubaida's (1989) critique of simplistic analyses that brand diverse realities as "Islamic" dynamics; such dynamics were built according to different and sometimes competing legacies. In *Beyond Islam* (2011), he argues that Islam is only an effective factor in the Middle East's diverse histories as part of the configurations of social relations and ideologies of economy, power, and institutions. Zubaida also eloquently recalls that capitalism was one of the most essential motors of modernity, and the imposition of modernity during colonization meant the imposition of a capitalist mode of economy that "Islam" had to accommodate. In his fascinating analysis, Zubaida shows how the overemphasis on "cultural" modes of resistance to modernity, often represented by Islamist movements, can be very misleading because it considers only the secular aspect and puts aside the more essential material effects. Thus I apply Zubaida's approach by not limiting my analysis to women's discourses and analyzing the material realities in which such discourses are grounded.

However, in line with Deeb's analysis (2006), I would argue that the definition of "modernity" is not the most productive question; it is far more interesting to explore the way ideas of modernity, Islam, and gender are expressed in relation to one another in Iraqi women activists' contexts. Throughout this book, my definition of feminism is broad. I define it mainly as "actions and mobilizations aimed at enhancing women's social, economic, and political rights," drawing attention to the context in which these rights are defined and analyzing the complex entanglement in which they are produced and expressed.

In *Secularism, Gender and the State in the Middle East: The Egyptian Women's Movement* (2000), Al-Ali proposes that "secular-oriented" forms of feminisms are characterized by the acceptance of the separation between religion and politics and stresses that such does not necessarily denote "antireligious" or "anti-Islamic" positions. According to Al-Ali, "secular-oriented women" in Egypt do not support *shari'a* as the main or sole source of legislation; they refer to civil law and human rights conventions adopted by the United Nations as frames of reference for their struggle. However, Al-Ali also highlights the heterogeneity of understandings and manifestations of secularism among Egyptian women activists and the need to analyze the continuum between religious and secular beliefs and practices in women's everyday lives, because "secular-oriented women" in Egypt can also be practicing Muslims (Al-Ali 2000: 130). Al-Ali (2000: 14) also insists on the necessity to provide a complex reading of the continuum between religious and secular activism, staying away from dichotomous views: "The very dichotomy of religious versus secular seems rather counterproductive as it only feeds into Islamist conceptualizations of secularists 'being against religion.'" Al-Ali also highlights how the Egyptian women's movement reflects the social and political postcolonial Egyptian context. However, I show that both secular and Islamist women's activism reflects the Iraqi social and political context. Akin to Salime's (2011) study of the Moroccan women's movement, I explore their activism in relation to one another, not as separate entities. Thus I show the diversity of both nonreligious/secular and religious feminisms. I deconstruct simplistic dichotomies in introducing a more complex approach in line with Hatem's (1994, 2005) and Abu-Lughod's (1998) work. I introduce an alternative way of understanding the visible secular/Islamist opposition by analyzing the relevance and meaning of "Islamic feminism" (Abou Bakr 2012, 2013; Badran 2009; Mir-Hosseini 1999, 2011) in the Iraqi context.

Finally, I look at the different political and communal legacies in which Iraqi women activists situate their activism for women's rights. In this regard, Hasso's (2005) historicized ethnography on gender, women's involvement, and sexuality in the ideologies and strategies of a transnational Palestinian political movement is of interest. It offers a way of understanding how gender defines and is defined by political agendas within movements in which the struggle against colonialism carries politicized gender dimensions. Looking at the different ways Iraqi women's rights activism is situated within broader political legacies can deepen understandings of their stands on gender and women's rights issues.

Iraqi Women Activists' Feminisms

As elsewhere, Iraqi women activists have diverse ways of understanding political activism and feminisms. Throughout out my interviews, I identified several trends of activism for women's rights and noticed that Iraqi women activists relate to political legacies very much linked to their personal belongings and life trajectories. In what follows, I have broken down these trends into four categories, from the most common to the most unique, while bearing in mind that such categories are not exclusive and are often imbricated.

Human Rights Feminists

"Human rights feminists" are the most common trend across the Iraqi women activist spectrum. This trend is very common among women who first got involved in women's civil society organizations after 2003 – those who had no prior familiarity with political activism or gender-specific issues. Human rights feminists often define their activism as "defending women's rights as a part of human rights" and became involved primarily "as women" within civil society organizations. Human rights feminists use international human rights conventions and the United Nation's regime of women's rights, such as the CEDAW and Security Council Resolution 1325, and advocate to preserve the unified PSC. These women activists also advocate a reform of the PSC that would "align Iraqi laws with international conventions of rights," but remain mostly very general in their stand, taking for granted the division between public and private. Thus, when asked to expand on the extent of such reforms, most question Penal Code articles related to *ta'dib al-zawja* ("disciplining the wife'), which allow domestic violence and lighten sentences for crimes committed in the "name of honor." They also demand abolishing legal requirements for women to have a *mahram* to travel and a *wali al-amr* to obtain a passport. Human rights feminists also suggest reforming the PSC to penalize marriages contracted outside the court, reinforce women's right to divorce, and penalize the excessive use of polygamy.

In my interviews Iraqi women activists whom I identify as human rights feminists do not demand a complete end to polygamy. Most human rights feminists insist on respecting Iraqi/Muslim culture and finding a common ground with religious authorities. The focus of their advocacy is directed to the public domain, such as struggling for the implementation of the 25 percent women's quota[6] in representative assemblies and women's participation in political, work, and education spheres. Most of their initiatives are related to notions of "women's leadership" and "empowerment," encouraging women to participate in "democracy building," voting, and civil society or political groups.

Having attended gender mainstreaming courses provided by international nongovernmental organizations (NGOs) and UN-Women since 2003, human rights feminist tend to have a consensual understanding of the notion of gender and often use the following expression: "women and men have as much rights as they have duties." Because human rights feminists focus on the public domain, most do not articulate a gender discourse that elaborates their understanding of women's rights issues and gender norms. In my interviews, while remaining vague in their definition of women's rights, human rights feminists all preferred to use the word *'adala* ("justice") or *insaf* ("fairness") instead of *musawa* ("equality"). For example, Lamia I., fifty-six, is a retired lawyer, mother of five, and prominent member of the al-Rafidain Women's Coalition. She explains her vision of political activism and the notion of gender and women's rights activism.

I was asked by three different political parties to run for them, but I refused, saying that I want to remain an independent civil society women's activist. My idea is to create a women's party, but no group supported this idea. Part of me believes that this is the future . . . We at the organization, we worked a lot on CEDAW in raising awareness among women, in encouraging them to participate in political life. We also worked a lot on the Constitution, lobbying to preserve Law No. 188 of the PSC and reform it in a way that aligns Iraq with international conventions of human rights . . . In terms of women's rights and the notion of gender, I think that we have to gather Western and Eastern views, because the best things are found in a middle ground. Very often people tell me that I carry the stick of the middle; I am not very liberal [she indicates her *hijab*] or fundamentalist. I think that the golden

---

[6] Thirty percent in Iraqi Kurdistan.

mean is the best thing. There are some organizations, very very few – they can be counted on one hand – that demand full equality. But most women's organizations demand reasonable things. We ask for the implementation of the concept of gender. Then there are secondary things, like we don't demand equality in the way men and women dress. We demand equality in ideas, work opportunities, and even the domestic sphere; we demand that domestic work should not only be on women's shoulders. My husband helps me a lot in domestic work, you know. He knows the conditions in which I work, that I do not always have the time to cook and clean every single day, especially when I am traveling in another province of Iraq several times a week for the organization. He understands that he has to learn how to do these things by himself, and we ended up agreeing on that.

Lamia's profile is very common among independent civil society women activists. Her words are representative of most pragmatic feminists, who have tried to find a middle ground between the radical and Islamist feminists that I present next. Like most human rights feminists I met, Lamia prefers staying away from political parties and remains an independent woman activist. However, she is very close to many women representatives, such as parliamentarians and members of Provincial Councils, who provide support to her organization and help her claims and demands reach governmental institutions. Like the majority of Iraqi women activists, Lamia does not tackle issues of sexuality, which she considers "too radical," and she promotes the framework of the nuclear middle-class family.

Islamist Activists

There are three different profiles of "Islamist activists": Sunni and Shi'a Islamists in Arab Iraq and Kurdish Islamists of Iraqi Kurdistan. As discussed previously, Sunni Islamists in Arab Iraq stand alongside "secular" (meaning plural) women activists in refusing Article 41 of the Constitution and any sectarian-based questioning of the PSC, such as the most recent Ja'fari Law proposition. However, Sunni Islamists' reading of issues related to gender and Islam are quite similar to the Shi'a Islamist perspective. Thus, regarding the PSC, both Shi'a and Sunni Islamists agree on a general and loose definition of "women's rights in Islam" characterized by a modern, middle-class, patriarchal understanding of women's issues and gender norms. Although both Sunni and Shi'a Islamists consider the PSC to be a fair and acceptable law, they also deem certain issues – such as polygamy and unequal shares in inheritance – as "untouchable" issues. For them, these issues are related to the "Law of God" – *shari'a* – and cannot be questioned. Some are more conservatives than others regarding women's dress and gender relations; for example, some consider the wearing of the *'abaya* (Shi'as) or long overcoats (Sunnis), in addition to the *hijab*, to be essential. Others consider issues of clothing to be secondary and focus their discourse on matters of religious practice that are less gendered, such as promoting both education and political activism as "religious duties."

However, all Islamist women activists in Iraq also simultaneously use human rights conventions, such as the CEDAW and Security Council Resolution 1325, and consider such conventions to be valid as long as the "principles of *shari'a*" are not questioned. Thus their use of international human rights conventions and the UN regime of women's rights is loose and ambiguous. Sallama A. is a prominent Shi'a Islamist, and her discourse on women's rights is very common among Islamists in Iraq. After praising Islam for the "perfect" and "ideal" status it reserves for women, she tackles issues of polygamy, inheritance, and the notion of *qiwama* ("male dominance").

Well, polygamy you know, Islam allows it but does not promote it. On the contrary, Islam limits polygamy to the maximum. If the law was easy to implement, a woman could say in her marriage contract that she refuses for her husband to take a second wife ... Regarding inheritance, we have an economic vision in Islam, and we would be very happy and at peace if this vision was implemented. The problem is not Islam; it is in the bad interpretation and implementation of Islam. We think that women should not carry the financial responsibility of their households and that they have the right to keep their money and wealth for themselves. The problem in Arab society is that women work outside, and then they look after the household and raise the children. And men in all of that, what do they do? A man only works outside, and he is just content in going in and out of the house like that; sometimes he also helps in raising the children. If women could avoid being economically in charge of the households, they could choose when and how they want to work. I know a lot of women who, after raising their children, decided to go back to work or university to study so that they can think for themselves. This is why on the issue of inheritance Allah says, "[f]or the men like for two women," in order to impose upon men the financial responsibility for the household. It is a whole economic vision; we do not want to give equal shares between men and women in order to free women from the economic charge of the household. Although, yes, today it is the case women are economically in charge of the household, we do not want this reality to become the rule ... On the *qiwama* issue, it is said in the Qur'an: "Men have a *qiwama* over women in what they spend and in what Allah has given them as privilege one from the other." This means that men are in charge of administrating the household, financially as well as morally. Thus he is in the service of the woman and not above her. He has a preeminence in what he spends for the household. Allah gave men physical strength in order for them to serve women and the needs of household. The *qiwama* is a charge more than a privilege.

Sallama's words represent a modern patriarchal view of gender relations built on an ideal of a middle-class or bourgeois family in which women can be exempt from "working outside" because men are supposed to be financially and morally in charge of the household. In this ideal view, women's roles within the family are primarily to bear children and manage the household, although men are considered their supreme managers. Sallama's modern understanding of issues related to gender and Islam represents a common trend among Shi'a and Sunni Islamists; such an understanding is representative of the transnational Islamist discourses that emerged in the 1970s in the Middle East (Burgat 1996; Göle 1993; Hatem 1994, 2005). However, when interrogated on issues related to gender and Islam, her argumentation is also very common to non-Islamist women activists. As Abu-Lughod (1998) and Hatem (1994, 2005) showed, the nuclear, patriarchal, bourgeois family model is common among Islamist and non-Islamist women activists across the Middle East. Although nuances exist among Islamist feminists in Iraq (e.g., some are closer to Muslim feminist discourses on gender and Islam than others), they all share, along with human rights feminists, a desire not to tackle issues of sexuality. While human rights feminists generally stay silent on the matter, unwilling to provoke the hegemonic social and religious conservatism of Iraqi society, Islamist feminists advocate for the defense of the heterosexual, patriarchal nuclear family and containing sexuality to the framework of marriage.

As discussed previously, Kurdish Islamist women have been more in favor of reforms in the field of women legal rights. In addition, the tension between Kurdish Islamist women activists and other women's organizations was lowered by the arbitration of the state and the "NGOization" of activism. As I showed through the example of Samya A., a prominent Islamist and women's rights activist, some Kurdish Islamist women went so far as to push the boundaries of the private domain in advocating for a reform of *shari'a* regarding women's issues. Thus many of them can be considered both Islamist and human rights feminists.

More generally, Islamist feminist activism is characterized by a focus on issues related to women's political participation and empowerment within the work and education spheres, as well as concrete humanitarian support through wide charity networks. Rather than articulating a clear gender discourse, Islamist feminists in Iraq develop loose and general rhetoric on "women's rights in Islam" that focuses on the role of women in the political sphere and dedicate most of their time to humanitarian, welfare, and social work. In addition to activities alongside other women's organizations, such as "democracy" and "women's empowerment" trainings, Islamist women's groups are involved on the ground in a wide range of activities that cover nearly all aspects of women's lives. Thus Hawa'una (the Muslim Women's Organization in Iraq), which is affiliated to the Shi'a Islamic Supreme Council of Iraq, provided activities on "graciousness" and "aesthetics" to a significant number of women along with its other activities, such as literacy, tutoring for schoolgirls, and sewing, media, and computer training sessions. According to Hawa'una's report, between 2004 and 2007, their activities and lectures on "graciousness" and "aesthetics" were far more important than their *fiqh* ("religious jurisprudence') lectures. As a significant example, their report indicates that between 2004 and 2007, they provided twenty-four *fiqh* lectures for 290 women, thirty-seven lectures on graciousness for 1,386 women, and ninety-eight aesthetics sessions for 588 women. The organization, like other Islamist groups, financially supports young couples and helps them to buy furniture. The organization also facilitates marriages, such as organizing collective wedding ceremonies. Although all their activities are framed inside a specific religious discourse, such organizations are very pragmatic on the ground and seek to answer the needs of the population concretely. Thus it is revealing that such organizations might privilege aesthetics and beauty classes over *fiqh* or proper Islamic formations. Among the groups I observed, the lectures and events always tried to address the genuine and concrete needs of their audiences, from advice on women's health to marriage coaching.

An Islamist woman activist working in Shi'a neighborhood insisted on the importance of addressing the basic and essential needs of women and families before proposing any kind of training on religious or women's rights issues.

Our organization has to begin with urgent matters. We are taking care of the people in need. Every day we have women coming to our offices; they are so poor, and they have children to feed. This woman comes to ask for help for her survival, not for listening to a conference or something theoretical. This is what I say to other civil society organizations: "how do you want to promote democracy and progress in our society when you cannot provide for the basic everyday needs of the people?" We first help them concretely, and then we propose that they listen to our ideas about political activism and Islam.

Islamist feminists can be characterized as conservative in terms of gender norms and representations because most promote a patriarchal understanding of women's legal rights within an ideal patriarchal family. Nevertheless, their feminism is deployed through the social and welfare support provided to women and families, especially through charities dedicated to orphans, widows, and elders. However, Islamist feminists' gender discourse is loose, both in *shari'a* and in the UN regime of rights, and this ambiguity allows nuances that can go as far as a human rights feminist repertoire. Thus I argue that Islamist feminists are the mirrors of the hegemony of religious conservatism in Iraqi society as much as they are its active reproducers.

Muslim Feminists

Most women activists that can be defined as "Muslim/Islamic feminists" are not Islamists women activists but more often women involved in "secular" organizations who, by personal conviction or as a pragmatic strategy, consider the use of antipatriarchal readings of Muslim jurisprudence, sacred texts, and religious discourses as an important tool in advocacy for women's rights and equality. In my interviews, all such activists preferred the word *musawa* ("equality") to *'adala* ("justice") or *insaf* ("fairness") in their advocacy for women's rights; their demands for reform of the PSC were similar to those advocated by human rights feminists. The difference between Muslim feminists and human rights feminists lies in the latter's choice to both leave the sphere of religious jurisprudence to religious scholars and exclusively base their advocacy on human rights conventions and the UN regime of rights. "Islam" or "Muslim culture" is advocated by human rights feminists mostly as part of Iraqi culture but not as a sphere of engagement. Since the PSC is a *fiqh*-based law, many human rights feminists turned to Muslim feminist discourses as a necessary strategic tool to promote egalitarian readings of the law. Nevertheless, they avoid getting into religious debates and prefer consulting with and seeking the support of religious scholars rather than going into the jurisprudence themselves.

Among non-Islamist women activists, Noor S. – head of the Women's Leadership Institute – is the only activist I met who had encountered a Muslim feminist transnational movement, because she attended a meeting organized by the international network Women Living under Muslim Laws. Noor S. can be described as a proper human rights feminist, and her views on the use of religious argumentation in advocacy for women's rights stands between those of human rights feminists and Muslim feminists.

I think that a good reading of the Qur'an, a meaningful reading, not a masculine reading, is necessary. The readings of the sacred texts are grounded in the society's context. The ones who interpret religious texts are the mirrors of their society and the way they have been taught to think. This is why I believe that we should reread the sacred texts, that it would benefit human dignity and favor it. I proposed to the Women Living under Muslim Laws network to be in charge of a project such as that in Iraq, to initiate new readings of religion and of the law, so that we can respond to religious fundamentalists and traditionalists and build a strong discourse in front of them. But you know, Zahra, the problem is that Muslim feminists, or Muslim feminist discourse, is too far away from the field, from the concrete realities of women. I met some of them in a meeting organized by Women Living under Muslim Laws, and I was telling them that their discourse was too intellectual. After attending their meeting, I started to understand their thoughts, but imagine, I am myself an academic and I taught at university, and it was hard for me before attending that meeting to understand their writings. Was it the language or the concepts? ... I think that the Muslim feminist movement should elaborate a discourse that is close to people. When we organize meetings in which we invite local religious scholars here in Baghdad, you can see the difference straightaway. The imam is often a simple man who speaks to people in their own words, and they completely relate to him and understand him because he is from them, whereas in big conferences, the words, the people, the attitudes are different and far away from people. I try to simplify things so that they are accessible to people. Even the concept of patriarchy, I try to explain it in the simplest way possible ... In reality, I do not use the religious repertoire very much, but I adapt myself. I do not feel uncomfortable with it, and I do not feel provoked in my dialogue with Islamists and Islamist women. I make the effort to understand. My international repertoire of thought is not against that; I think I can talk to anyone with a human register of discourse. You know, readings and interpretations of religious texts are so diverse, not anyone can deal with them. And also, in Iraq, we have so many trends, *mazahab*, schools, and belongings ... I believe that a fair state, based on law, can protect me, the religious person, the tribal Shaikh, the Christian, the poor, and the rich. Our issue is that we do not have strong state institutions. This is why religious issues are so sensitive.

Noor's focus on the importance of developing a strong state and state institutions in order to implement the rule of law was expressed by all Iraqi women activists. Because "state-building" after the invasion and occupation was, in fact, an "international" or US-led endeavor, it is revealing that local activists prefer relying on an international register of rights to advocate for women's rights. In a context marked by sectarian divisions and a weak state, Noor – whose organization is funded by international and UN donors – privileges the use of a global register of rights in building a common understanding of women's rights at the local level. Moreover, Noor's critique of the intellectualism and disconnectedness of Muslim feminist dynamics also reveals the gap between the global context, in which transnational Muslim feminist discourses have been produced, and the local contexts of the supposed audience. Thus, according to Noor, the fact that Muslim feminist transnational dynamics use Muslim rhetoric does not make it more useful or understandable to locals. She does not consider an argument's "Islamic" dimension to be enough for it to be taken as "indigenous," because her approach to "Iraqi culture" is complex and not simplistic. Noor's use of a global register of rights allows her to situate herself outside sectarian and party-backed ideologies and stand as "a human" for women's rights. It is very interesting to note that the use of a global register of rights, as well as NGO spaces, constituted for many women activists the only spheres situated outside the sectarian party-backed lines. Despite being limited, these spheres allowed activists to stand apart from the sectarian political conflicts dividing society and its political elite. Thus, despite the fact that her reading of Islam can be deemed as Muslim feminist, her activism for women' rights corresponds to the human rights feminist category.

Samya A., the Kurdish Islamist activist introduced in Chapter 5, is a typical Muslim feminist, in that she chose to articulate both a human rights repertoire and a feminist understanding of religious thought and jurisprudence. She criticizes dominant Islamic thought for being patriarchal and having betrayed the essential "egalitarian message" of Islam and calls for a rereading of religious texts inspired by an egalitarian understanding of gender. Islamic/Muslim feminist movements have emerged as transnational intellectual dynamics for about two decades, proposing antipatriarchal readings of religious texts (Qur'an and Sunna) and *fiqh*. The use of *ijtihad* is, according to them, one of the main tools to implement reform of the patriarchal *fiqh*. Muslim feminism situates itself at the crossroads of critical, postcolonial, and Black feminism, on the one hand, and reformist – from modernist to radical – Islamic thought, on the other (Ali 2012). In the context of North America and Europe, where Muslims represent a minority, Muslim feminisms work as a tool against Islamophobia and racism, as well as questioning secularist and antireligious forms of feminisms. In its pietist forms, Muslim feminisms also challenge normative readings of modernity and propose alternative modern identities grounded in the intersection of dynamics of faith and pluralistic notions of citizenship (Ali 2012). In Muslim majority countries, Muslim feminisms are expressed in a different context, one marked by the hegemony of Islamization, *shari'a*-based personal laws, and, in some, the power of conservative Islamists. Thus Muslim feminist rhetoric imposed itself in a context where the law itself, and the overall cultural climate, is Islamized. For many women's rights activists, the use of Muslim feminist rhetoric is mainly a matter of strategy because the call for the secularization of law proves difficult when conservative religious discourse has hegemony (Ali 2012).

However, some Iraqi women activists – mostly non-Islamists but also some Islamists such as Samya A. – develop a Muslim feminist standpoint similar to those developed in Malaysia (Anwar 2012), Egypt (Abou Bakr 2012), and Iran (Mir-Hosseini 1999). Without constituting a proper organization such as the Sisters in Islam in Malaysia or being part of a transnational Muslim feminist movement such as Musawah, these activists developed a feminist understanding of Islamic thought and jurisprudence and defined their activism as such. For example, Amel F., a lawyer specializing in women's rights issues, has developed a Muslim feminist understanding of religious laws despite being involved in secular women's networks.

For me, on the contrary, I have a lot of good relations with Islamists; I am very close to many of them. Because my work is related to Islamic law, I speak about issues I have studied according to an Islamic point of view. When I have to argue against fundamentalists, I manage to convince them by using religious law argumentation. When there are conflicts with the secularist kind of activists, Islamists women come and ask for my help: "Can you explain to them, because they don't understand." Some secular activists, not all of them, but many of them have a superficial understanding of the laws related to women. They focus only on the discourses and do not do the job of analyzing the law itself and building an argument change the law. I believe that working on the religious argument is the only way to make things change, and we have to get involved in the rereading of religion, both secular and religious activists.

Amel's words are common among women activists involved in secular organizations who developed a Muslim feminist argument, deepening their knowledge and skills on religious thought and jurisprudence. Many such activists managed to build bridges with Islamist activists and open spaces of discussion and negotiation.

Women who stand between religious and nonreligious activism can also be called Muslim feminists. Bashaer B., forty-five, is neither an Islamist woman activist like Samya A., despite the fact that she is from a religious Najafi family, nor a secular women activist like Amel F. Bashaer, is a Muslim feminist thinker, has Ph.D. in law philosophy from Kufa University, and is involved in politics as an independent parliamentarian and prominent activist. Bashaer, after deploring the fact that Muslim feminist thought is absent from Iraq due to its disconnection from transnational Muslim feminist movements, explained her own views on women and gender issues.

I believe in total equality, and I use the word "equality" while believing in the superiority of women over men. Women can and do more than men; maternity makes them superior biologically, capable of far more, capable of creating human lives. Deeply, men are aware of this superiority, and because of this, they try to fabricate laws and rules in order to limit the natural superiority of women. In my view of Islam and antipatriarchal readings of Islam, I can say that no Islamist woman represents me. I relate to none of them. I can say that the only woman that represents my thought is Dr. Sundus Abbas. But you know, because I look like them, the Islamists [indicating her *hijab* and long overcoat], my discourse can have an impact. I come from a religious family from Najaf, and people trust me. It is important to be trustworthy and gain people's trust so that they think we are not going to destroy culture and religion. Because of my look and background, I am allowed to be very critical and propose reforms. Because I come from the inside, I am not accused of creating divisions. I do not want to lose my legitimacy as a religious person.

Bashaer's views on Islam are very close to the perspective of prominent and controversial Shi'a religious scholar Ahmed al-Gubenchi. In *Al-Mar'a, al-Mafahim wal-Huquq* (Woman, Concepts and Rights), al-Gubenchi (2009) developed what could be considered as a Muslim feminist discourse, advocating for a radical reform of Muslim thought and jurisprudence that goes "back to the essential egalitarian message of Islam." Bashaer and Ahmed al-Gubenchi are often invited by various civil society groups to talk about the "rights of women in Islam" from their Muslim feminist standpoint. Despite being considered unorthodox by many conservative Islamists, they managed to gain trust and consideration among Islamists and non-Islamists alike. Within Islamists spheres, they are often considered to be "liberals"; within secular spheres, they are deemed "religious." However, Bashaer and Ahmed al-Gubenchi represent a third space between Islamist and secular activists because they gather a conflicting repertoire of discourses using an egalitarian reading of women and gender issues within the framework of religion.

Muslim feminists in Iraq do not represent a coherent group or network such as those found in Egypt, Iran, or Malaysia, and their Muslim feminist stand does not constitute a proper agenda. Believing that gender equality is embedded within the "message of Islam, which has been corrupted and must be radically reformed" is a widespread opinion among Iraqi women activists, including among human rights, leftist, and radical feminists. Nevertheless, Muslim feminists believe the religious argument to be a useful and valid tool of advocacy for women's rights in the context of Iraq; human rights, leftist, and radical feminists, by contrast, do not consider religious argumentation as an essential strategic tool in their activism. However, the activists developing a Muslim feminist awareness or discourse, either in their advocacy work or as a matter of conviction, all believe in breaking the West/East dichotomy and approaching "Iraqi culture" as dynamic, not static. Gender equality and feminism, according to such Muslim feminists, are not Western concepts; on the contrary, because they consider Islam as essentially egalitarian, they also consider gender equality and feminism as endogenous to Iraqi culture. However, even if Muslim feminists engage in religious debate on private matters – something that human rights feminists refuse to do – and consider advocacy for women's rights in the public sphere to be insufficient – something that Islamist essentially do – Muslim feminists in Iraq do not tackle issues of sexuality because they choose to stay within the lines of the "culturally acceptable."

Leftist and Radical Feminists

"Leftist and radical feminists" advocate for the most radical understanding of gender equality and women's rights. Many leftist and radical feminists are affiliated with al-Rabita and are close to the Iraqi Communist Party; others are active within social and development organizations, such as al-Amel. For example, the Organization for Women's Freedom in Iraq (OWFI), which falls into this category, has members close to the Worker-Communist Party and members who are independent activists. Several prominent female intellectuals and scholars are radical feminists. However, the existing scholarship on the matter is very thin, and most such intellectuals deplore the lack of theoretical material for developing proper feminist thought in Iraq.

Rabab H. – a founding member of al-Amel and the IWN and former figure of al-Rabita – can be deemed a leftist feminist. She cited Rosa Luxembourg as the person who embodies her vision of feminism, situating gender equality within the global struggle for social justice. Like most Iraqi women activists, Rabab insisted on being close to and understood by people from all backgrounds, especially the more disenfranchised, and the importance of getting men involved in the "Iraqi women's movement."

You know, I always adapt my discourse to the social and cultural level of the context. I do not use incomprehensible vocabulary when I talk to people about the concept of gender because what is more important for me is to influence general awareness. I want to contribute by spreading human values, ethical values at the level of the society. If we speak a language that is too complicated and far away from people's realities, we are not going to have any impact. Nobody will relate to us. When I talk to a woman, I also talk to men, from all backgrounds, either educated or illiterate, either men of religion or tribal shaikhs; we talk to everybody. And in that way, we manage to build bridges and cross boundaries. I remember in 2000, we [al-Amel] were among the first organizations to introduce the concept of gender in Iraqi Kurdistan. At the time, we had to bring two specialists, one Egyptian and one British, and we organized training sessions in Erbil and Sulaymaniyah on gender and development. A lot of activists attended. It was the first time that gender was tackled. Here most people think it is a Western concept. So we also started to look at gender in the field of religion in Islam and show that there were false representations and ideas. We tackled issues of gender roles and norms. And we always integrated men in our movement, especially specialists, thinkers, lawyers, researchers in social sciences who conducted studies on the matter. We are very proud to have men in the women's movement, although there are not that many, but their presence is visible and their support is very clear. It is important. Although we try to adapt, we do not make any concessions on the principle of equality. It is an essential and fundamental principal. We do not make any concessions on that. In the Constitution, or in any subject, equality is equality. Why are we against Article 41? Because it does not allow equality. Some suggest that we use *'adala* ["justice"] or *takamul* ["complementarity"] instead of equality. I reply, "no, I want equality." Equality for everyone, for social justice, for every level of society.

OWFI is one of the most radical women's organizations in Iraq; it defines itself as leftist, feminist, and anti-imperialist. Through its journal, *Jaridat al-Musawat*, OWFI advocates for gender equality and is one of the few organizations tackling issues of prostitution, sexual violence, and homophobia.[7] OWFI offers help and support to women victims of sexual violence, forced prostitution, and incarceration. The OWFI activists I interviewed were the most outspoken about women's sexual freedom, sexual violence, and homophobia. Very critical of Islamist parties, they advocate for the complete secularization of the PSC. Not only were OWFI activists critical of Islamists, but they also seemed to address their critique to religion itself. OWFI is the only organization that has opened shelters for women victims of abuse because they are still illegal in Arab Iraq despite being sponsored by the government in Iraqi Kurdistan. Since the invasion of Mosul, OWFI has also open shelters for women and children victims of violence and sexual abuse at the hands of IS soldiers.

Many leftist activists I met in Iraq, despite not being involved in gender-specific organizations, developed a radical understanding of gender equality and women's issues within the framework of class-based inequalities. Thus these leftist activists consider the questioning of patriarchy as one essential dimension of their struggle for social justice. Such was the case for the women activists I met who are involved in social and development organizations such as al-Amal or the Tammuz Organization for Social Development. More generally, many members of al-Rabita are leftist feminists and have developed an understanding of social justice and equality that considers gender equality as the core of their project for social change. The difference between most leftist feminists and radical feminists, who are often leftist activists as well, is that leftist feminists' discourse about sexuality is more limited and does not cross the boundaries of what they consider "acceptable to society." Thus, although leftist and radical feminists are often in agreement about sexual freedom and homophobia, radical feminists tend to be more outspoken about these

---

[7] See, for example, *Jaridat al-Musawat*, March 8, 2012, vol. 9, issue 9, p. 6.

issues. Nevertheless, leftist and radical feminists both avoid debates about religion; on this matter, they stand alongside human rights feminists because they consider religion to be a part of "culture" but do not engage within the religious itself.

Iman A., forty-two, is a sociologist and researcher at Baghdad University, and she is also one of the most radical feminists I met in Iraq. Before the fall of the regime, Iman published several studies on gender for the General Federation of Iraqi Women (GFIW). Since the fall, she has been very active around gender and women's rights issues. Along with other Iraqi scholars, Iman is one of the founders of the Iraqiyat Studies Center, which is dedicated to gender issues. The Iraqiyat Studies Center was very active until 2010, especially through the publication of its two reviews. Iman also published several articles and studies on women's conditions since the invasion and occupation in sociological journals. She speaks about getting involved in women's organizations and networks after the fall of the regime and the fact that she was one of the few who had been trained in gender matters from the GFIW. She explains her views on gender equality, as well as on the implementations of such views in Iraq.

I advocate for total equality. I am very familiar with and close to what is called the third-wave of feminism, demanding the questioning of the very meaning of gender hierarchies and differences. Until very recently, I was living a life coherent with my ideas. I chose neutral clothes, neither feminine nor masculine, and I promoted these kinds of ideas. But here, you know, we cannot claim these kinds of things; it is not the right time. And I really believe that ideas and laws that do not follow the development of society are not useful and won't provide anything. In the West, feminism followed social, economic, and life development. I respect the thought developed by third-wave feminism, but it is really not the time to implement it in Iraq. When we reach all the steps achieved by first- and second-wave feminism in the West, especially in terms of feminist activism, then we can start talking about questioning gender divisions. At the moment, we want to advocate for human rights for women, for women's humanity to be acknowledged. Tribal mores are very heavy on women; there is an enormous regression in women's conditions in Iraq. Now, you know, the fact that a young girl is escorted by her brother to go to university or that she uses *khat* [private driver shared with other people] to move around, it affects her very freedom of movement. When I was a student, I used to take the bus, and it allowed me more freedom. This is not possible for female students today, even in open-minded families, because of the context we are living in now. Young girls have limited horizons as a result, a limited experience, a limited life. This is why I am very pessimistic about the new generation, the one that spent its youth in such conditions. I believe this generation is worse than ours.

Iman is one of the few activists with whom it was possible to open the subject of sexualities. In a half-serious, half-joking way, she said:

You know, I go as far as questioning the fact that women should epilate. I tried not to epilate for a while, but I ended up doing it because my legs looked like nothing [laughing] ... I am among the ones who promote sexual freedom, even the freedom of homosexuality. I see no problem with that; I believe it is part of individual freedom. On the contrary, I promote it in order to put an end to male domination! [laughing] If women told themselves that they were truly independent beings and do not need men, there wouldn't be male domination anymore. But because all of them are in search of a husband and want a married life, like everyone ... they limit themselves. I am one of them as a married woman.

Iman spoke about her two marriages. She was first married at the age of thirty-five, but this marriage did not work. She got married again two years later and now has a young child. She explained how married life forced her to live in complete contradiction to her beliefs. Despite the fact that Iman is financially in charge of her household, she is also in charge of all domestic work and takes care of her baby on her own. Iman added that her husband only washes the dishes on holidays and thinks that he should be "celebrated for it." Iman's depiction of living a life that contradicts her beliefs in gender equality is common among many activists I met. Nevertheless, as I later show, many women activists choose to never get married.

Iman, like many activists, deplores the lack of "proper feminist thought" in Iraq. According to her, this dearth is the result of the crisis in the education system and Iraq's more than two decades of intellectual isolation. Iman is very critical of the lack of feminist thinking in women's organizations and networks that emerged after 2003. According to her, Iraqi women's activism since 2003 does not constitute a proper movement with a common feminist agenda; it is more a gathering of feminist personalities and women's groups.

We do not have a feminist movement in Iraq, because we do not have feminist thinkers or theorists. We have many initiatives done in partnership with international organizations and mobilizations that are very critical of women's oppression. Our problem is that we do not have pioneers, leaders, women who would develop a proper feminist thinking, theories, and concepts. Our women's groups do not even agree on a common feminist project. Some Iraqi women are prominent intellectuals, but not in the feminist domain; they do not adopt a feminist thought and, many times, do not even identify as feminists. We have great women, but none of them are feminist personalities. So, in Iraq, we have women's activism, but not a feminist movement. There is no feminist vision, no feminist concepts or thinking. Now many women are training themselves in these concepts. To be honest, I am quite sure that if you clarify the concept of gender and feminist ideas to many prominent women activists, they would deny being feminist and struggle against it.

Iman's very critical depiction of Iraqi women's activism is quite unique. Although many activists deplore the absence of developed and clearly articulated feminist thought in Iraq, most consider being part of a proper women's movement, especially through networks such as the IWN that gather a wide range of activists around a similar agenda. I concur with Iman's depiction of the social, economic, and educational realities that have led to a dearth of proper feminist scholarship in Iraq. Such scholarship has been developed in other countries, such as in Europe and North America, since the 1970s through academia and the opening of departments dedicated to women and gender studies.

Tensions exist across the Iraqi feminist spectrum around the issue of women's dress code, either the *hijab* or the *'abaya*. It is not possible to generalize on this matter because opinions vary within each category over the issue of women's dress code. The wearing of the *hijab* has been widespread in urban Iraq since the 1990s, and most women activists wear the *hijab*, albeit in a variety of ways. Some human rights feminists are very critical of the *hijab*; many others wear the *hijab* themselves. Some leftist and radical feminists do not consider women's dress code as a relevant issue to tackle, while others were very outspoken in their rejection of the *hijab* and *'abaya*, which they consider "clothes of women's oppression." Most Islamists feminists consider the *hijab* an essential issue because it supposedly guarantees women's modesty and the *'abaya* as secondary. As for Muslim feminists, some are veiled and some not, but none consider it an important issue to tackle publicly; instead, women's personal choice is the most essential element of their argument about women's dress code.

The IWN is the most important women's rights networks in Iraq. Its most famous figure, Hanaa Edwar, is also a founding member of al-Amel and prominent figure in al-Rabita. The IWN gathers a wide range of women's organizations and activists from across Iraq. Through its meetings, gatherings, demonstrations, and publications, such as *al-Nashra*, the IWN has managed to gather human rights, Muslim, leftist, and radical feminists, as well as some Islamist feminist personalities. It has not only been a unifying network for women activists from divergent trends of women's rights advocacy but also a politically unifying force because it advocates for the preservation of *al wahda al-wataniyya* ("the unity of the nation") against sectarianism and the fragmentation of Iraqi citizenship and territories. Along with its struggle for women's rights, especially legal rights, the IWN also advocates for broader political issues, such as Iraq's independence from US-led and regional interferences. Activists of the IWN are at the forefront of civil society initiatives related to the struggle against corruption, ending sectarian violence, respecting human rights, freedom of speech, and the implementation of a functional democratic political system.

However, despite its success in gathering groups, organizations, and personalities around common aims, the IWN's work has faced great challenges, just like all other women's groups and activities. As shown earlier, the context of post-2003 Iraq is marked by sectarian war; a dysfunctional and weak state; generalized poverty; a crisis of the education, social, and welfare systems; and social, political, and religious conservatisms. I now turn attention to these dimensions' concrete impacts on the lives of women activists and their personal choices and trajectories.

The Personal Is Political: On Respectability and Womanhood

Being a Single Woman Activist: Respectability and Moral Judgment

From Islamist to radical feminists, all expressed their difficulty in balancing their activism, which requires "working outside," and family life. While almost all Islamist feminists are married and have children, many human rights, Muslim, leftist, and radical feminists are not married: some are divorced, some are widows, but most have simply never been married. In a context where marriage is the norm and where relationships outside the framework of marriage are very difficult, being nonmarried carries stigma and difficulties. Nevertheless, the nonmarried activists presented this situation as an "opportunity" to "work freely," or the "best of bad choices." Such was the case of Fatima A., forty-five, a prominent woman activist.

No, I am not married, and I do not have children. This explains also why I have been able to get involved fully, because I have freedom of movement. Of course, marriage is not necessarily an obstacle to involvement and work; my sisters are married and they work ... but the nature of my involvement in the Municipal Council and in civil society organizations demands full availability and great freedom of movement. Getting married wouldn't have allowed me this freedom because of all the responsibilities that are linked to it ... a house, children.

Sarah H., forty-two, is a prominent figure of the al-Rafidain Women's Coalition. Her husband was killed by the US-led coalition bombings of 2003. After his death, she decided not to return with her two children to her parents' house, which is common practice for widows or divorced women. Instead, Sarah decided to stay in al-Saidiyya – a neighborhood very much targeted by sectarian militias, especially for a "mixed" family like hers, because Sarah's husband was Shi'a and she is Sunni. After staying home for a while, she returned to work in the petrochemical sector and also became involved in women's rights organizations. Sarah speaks about the difficulties of being a "single woman" in the sphere of women's activism and the insecurity to which women activists are exposed. Sarah decided to hide the fact that she is widowed and kept wearing her wedding ring. According to Sarah, appearing as married was the only way for her to be respected and considered moral as a women's rights activist.

After what happened to my husband, I decided not to go to my parents' house. I lived on my own and refused the idea of going back to my family house. I live in al-Saidiyya. It is still a very dangerous area, to the extent that even my brother and son have left the neighborhood. We stayed, my daughter and I, on our own in the house. Many people have told me that it is too dangerous. But I resisted the idea of leaving the house and going to my parents. After the death of my husband in 2003, I started driving my own car again, in the middle of the hardest time we experienced in al-Saidiyya! [She laughs.] Because it needs to be like that; I do not want to be dependent on others. The streets of Baghdad teach you a lot; it makes you stronger, strong enough to face anything . . . So I go to my workplace two days a week. I will have to go three days now that we moved to another place because our offices were destroyed by a car bombed attack. The rest of my time I dedicate to the al-Rafidain Women's Coalition, for which I often also work from home, when dealing with emails, for example. But being physically present in the organization office is very important, so I am there most of the time. I come all the way from al-Saidiyya. At the end of the afternoon, I stop working, any invitation or call after 4 P.M. I declined because I have my family, my children. It has been two years that I have worked that way. You know, people, when they see a young woman working, they think straight away that they can call her at any time. So I switch off my phone at 4 P.M. I can go on the Internet for one or two hours at home, but I do not accept calls for the organization after 4 P.M. I had to hide to fact that I am a widow; I always keep my wedding ring when I am outside. If people, especially men, ask me what I do after a meeting or a gathering, I say that I have to go home, because my husband is waiting for me. But you know, despite that, I have experienced some kind of harassment and difficult situations with men, just because I am a woman activist. They think that I am liberated, that I am open to do with them certain things, just because I am a women's rights activist. I have to gain respect; I have to be perceived as respectable. It is tiring, but it is necessary. So I just lie about my status, and all the other activists in the organization know that I am a widow, but they cover me as well . . . Of course, I want to get married again, but I protect myself. Women who work in women's organizations, many people think "these women, they want freedom to do anything." And they mean bad things, of course. So they take the freedom to behave with us in inappropriate ways. Society pushes us to lie. I am heartbroken for the other women activists who are single women, unmarried, widows, or divorced. There is such a demeaning vision of nonmarried women and divorced women, even of widows. They all face discrimination, fear for their reputation, and accusations of being too liberated.

Sarah's account of her life as an employee in the petrochemical sector and member of the al-Rafidain Women's Coalition and how she moves from one area of Baghdad to another reveals the many challenges faced by women in postinvasion Iraq. Sectarian violence represents a real threat for her because she lives in a very dangerous area and has a mixed background (Sunni and Shi'a). The limits she imposes on herself and cautions she takes, such as switching off her phone after work and lying about her marital status, reveal how much she fears for her reputation and wishes to be seen as respectable. Interestingly, the judgments about women activists that Sarah describes are not particularly linked to religious conservatism because Islamist women are political activists and even religious figures in Iraq have promoted women's political activism. Society looks at Iraqi women's rights activists through a lens of social conservatism. Islamist women activists, despite considering their activism to be a "religious duty," also face judgments and fear for their reputations, especially when working in non-gender-segregated spaces. I heard similar accounts from activists of various backgrounds: Islamist, human rights, leftist, and radical feminists. It shows the tenseness of issues related to women's behavior and how women activists are subjected to moral judgments about their respectability, especially when single. For single women activists, the quest for respect while struggling for women's rights is subject to social limits. Thus they have to face religious, political, and social conservatisms at the same time.

Despite the difficulty of being single and the social burden it represents, some activists have chosen not to get married. Reema B., forty-three, is woman's rights activist, lawyer, and professor of law at Baghdad University. She speaks about her views on marriage.

No, I will never get married. I refuse the idea of getting married; it will destroy me. I cannot bear the idea of being tied to someone. The Oriental man, whoever he is, will never accept a woman like me. And even if he accepts, the people around him will not accept it and will pressure him. I have my social and professional status; I do not want to lose it. I am fine the way I am. I do not need a man in my life; it will make me regress instead of progressing. I do not want people to think that I have issues, that I am not normal. I respect men. I have a lot of men who are my friends. But I do not authorize a relationship to go further than friendship ever . . . I am also a religious person. My father was a well-known communist activist, and he was religious too – he was practicing. He was not corrupt; he had principles. My sisters and I, we are religious. We read the Qur'an very often, and I pray every day. I am also, despite my look [she indicates her long hair and knee-length skirt], very religious. I finish reading the Qur'an around four or five times a year. My older sister is veiled; my other sister and I are not, but we are very pious. I respect my religion, my prayers, my God. I do not harm anyone; I respect everyone. This is to be religious after all.

Reema's characterization of the "Oriental man," who would have difficulty accepting a spouse who does not stick to traditional social expectations, is a feature that can be found anywhere else in the world, across many places and cultures. Nevertheless, the postinvasion Iraqi context adds multiple forms of conservatism, which have politicized and thus exacerbated gender norms and relations to a context already steeped in patriarchal gender relations. Reema insisted several time on her refusal to allow a relationship with a man go further than friendship, indicating that she is "a moral person." The link she spontaneously made between having male friends and being religious reveals how much issues of gender and sexuality are linked to religious norms and expectations. Thus her refusal to get married, her attitude toward relationships with men outside of marriage, and her insistence on her piety reveal the concrete social and religious conservatisms in relation to women's and gender issues. Reema's lack of hope in finding a spouse that accepts "a woman like her" is a feeling expressed by many single women activists. Fatima's, Sarah's, and Reema's accounts show the expectations and norms imposed on women due to their gender: they are supposed to privilege the domestic over the public, as well as limit their behavior when dealing with men, in order to prevent accusations of being sexually loose.

More generally, most of the women activists I met expressed their feelings about Baghdad's overall tense and conservative climate. I can still sense the discomfort of a situation I experienced with Reema because she is one of the few lecturers at Baghdad University who wears clothes considered by many as "inappropriate" in the context of rising conservatism. Her makeup is heavy, her long brown hair is loose over her shoulders, her top is slightly low necked, and her shirt is a little shorter than the average knee-length skirt, showing her legs highlighted by high-heels. We sat on a sofa in the corner of the professors' room in the Law Department. It was midday during the exam period, and the room was full of old and middle-aged male lecturers and professors. After ordering tea and bottle of water from the cafeteria counter and greeting from a distance the group of male academics sitting on the sofas across the room, we began discussing the heat and the traffic. After fifteen minutes of informal conversation, she suddenly lowered her voice and indicated with her eyes the group of men sitting across the room. She told me: "Look at the way they look at me. I cannot stand staying here anymore. We really have to leave, Zahra." Her discomfort was obvious, and her face looked tense. We moved to her colleague's office, where we pursued our discussion in private.

More generally, living in Baghdad and observing its different spaces – such as its women's organizations' offices and university campuses – felt like existing feels like living on little islands on little islands scattered in a city of constant war, where violence and armed male soldiers represent a part of everyday reality. Inside the houses, university campuses, libraries, cultural centers, and activists' offices, one sometimes feels that one is on an island far removed from the realities of insecurity and violence. Women travel from one place to another, accompanied door to door, from one island of social life to another. For a short while at least, Baghdad's constant state of war can be forgotten. Reema tries to live her life as she wants and dress the way she wants, surrounded by signs and walls that remind her of the "abnormality" of her normality. Of course, a woman's discomfort in a space full of men, whatever clothes she wears, is common any place in the world. The anecdote about Reema is not interesting because of how she dressed but because of her attempt to negotiate her dress outside the "conservative-dominant code" in the few areas in which she circulates on her own: the university campus where she works, the cultural centers where she often gives speeches and training sessions on women's rights, and the women activist organizations' offices.

The difficulty of a woman living on her own in Baghdad was highlighted by many activists. Huda, an OWFI member and the youngest activist I interviewed, mentions the difficulties faced by young women in the current context. She speaks about all the barriers she faces as a young, independent woman activist.

Where I live, I pay attention to the way I dress and to the way I behave. The pressure and harassment of the militias are just crazy. I do not understand why the whole world is leaving us in the middle of this situation of violence and craziness. You know, I do not think that I will ever find a man that will take me, as radical as I am. Even if he is okay with the way I am, his family would not believe in equality, and he would be pressured by society. Young people here can't experience love; there are too many barriers. Even a woman who wants to rent a place on her own gets so many critiques. She would be accused of doing bad things in her apartment. People would say, "God knows how many men visit her every night." She risks being harassed by militias, and she could get killed for an inappropriate behavior. In Europe, I heard that girls are independent at the age of eighteen, that they rent their own apartments. I work, I look after myself, I do not rely on my family, but I can't rent a place on my own here in Baghdad.

Among the married activists, many expressed their difficulty finding a husband and dealing with married life while being political activists. Khanum H., thirty-four, is a young activist from Sulaymaniyah and the editor-in-chief of *Rewan*, one of the main women's journals in Iraqi Kurdistan; we met at the *Rewan* office several times. She got married at the age of twenty-five and has a very young daughter, who was present during our interviews, playing and running around. Khanum talks about her marriage and the difficulties she faced due to her activism.

My generation is among those who did not know women's organizations. When I decided to get involved, I knew it would be difficult to get married. I thought to myself, what will people think of me if I end up old and lonely? Also, people follow my work: what I write and what I say on women's rights. But I struggled against my own fear of people's judgment, even of my family's judgment. So it was hard for me to find a husband. I thought that I would stay an old maid when I started to get involved in *Rewan*, but I found someone. He is not an activist; he comes from a very close background, very tribal. But we agreed. I explained to him how I am and that I do not have the intention to change what is fundamental for me. Despite that, my political activism is still the main source of conflict between my husband and me. You know, things are not easy. Ten days after giving birth to this little girl, I came back to the journal because, at the time, everything was being built; it was just the beginning of the journal.

The "double workday" is a reality shared by most middle-class and poor women in the world because they are in charge of domestic work and child care in addition to their jobs. A woman activist in Europe would also face difficulties finding a suitable partner because the realities of traditional gender norms and patriarchy are still prevalent in most contexts around the world. Nevertheless, Iraqi women activists experience overlapping limits and constraints. Social, political, and religious conservatisms that impose a set of normative representations and behaviors for women are the product and mirror of decades of war, militarization, and economic, political, and educational crises. The "sectarianization" of the state and society, as expressed through violence, exacerbated the already existing social, political, and religious conservatisms. This exacerbation of conservatisms shaped gender norms and relations, as well as the way notions of morality and respectability are imposed on women.

Being Equal Yet Different: Defining Womanhood

The notion of gender disseminated among women's groups in Iraq – via gender mainstreaming campaigns – was defined, interpreted, and appropriated in various ways. Introduced by UN-Women, gender was presented as a notion that breaks with normative gender norms associating men with the public sphere and women with the private sphere. Gender, defined as the "social sex," highlights the social and historical construction of gender norms and practices, as well as notions of femininity and masculinity. Situating the construction of gender representations in social and historical perspective aims to question patriarchal social relations and place equality as the basis of gender relations. In addition, the notion of gender also pushes for women's social and political participation in the public domain. The notion of gender as introduced by UN-Women and many other NGOs provoked many Islamists, who considered this a "Western concept." As mentioned previously, nevertheless, many Islamist women were funded by international donors and NGOs that promoted gender mainstreaming campaigns. Some Islamist women, while choosing to avoid using the word "gender" – in English, because it has no equivalent in Arabic – attended and organized workshops about "defending Muslim women's dignity" or "defending women's glorious status in Islam." In these workshops, the notion of gender was applied in the public domain – e.g., education, work, and political activism – and the private domain was left to *shari'a*. The Sunni Islamists used the PSC as a basis of demonstration, showing that women's rights must be defended within the "limits of *shari'a*." Islamist feminists tend to advocate for a less radical reform of the *fiqh* than Muslim feminists.

Islamist and radical feminists fall at the two extremes of the feminist spectrum of Iraqi women activists. These two poles stand at odds in how they define gender norms and relations, as revealed by their oppositional stand on the women's dress code. Islamist feminists, however, are situated in a more powerful position than radical feminists. In a context of hegemonic religious, social, and political conservatism, radical feminists are marginalized. Nevertheless, in between these two extremes, human rights, Muslim and many leftist feminists developed a similar understanding of gender norms and practices. Some define the notion of gender or feminism as Western; others propose approaches that include culture and religion and go beyond the Western/Muslim-Oriental dichotomy. Thus I noticed common grounds between most human rights, Muslim, and leftist feminists in Iraq around the notion of gender and the definition of women's activism/feminism. Wafa S., for example, is a leftist feminist, engineer, and founding member of both the IWN and the Iraqiyat Studies Center. How she approaches the notion of gender and feminist activism reflects this common ground.

The notion of gender, as it is taught by UN-Women and NGOs, of course, and not the way it is defined in feminist academic work, is to question the division of the sexes on which society is built. Now the ideas that emerged with the development of feminist concepts in the 1970s, that women could carry exactly the same kind of work as men, regardless of their biological constitution, is not the way I define gender. Women cannot do the same things that men do; they are not biologically like men. So gender is not about forgetting biological difference, no, but about demanding equality in dignity. A human being has natural rights that must be preserved, whatever is his gender, whoever he is. The idea of social gender is that men and women's roles in society should not be predetermined. Of course, we do not demand that men get pregnant and give birth, but we can ask for paternal leave just like maternal leave. Women's and men's roles can be complementary, and society should make it possible that anyone could, regardless of gender, choose the role that suits him. We do not take extremists ideas about gender; we take the essential and general idea. We take the gender mainstreaming vision in the way it is taught by programs and training sessions and implement it in ours. Of course, on a very personal level, these radical ideas of gender developed by some academics can interest me, but I have a social role to play, and I have a legitimacy to preserve as a woman activist. I can't take an idea, for example, developed by a French thinker that questions and deconstructs everything and come here and propose to implement it. It is unthinkable ... I promote any initiative that puts women forward and contributes to enhancing her social, economic, and legal position from whatever ideology. So I do not limit myself to social class analysis of women's oppression. I have to be open to all kinds of contributions to the improvement of women's position ... My priority is to struggle against poverty and for education. Poverty is a women subject. There is today a politics of ignorance; the level of instruction is catastrophic. We have a generation of illiterates emerging. Conservative religious discourse is replacing education, and this discourse is sectarian.

Like most human rights, Muslim, and leftist feminist activists in Iraq, Wafa is also invested in activities related to social and cultural development, as well as nonsectarian civil society initiatives for the promotion of democracy, the struggle against corruption, and the safeguarding of human rights. Her approach to gender and feminism, according to my research, is most common among human rights, Muslim, and leftist feminists. It relies on a socially acceptable notion of gender, which highlights biological differences between men and women, promotes the notion of natural human rights and dignity, and associates women's issues with broader issues of social and cultural development. Like Wafa, most Iraqi women activists tend to avoid what they call "extreme feminist views" in their discourse in order to "preserve their legitimacy" and stay "close to people." For them, equality does not mean similarity; many associate what they call "extremist gender views" with advocacy for the sameness of the sexes and unlimited sexual freedom.

Nevertheless, when asked about their approaches to femininity and masculinity, most activists remained vague and imprecise. With the exception of some radical feminists, whose views deconstruct the very existence of gender differences, I found three main features in Iraqi women activists' approach to the notions of femininity and womanhood. Some consider these features as essential differences between men and women, and others see these features as contextual and constructed.

Womanhood as Provider of Peace and Nonviolence   This idea is generally associated with the women's maternal role and biological characteristics. It is the idea that women, because they carry life, give birth, and are limited in their physical strength compared with men, tend to advocate for peace and oppose violence. This view is shared by many activists, such as Bushra B., forty, who is a women's rights activists and member of a social development organization in Baghdad.

I refuse any violent action. It is as a feminist activist that I refuse violence, essentially. I consider that women's action is based on peace, and on refusing violence and the use of weapons. History showed us that the use of violence is useless and affects women primarily. It affects women and their conditions of giving birth, as well as their families, and it provokes the rise of widows and orphans.

Womanhood as Delicacy and in Need of Special Consideration   Most activists relate the idea of "women as providers of peace" to an idea of womanhood that considers the biological and social aspects of women's functions. As the provider of life and in her biological constitution, a woman is more delicate than a man and in need of special care. Zahra B., thirty-four, is an active member of a social development and charity organization, she explains:

You know, in concrete terms, equality is impossible. We see it in biological differences. We women have special dimensions in our bodies. Men were made rougher and more physically capable of bearing things that we cannot bear. The other day I was watching a documentary on a Western country. They showed a woman whose job was to serve oil at a gas station, and she was dressed exactly like a man. I was so sad for this woman. Woman has femininity; she is made delicate. It is not her place to do this kind of rough job. They also showed a woman who was building a wall, a woman builder, dressed like a man. Of course, I am not against the fact that women can access any job. But we can't force women to work jobs that contradict their biological constitution, in contradiction to herself, just because we want equality. Women are in need of special care and consideration.

The Idealized Mother: al-Hejiyya, the One Who Sacrifices   The figure of *al-Hejiyya* – a word used in Iraqi dialect to describe elderly women[8] – was invoked by most activists to describe either their own mothers or women from the previous generation. *Al-Hejiyya* is considered one of the main role models and sources of inspiration for Iraqi women activists. She is described as strong and resilient; everything about her is synonymous with hardship and pain, as well as dignity and courage. *Al-Hejiyya* is the antonym of selfishness; she is all about giving and sacrifice. Depending on social background and generation, *al-Hejiyya* is the illiterate or noneducated woman who has supported her daughters' education and financial independence; she is the mother or widow of *al-shahid* ("martyr"), a man killed at the front, in detention, or in uprisings; she is the one who saved the family from hunger during the sanctions period by working outside or managing the family economy (sewing, making bread, selling homemade sweets and meals).

These three features are present in most women activists' narratives about womanhood and femininity and reveal significant dimensions of Iraqi women's social history. In the 1960s and 1970s, Iraqi women had remarkable access to higher education and the work sphere. As some of the most educated women in the region, most Iraqi middle-class women worked in various spheres, primarily in the public sector. Like women in other parts of the world, their high level of education and investment in "work outside" did not exonerate them from their primary role as mother and domestic caregiver. Nevertheless, until the 1980s, good child care, health, and maternity services were provided by the state. The deterioration of women's condition in the 1980s and 1990s was due to war, sanctions, and the weakening of state services used by women, such as maternity health support, child care, and jobs in the public sector. The figure of *al-Hejiyya* embodied this situation because women, through wars and economic sanctions, became the primary caretakers of the household and the main agents of its survival. Poverty, war, and militarization affected social values by enhancing normative gender representations and practices, celebrating values of dominant masculinity, and placing women in situations of vulnerability and dependency. In such a situation, the definition of women as peace providers finds its legitimate place. Moreover, the claim of "respecting women's specific biological being" also takes on its whole meaning in a context where the social and economic burdens imposed on women added to their already difficult conditions of maternity and life.

---

[8] It is based on the assumption that elders have accomplished al-Hajj.

Conclusion: Contextualizing Feminisms

With the exception of Shi'a Islamist women's political organizations, Iraqi women's political groups, independent associations, and networks – such as the al-Rafidain Women's Coalition or the IWN – mobilized against Decree 137, Article 41, and the Ja'fari Law proposition. They submitted petitions and open letters to the Ministry of Women's Affairs and the government asking for the preservation of Law No. 188 in the name of Iraq's unity and the defense of women's rights. More important, women activists, after organizing dozens of meetings of lawyers and legal experts, submitted a draft proposal for amending discriminatory laws to the government. They proposed to reform Penal Code articles dealing with *ta'dib al-zawja*, or crimes committed in the "name of honor," and the abolition of women's requirement for a *mahram* to travel and *wali al-amr* to obtain a passport. They advocate for the elaboration of laws that protect women from domestic violence, along the lines of the laws adopted in 2011 in Iraqi Kurdistan. Several women scholars, sociologists, legal experts, and specialists also contribute to this effort by producing articles, and books on the subject, which were disseminated during meetings.

In a context of widespread insecurity, where armed groups threaten women activists and the political leadership is dominated by conservative Shi'a Islamist political parties, activists' demands, with few exceptions, have been very cautious. At the two ends of the Iraqi feminist spectrum, radical feminists advocate for a radical reform of the PSC and its secularization toward full equality (in inheritance, marriage and divorce, the interdiction of polygamy, etc.), and Shi'a Islamists advocate for questioning the PSC on a conservative sectarian basis. In between, human rights, Muslim, and leftist feminists insist on preserving the actual PSC, despite its weaknesses, and concentrate their campaigns on the UN regime of rights, such as the CEDAW and Security Council Resolution 1325. The UN regime of rights, mostly the CEDAW, Security Council Resolution 1325, and international human rights vocabulary, is used as the main framework of advocacy for women's legal rights, along with references to Islam and affirmations of the "Muslimness" of the PSC. The way women activists mobilize around legal rights issues, whether from an Islamist, nationalist, leftist, communal, or "secular" perspective, has been characterized by overlapping references using "Iraqi culture," the United Nation's regime of rights, and the Islamic regime of rights. "Secular" means here pluralistic rather than nonreligious because Christian women groups are included in this denomination and because many Iraqi women activists consider religion to be an important dimension of their lives and beliefs. These overlapping discourses are mostly characterized by a loose understanding of human and women's rights, a preference for the word *'adala* ("equity") or *takamul* ("complementarity") over *musawa* ("equality") and a very general reference to culture and religion. Activists from different backgrounds found commonalities in the imprecision of their stands and declarations of women's rights, Islam, *shari'a*, Iraqi culture, justice, and equality/equity as slogans referring to different understanding and definitions.

In presenting elements that characterize the concrete realities of Iraqi women activists' lives, I show the necessity of analyzing different feminisms in relation to the concrete realities in which they are expressed. I show that notions of "morality" and "respectability" are framed by multiple forms of conservatisms. Thus Iraqi women activists' "multiple moral rubrics" are characterized by social, political, and religious conservatisms that shape patriarchal gender norms and relations, affecting women's everyday lives. Thus, while some women activists use a religious argument to advocate for women's rights, such as Muslim feminists, others use it as a tool in a context marked by *shari'a*-based laws and the hegemonic power of conservative Islamist parties. In such a context, the "secular" and the "religious" have to be contextualized and analyzed in the framework of gender and nation, state and religion, and not as simply pro- and anti-*shari'a*.

In a context of both the "NGOization" of women's rights activism and the "sectarianization" of Iraqi society and politics, international and human registers of rights imply different meanings. For human rights feminists, the international and human registers of rights represent a framework for political, nonsectarian actions, because their advocacy for women's rights as human rights constitutes an independent political position in the postinvasion Iraqi context. For Islamist women activists, the international and human registers of rights constitute a framework adjustable to their Islamist women's rights agenda. For Sunni Islamists, these registers are tools for advocacy of a nonsectarian legal framework of rights, whereas Shi'a Islamists select "freedom of belief" as an essential human right in order to advocate for their specific regime of rights.

At a theoretical level, I insist on the importance of contextualizing notions of women's rights and feminisms, secular and religious, and conservative and progressive. In doing so, I have attempted to enrich the approach of both Al-Ali (2000) and Salime (2011) by showing that both secular and Islamist forms of activism are grounded in the specificities of Iraqi social and political culture. Post-2003 Iraqi political culture is dominated by conservative Shi'a Islamist parties; thus Shi'a Islamists represent the voice of power, whereas Sunni Islamists and other women's rights groups try to negotiate their advocacy from a less powerful position. The current Iraqi context is characterized by conflicting gendered national imaginaries in which social, political, and religious conservatisms are articulated in complex ways. If Islamists can be deemed as feminists in their provision of women's welfare and support for political activism, they are conservative in their definition of gender norms and relations. Moreover, since Sunni and Shi'a national imaginaries have competed for power since 2003, they take different positions on conservatisms: Shi'a Islamists advocate for sectarian conservatisms, whereas Sunni Islamists advocate against political conservatisms and align with secular women's groups on the PSC. Finally, even though Islamist and radical feminist divisions are insurmountable, the latter can barely express their views in a context where conservative Islamists and their militias represent the hegemonic social and political power. Thus, in line with Hasso (2005), I have shown that gender norms and representations, as well as women's political activism, are defined by conflicting political agendas.

Conclusion
Making Sense of Violence as a Feminist Praxis

Since the IS invasion of parts of northern Iraq, images of women brutalized by the terrorist group, especially from minority communities such as the Yazidis, were spread across global media and social networks. The systematic use of enslavement and rape of women and girls from ethnic and religious minorities by IS fighters characterizes one of the most horrific forms of sexual violence. According to the United Nations, the number of civilians displaced since the beginning of the military operation in Mosul has reached half a million, and the number of victims is still unknown as the war against IS reaches its final stages. Civilians have been taken hostage by IS and have been victims of the US airstrikes and the Iraqi army military advancement into the city. Mass graves of civilians killed by IS have been found in the outskirts of the city as the Iraqi population and the world slowly uncover the atrocities and brutality experienced by the population of the area occupied by the terrorist organization since its takeover of Mosul in June 2014.

There is a strong unevenness between the attention and emotion expressed regarding IS sexual violence against Yazidis women and the attention given to the violence experienced by the Iraqi population since the beginning of the offensive against IS in Mosul. Moreover, the political and media discourse is dominated by the ease with which the world has fallen into a cultural interpretation of IS violence and the essentialist reading lens that sees the conflict as the "civilized" against the "barbarians." Throughout my ongoing fieldwork, I have witnessed the consequences of this discourse inside the country: growing sectarian tension and violence, military bashing, celebration of masculine violence, and a state of emergency that allows the government to repress, silence, and undermine critiques and opposition to its politics under the pretence that the country's identity and borders are under threat. As demonstrated throughout this book, the unspeakable violence faced by women under IS cannot be understood without considering the continuum of structural violence occurring in Iraq since at least the 1980s through militarization,

291

harsh patrimonial authoritarianism, devastating economic sanctions, and US-led military invasion and occupation that have exacerbated ethnosectarian, social, and political tensions.

In this extremely difficult context, Iraqi women political activists since 2003 have been caught between fighting to preserve their existing rights under threat from conservative social forces and struggling to preserve their essential rights to security and dignity questioned by the violent crisis provoked by the invasion and occupation. However, the emergence since 2011 of a movement of protest contesting the legitimacy of the post-2003 regime has also given women's rights activists a platform to relate their advocacy for gender equality to broader social and political agendas. It has opened horizons both beyond the "NGOization" of the civil society sphere and party or communal backed political groups. Struggling for a "civil state" – *dawla medeniyya* – is today the main point of convergence between civil society, youth movements, and feminist activists in Iraq.

The context following the invasion of IS exacerbated the post-2003 situation by militarizing the ethnosectarian conflict. Iraqis witnessed in horror this invasion and were subject to a hypermilitarized and ethnosectarian state discourse. However, in this context of extreme crisis, ordinary citizens launched a strong grassroots movement on July 31, 2015, that was then followed by civil society, women's rights, and political activists. From Basra to Baghdad's Tahrir Square across Iraq, this movement has expressed citizens' general exasperation at the corruption and mismanagement of the post-2003 government – corruption and mismanagement epitomized by electricity cuts during the unbearable summer heat even in the month of Ramadan and the general lack of basic public services. These protests quickly turned into a massive popular movement – supported even by the prominent religious figure Ayatollah Sistani – vilifying Iraq's postinvasion regime and demanding radical reforms. Every Friday since then, demonstrators have gathered in the main public squares of Iraq's big cities, including Najaf, Nasiriyah, and Basra, and echoed the slogans of the protestors in central Baghdad: *Biism il-din baguna al-haramiyya* ("In the name of religion, we have been robbed by looters") and *Khubz, Huriyya, Dawla Medeniyya* ("Bread, Freedom, and a Civil State"). Demonstrators consider the new regime's corruption and sectarian politics to be directly responsible for the formation and spread of IS.

Many women's rights activists who participated actively in this movement of protest emphasized the importance of linking gender-equality advocacy with the struggles for religious, social, and class equality. IWN activists insist on the preservation of equal citizenship for Iraqis from all ethnic and religious backgrounds as a cornerstone of the preservation of women's legal rights. As part of their advocacy for the abolition of the ethnosectarian quota system and the denunciation of corruption, the demonstrators are calling for a reform of the Electoral Law in order for it to include nonsectarian, small, and secular parties.

However, these mobilizations face harsh repression from the government, as well as from armed militia groups who threaten, harass, assault, kidnap, and sometimes also kill demonstrators, journalist, and political activists. The "War on Terror" is used by the state and these armed sectarian groups to silence political dissent and any alternative political discourse, and activists of the opposition are often accused of being supportive of Ba'thism or terrorism. The popularity of the Iraqi army, as well as the popular army called *al-Hashd al-Sha'bi* formed of ordinary citizens following the call of Ayatollah Sistani "to protect the Iraqi nation against IS invaders" in June 2014, is at its highest point since these forces took Mosul back from IS in 2017. The official narrative on the war against IS is a discourse of "success against terror," and it dominates and polarizes the political and media sphere, rendering ineffective any critic of the unspeakable destruction of part of Mosul itself and the mismanagement of the humanitarian crisis provoked by the war.

The proliferation of arms and their distribution to members of the paramilitary forces formed by civilians since the invasion of IS not only have exacerbated militarization but also have started a new cycle of generalized armed violence. Clashes have already occurred between armed soldiers standing at checkpoints and young armed soldiers coming back from the Mosul front, and no clear plan or process of disarmament of paramilitary forces has been undertaken. Moreover, all the militias and armed groups that are now in possession of arms have reached a particular status in society, and their integration into the army does not seem to be a legitimate option for them. There is total impunity for the armed groups who have committed crimes such as the killing or kidnapping of activists or journalists who criticized the military campaign in Mosul or offered any other critique of the army or *al-Hashd al-Sha'bi*.

Human rights abuse at the hands of the state, the army, or paramilitary forces and the threat represented by armed militia groups in the Iraqi streets represent a striking feature of the post-2003 regime. Far from being "democratic," this regime has proved to be dysfunctional, repressive, and unable to provide access to essential rights and resources to its population. Struggles between different political powers in Iraq are expressed through violence and the extreme militarization, and the normalization of armed violence has had a deep impact on the social and cultural fabric of Iraqi society. While I am writing these lines, the Iraqi Parliament has approved the principle of a reform of the Personal Status Code (PSC) along sectarian lines. Use of the "War on Terror" by dominant conservative Islamist parties to assert its ethnosectarian version of Iraqi identity is again played upon women's legal rights. Not only are the "War on Terror" politics characterized by a celebration of militarization and sectarianism, but they are eluding alternative political approaches targeting the roots of terrorism and the very nature of structural political, economic, and social violence resulting from wars, authoritarianism, the US-led imperialist war, and neoliberal politics.

Bibliography

Abdelrahman, Maha. 2007. NGOs and the Dynamics of the Egyptian Labour Market. *Development in Practice* 17(1): 78–84.

Abdo, Nahla. 1999. Gender and Politics under the Palestinian Authority. *Journal of Palestine Studies* 28(2): 38–51.

Abdul-Hadi, Rabab. 1998. Palestinian Women's Autonomous Movement: Emergence, Dynamics and Challenges. *Gender and Society* 12(6): 649–73.

Abdul Hussein, Lahay. 2006. *Ather al-Tanmiyya wal-Harb "ala Nisa" al-'Iraq 1968–1988.* Baghdad: Dar al-Shu'un al-Thakafiyya.

Abdullah, Badrea S. 2015. *Al-Dawr al-Siyasi lil Mar'a al-Iraqiyya.* Jame'at Baghdad: Merkez al-Dirasat al-Istratejiyya wal Du'aliyya.

Abdullah, Thabit. 2003. *A Short History of Iraq.* Iowa City, IA: Pearson Education.

Abou-Bakr, Omaima. 2013. *Feminist and Islamic Perspectives: New Horizons of Knowledge and Reform.* Cairo: Women and Memory Forum.

2012. Le féminisme islamique et la production de la connaissance: perspectives dans l'Egypte postrévolutionnaire, in Z. Ali (ed.), *Féminismes Islamiques.* Paris: La Fabrique: 165–84.

Abu-Lughod, Lila.2013. *Do Muslim Women Need Saving?* Cambridge, MA: Harvard University Press.

2002. Do Muslim Women Really Need Saving? Anthropological Reflections on Cultural Relativism and Its Others. *American Anthropologist* 104(3): 783–90.

(ed.).1998. *Remaking Women: Feminism and Modernity in the Middle East.* Princeton, NJ: Princeton University Press.

1993. *Writing Women's Worlds: Bedouin Stories.* Berkeley, CA: University of California Press.

1991. Writing against Culture, in R. G. Fox (ed.), *Recapturing Anthropology: Working in the Present*, Santa Fe, NM: School of American Research Press: 137–54.

1986. *Veiled Sentiments: Honor and Poetry in a Bedouin Society.* Berkeley, CA: University of California Press.

Abu-Nimer, Mohammed. 1996. Conflict Resolution Approaches: Western and Middle Eastern Lessons and Possibilities. *American Journal of Economics and Sociology* 55(1): 35–52.

Afshar, Haleh (ed.). 1996. *Women and Politics in the Third World.* London: Routledge.

Ahmed, Leila. 2011. *A Quiet Revolution: The Veil's Resurgence from the Middle East to America*. New Haven, CT: Yale University Press.

1992. *Women and Gender in Islam: Historical Roots of a Modern Debate*. New Haven, CT: Yale University Press.

1982. Feminism and Feminist Movements in the Middle East, a Preliminary Exploration: Turkey, Egypt, Algeria, People's Democratic Republic of Yemen. *Women's Studies International Forum* 5(2): 153–68.

Al-Ali, Nadje. 2007. *Iraqi Women: Untold Stories from 1948 to the Present*. London: Zed Books.

2000. *Secularism, Gender and the State in the Middle East: The Egyptian Women's Movements*. Cambridge: Cambridge University Press.

Al-Ali, Nadje, Al-Jeboury, Irada, et al. 2012. *Female Iraqi Academics in Postinvasion Iraq: Roles, Challenged and Capacities*. London: Zed Books.

Al-Ali, Nadje, & Pratt, Nicola. 2011. Between Nationalism and Women's Rights: The Kurdish Women's Movement in Iraq. *Middle East Journal of Culture and Communication* 4(3): 339–55.

2009a. *What Kind of Liberation? Women and the Occupation of Iraq*. Berkeley, CA: University of California Press.

(eds.). 2009b. *Woman and War in the Middle East*. London: Zed Books.

2008. Women Organizing and the Conflict in Iraq since 2003. *Feminist Review* 88: 74–85.

Al-Ali, Zaid. 2014. *The Struggle for Iraq's Future: How Corruption, Incompetence and Sectarianism Have Undermined Democracy*. New Haven, CT: Yale University Press.

Al-Derbendi, Abdel Rahman. 1968. *Al-Mar'a al-'Iraqiyya al-Mu'asera*. Baghdad: Dar al-Basra.

Al-Dulaimi, Naziha, 1952. *Al-Mar'a al-'Iraqiyya*. Baghdad: Matba'at al-Rabita.

Alexander, Jacqui, & Mohanty, Chandra Talpade. 1997. *Feminist Genealogies, Colonial Legacies, Democratic Futures*. London: Routledge.

Al-Gubenchi, Ahmed. 2009. *Al-Mar'a, al-Mefahim wal Huquq: Qira'e jedida li Qezaya al-Mar'a fi al-Khitab al-Dini*. Beirut: Al-intishar al-'arabi.

Ali, Ala. 2014. Security, Religion and Gender in al-Anbar Province, Iraq: A Focused Group-Based Analysis. Paper presented at the Gunda Werner Institute in Berlin, November 27, 2014.

Alinia, Minoo. 2013. *Honor and Violence against Women in Iraqi Kurdistan*. New York, NY: Palgrave Macmillan.

Ali, Zahra. 2017. The Fragmentation of Gender in Post-Invasion Iraq, in Amal Ghazal & Jens Hanssen (eds.), *The Oxford Handbook of Contemporary Middle-Eastern and North African History*. Oxford: Oxford Handbooks Online.

2017. Reflecting on Multiple Fragmentations in a City of Men. *Jadaliyya*, November 15, available at www.jadaliyya.com/Details/34665/Reflecting-on-Multiple-Fragmentations-in-a-City-of-Men.

2016. Young Grassroots Activism on the Rise in Iraq: Voices from Baghdad and Najaf. *Open Democracy*, May 5, available at www.opendemocracy.net/north-africa-west-asia/zahra-ali/young-grassroots-activism-on-rise-in-iraq-voices-from-baghdad-and-najaf.

2013. Le mouvement des femmes de l'Irak post-Saddam. *L'Homme et la société, Sexe et Politique* 189–90 (February): 223–43.

2013. Le mouvement des femmes dans l'Irak post-Saddam: entre Genre, Nation et Religion. Héritages passés et défis présents. *Genesis* XII(1): 71–99.

(ed.) 2012. *Féminismes Islamiques*. Paris: La Fabrique.

Al-Jawaheri, H. Yasmin. 2008. *Women in Iraq: The Gender Impact of International Sanctions*. New York, NY: I.B. Tauris.

Al-Khafaji, Isam.2003. A mi-chemin de la démocratie: les options de transitions de l'Irak, in Hamit Bozarslan & Dawod Hosham (eds.), *La Société Irakienne: Communautés, Pouvoirs et Violences*. Paris: Karthala.

1986. State Incubation of Iraqi Capitalism. *Middle East Report* 142 (September–October): 16.

Al-Khalil, Samir. *Republic of Fear: The Politics of Modern Iraq*. Berkeley, CA: University of California Press.

Al-Khayyat, Sana.1990. *Honour and Shame: Women in Modern Iraq*. London: Saqi.

Al-Musawi, J. Muhsin. 2006. *Reading Iraq: Culture and Power in Conflict*. New York, NY: I.B. Tauris.

Al-Nadawi, Nahla. 2010. *Al-Ada' al Barlamani lil Mar'a al-'Iraqiyya*. Baghdad: Shabakat al-Nisa' al-'Iraqiyyat.

Alnasrawi, Abbas. 2002. *Iraq's Burdens: Oil, Sanctions*. Westport, CT: Greenwood Press.

1994. *The Economy of Iraq: Oil, Wars, Destruction of Development and Prospectus, 1950–2010*. Westport, CT: Greenwood Press.

Al-Rachid, Loulouwa. 2010. L'Irak de l'embargo à l'occupation: dépérissement d'un ordre politique (1990–2003). Ph.D. thesis, Paris: Institut d'Etudes Politiques.

Al-Rachid, Loulouwa, & Méténier, Edouard. 2008. A propos de la violence "irakienne." Quelques éléments de réflexion sur un lieu commun. *A Contrario* 5(1): 114–33.

Al-Sharqi, Amel. 1982. The Emancipation of Iraqi Women, in T. Niblock (ed.), *Iraq: The Contemporary State*. London: Palgrave Macmillan: 74–87.

Al-Wardi, Ali.1978. *Lamahat Ijtima'iyya min Tarikh al-'Iraq al-Hadith*. Baghdad: Matba'at al-Adis al Baghdadiyya.

1965. *Dirasa fi Tabi'at al-Mujtama' al-'Iraqi*. Baghdad: Matba'at al-'Ani.

Al-Zublef, Abdul Husein, & Said, Hamid. 1980. *Al-Mar'a wal Ta'lim al-Nizami 1920–1979*. Baghdad: Wizarat al-Thaqafat wal Ta'lim.

Amnesty International. 2014. Escape from Hell: Torture and Sexual Slavery in Islamic State Captivity in Iraq, December 2014, available at www.amnesty .org.uk/files/escape_from_hell-torture_and_sexual_slavery_in_islamic_sta te_captivity_in_iraq-_english_2.pdf.

2013. Iraq: A Decade of Abuses, March 11, available at www.amnesty.org/en/ documents/MDE14/001/2013/en/.

2011. Broken Bodies, Tortures Minds: Abuse and Neglect of Detainees in Iraq, February 8, available at www.amnesty.org/en/documents/MDE14/001/201 1/en/.

Anderson, J. N. D. 1963. Changes in the Law of Personal Status in Iraq. *International and Comparative Law Quarterly* 12(3): 1026–31.

1960. A Law of Personal Status for Iraq. *International and Comparative Law Quarterly* 9(4): 542–63.

1953. A Draft Code of Personal Law for Iraq. *Bulletin of the School of Oriental and African Studies, University of London* 15(1): 43–60.

Anthias, Floya, & Davis, Nira Yuval (eds.). 1989. *Woman-Nation-State*. London: Palgrave Macmillan.

Anwar, Zainah. 2012. Négocier les droits des femmes sous la loi religieuse en Malaisie, in Zahra Ali (ed.), *Féminismes Islamiques*. Paris: La Fabrique.

Arato, Andrew. 2009. *Constitution Making under Occupation: The Politics of Imposed Revolution in Iraq*. New York, NY: Columbia University Press.

Asad, Talal. 2003. *Formations of the Secular: Christianity, Islam, Modernity*. Stanford, CA: Stanford University Press.

Babakhan, Fa'iza. 2009. *Al-Qiwanin al-'Iraqiyya al-Khasa bi Huquq al-Mar'a fi Zaw Itifaqiyyat Sidaw. Dirasa Muqaranat*. Baghdad: Dar al-Riwad al-Muzdahira.

2009. *Al-Waza' al-Qanuni li Huquq al-Mar'a fi al-Tashri'at al-'Iraqiyya. Dirasa Muqarana*. Baghdad: Dar al-Riwad al-Muzdahira.

Badran, Margot. 2009. *Feminism and Islam: Secular and Religious Convergences*. London: One World Publications.

1995. *Feminists, Islam, and Nation: Gender and the Making of Modern Egypt*. Princeton, NJ: Princeton University Press.

Barakat, Sultan. 2005. Post-Saddam Iraq: Deconstructing a Regime, Reconstructing a Nation. *Third World Quarterly* 26(4–5): 571–91.

Barakat, Sultan, & Wardell, Gareth. 2002. Exploited by Whom? An Alternative Perspective on Humanitarian Assistance to Afghan Women. *Third World Quarterly* 23(5): 909–30.

Baram, Amatzia. 1997. Neo-Tribalism in Iraq: Saddam Hussein's Tribal Policies 1991–96. *International Journal of Middle East Studies* 29: 1–31.

1994. A Case of Imported Identity: The Modernizing Secular Ruling Elites of Iraq and the Concept of Mesopotamian-Inspired Territorial Nationalism, 1922–1992. *Poetics Today* 15(2): 279–319.

Baram, A. Ronen, Rohde, Achim, & Amatzia, Zeidel R. (eds.). 2010. *Iraq between Occupations: Perspectives from the 1920 to the Present*. London: Palgrave Macmillan.

Baron, Beth. 2005. *Egypt as a Woman: Nationalism, Gender, and Politics*. Berkeley, CA: University of California Press.

Bashkin, Orit. 2011. Hybrid Nationalisms: Watani and Qawmi Visions in Iraq under 'Abd Al-Karim Qasim (1958–1961). *International Journal of Middle East Studies* 43: 293–312.

2009. *The Other Iraq: Pluralism and Culture in Hashemite Iraq*. Stanford, CA: Stanford University Press.

2008. Representations of Women in the Writings of the Intelligentsia in Hashemite Iraq, 1921–1958. *Journal of Middle East Women's Studies* 4(1).

Batatu, Hanna. 1991. The Old Social Classes Revisited, in Robert A Fernea & William Roger Louis (eds.), *The Iraqi Revolution of 1958: The Old Social Classes Revisited*. New York: I.B. Tauris: 211–22.

1989. Shi'i Organizations in Iraq: al-Da'wah al-islamiyah and al-Mujahidin, in Juan R. I. Cole & Nikki R. Keddie (eds.), *Shi'ism and Social Protest*. New Haven, CT: Yale University Press.

1986. State and Capitalism in Iraq: A Comment. *MERIP Middle East Report No. 142*, September–October: 10–12.

1978. *The Old Social Classes and the Revolutionary Movements of Iraq: A Study of Iraq's Old Landed and Commercial Classes and of Its Communists, Ba'thists, and Free Officers*. Princeton, NJ: Princeton University Press.

Bayt al-Hikma. 2011. *Bina' al-'Iraq. A'mal al-Mu'tamar al-Merkezi al-Sanawi al-Thani li Bayt al-Hikma*. Baghdad: Bayt al-Hikma.

2010. *Al-Hikma*, vol. 48. Baghdad: Bayt al-Hikma.

2010. *Dirasat Ijtima'iyya*, vol. 22. Baghdad: Bayt al-Hikma.

2009. *Al-'Iraq 700 sena min al-Hazara. Al-Taqrir al-Watani li-hal al-Tanmiyya al-Bashariyya*. Baghdad: Wizara al-Takhtit/Bayt al-Hikma.

Begikhani, Nazand, Hague, Gill, & Gill, Aisha. 2012. "Honour"-Based Violence in Kurdish Communities. *Women's Studies International Forum* 35(2): 75–85.

2005. Honour-Based Violence among the Kurds: The Case of Iraqi Kurdistan, in Lynn Welshman & Sarah Hussain (eds.), *Honour Crimes, Paradigms, and Violence against Women*. New York: Zed Books: 209–30.

Bint al-Rafidain/UNIFEM.2006. *Dirasa Qanuniyya li-Waqe 'al-Ahwal al-Shakhsiyya fi Manadiq al-Furat al-Awsat*. Babel/Karbala/Najaf/Diwaniyya/Waset.

Booth, Marilyn.2001. Woman in Islam: Men and the "Women's Press" in Turn-of-the-20th-Century Egypt. *International Journal of Middle East Studies* 33(2): 171–201.

1998. The Egyptian Lives of Jeanne d'Arc, in Lila Abu-Lughod (ed.), *Remaking Women: Feminism and Modernity in the Middle East*. Princeton, NJ: Princeton University Press.

Bourdieu, Pierre. 1980. *Le sens pratique*. Paris: Ed. de Minuit.

Bozarslan, Hamit. 2009. *Conflit kurde*, Paris: Autrement.

2008. *Une histoire de la violence au Moyen-Orient. De la fin de l'Empire ottoman à Al-Qaida*. Paris: La Découverte.

(eds.). 2007. L'Irak en Perspectives. *REMMM* 2007: 117–18.

Bozarslan, Hamit, & Dawod, Hosham (eds.). 2003. *La Société Irakienne: Communautés, Pouvoirs et Violences*. Paris: Karthalat.

Brah, Avtar, & Phoenix, Ann.(2004). Ain't I a Woman? Revisiting Intersectionality. *Journal of International Women's Studies* 5(3): 75–86.

Brown, Lucy, & Romano, David. 2006. Women in Post-Saddam Iraq: One Step Forward or Two Steps Back?, *NWSA Journal* 18(3): 51–70.

Burgat, François. 1996. *L'islamisme en face*. Paris: La Découverte.

2005. *L'islamisme à l'heure d'Al-Qaida*. Paris: La Découverte.

Carroll, Katherine Blue. 2011. Tribal Law and Reconciliation in the New Iraq. *The Middle East Journal* 65(1): 11–29.

Charrad, M. Mounira. 2011. Central and Local Patrimonialism: State-Building in Kin-Based Societies. *Annals AAPSS* 636: 49–68.

2011. Gender in the Middle East: Islam, State, Agency. *Annual Review of Sociology* 37: 417–37.

2001. *States and Women's Rights: The Making of Postcolonial Tunisia, Algeria and Morocco*. Berkeley, CA: University of California Press.

Chatelard, Geraldine, & Dorai, Kamel. 2009. La présence irakienne en Syrie et en Jordanie. Dynamiques sociales et spatiales, et modes de gestion par les pays d'accueil. *Maghreb-Machrek* 199: 43–60.

Cobett, Deborah. 1986. Women in Iraq, in *Saddam's Iraq: Revolution or Reaction?* London: Zed Books: 120–37.

Cole, Juan. 2009. Struggles over Personal Status and Family Law in Post-Baathist Iraq, in Kenneth M. Cuno & Manisha Desai (eds.), *Family, Gender, and Law in a Globalizing Middle East and South Asia*. Syracuse, NY: Syracuse University Press: 105–25.

Coleman, Isabel. 2010. *Paradise Beneath Her Feet: How Women Are Transforming the Middle East*. New York, NY: Random House.

Collins Hill, Patricia. 1990. *Black Feminist Thought: Knowledge, Consciousness, and the Politics of Empowerment*. New York, NY: Routledge.

1989. The Social Construction of Black Feminist Thought. *Signs* 14(4): 745–73.

Collins Hill, Patricia, & Bilge, Sirma. 2016. *Intersectionality*. Malden, MA: Polity Press.

Colp Rubin, Judith. 2008. Women in the New Iraq. *Global Politician*, available at www.globalpolitician.com/25202-iraq.

Crenshaw, Kimberlee. 1991. Mapping the Margins: Intersectionality, Identity Politics, and Violence against Women of Color. *Stanford Law Review* 43(6): 1241–99.

1989. Demarginalizing the Intersection of Race and Sex: A Black Feminist Critique of Antidiscrimination Doctrine, Feminist Theory, and Antiracist Politics. *University of Chicago Legal Forum* 1989: 139–67.

Da'ud, Sabiha al-Shaikh. 1958. *Awwal al-Tariq Ila al-Nahda al-Niswiyya fi al-'Iraq*. Baghdad: Matba'a al-Rabita.

Damaluji, Mona. 2010. Securing Democracy in Iraq: Sectarian Politics and Segregation in Baghdad, 2003–2007. *Traditional Dwellings and Settlements Review* 21(2): 71–87.

Davis, Angela. 1981. *Women, Race and Class*. New York, NY: Random House.

Davis, Eric. 2005. *Memories of State: Politics, History, and Collective Identity in Modern Iraq*. Berkeley, CA: California University Press.

Dawisha, Adeed. 2009. *Iraq: A Political History from Independence to Occupation*. Princeton, NJ: Princeton University Press.

Dawod, Hosham. 2003. The "State-ization" of the Tribe and the Tribalization of the State: The Case of Iraq, in Hosham Dawod & Jabar A. Faleh (eds.), *Tribes and Power: Nationalism and Ethnicity in the Middle East*. London: Saqi: 110–35.

Dawod, Hosham, & Faleh, Jabar A. (eds.). *Tribes and Power: Nationalism and Ethnicity in the Middle East*. London: Saqi.

Dayan-Herzbrun, Sonia. 2013. La théorie critique au-delà du postcolonial. *Illusio* 10–11: 109–19.

2005. *Femmes et politique au Moyen-Orient*. Paris: L'Harmattan.

Deeb, Lara. 2006. *An Enchanted Modern: Gender and Public Piety in Shi'i Lebanon*. Princeton, NJ: Princeton University Press.

Deeb, Lara, & Harb, Mona. 2013. *Leisurely Islam: Negotiating Geography and Morality in Shi'ite South Beirut*. Princeton, NJ: Princeton University Press.

Dodge, Toby. 2013. *Iraq: From War to a New Authoritarianism* (Adelphi Series). London: Routledge.

2005. *Iraq's Future: The Aftermath of Regime Change* (Adelphi Series 372). London: Routledge.

2003. *Inventing Iraq: The Failure of Nation Building and a History Denied*. New York, NY: Columbia University Press.

Droz-Vincent, Philipe. 2008. Où sont donc les "sociétés civiles" au Moyen-Orient?, *Humanitaire* 20.

Dussel, Enrique. 2000. Europe, Modernity, and Eurocentrism. Nepantla. *Views from South* 3: 465–78.

Enloe, Cynthia.2004. *The Curious Feminist: Searching for Women in a New Age of Empire*. Berkeley, CA: University of California Press.

Efrati,Noga. 2012. *Women in Iraq: Past meets Present*. New York, NY: Columbia University Press.

2008. Competing Narratives: Histories of the Women's Movement in Iraq, 1910–1958. *International Journal of Middle East Studies* 40(3): 445–66.

2005. Negotiating Rights in Iraq: Women and the Personal Status Law. *Middle East Journal* 59(4): 575–95.

2004. The Other "Awakening" in Iraq: The Women's Movement in the First Half of the Twentieth Century. *British Journal of Middle Eastern Studies* 2004: 153–73.

1999. Productive or Reproductive? The Roles of Iraqi Women during the Iraq-Iran War. *Middle Eastern Studies* 35(2): 27–44.

Esposito, L. John, & Haddad, Yvonne (eds.). 1998. *Islam, Gender, and Social Change*. Oxford: Oxford University Press.

Fanon, Frantz. 1961. *Les Damnés de la Terre*. Paris: Maspero.

1952. *Peau noire, masques blancs*. Paris: Seuil.

Farouk-Sluglett, Marion. 1993. Liberation or Repression? Pan-Arab Nationalism and the Women's Movement in Iraq, in D. Hopwood, H. Ishow, T. Koszinowski (eds.), *Power and Society*. Oxford: Ithaca Press, St. Antony's College.

1991. Irak: rente pétrolière et concentration du pouvoir. *Monde arabe Maghreb-Machrek* 131: 3–12.

Farouk-Sluglett, Marion, & Sluglett, Peter. 1991. The Historiography in Modern Iraq. *American Historical Review* 96(5): 1408–21.

1987. *Iraq since 1958: From Revolution to Dictatorship*. New York, NY: I.B. Tauris.

Fattah, Hala. 2012. What Did It Mean to Be an Iraqi during the Monarchy? A Preliminary Investigation Based on Oral Interviews with Iraqis in Jordan and the United Kingdom, in Jordi Tejtel, Peter Sluglett, Riccardo Bocco & Hamit Bozarslan (eds.), *Writing the Modern History of Iraq: Historiographical and Political Challenges*.London: World Scientific Publishing: 95–103.

Ferguson, Susanna. 2015. Listening to Rights Talk in Damascus: Women's Rights, Human Rights, and the State in Syria, 2009–11. *Comparative Studies of South Asia, Africa and the Middle East* 35(3): 557–74.

Fernea, Robert, & Rogers, Louis (eds.). *The Iraqi Revolution of 1958: The Old Social Classes Revisited*. New York, NY: I.B. Tauris.

Fischer-Tahir, Andrea. 2010. Competition, Cooperation and Resistance: Women in the Political Field in Iraq. *International Affairs* 86(6).

2009. *Brave Men, Pretty Women? Gender and Symbolic Violence in Iraqi Kurdistan Urban Society.* Berlin: Europäisches Zentrum für Kurdische Studien.

Fleischmann, Ellen. 1999. The Other "Awakening": The Emergence of Women's Movements in the Middle East, c. 1900–1940, in Margaret L. Meriwether & Judith E. Tucker (eds.), *A Social History of Women and Gender in the Modern Middle East.* Boulder, CO: Westview Press: 89–140.

Foucault, Michel. 1966. *Les mots et les choses. Une archéologie des sciences humaines.* Paris: Gallimard.

Glissant, Edouard. 1997. *Traité du Tout Monde.* Paris: Gallimard.

1990. *Poétique de la Relation.* Paris: Gallimard.

Göle, Nilüfer. 1993. *Musulmanes et Modernes. Voile et civilisation en Turquie.* Paris: La Découverte.

Gordon, Joy. 2010. *Invisible War, the United States and the Iraq Sanctions.* Cambridge, MA: Harvard University Press.

Greenberg, Marcia E., & Zuckerman, Elaine. 2006. The Gender Dimensions of Post-Conflict Reconstruction: The Challenges in Development Aid. Research Paper No. 2006/62, UNU-WIDER, available at www.wider.unu.edu/publications/rps/rps2006/rp2006-62.pdf.

Grewal, Inderpal, & Kaplan, Caren (eds.). 2006. *Scattered Hegemonies: Postmodernity and Transnational Feminist Practices.* Minneapolis, MN: University of Minnesota Press.

Haddad, Fanar. 2014. A Sectarian Awakening: Reinventing Sunni Identity in Iraq after 2003. *Current Trends in Islamist Ideology* 14: 70.

2010. Sectarian Relations in Arab Iraq: Competing Mythologies of History, People and State. Ph.D thesis, University of Exeter.

Hall, Stuart. 1997. The Local and the Global: Globalization and Ethnicity, in A. D. King (ed.), *Culture, Globalization and the World-System: Contemporary Conditions for the Representation of Identity.* Minneapolis, MN: University of Minnesota Press.

1996a. Introduction: Who Needs Identity?, in S. Hall & P. du Gay (eds.), *Questions of Cultural Identity.* London: Sage: 1–17.

1996b. New Ethnicities, in D. Morley & K. Hsing Chen (eds.), *Stuart Hall Critical Dialogues in Cultural Studies.* New York: Routledge: 442–41.

1990. Cultural Identity and Diaspora, in J. Rutherford (ed.), *Identity: Community, Culture, Difference.* London: Lawrence & Wishart: 222–37.

1986. On Postmodernism and Articulation: An Interview by Stuart Hall with Lawrence Grossberg. *Journal of Communication Inquiry* 10(2): 45–60.

Hamoudi, Haider Ala, Al-Sharaa Wasfi, H. and Al-Dahhan, Aqeel. 2015. The Resolution of Disputes in State and Tribal Law in the South of Iraq: Toward a Cooperative Model of Pluralism, in Michael A. Helfand (ed.), *Negotiating State and Non-State Law: The Challenge of Global and Local Legal Pluralism.* Cambridge: Cambridge University Press: 215–60.

Haraway, Donna. 1988. Situated Knowledges: The Science Question in Feminism and the Privilege of Partial Perspective. *Feminist Studies* 14(3): 575–99.

Hardi, Choman, 2011. *Gendered Experiences of Genocide: Anfal Survivors in Kurdistan-Iraq*. London: Routledge.

Harding, Sandra. 1992. Rethinking Standpoint Epistemology: What Is "Strong Objectivity"? *Centennial Review* 36(3): 437–70.

Harling, Peter. 2012. Beyond Political Ruptures: Towards a Historiography of Social Continuity in Iraq, in Jordi Tejtel, Peter Sluglett, Riccardo Bocco, & Hamit Bozarslan (eds.), *Writing the Modern History of Iraq: Historiographical and Political Challenges*. London: World Scientific Publishing: 61–86.

Hasso, Frances S. 2005. *Resistance, Repression, and Gender Politics in Occupied Palestine and Jordan*. Syracuse, NY: Syracuse University Press.

2001. Feminist Generations? The Long-Term Impact of Social Movement Involvement on Palestinian Women's Lives. *AJS* 107(3): 586–611.

1998. The "Women's Front": Nationalism, Feminism, and Modernity in Palestine. *Gender and Society* 12(4): 441–65.

Hatem, Mervat.2005. Secularist and Islamist Discourses on Modernity in Egypt and the Evolution of the Post-Colonial Nation-State, in Moghissi Haideh (ed.), *Women and Islam: Images and realities*, Abingdon: Taylor & Francis.

1998. The Secularist and Islamist Discourses on Modernity in Egypt and the Evolution of the Post Colonial Nation-State, in Yvonne Haddad and John Esposito (eds.), *Islam, Gender and Social Change*. Oxford: Oxford University Press.

1994. Egyptian Discourses on Gender and Political Liberalization: Do Secularist and Islamist Views Really Differ?. *Middle East Journal* 48(4).

1993. Toward the Development of Post-Islamist and Post-Nationalist Feminist Discourses in the Middle East, in Judith E. Tucker (ed.), *Arab Women: Old Boundaries, New Frontiers*. Bloomington, IN: Indiana University Press, 29–48.

Henrizi, Anika. 2015. Building Peace in Hybrid Spaces: Women's Agency in Iraqi NGOs. *Peacebuilding* 3(1): 75–89.

hooks, bell. 1986. Sisterhood: Political Solidarity between Women. *Feminist Review* 23: 125–38.

Hopwood, Derek, Ishow, Habib, & Koszinowski, Thomas. 1993. *Power and Society*. Oxford: Ithaca Press, St. Antony's College.

Human Rights Watch. 2003. Climate of Fear: Sexual Violence and Abduction of Women and Girls in Baghdad, available at www.hrw.org/reports/2003/iraq0703/.

Hussein, Sadam. 1979. *Social and Foreign Affairs in Iraq*. London: Routledge.

International Crisis Group. 2013. Make or Break. Iraq's Sunnis and the State. Middle East Report No. 144, August.

2008a. Iraq after the Surge. II: The Need for a New Political Strategy. Middle East Report No. 75, April 30.

2008b. Iraq after the Surge. I: The New Sunni Landscape. Middle East Report No. 74, April 30.

Iraqiyat Studies Center. 2006. *Muraja'at fi al-Distur al-Iraqi*. Baghdad: al-Atlas.

2007. *Muraja'at fi al-Tashri' at wal Qawanin al-'Iraqiyya al-Khasa bil Mar'a*. Baghdad: al-Atlas.

Ishow, Habib. 2003. *Structures Sociales et Politiques de l'Irak Contemporain. Pourquoi un Etat en crise?* Paris: L'Harmattan.

Ismael,Jacqueline S., & Ismael, Shereen T.2008. Living through War, Sanctions and Occupation: The Voices of Iraqi Women. *International Journal of Contemporary Iraqi Studies* 2(3): 409–24.

2007. Iraqi Women under Occupation: From Tribalism to Neo-Feudalism. *International Journal of Contemporary Iraqi Studies* 1(2): 247–68.

2000. Gender and State in Iraq, in Joseph Suad (ed.), *Gender and Citizenship in the Middle East*. Syracuse, NY: Syracuse University Press.

Ismael, Jacqueline S. & Ismael, Tareq Y. 2015. *Iraq in the Twenty-First Century: Regime Change and the Making of a Failed State*. London: Routledge.

Issa, Ali. 2015. *Against All Odds: Voices of Popular Struggle in Iraq*. Washington, DC: Tadween Publishing and War Resisters League.

Jabar, A. Faleh. 2003. *The Shiite Movement in Iraq*. London: Saqi.

2003. Shaikhs and Ideologues: Deconstruction and Reconstruction of Tribes under Patrimonial Totalitarism in Iraq, 1968–1998, in Hosham Dawod & A. Faleh Jabar (eds.), *Tribes and Power: Nationalism and Ethnicity in the Middle East*. London: Saqi: 69–135.

Jad, Islah.2007. NGOs: Between Buzzwords and Social Movements. *Development in Practice* 17(4–5): 622–29.

2003. The NGO-isation of Arab Women's Movements. *IDS Bulletin* 35(4): 34–42, available October 2004 at http://76.163.8.31/english/doc/images/Isl ah%2520Jad%2520NGOization.pdf.

Jameel Rashid, Asma. 2010. Al-Tamthil al-Siyasi lil Mar'a al-'Iraqiyya. *Shu'un 'Iraqiyya* 4: 213–30.

2006. Al-Mar'a al-'Iraqiyya Be'd thalath sanawat min al-Taghir. *Al-Thakafat al-Jadida* 318 (May): 35–46.

Jawad, Saad N., & Al-Assaf, Sawsan. I. (2014), The Higher Education System in Iraq and Its Future. *International Journal of Contemporary Iraqi Studies* 8(1): 55–72.

Jayawardena, Kumari. 1986. *Feminism and Nationalism in the Third World*. London: Zed Books.

Joseph, Suad. 2000. *Gender and Citizenship in the Middle East*. Syracuse, NY: Syracuse University Press.

1991. Elite Strategies for State Building: Women, Family, Religion and the State in Iraq and Lebanon, in Deniz Kandiyoti (eds.), *Women, Islam, and the State*. London: Macmillan: 176–200.

Kaplan, Karen, Alarcon, Norma, & Moalled, Minoo (eds.). 1999. *Between Woman and Nation: Nationalisms, Transnational Feminisms, and the State*. Durham, NC: Duke University Press.

Kandiyoti, Deniz. 2007a. Between the Hammer and the Anvil: Post-Conflict Reconstruction, Islam and Women's Rights. *Third World Quarterly* 28(3): 503–17.

2007b. Old Dilemmas or New Challenges? The Politics of Gender and Reconstruction in Afghanistan. *Development and Change* 38(2): 169–99.

1999. Identity and Its Discontents: Women and the Nation. *Millenium* 20(3): 429–43.

1996a. Contemporary Feminist Scholarship and Middle East Studies, in *Gendering the Middle East: Emerging Perspectives*. London: I.B. Tauris: 1–29.

(ed.). 1996b. *Gendering the Middle East*. London: I.B. Tauris.

1991. *Women, Islam and the State*. Philadelphia, PA: Temple University Press.

1988. Bargaining with Patriarchy. *Gender & Society* 2(3): 274–90.

Kamp, Martina. 2009. Fragmented Citizenship: Communalism, Ethnicity and Gender in Iraq, in Nadje Al-Ali & Nicola Pratt (eds.), *Women and War in the Middle East: Transnational Perspectives*. London: Zed Books.

Karam, Azza. 1998. *Women, Islamisms and the State. Contemporary Feminisms in Egypt*. London: Palgrave Macmillan.

Khattak, Saba Gul. 2002. Afghan Women: Bombed to Be Liberated? *Middle East Report No. 222* (Spring): 18–23.

Khayun, Rashid, & Badurzeki, Mohamed. 2006. *Al-Distur wa al-Mar'a*. Baghdad: Ma'had al-Dirasat al-Istratajiyya.

Khoury, Dina Rizk. 2013. *Iraq in Wartime: Soldiering, Martyrdom, and Remembrance*. Cambridge: Cambridge University Press.

2012. The 1991 Intifada in Three Keys: Writing the History of Violence, in *Writing the Modern History of Iraq*, In, Jordi Tejtel, Peter Sluglett, Riccardo Bocco, & Hamit Bozarslan (eds.), *Writing the Modern History of Iraq: Historiographical and Political Challenges*. London: World Scientific Publishing: 245–67.

Kian-Thiebaut, Azadeh (ed.). 2010. Genre et perspectives postcoloniales, in *Les Cahiers du Cedref*. Paris: Université Paris Diderot.

King, Diane. 2014. *Kurdistan on the Global Stage: Kinship, Land, and Community in Iraq*. New Brunswick, NJ: Rutgers University Press.

Krook, Mona Lena, O'Brien, Diana Z., & Swip, Krista M. 2010. Military Invasion and Women's Political Representation. *International Feminist Journal of Politics* 12(1): 66–79.

Kutschera, Chris. 2005. *Le Livre Noir de Saddam Hussein*. Paris: Oh! Editions.

Lafourcade, Fanny. 2012. How to "Turn the Page"? The National Iraqi Leadership after 2003 and the deba'thification Issue, in Jordi Tejtel, Peter Sluglett, Riccardo Bocco, & Hamit Bozarslan (eds.) *Writing the Modern History of Iraq: Historiographical and Political Challenges*. London: World Scientific Publishing: 181–201

2007a. *Le chaos irakien. Dix clés pour comprendre*. Paris: La Découverte.

2007b. Retour sur l'échec de la "Reconstruction." La question de la "société civile" irakienne. *REMMM, L'Irak en perspective* 2007: 117–18.

Latte Abdallah, Stéphanie. 2009. Vers un féminisme politique hors frontières au Proche-Orient: Regard sur les mobilisations en Jordanie (années 1950–années 2000), in *Vingtième Siècle, Revue d'histoire*, vol. 103: *Proche-Orient: foyers, frontières et fractures*. 177–95.

Lazreg, Marnia. 1994. *The Eloquence of Silence: Algerian Women in Question*. London: Routledge.

Lorde, Audre. 1984. *The Transformation of Silence into Language and Action*. Berkeley, CA: Ten Speed Press.

Lugones, Maria. 2010. Towards a decolonial feminism. *Hypathia* 25(4): 742–49.

Luizard, Pierre-Jean. 2002. *La Question Irakienne*. Paris: Fayard.

1991. *La formation de l'Irak contemporain, Le rôle politique des ulémas chiites à la fin de la domination ottomane et au moment de la création de l'Etat irakien.* Paris: CNRS.

Luizard, Pierre-Jean (eds.). 2006. Le choc colonial et l'islam, Les politiques religieuses des puissances coloniales en terres d'islam, in *Actes du colloque du GSRL Colonisation, laïcité et sécularisation. Les non-dits de la politique religieuse des puissances coloniales dans les pays musulmans des 22–25 novembre 2004.* Paris: La Découverte.

Mahmood, Saba. 2005. *Politics of Piety: The Islamic Revival and the Feminist Subject.* Princeton, NJ: Princeton University Press.

Malak, Abdulhusein Suhayla. 1978. *Biblioghraphiyya Mawzu'iyya 'an al-Mar'a al-'Iraqiyya.* Baghdad: Al-Itihad al-'Am li Nisa' al-'Iraq, al-Dirasat wal Buhuth.

Marr, Phebe. 1985. *The Modern History of Iraq.* Boulder, CO: Westview Press.

Masarat. 2010. *Masihiyun al-'Iraq*, vol. 14 (Year 5).

2009. *Yahud al-'Iraq*, vol. 13 (Year 4).

Mekki, Ilham. 2010. Al-Thakafa al-Siyasiyya lil Barlamaniyyat al-'Iraqiyyat. Master's dissertation, University of Baghdad.

Meriwether, Margaret L., & Tucker, Judith E. (eds.). 1999. *A Social History of Women and Gender in the Modern Middle East.* Boulder, CO: Westview Press.

Metcalfe, Dawn Beverly. 2008. Women, Management and Globalization in the Middle East. *Journal of Business Ethics* 83(1): 85–100.

Mikdashi, Maya. 2013. Queering Citizenship, Queering Middle East Studies. *International Journal of Middle East Studies* 24(2).

Milic, Andjelka. 2004. The Women's Movement in Serbia and Montenegro at the Turn of the Millennium: A Sociological Study of Women's Groups. *Feminist Review* 76: 65–82.

Minoo, Alinia. 2013. *Honor, Violence against Women in Iraqi Kurdistan.* London: Palgrave Macmillan.

Mir-Hosseini, Ziba. 2011. Beyond Islam vs. Feminism. *IDS Bulletin* 42(1).

1999. *Islam and Gender: The Religious Debate in Contemporary Iran.* New York: I.B. Tauris.

Mlodoch, Karin. 2012. Fragmented Memory, Competing Narratives: The Perspective of Women Survivors of the Anfal Operations in Iraqi Kurdistan, in Jordi Tejtel, Peter Sluglett, Riccardo Bocco, & Hamit Bozarslan (eds.), *Writing the Modern History of Iraq: Historiographical and Political Challenges.* London: World Scientific Publishing: 205–26.

Mofarah, Kasra. 2008 Confusion en Irak. *Humanitaire* 20, available at http://humanitaire.revues.org/326.

Moghadam, M. Valentine.2009. *Globalization and Social Movements Islamism, Feminism and the Global Justice Movement.* Lanham, MD: Rowman & Littlefield.

(ed.). 1994. *Gender and National Identity: Women and Politics in Muslim Societies.* London: Zed Books.

Moghissi, Haideh. 1999. *Feminism and Islamic Fundamentalism: The Limits of Postmodern Analysis.* London: Zed Books.

Mohanty, T. Chandra. 2003. *Feminism without Border: Decolonizing Theory, Practicing Solidarity*. Durham, NC: Duke University Press.

2003. "Under Western Eyes" Revisited: Feminist Solidarity through Anticapitalist Struggles, in Chandra T. Mohanty (ed.), *Feminism without Border: Decolonizing Theory, Practicing Solidarity*. Durham, NC: Duke University Press: 192–221.

1988. Under Western Eyes: Feminist Scholarship and Colonial Discourses. *Feminist Review* 30: 61–88.

Mohanty, C. Talpade, Russo, Ann, & Torres Lourdes (eds.). 1991. *Third World Women and the Politics of Feminism*. Bloomington, IN: Indiana University Press.

Mojab, Shahrzad. 2009. Imperialism, "Post-War Reconstruction" and Kurdish Women's NGOs, in Nadje Al-Ali and Nicola Pratt (eds.), *Women and War in the Middle East: Transnational Perspectives*. London: Zed Books: 99–128.

2007. Women's NGOs under Conditions of Occupation and War, available at www.solidarity-us.org/node/576.

2004. No "Safe Haven": Violence against Women in Iraqi Kurdistan, in W. Giles & J. Hyndman (eds.), *Sites of Violence: Gender and Conflict Zones*. Berkeley, CA: University of California Press: 108–33.

2004. The Particularity of "Honour" and the Universality of "Killing": From Early Warning Signs to Feminist Pedagogy, in Mojab Shahrzad & Nahla Abdo (eds.). *Violence in the Name of Honour: Theoretical and Political Challenges*. Istanbul: Istanbul Bilgi University: 15–37.

2003. Kurdish Women in the Zone of Genocide and Gendercide. *Al-Raida* XXI(103): 20–25.

2001. *Women of a Non-State Nation: The Kurds*. Costa Mesa, CA: Mazda Publishers.

Molyneux, Maxine.1985. Mobilization without Emancipation? Women's Interests, the State, and Revolution in Nicaragua. *Feminist Studies* 11(2): 227–54.

Najmabadi, Afsaneh. 2000. (Un)Veiling Feminism. *Social Text* 18(3): 29–45.

Nakash, Ytizhak. 1994. *The Shi'is of Iraq*. Princeton, NJ: Princeton University Press.

Niblock, Tim (ed.). 1982. *Iraq: The Contemporary State*. London: Palgrave Macmillan.

Norton Augustus, Richard. 1993. The Future of Civil Society in the Middle East. *Middle East Journal* 47(2): 205–16.

Omar, Suha. 1994. Women: Honour, Shame and Dictatorship, in Fran Hazelton (ed.), *Iraq since the Gulf War: Prospects for Democracy*. London: Zed Books: 60–71.

Organization of Women's Freedom in Iraq. 2010. *Prostitution and Trafficking of Women and Girls in Iraq* (published for the CSW 54th session). New York, NY.

Panday, Pranab Kumar. 2008. Representation without Participation: Quotas for Women in Bangladesh. *International Political Science Review* 29(4): 489–512.

Pateman, Carol, Hirschmann, Nancy J., & Powell, Bigham, Jr. 1992. Political Obligation, Freedom and Feminism. *American Political Science Review* 86(1): 179–88.

Pieri, Caecilia. 2014. Can T-Wall Murals Really Beautify the Fragmented Baghdad. *Jadaliyya*, May 18, available at www.jadaliyya.com/pages/index/1 7704/can-t-wall-murals-really-beautify-the-fragmented-b.

Phillips, Anne. 2002. Does Feminism Need a Conception of Civil Society?, in Will Kymlicka & Simone Chambers (eds.), *Alternative Conceptions of Civil Society* (Ethikon Series in Comparative Ethics). Princeton, NJ: Princeton University Press: 71–89.

Pietrobelli, Marta. 2013. Institutionalizing Gender: Women's Political Participation in Jordan. Ph.D. thesis, Centre for Gender Studies at SOAS, London.

Pursley, Sara. 2013. The Stage of Adolescence: Anticolonial Time, Youth Insurgency, and the Marriage Crisis in Hashimite Iraq. *History of the Present* 3(2): 160–97.

2012. Building the Nation through the Production of Difference: The Gendering of Education in Iraq, 1928–1958, in Jordi Tejtel, Peter Sluglett, Riccardo Bocco & Hamit Bozarslan (eds.), *Writing the Modern History of Iraq: Historiographical and Political Challenges*. London: World Scientific Publishing : 119–41.

2012. Daughters of the Right Path: Family Law, Homosocial Publics, and the Ethics of Intimacy in the Works of Shi'i Revivalist Bint Al-Huda. *Journal of Middle East Women's Studies* 8(2): 51–77.

Rassam, Amal. 1992. Political Ideology and Women in Iraq: Legislation and Cultural Constrains, in J. G. Jabbra & N. W. Jabbra (eds.), *Women and Development in the Middle East and North Africa*. Leiden: Brill: 82–95.

1982. Revolution within the Revolution? Women and the State in Iraq, in T. Niblock (eds.), *Iraq: The Contemporary State*. London: Palgrave Macmillan: 88–99.

Rehn, Elisabeth, & Johnson Sirleaf, Elaine. 2002. *Women, War and Peace: The Independent Experts' Assessment on the Impact of Armed Conflict on Women and Women's Role in Peace-Building*. New York, NY: UNIFEM.

Reilly, Niamh. 2011. Rethinking the Interplay of Feminism and Secularism in a Neo-Secular Age. *Feminist Review* 97: 5–31.

Richter-Devroe, Sophie. 2009. "Here, It's Not about Conflict Resolution: We Can Only Resist": Palestinian Women's Activism in Conflict-Resolution and Non-Violent Resistance, in Nadje Al-Ali & Nicola Pratt (eds.), *Women and War in the Middle East*. London: Zed Books.

2008. Gender, Culture, and Conflict Resolution in Palestine. *Journal of Middle East Women's Studies* 4(2): 30–59.

Rohde, Achim. 2010. Gender Policies in Ba'athist Iraq, in *State-Society Relations in Ba'thist Iraq*. London: Routledge: 75–118.

2006. Opportunities for Masculinity and Love: Cultural Production in Ba'thist Iraq during the 1980s, in Lahoucine Ouzgane (ed.), *Islamic Masculinities*. London: Zed Books.

Romano, David. 2014. Iraq's Descent into Civil War: A Constitutional Explanation. *Middle East Journal* 68(4): 547–66.

Sabbagh, Suha (ed.), 1996. *Arab Women: Between Defiance and Restraint*. Ithaca, NY: Olive Branch Press.

Said, Edward. 1994. *Culture and Imperialism*. New York, NY: Vintage Books.

1977. *Orientalism*. London: Penguin Books.

Sakai, Keiko. 2003. Tribalization as a Tool of State Control in Iraq: Observations on the Army, the Cabinets and the National Assembly, in, Hosham Dawod & Jabar A. Faleh (eds.), *Tribes and Power: Nationalism and Ethnicity in the Middle East*. London: Saqi: 136–61.

Salime, Zakia. 2011. *Between Feminism and Islam: Human Rights and Sharia Law in Morocco*, vol. 36. Minneapolis, MN: University of Minnesota Press.

Sassoon, Joseph. 2016. Iraq's Political Economy Post 2003: From Transition to Corruption. *International Journal of Contemporary Iraqi Studies* 10(1–2):17–33.

2012a. *Saddam Hussein's Ba'th Party: Inside an Authoritarian Regime*. Cambridge: Cambridge University Press.

2012b. The Brain Drain in Iraq after the 2003 Invasion in Writing the Modern History of Iraq, in Jordi Tejtel, Peter Sluglett, Riccardo Bocco, & Hamit Bozarslan (eds.), *Writing the Modern History of Iraq: Historiographical and Political Challenges*. London: World Scientific Publishing: 379–89.

Shaaban, Abdul Hussein. 2010. *Jadal al-Hawiyyat fi al-'Iraq. Al-Dawla wal-Muwatana*. Beirut: Arab Scientific Publishers.

Shakry, Omnia. 1998. Schooled Mothers and Structured Play: Child Rearing in Turn-of-the-Century Egypt, in Lila Abu-Lughod (ed.), *Remaking Women: Feminism and Modernity in the Middle East*. 126–70.

Sharabi, Hisham. 1988. *Neopatriarchy: A Theory of Distorted Change in Arab Society*. Oxford: Oxford University Press.

1966. *Nationalism and Revolution in the Arab World*. New York, NY: Van Nostrand.

Shohat, Ella. 2006. *Taboo Memories, Diasporic Voices*. Durham, NC: Duke University Press.

Sousa Santos, Boaventura. 2007. Beyond Abyssal Thinking: From Global Lines to Ecologies of Knowledges. *Review* 30(1): 45–89.

Spivak, Ch. Gayatri. 1999. *A Critique of Postcolonial Reason: Toward a History of the Vanishing Present*. Cambridge, MA: Harvard University Press.

1988. Can the Subaltern Speak?, in C. Nelson & L. Grossberg (eds.), *Marxism and the Interpretation of Culture*. Basingstoke: Macmillan Education: 271–313.

Tejtel, Jordi, Sluglett, Peter, Bocco, Riccardo, & Bozarslan, Hamit (eds.). 2012. *Writing the Modern History of Iraq: Historiographical and Political Challenges*. London: World Scientific Publishing.

Tripp, Charles. 2000. *A History of Iraq*. Cambridge: Cambridge University Press.

Tucker, E. Judith (ed.). 1993. *Arab Women: Old Boundaries, New Frontiers*. Bloomington, IN: Indiana University Press.

UNDP. 2001. *Gender Approaches in Conflict and Post-Conflict Situations*. Rome: United Nations Development Programme.

UNIFEM. 2004. *Gender Profil – Iraq*, available at http://sites.utoronto.ca/wwdl/
bibliography_war/UNIFEM%20-%20Iraq%20-%20women%20war%20an
d%20peace.htm.
WILPF. 2014. *Women and Explosive Weapons*. Geneva: Women's International
League for Peace and Freedom.
Wien, Peter. 2012. From Forty-One to *Qadisiyyat Saddam*: Remarks on an
Iraqi Realm of Memory, in Jordi Tejtel, Peter Sluglett, Riccardo Bocco &
Hamit Bozarslan (eds.), *Writing the Modern History of Iraq:
Historiographical and Political Challenges*. London: World Scientific
Publishing: 105–18.
      2006. *Iraqi Arab Nationalism: Authoritarian, Totalitarian and Pro-Fascist
Inclinations, 1932–1941* (SOAS Routledge Studies of the Middle East).
London: Routledge.
Wizarat al-Ta'lim al-'Ali wal Bahth al-'Ilmi, Merkez ahya' al-Turath al-'Ilmi al-
'Arabi Ma'a al-Itihad al-'Am li Nisa' al-'Iraq. 1977. Dawr al-Mar'a al-
Arabiyya fi al-Haraka al-'Ilmiyya. Bagdad: Jame'at Baghdad.
Yousif, Bassam. 2016. Iraq's Stunted Growth: Human and Economic
Development in Perspective. *Contemporary Arab Affairs* 9(2): 212–36.
      2013. *Human Development in Iraq, 1950–1990*. London: Routledge.
      2010. The Political Economy of Sectarianism in Iraq. *International Journal of
Contemporary Iraqi Studies* 4(3): 357–67.
Yuval-Davis, Nira. 2007. Identity, Identity Politics and the Constructionism
Debate. Paper presented at the BSA conference, UEL, available at www
.uel.ac.uk/ipsa/documents/bsa2.pdf.
      1997. *Gender and Nation*. London: SAGE.
Zangana, Haifa. 2007. *City of Widows: An Iraqi Woman's Account of War and
Resistance*. New York: Seven Stories Press.
Zubaida, Sami. 2011. *Beyond Islam: A New Understanding of the Middle East*.
London: I.B. Tauris.
      2002. The Fragments Imagine the Nation: the Case of Iraq. *International
Journal of Middle East Studies* (Special Issue) 34(2): 205–15.
      1989. *Islam, the People and the State*. London: Routledge.
      1991. Community, Class and Minorities in Iraqi Politics, in Robert A Fernea &
William Roger Louis (eds.), *The Iraqi Revolution of 1958: The Old Social
Classes Revisited*. London: I.B. Tauris: 197–210.
Zuhdi, Khanem. 2008. *Sahafat min Tarikh al-Harakat al-Nisa'iyya al-'Iraqiyya*.
Baghdad: Dar al-Riwad al-Muzdahirah.

Organizations' Documentation

Al-Itihad al-Islami li Akhawat Kurdistan. 2010. *Nebza 'an Al-Itihad al-Islami li
Akhawat Kurdistan (1994–1415)*.
      2007. *Al-Mustaqbel*, vol. 99. (Year 10).
Al-Itihad Nisa' Kurdistan. 2010. *Kana*, vol. 5.
      2010. *Kana*, vol. 4.
      2009. *Kana*, vol. 3.
      2009. *Kana*, vol. 2.

2008. *Kana*, vol. 1.

2008. *Kana*, vol. 0.

Jam'iyyat al-Ansar. 2010. *Hamla Muhammad Qudwatana*.

2010. *Mashari' wa a'mal*.

2008. *Mashari' wa a'mal*.

2006. *Mashari' wa a'mal*.

Jam'iyyat al-'Iraqiyya li Huquq al-Insan. 2009. *Sawt al-Insan*, vol. 72 (July).

2009. *Sawt al-Insan*, vol. 73 (September).

Jam'iyyat Nisa' Baghdad. 2007. *Ma'an*, vol. 1 (April–June).

2007. *Ma'an*, vol. 2 (July–September).

2007. *Ma'an*, vol. 2 (January–March).

Ma'had al-Mar'a al-Qiyadiyya. 2009. *Al-Mar'a al-Qiadiyya*, vol. 30 (September).

2009. *Al-Mar'a al-Qiadiyya*, vol. 28 (June).

2009. *Al-Mar'a al-Qiadiyya*, vol. 27 (March).

Majles al-'Iraqi lil Silm wal Tazamun. 2012, 12 (April).

Munazamat al-Mar'a al-Muslima fi al-'Iraq. *Hawa'una*, vol. 54.

2010. *Hawa'una*, vol. 22.

2008. *Hawa'una*, vol. 42.

2008. *Hawa'una*, vol. 29.

2008. *Mashari' wa A'mal*. 2004–7, Baghdad.

2007. *Hawa'una*, vol. 21.

Munazamat Huriyyat al-Mar'a fi al-'Iraq. 2012. *Al-Musawat*, vol. 20 (Year 9, March).

Rabitat al-Mar'a al-'Iraqiyya. 2010. *Miswadat warqat 'amal ta'ni bil tifl wal tufula*.

2009. *Bayan bi munasebat 'Id al-Mar'a al-'Alami* (March).

2008. *Al-Mu'tamar al-Sades, al-Ahdaf wal Nizam al-Dakhili*.

2008. *Nidal al-Mar'a*, vol. 2, year 56 (July).

Rabitat al-Um al-'Iraqiyya. 2012. *Nusf al-Qima*, vol. 50 (May).

Rabitat al-Mar'a al-Kurdistaniyya fi al-'Iraq. 2007. *Al-Barnamaj wal Nizam al-Dakhili, al-Mu'tamar al-Rabe'* (November).

Shabakat al-Nisa' al-'Iraqiyyat. 2006. *Al-Nashra*, vol. 3 (November).

2006. *Al-Nashra*, vol. 2 (August).

Tahaluf Nisa' al-Rafidain. 2008. *Zahrat al-Rafidain*, vol. 1 (May, June, July).

Index

'Arif Brothers, 68; 1963 military coup
against Ba'th regime, 71, 78; adoption of
Islamist discourse, 72; nationalist measures, 71; oppression of Shi'a, 71
'ulemas: 'Abd al-Karim Qasim, 64; and
PSC, 64, 80; criticism by both Sunni and
Shi'a, 62; in relation to state authority,
62; Law no. 188 and, 63; PSC and, 62;
relationship between colonial state and
different groups, 39, 45, 53; Shi'a, 46, 48;
struggles between social and political
forces, 39; Sunni and Shi'a, 63, 232;
Sunni Arab religious, political, and economic figures, 48
1920 Revolution, 56, 66
1948 al-Wathba, 56
1952 *intifada*, 56
1991 *intifada*, 305

Abou-Bakr, Omaima, 261, 270, 295
Abu-Lughod, Lila, xii, 12, 13, 17, 19, 20,
24, 43, 44, 166, 191, 240, 244, 245, 246,
261, 266, 295
agriculture industry, 86, 87
Agriculture, Center for, 117
Ahmed, Leila, 11, 42, 43, 260
al-'Askeri shrine in Samarra attack, 24
Al-Ali, Nadje, xii, 17, 21, 23, 64, 67, 93, 96,
100, 102, 110, 115, 125, 166, 167, 172,
191, 205, 209, 210, 212, 232, 261,
287, 289
al-Amal: organization, 180; women's activism, 168, 174, 274
al-Bakr, Ahmed Hassan, 85
Al-Derbendi, Abdel Rahman, 53, 55, 296
al-Dulaimi, Naziha, 47, 57, 58, 60, 63,
70, 249
al-Ghazali, Nazem, 197
al-Gubenchi, Ahmed, 272
al-Hashd al-Sha'bi, 293
al-Huda, Bint, 80, 81, 226, 249, 308
al-Husri, Sati', 50, 54

Alinia, Minoo, 202, 203, 204, 212,
297, 306
al-Ja'fari, Ibrahim, 147
al-Kazimiyya, xi, 1, 25, 29, 30, 37, 68, 97,
120, 122, 140, 148, 224
Al-Kerrada, 6, 25, 29, 30, 63, 97, 99, 148,
153, 183, 189, 241, 251
Al-Khafaji, Isam, 72, 86, 87, 297
Al-Khayyat, Sana, 92, 297
al-Mala'ika, Nazik, 249
Al-Mutannabi Street, 3, 4, 5, 137; car bomb
attack, 4
Al-Nashra, 277, 311
al-Rafidain Women's Coalition (RWC),
xiv, 142, 169, 179, 180, 181, 183, 229,
241, 250, 263, 278, 279, 280, 288
Al-Rashid Street, 2, 3
al-Roaa Network, 181
al-Sadr, Moqtada, 175, 189
al-Sadr, Muhammed Baqer, 35, 80, 82,
83, 249
al-Shaikh Da'ud, Sabiha, 53, 54, 57, 58, 59,
60, 249, 252
al-Shaikhly, Azhar Abdel Karim, 150,
153
al-Suwaydi, Shaikh Yusef, 56
al-Taman, Ja'far Abu, 56
al-Wardi, Ali, 45, 46, 297
al-Zahawi, Jamil Sidqi, 47, 53
Anthias, Floya, 18, 42, 76, 118
Anwar, Zainah, 270, 298
Arab Women Lawyers Network,
181
Arab Women's Tribunal, 180
armed group, 173
armed groups, 138, *See* militia(s)
Asad, Talal, 248, 255
Association for Women's Revival, xiv
Association of Women for Women, xiv
Assyrian Women's Association, xiv
Assyrian Women's Union, 181, 217, 218
Asuda, xiv, 83, 180

Books in the Series